PAGE 34

ON THE ROAD

YOUR COMPLETE DESTINATION GUIDE
In-depth reviews, detailed listings and insider tips

PAGE 249

SURVIVAL GUIDE

VITAL PRACTICAL INFORMATION TO HELP YOU HAVE A SMOOTH TRIP

THIS EDITION WRITTEN AND RESEARCHED BY

Emily Matchar
Tom Masters

welcome to The Bahamas

Glitz & Glamour

The rich and famous (and the merely rich) flock to the Bahamas for posh resorts, slick restaurants and A-list treatment. You too can live the high life at one of the country's star-spangled hotspots, provided you've got the cash and the flash (or just the cash). Nassau, the go-go capital, is the place for old-school elegance, with chic colonial hotels, James Bond–approved cocktail lounges and an ultra-cool cigar factory. Across the bridge, high-rollers test their luck at the Atlantis casino while the paparazzi snap starlets suntanning on Cabbage Beach. A short skip away, Harbour Island plays host to rock stars and CEOs, though the low-key locals don't make a fuss about it. Yachties point their compasses toward the Abacos, the sailing capital of the world.

Sand & Solitude

Life in the fast lane not your style? Head for the 'Out Islands' (also known as the Family Islands) – that is to say, all the islands besides New Providence and Grand Bahama – which share a grand total of one traffic light between them. Life isn't just slower here, life is actually asleep in a hammock with a half-drunk bottle of Kalik by its side. Fishermen untangle their nets by quiet harbors, donkeys graze on the side of muddy roads, *potcakes* (stray dogs) snooze beneath hibiscus bushes. Rent snorkel gear and explore a sun-dappled cove in the Exumas.

Strolling Pink Sands Beach

2 Celebs like Mick Jagger, Elle Macpherson and Harrison Ford have all been snapped frolicking on the rosy shores of Harbour Island's Pink Sands Beach (p139). Why not join them? Everyone is welcome on this world-famous stretch of sand, whose ethereal color comes from finely pulverized red coral. If you do spot a star, just follow the locals' lead and say 'good afternoon.' Harbour Islanders treat everyone – A-listers and mere commoners alike – with the same laid-back friendliness, which is part of what makes it such an appealing getaway.

Snorkeling

3 With nearly 100,000 sq miles of ocean, the Bahamas has more to see underwater than above. So pop on a mask and flippers and hop in to explore. Snorkelers will thrill to the gin-clear waters of the Exumas (p158), the strange underwater 'road' of the Biminis (p99), the bottomless blue holes of Andros (p101), and the secluded cays of the Southern Bahamas (p181). Look out for lantern-jawed groupers the size of VW Beetles, marching columns of spiny Caribbean lobsters, color-changing octopi, angelically floating eagle rays, and the occasional curious dolphin.

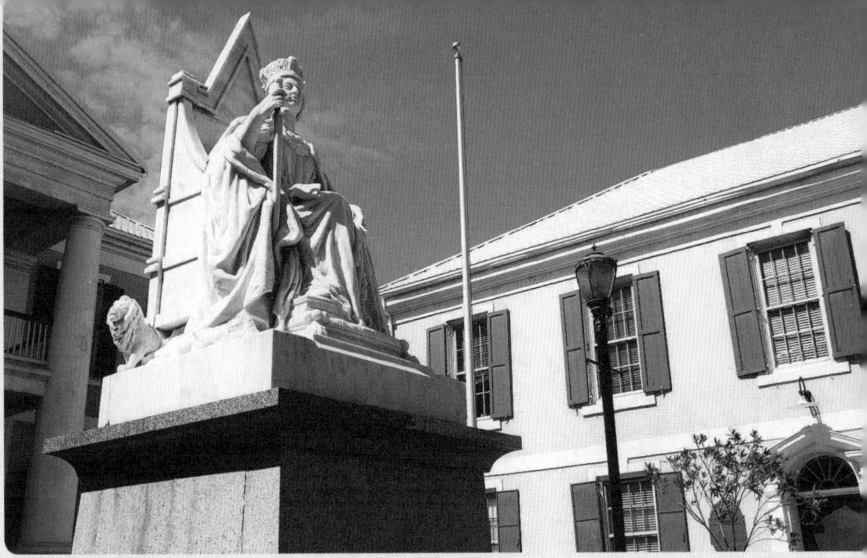

Wandering Colonial Nassau

4 Many visitors to Nassau (p40) never make it past the duty-free shops of Bay St. Their loss. Downtown Nassau is a pink-and-white colonial jewel, with government buildings as ornate as wedding cakes, 18th-century forts complete with canons and dungeons, and crumbling graveyards full of pirates and those who hunted them. Surveying the city from the top of Fort Fincastle, you can almost hear the 'arrrg!' of notorious scourges like Blackbeard and Calico Jack. Several interesting history museums illuminate the city's past and provide helpful walking maps.

Climbing Mt Alvernia Hermitage

5 Sitting atop the highest peak in the Bahamas (a not-quite-Himalayan 206ft above sea level), this atmospherically crumbling monastery (p171), on Cat Island, graces many a postcard. Built by Father Jerome, an itinerant priest and architect, it resembles a miniature version of the medieval churches of the father's native England. The trek to the hermitage is truly awe inspiring, as are the panoramic views for the peak. Try to visit just before sunset, when the pink light illuminates the pale gray stone.

Island Hopping

6 Is there a more glamorous phrase in the English language than 'island hopping'? The Bahamas, with its 29 islands and innumerable cays, is the perfect place to practice the jetsetter's art. Though all the major islands of the Bahamas are connected to Nassau via air, they're not all connected to each other, so plan ahead. We suggest touching down in Nassau, hopping over to the Abacos to explore the Loyalist Cays (p122) via ferry, then flying to Eleuthera to stroll barefoot on Harbour Island's Pink Sands Beach (p139).

RICHARD CUMMINS/LONELY PLANET IMAGES ©

Drinking, Dancing & Partying

7 Booze- and beats-fueled hedonism is always on offer in the Bahamas, whether that means cracking open an icy cold Kalik beer at a laid-back beach bar or shaking your bootie at a throbbing Nassau nightclub. Nassau's Paradise Island (p65) is undoubtedly the country's party capital, though the beach bars of Grand Bahama (p86) and the chic cocktail lounges of Eleuthera's Harbour Island (p139) give it a run for its money. Don't leave without trying a Goombay Smash or dancing till dawn to soca beats.

OLIVIER GOUJON/ALAMY

GREG JOHNSTON/LONELY PLANET IMAGES ©

Staking Out a Secluded Cay

8 With more uninhabited cays than inhabited ones, it's easy to find your own secluded stretch of sand in the Bahamas. To get off the beaten path, try the Berry Islands (30 islands, 800 people; p111), the 365 sun-spangled Exuma Cays (p166), or the little-visited islands of the Southern Bahamas (p181). The seaworthy can rent their own boat for solo exploration, while landlubbers should charter a vessel with a captain. Find an empty cove, drop anchor, and ahhhhh...It's a cliché to ask, but ask yourself anyway: does life really get any better than this?

Kayaking

9 The Bahamas is a paddler's paradise, full of mangrove swamps, shallow reefs and offshore islets, all waiting to be explored by kayak. Most of the more developed islands have kayak tours or rentals, but you may have to pack your own gear if you want to paddle further afield. Top spots include the fringing reef off Andros (p101), the sunny shallows west of the Exumas, Grand Bahama's Lucayan National Park (p90), and the mangrove wetlands of the Abaco Marls (p117) or North Bimini (p95).

GREG JOHNSTON/LONELY PLANET IMAGES ©

Atlantis Revelry

10 The steroid-pumped love child of Disney World and Indiana Jones, Paradise Island's gargantuan Atlantis (p58) is a full-immersion, 24/7 vacation bacchanalia. Many visitors to Atlantis never leave the resort grounds. Why would you? You can plunge down 200ft waterslides at the on-site water park, explore faux archaeological ruins, eat live conch at a celebrity chef–run sushi bar, test your luck at the vast casino. And more. Way more.

JULIET COOMBE/LONELY PLANET IMAGES ©

need to know

Currency

» Bahamian dollar ($) or US dollar ($) The currencies are equivalent, and both are accepted throughout the country.

Language

» English

When to Go

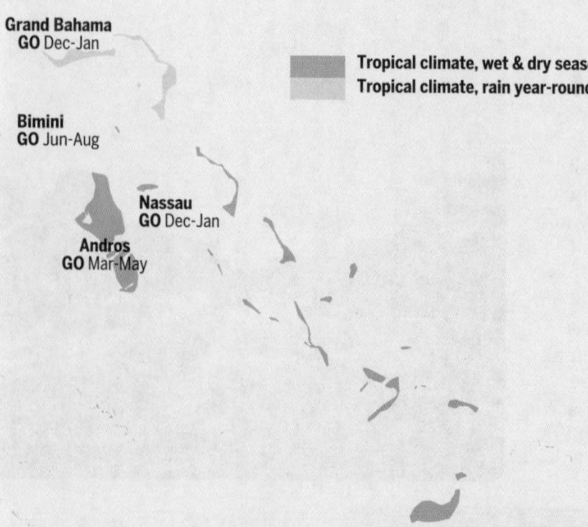

High Season
(Dec–Feb)

» Winter in the US and Europe drives crowds to the Bahamas, and prices skyrocket.

» Expect sunny, warm days and slightly chilly nights.

Shoulder
(Mar–Aug)

» In March and April, Spring Breakers turn Nassau and Grand Bahama into party central.

» Spring is balmy, summer is steamy.

» Destinations such as Andros and the Biminis have their high season in spring, when fishing is best.

Low Season
(Sep–Nov)

» Fall hurricane season means few crowds and rock-bottom prices, but it can also mean… hurricanes.

» Days are mild, though sometimes rainy.

Your Daily Budget

Budget less than
$150

» Rent a cottage with friends or family for $600–$1000 per week

» Stock up at the supermarket: (dinner for two) $20–$30

» Swim, sun, snooze in a hammock – all free

Midrange
$150–$300

» Double room in decent hotel: $150–$250

» Local cafes and conch stands: $6–$20

» Snorkel trip or guided tour once or twice: $60

Top end over
$300

» Luxury hotel room: from $200

» Eat at celebrity-chef restaurants: (dinner for two), $200

» Charter a yacht from $3000 per week

Money

» ATMs widely available on Nassau and Grand Bahama, much rarer in the Out Islands. Many restaurants and many Out Island hotels don't accept credit cards.

Visas

» Generally not needed for stays of up to 90 days.

Cell Phones

» Local SIM cards can be used in unlocked phones. Locked American phones must be set to global roaming.

Driving

» Drive on the left side of the road, though most cars are American and have a left-side steering wheel.

Websites

» **Lonely Planet** (www.lonelyplanet.com/the-bahamas) Destination information, hotel bookings, traveler forum and more

» **Islands of the Bahamas** (www.bahamas.com) Official tourism site; gives useful island-by-island info

» **Grand Bahama Vacations** (www.grandbahamavacations.com) Helpful guide for island getaways

Exchange Rates

Australia	A$1	$1
Canada	C$1	$1
Eurozone	€1	$1.40
Japan	¥100	$1.22
New Zealand	NZ$1	$0.74
UK	£1	$1.62
US	$1	$1

For current exchange rates see www.xe.com

Important Numbers

You need to dial 1 plus the country code when calling between the various islands of the Bahamas.

Country code	☎242
International access code	☎1-242
Emergency numbers	☎911 or ☎919

Arriving in the Bahamas

» **Nassau**

Taxis meet flights at Lynden Pindling International Airport; set fares $22/35 to Cable Beach/Paradise Island. Cruise ships dock at Prince George Wharf (p42).

» **Grand Bahama**

Taxis meet flights at the international airport.
Cruise ships dock at Freeport Harbour; taxis and buses meet shipping schedules (p89).

» **Out Islands**

Taxis or minibuses generally meet flights at all Out Island airports.

Planning a Dive

The Bahamas is a world-class diving destination, with jaw-dropping barrier reefs, multihued sea life and eerie shipwrecks. Unique Bahamas dive experiences include swimming with wild dolphins and 'wall-dives' – plunges off the continental shelf into deep ocean trenches. Nassau and Grand Bahama both have numerous well-regarded outfitters. Many popular dives, especially dolphin experiences or shark encounters, will sell out well in advance, so it's important to book ahead. On the Out Islands, dive outfitters are smaller, but are often highly experienced. Always check for PADI or equivalent accreditation. Many hotels in popular dive areas offer dive packages, with rates that include accommodations and multiple daily dives. Remember, plan your last dive for more than 24 hours before flying.

what's new

For this new edition of the Bahamas, our authors have hunted down the fresh, the transformed, the hot and the happening. These are some of our favorites. For up-to-the-minute recommendations, see lonelyplanet.com/the-bahamas.

Baha Mar, New Providence

1 As we write, this megaresort is poised to break ground on Cable Beach, a popular vacation area just west of downtown Nassau. The massive project, which threatens to rival Paradise Island's Atlantis in size, will include hotels, shopping and entertainment districts. When finished, Cable Beach will be a very different, much glitzier place. Two existing hotels, the Sheraton and the Wyndham, have already been renovated for takeover (p51).

Grabber's, Great Guana Cay, Abaco

2 The beachfront tiki bar at this laid-back new resort is quickly becoming a go-to island hangout for party-happy expats and visitors (p127).

Bimini Sands Recreation & Activities Center, Bimini

3 Bimini got a whole lot more family-friendly with the opening of this all-purpose outfitter, whose friendly managers offer snorkeling trips, nature tours, shark encounters, kayaking and much more (p98).

Bimini Big Game Club, Bimini

4 Defunct for years, this legendary angler's resort just got a luxury facelift by renowned sea-life painter Guy Harvey (p99).

Shannas Cove Resort, Cat Island

5 On the far north of the island, this charming new family-run resort is aimed at divers and couples looking for total tranquility (p176).

Pineapple Fields, Eleuthera

6 This luxe new condo resort is helping mainland Eleuthera shake off its underdog reputation; several excellent nearby restaurants add to the buzz (p152).

Garden of the Groves, Grand Bahama

7 Completely redone, this lush botanical oasis is now one of the island's must-see sights, with well-kept hiking trails and splendid birds flitting from limb to limb (p75).

Junkanoo Beach Club, Grand Bahama

8 This wildly popular beach club, with free beach access, kayaks and changing facilities, has become the island's top choice for an afternoon of fun (p80).

Long Island Breeze Resort, Long Island

9 The island's first major development in years is shaping up to be a winner, with eight luxury rooms (and 40 more on the way) and innovative, local management (p187).

if you like...

Diving & Snorkeling

With almost 100,000 sq miles of glittering aquamarine ocean, the Bahamas is a world-class snorkeling and diving destination. Divers explore psychedelic reefs, stalactite-filled blue holes, eerie WWI-era wrecks and bottomless ocean caverns. Snorkelers can explore solo or join group trips to hidden coves and fish-filled reefs. Tops on everyone's lists are the wildlife encounters – swimming alongside playful wild dolphins, feeding fang-toothed sharks.

Tongue of the Ocean Just off the coast of Andros, this 6000ft-deep canyon is the site of a dramatic wall-dive (p107)

UNEXSO Grand Bahama's renowned dive center offers a wildly popular dolphin encounter (p77)

Exuma Cays These 365 tiny islands are a dreamy spot for solo snorkeling (p166)

Bimini Road Is it the lost city of Atlantis? Or just a pile of rocks? Snorkel over to Bimini and find out (p99)

Stuart Cove's Dive & Snorkel Bahamas Nassau's premiere dive and snorkel outfitter has trips for all ages and levels (p52)

Stunning Beaches

The ugliest beaches in the Bahamas are still pretty jaw-dropping, so it's hard to go wrong here. The beaches of Nassau and Grand Bahama tend to be more crowded, which is great if you're looking for a margarita or a banana-boat ride. On the Out Islands, it's likely to be just you, the sand, and a few curious sea birds.

Pink Sands Beach Harbour Island's legendary stunner, its rosy color the result of finely crushed coral (p139)

Gold Rock Beach A few miles from downtown Freeport, Grand Bahama's most gloriously vacant beach (p79)

Cabbage Beach On Paradise Island, a vision of white sand and warm aqua water (p51)

Cat Island Swaying coconut palms, powdery sand and gin-clear waters make this a secluded favorite (p170)

Treasure Cay Beach In the Abacos, this bone-white stretch of sand is the supermodel of the beach world (p134)

Secluded Coves

With nearly 700 islands and cays, the Bahamas has plenty of seclusion to go around. Even in mile-a-minute Nassau, blissfully peaceful stretches of sand are easy to find, if you know where to look. On the Out Islands, it sometimes seems like there are more beaches than people. Bring a picnic, a bottle of water and a good book, and live out your Hollywood shipwreck fantasies.

Lighthouse Bay In south Eleuthera, the impossibly rutted road keeps the crowds away from this pink-sand stunner (p154)

Exuma Cays You can go for days without seeing another soul in this watery wonderland of some 360 tiny islands (p166)

Berry Islands Islands: 30. Human population: 800. Secluded coves: uncountable (p111)

Tahiti Beach On Elbow Cay, this hidden stretch of sand overlooks a shallow turquoise bay (p123)

Grotto Beach On little-visited San Salvador, this is a top snorkeling spot (p180)

» Loggerhead turtle swimming among a wreck

Party Nightlife

C'mon, you can sleep when you're dead! Nassau is the place for nightclubs, from tequila-fueled Spring Break dives to swanky, starlet-filled pleasure palaces. Grand Bahama has its share of pubs and clubs, too, especially in the resort suburb of Lucaya. On the Out Islands nightlife might mean a bottle of rum, a guitar and a crowd of rumbustious locals.

Fish Fry On weekends, Nassau's Arawak Cay becomes an open-air party, fueled by Junkanoo beats and a potent concoction called sky juice (p62)

Aura The beautiful people dance the night away at Paradise Island's most chic nightclub (p66)

Elvina's Lenny Kravitz is a regular at this unassuming white cottage in Eleuthera's Gregory Town, which explodes with music on Tuesday and Friday nights (p150)

Nipper's Beach Bar & Grill Yachties and locals get wild at this legendary Great Guana Cay beach bar (p127)

Port Lucaya Marketplace Most of Grand Bahama's nightlife is centered around this pastel-pretty shopping village (p75)

Romantic Getaways

Pink sand beaches. Secluded coves. Coral-colored sunsets. Opulent colonial-era hotels. Hushed spas. There's a reason the Bahamas is a top wedding and honeymoon destination. If you can't get that lovin' feeling here, you might want to consider whether you're actually a robot.

Downtown Nassau Horse-drawn carriage rides, atmospheric old hotels, sweet side-street bistros (p41)

Cove Atlantis Paradise Island's most adult property, popular with honeymooners (p59)

Sandals at Emerald Bay This all-inclusive couples-only resort pulls out all the stops (p164)

Harbour Island Swank hotels, pink-sand beaches, world-class restaurants, all with a dose of laid-back small-town charm (p139)

Andros Get away from the crowds at one of Andros' remote resorts, accessible only by boat (Kamalame Cay p106; Tiamo p111)

Spas Luxuriate in a beachfront massage *à deux* at one of Nassau's many spas (p55)

History

The history of the Bahamas is a colorful story of Spanish piracy, African culture and British rule. While Nassau bears the most obvious traces of the past, with colonial buildings and ruined 18th-century forts, most of the islands have unique historical sights, from crumbling Spanish churches to caves once inhabited by the Lucayan people.

Downtown Nassau The past comes to life in ornate colonial buildings, imposing stone cathedrals and colorful pirate museums (p41)

Loyalist Cays These Abaco islands were settled by Loyalists fleeing America after the Revolutionary War, and their influence is still obvious in the New England–style architecture and the locals' old-fashioned accents (p122)

Mt Alvernia Hermitage This hilltop monastery was built by Father Jerome, the Bahamas' beloved wandering priest (p171)

Lucayan National Park Skeletons of indigenous Lucayan people were found at the bottom of this park's blue holes (p90)

If you like... pirates, Nassau's Pirates of Nassau museum will shiver your timbers, while the nearby statue of pirate-fighter Woodes Rogers will make you say 'arrrrgh!' (p41)

Wildlife Watching

Whether you're an amateur marine biologist or a passionate birdwatcher, the Bahamas offers an abundance of wildlife for your viewing pleasure. Birders should look out for the Bahamas swallow, Bahamas woodstar, Greater Antillean bullfinch and the Cuban emerald hummingbird. Undersea, keep your eyes peeled for the Nassau grouper, the Atlantic spotted dolphin and the lemon shark.

Grand Bahama Tops for birdwatching, especially in the Garden of the Groves botanical garden (p75)

Berry Islands Several of these remote, uninhabited islands are given over to private nature preserves (p111)

Staniel Cay Splash around with the famous swimming pigs of the tiny cay neighboring this Exuma island (p167)

Exuma Cays Land & Sea Park Fearsome-looking rock iguanas abound in the Exumas (p167)

Ardastra Gardens, Zoo & Conservation Center Nearly 300 species of animals, many indigenous to the Bahamas, live at this Nassau zoo. Don't miss the march of the flamingos! (p48)

Shopping

Duty-free diamonds, watches, perfumes, cigars and handbags lure shoppers to the Bahamas. But there's more to the island's shopping scene than luxury goods. The Bahamas also produces gorgeous straw work, Androsia batik fabric, wood carvings, conch jewelry and folk-art paintings. Food-wise, look out for rum cakes, coconut candies and Eleutheran pineapple jam.

Bay Street Downtown Nassau's iconic shopping strip is lined with duty-free jewelry stores, luxury boutiques and souvenir shops (p67)

Androsia Ltd On Andros, you can watch the famous batik fabric being made, then buy some of your own at the onsite store (p107)

Graycliff Cigar Co In this small Nassau factory, a team of expert Cubans roll top-end stogies. Best of all, they're kosher for import into the US (p45)

Dunmore Town The fancy-pants boutiques of central Harbour Island are some of the country's best (p147)

Port Lucaya Marketplace Grand Bahama's postcard-pretty shopping district offers batik clothing, crafts, watches and gems (p87)

Fishing

Anglers rhapsodize over the Biminis, Andros and the Abacos, all world-class fishing destinations. Bimini, on the edge of the Gulf Stream, is renowned for its big-game fishing – wahoo, marlin, sailfish, tuna. The flats and shallows of Andros and the Abacos are tops for bonefishing, an addictive type of catch-and-release fishing.

Bimini Big Game Club This luxury hotel and marina is the place to swap big fish stories with fellow anglers (p99)

Grand Bahama Freeport-based bonefishing guides whisk guests directly to eastern Grand Bahama's rich sandy-bottomed flats (p78)

Marls of Abaco On the southwestern side of Abaco, these endless mangrove wetlands are prime grounds for bonefishing (p117)

Cargill Creek Area Remote southern Central Andros is bonefishing heaven, with a number of rustic bonefish lodges set directly on the shallow bights (p108)

month by month

Top Events

1 **Nassau New Year's Day**, January

2 **Family Island Regatta**, April

3 **Eleuthera Pineapple Festival**, June

4 **Emancipation Day**, August

5 **Junkanoo**, December

January

The first half of the month, which coincides with American winter vacation, is busy and crowded. Weather is warm in the day, crisp at night and locals are still buzzing from all the Junkanoo festivities.

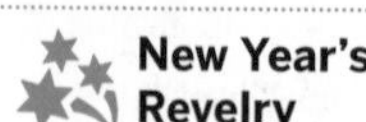

New Year's Revelry

New Year's Day brings country-wide Junkanoo festivities, a kaleidoscope of masked dancers, music, parades and all-around high spirits. Nassau and Grand Bahama have the wildest parties, while Out Island celebrations are more low key. Nassau also has a spectacular parade down Bay St.

March

The weather's balmy, though still a tad chilly at night. Spring Break brings hoards of Jell-O shot-loving American college students to Nassau and Grand Bahama for a week of revelry. Whether this is heaven or hell is a matter of taste and age.

Fishing Season on Andros

While high season begins to wind down in most of the country, Andros' busy time is just heating up. Fishing is best in early spring, so book your bonefishing lodge well ahead of time.

Bacardi Rum Billfish Tournament

This three-day fishing tournament brings hundreds of competitive big game fishermen and -women to Grand Bahama's Port Lucaya. Look out for lots of sunburned faces and rum-fueled parties.

April

Spring Break traffic slows to a trickle, signaling the beginning of the Bahamian shoulder season. Rooms are slightly cheaper, crowds thinner and weather warmer.

Family Island Regatta

Since 1954, Bahamian sailors have gathered in George Town, Exuma for an extravaganza of sailing contests, cultural events and merry-making (p162). Designed to keep old-fashioned boat-building alive, the regatta only allows wooden-hulled vessels with canvas sails.

May

Long Island Regatta

As spring rolls into high gear, the weather is warm and flowers burst from every corner. More than 40 locally built sailing sloops, representing each of the Bahamian islands, compete for prizes (p187). Onshore rake 'n' scrape bands, sporting activities and Bahamian food keep it lively.

June

Summer is solid shoulder season in most of the Bahamas, except in Bimini, where warm waters in the Gulf Stream mean better big-game fishing and bigger crowds.

Eleuthera Pineapple Festival

Held in the Bahamas' historical center of the

pineapple trade, Gregory Town, this four-day fete celebrates the sweet fruit, with cooking demos, pineapple eating contests, pineapple-themed sports competitions and the crowning of a Miss Teen Pineapple Princess (p150).

Bahamas Boating Flings

All month long through mid-August, lead boats guide flotillas of yachts across the Gulf Stream from Fort Lauderdale, Florida, to Bimini to kick off the deep-sea fishing season. Think road trip, but with boats (p99).

July

As summer rolls along, the weather turns distinctly steamy. Americans flood in for the Fourth of July, which many Bahamian resorts honor with fireworks and festivities. Less than a week later, Bahamian Independence Day means country-wide festivities.

Independence Day

On July 10, 1973, the Bahamas became fully independent from Great Britain, though it remains a member of the commonwealth. Independence Day is celebrated country-wide with parades, fireworks and other festivities.

August

The hottest month of the year, August marks the beginning of the Atlantic hurricane season. Tourism begins to slow, especially toward the end of the month.

Emancipation Day

On the first Monday of the month, the Bahamas joins many other Caribbean nations in celebrating the passing of the Slavery Abolition Act, which ended slavery in the British colonies in 1834. In Nassau, celebrations are centered around the community of Fox Hill (p48).

Cat Island Regatta

Held on Emancipation Day, this is the biggest event of the year on Cat Island (p172). Sailboat races, domino tournaments, fried conch and rake 'n' scrape music keep crowds entertained late into the night.

October

As the hurricane season wears on, hotel prices nosedive and once-crowded beaches are nearly empty. If you love solitude and don't mind the minor risk of a storm, this is a prime time of year to visit.

North Eleuthera Sailing Regatta

This three-day racing pageant features scores of locally built sloops vying for the championship while onshore festivities are roaring. Boats sail between North Eleuthera, Harbour Island (p143) and Spanish Wells.

McLean's Town Conch Cracking Festival

Watch the conch shells fly at this one-of-a-kind Grand Bahama event, where competitors vie to break open the most conchs in a short time period. There's even a category for tourists! All manner of other conch-related festivities make this a fun day for all (p81).

November

Grand Bahama Conchman Triathlon

As hurricane season ends, the weather turns nippy at night. Hundreds of competitors descend on Grand Bahama to swim, bike and run until they fall face forward into the sand (p81). Join them, or just buy them a beer at the Port Lucaya Marketplace afterward.

Bahamas Wahoo Challenge

Grizzled deep-sea fishermen and -women come to Bimini to show off their wahoo-wrangling chops (p99). The Bimini Big Game Club plays host, though all the hotels on the island tend to book up.

December

High season gets rolling mid-month, as Americans and Europeans begin their winter holidays. Christmas is big on the islands, with most resorts staging big celebrations. And then, of course,

there's Junkanoo, the island's biggest fete.

Christmas

The weeks leading up to Christmas bring holiday boat parades, caroling concerts and craft fairs to many islands. Christmas itself is traditionally celebrated with baked ham, peas 'n' rice, black cake (a type of fruit cake) and plenty of spicy rum and eggnog.

Junkanoo

The national street party of the year starts in the early hours of Boxing Day across the islands. Comparable to New Orlean's Mardi Gras or Brazil's Carnival, Junkanoo is a swirl of parades, street concerts, masked dancers and more. A don't-miss.

itineraries

Whether you've got six days or 60, these itineraries provide a starting point for the trip of a lifetime. Want more inspiration? Head online to lonelyplanet .com/thorntree to chat with other travelers.

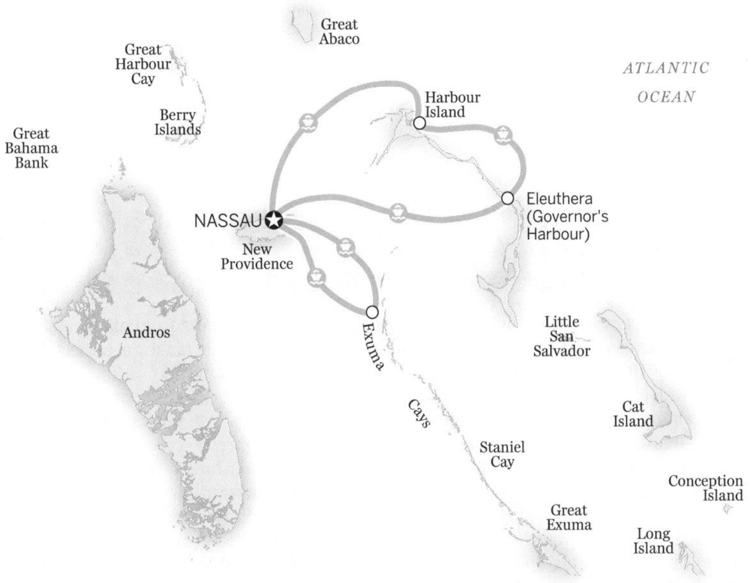

One Week
Essential Bahamas

Touch down in **Nassau**, the country's glitzy capital. Spend a morning taking in the ornate pink-and-white buildings of the historic downtown, then head straight for Cable Beach for jet skiing or daiquiri-sipping. The next day, cross the arched bridge to Atlantis on **Paradise Island**. You can spend 24 hours gambling, riding waterslides through shark tanks and dancing at glam nightclubs. On the third day, head to western New Providence to explore the uncrowded beaches and sip sunset cocktails at a swanky Nassau resort. On the fourth day, catch a fast ferry to Eleuthera's **Harbour Island** to stroll the iconic Pink Sands Beach, and perhaps spot a celeb or two. The next day, take a water taxi to the 'mainland', **Eleuthera**, to explore hidden beaches and photograph the famous Glass Window Bridge. Hop on the ferry back to New Providence in time for some snorkeling or a day-trip to play with dolphins at the **Blue Lagoon**. On your last day, take a powerboat ride to visit the rock iguanas on a remote cay in the **Exumas**.

One Month
Island Hopping

After a few days of living it up in **Nassau** and **Paradise Island**, spend a day or two on **Harbour Island**, wandering the stunning Pink Sands Beach, shopping at deluxe boutiques and dining among the glitterati at the Landing Restaurant. Then catch a water taxi to mainland **Eleuthera** and rent a car to explore the skinny 100-mile-long island, stopping for steak and revelry at the Rainbow Inn & Restaurant and spending at least a whole day at stunning, isolated **Lighthouse Beach**. In week two, grab a flight to **Abaco** for a week of exploring the Loyalist Cays via ferry or rental boat. Don't miss the Sunday pig roast at Nipper's Beach Bar & Grill on Great Guana Cay. Week three, fly back to Nassau and on to **Exuma** to visit Stocking Island and snorkel at **Thunderball Grotto**. Then fly onto pretty **Long Island** to see the striking churches of **Clarence Town** and the world's deepest undersea blue hole at **Turtle Cove**. In week four, it's back to Nassau, then on to **Andros** for bonefishing and blue hole exploring before catching the puddle-jumper to **Grand Bahama** to spend your last few days relaxing on peaceful **Lucaya Beach**.

Three Days
A Quick Nassau Getaway

Just a few hours from many major US cities, Nassau makes a perfect quick 'n' dirty getaway for a long weekend.

Spend your first morning getting oriented with a self-guided walking tour of the pastel-pretty colonial **downtown**. Learn about dastardly sea villains at the **Pirates of Nassau** museum, then head up the **Queen's Staircase** to **Fort Fincastle** for panoramic views over the harbor. In the afternoon, hit **Cable Beach** for sunning and water sports, then head downtown for dinner at the atmospherically Gothic **Graycliff Restaurant** (be sure to buy a stogie at the adjacent **cigar factory**). The next day, take the bridge to Paradise Island for a day of theme-park fun at the enormous **Atlantis** resort. Ride on waterslides, gawk at sharks through the lobby's aquarium windows, shop for duty-free diamonds and test your luck at the casino, then dine on avant-garde sushi at celebrity chef-run **Nobu**. On your last day, watch the famous flamingos march at **Ardastra Gardens, Zoo & Conservation Park** then take an afternoon **snorkeling trip** to nearby reefs before hopping on an evening flight back home.

Five Days

Relaxing Grand Bahama

Built specifically as a tourism destination in the 1950s, clean, peaceful, modern Grand Bahama is an ideal spot for a no-fuss holiday. From the airport take a taxi to **Lucaya**, the tidy coastal suburb that's home to most of the hotels and restaurants. Spend an afternoon exploring the duty-free shops, straw markets and cafes of pastel-pretty Port Lucaya Marketplace, then strolling over to dinner at trendy Sabor. The next day, lie on silvery **Lucaya Beach** for hours and don't move a finger (except maybe to grab lunch at Billy Joe's on the Beach). On day three, rent a car or catch a cab to **Garden of the Groves** for strolling and birdwatching, then on to the Junkanoo Beach Club for DIY snorkeling and kayaking, finishing up by enjoying fried turbot and listening to rake 'n' scrape at the Smith's Point Fish Fry. On day four, go eastward for hiking in **Lucayan National Park** and splendiferous empty sands at **Gold Rock Beach**. For your last day, treat yourself to a custom-made scent at the Freeport's Perfume Factory and a peek at the eerie International Bazaar before heading back to the airport.

Two Weeks

Out Island Adventure

Start off in vast but undeveloped **Andros**, a pristine wilderness of pineyard forest, barrier reef (one of the largest in the world) and hidden blue holes. Divers head to Small Hope Bay Lodge, a laid-back ecoresort in Central Andros. From here, culture vultures should explore the Bahamas African heritage on **Cat Island,** where the mysticism of obeah folk magic still reigns. Canoe around quiet **Turtle Cove** and take in the sunset from atop the striking **Mt Alvernia Hermitage**. Remote and unspoiled, the **Crooked Island District** offers a remote natural setting with a few splendid beaches, bat caves, birds (especially flamingos) and nesting turtles. **Mayaguana** is one of the least developed Bahamian islands, known for fantastic diving, populations of iguanas and its flamingos and isolated beaches. Finally, head for semiarid, scrub-covered **Great Inagua**. Nature rules here, with a **turtle reserve** at Union Creek and the famous **Bahamas National Trust Park**, where a hike takes you into the heart of one of the world's largest flocks of flamingos. Unfortunately none of the islands are connected by air to each other, so you'll have to zip in and out of Nassau regularly.

Diving in the Bahamas

Best Dolphin Encounter

Bill & Nowdla Keefe's Bimini Undersea (p98) Wild Atlantic spotted dolphins frolic alongside divers, coming and going as they please with no human pressure.

Best Wall Dive

Andros Plunge over the lip of the Continental Shelf and into the 6000ft-deep Tongue of the Ocean (p107).

Scariest Shark Experience

Underwater Explorers Society (UNEXSO; p77) Get up-close and personal with reef sharks while diving with this renowned Grand Bahama outfitter.

Wildest Drift Dive

Current Cut (p146) The fast-moving waters of this Eleuthera channel whisk divers past reefs and shipwrecks.

Best Wreck

Theo's Wreck (p76) Divers can penetrate the engine rooms and cargo holds of this 240ft-long freighter, sunk in 110ft of water off Grand Bahama.

Planning Your Dive

When to Go

During the coolest months (December through April), water temperatures are usually between 72°F (22°C) and 76°F (24°C). Summer water temperatures range from a balmy 78°F (25°C) to 84°F (28°C). You won't need anything more than a 3mm wetsuit.

Conditions are optimal year-round. Gin-clear visibility is the norm – it runs to 100ft and more – although the occasional winds can roil the waters. The lack of pollution and run-off is a definite bonus. Current conditions vary, but are generally imperceptible to mild.

What to See

The Bahamas is one of the richest marine realms in the Caribbean. Its warm tropical waters hold one of the greatest varieties of sea life found in the region. Dream of encountering the beasts? You can mingle with Caribbean reef sharks and nurse sharks, barracuda, bottlenose dolphins and spotted dolphins. Prefer smaller, technicolor critters? You'll spot loads of reef fish, including angelfish, snapper, jacks, grunts, parrotfish, lobsters, cardinal fish, damselfish, Nassau groupers, stingrays and moray eels. Want to see invertebrates? The vertical walls drip with gorgonians, hard corals, sponges and crinoids, combining to create a vivid and sensual tapestry.

Prices & Offerings

In Nassau, Grand Bahama and other well-trafficked areas, dive centers offer a full range of services and products, such as introductory dives, night dives, exploratory dives, specialty dives (such as blue holes, drift dives, Nitrox dives) and certification programs (usually PADI or NAUI).

While most dive shops are owned and operated independently of the island hotels, you may be able to book a dive package that includes both diving and lodging at a reputable hotel or resort. Generally, dive operations provide transfers to and from hotels.

Below are some dive costs. Note, two-, five- and 10-dive packages are much cheaper:

» introductory dive – including lessons and equipment $190

» single dive – with only a tank and weights supplied, $80 to $110 (much more for a specialty dive, such as shark dives or dolphin dives)

» equipment rental – an extra $45 per dive

» an Open Water certification course costs about $650

Island-by-Island Guide

All the islands of the Bahamas have spectacular diving, though some are more renowned than others. The following descriptions are by no means exhaustive. Local dive centers and tourist offices can provide specific location details and help you plan your trip. For information on diving organizations, see also p253.

Abacos

The Abacos are a diver's treat, with a good mix of caves, reef dives, wrecks and inland holes. Of particular interest is the ***San Jacinto***, which sank in 1865. Her remains are strewn on a gentle slope in less than 50ft. You'll see its big boilers, engine, propeller, stern and other structures. There's abundant fish life hanging around, including schools of grunts, snapper, goatfish, groupers and spotted eels. Further south, the ***Debra K*** is another fish haven, at about 45ft. It's also broken up, but is very atmospheric.

The Loyalist Cays have some of the country's most spectacular reefs, all psychedelic sponges and eye-popping sea fans:

» **Pelican Cays Land and Sea Park** Most outfitters will take you to this protected marine area, vibrant with grouper, moray eels and green sea turtles.

» **Fowl Cay** Another protected marine area to visit with an outfitter.

» **Mermaid Reef** Just off Marsh Harbour, close to the Loyalist Cays, this reef is shallow and best for snorkeling; keep your eyes open for the resident barracuda.

Andros

A mere 15-minute plane hop from Nassau opens up a whole new world of diving. Andros is one of the most intriguing islands in the Bahamas, with a sense of frontier diving. Another attraction is the presence of oceanic and inland blue holes. Over the years Andros has become the epicenter of blue-hole diving. While inland blue holes are for highly trained specialty divers only, there are some exceptional oceanic blue holes that are perfectly suitable for novice and intermediate divers.

» **Andros Wall** This awesome drop-off plummets down 6000ft into the Tongue of the Ocean. It is adorned with sponges, sea whips and gorgonians, and riddled with overhangs, chimneys, arches and caverns, such as those in Diana's Dungeons, Alec's Cavern, Hole in the Wall and Over the Wall, four fantastic sites at the edge of the wall. Keep your eyes peeled for big pelagics. There are also numerous shallow reef dives in the area.

» **Big Blue Hole** Originated from a collapse of the sea wall. This magical site features an enormous cavern system endowed with huge tunnels, boulders and other massive geological structures. You'll feel like you're floating in a lunar landscape. Unforgettable.

Biminis

The Biminis are famous for the **wild dolphin excursions** offered by Bill & Nowdla Keefe's Bimini Undersea dive center (p98). The experience differs completely from the Dolphin Encounter programs in Grand Bahama. Here it's much more spontaneous. You'll frolic with a pod of wild Atlantic spotted dolphins in their natural habitat on a flat northeast of the island – it requires a 1½-hour boat trip from the marina. While the encounter is not exactly guaranteed, the outfit claims a success rate of 80%. The dolphins are never forced to do anything they don't want to, and they are never rewarded with food.

Diving in the Biminis is not limited to dolphin encounters:

» **Bimini Barge** Wreck buffs should explore this magnificent barge, sitting upright in about 90ft near the edge of the drop-off.

BLUE HOLES

Blue holes are water-filled sinkholes that can occur inland or under the sea. The Bahamas, especially Andros, is famous for numerous, massive and mysterious blue holes, some of which make for fantastic diving. Among the best-known holes are Long Island's **Dean's Blue Hole** (at 663ft, the world's deepest ocean hole), inland Andros' stalactite-filled **Stargate**, Abaco's **Dan's Cave**, and Grand Bahama's **Owl's Hole**. Many inland holes have elaborate subterranean tunnels leading to the sea, so don't be surprised if you see a rogue shark or sea turtle in what looks like a country pond! Because the water at the bottom of the holes lacks oxygen, organic matter like ancient fish skeletons can remain preserved for ages, making many blue holes rich archaeological troves.

» ***Sapona*** The wreck sits half in and half out of the water and is surrounded by a smorgasbord of reef fish and decorated with a kaleidoscope of delightful corals and sponges.

» **The Wall** A sensational, high-voltage drift dive in the nutrient-rich Gulf Stream, over the edge of the continental shelf.

» **The Strip** A colorful night dive along a strip of reef surrounded by sand.

» **Bimini Road** An unusual site with a double line of large, neat square slabs, said to be the remnants of the legendary civilization of Atlantis.

Cat Island

Less-visited Cat Island is a true gem, with numerous untouched sites for those willing to venture away from the tourist areas. The dramatic seascape is the main drawcard, with an outstanding vertical wall that borders the south end of the island. It is peppered with numerous chasms, coral canyons, sandy valleys, gullies, faults and swim-throughs. Pelagics, especially sharks, regularly patrol the area. There are also elaborate shallow reefs and coral gardens inside the reef.

Recommended sites:

» **Hole in the Wall** An L-shaped channel in the wall, teeming with snappers, groupers, jacks and lots of soft and hard corals.

» **The Trench** An impressive groove in the reef, with an exit over the vertical wall.

» **The Playground** At the tip of Devil's Point, a varied site with a prolific fish life, including turtles, jacks, groupers, lobsters, squirrelfish and nurse sharks hanging under ledges.

» **Tartar Bank** An offshore pinnacle 3 miles from the coast, its near-constant current attracts plenty of schooling fish, along with nurse sharks and turtles.

Eleuthera

Eleuthera offers a wide range of diving experiences, ranging from wall-diving to drift dives and wreck dives. Most sites are located in the north, out of Harbour Island. The **Plateau**, the **Arch**, the **Grotto** and the **Blow Hole**, as their names suggest, boast a dramatic topography, with canyons, grooves, ledges, tunnels and crevices, all harboring large and small tropical fish.

Must-see dives:

» **Current Cut** If you want a thrilling ride try this narrow channel between the western tip of North Eleuthera and Current Island. During tidal exchange, divers are sucked into the pass and propelled through the funnel by the powerful current. For about 10 minutes, you'll feel as though you're gliding, accompanied by a procession of fish, both reef species and pelagics. The ride of a lifetime!

» **Devil's Backbone Wrecks** For wreck enthusiasts. The treacherous Devil's Backbone reef has snared many vessels, such as the *Cienfuegos*, a 292ft American steamship that ran aground on the reef in 1895, the *Potato & Onion* wreck and the *Carnarvon*, another freighter. They are mostly dismembered but some of their structures are still recognizable.

The Exumas

If you want relaxed diving, the Exumas will appeal to you. There are some excellent reef dives off George Town, near Stocking Island – the barrier reef is in pristine condition, ablaze with colorful life, and you'll have the sites to yourself. Another highlight is the numerous caves and blue holes that are hollowed out in the reef. They are far less intimidating than those at Andros and are a perfect introduction to blue-hole diving.

» **Fowl Cay Reef** A shallow reef with a rainbow of tiny darting tropical fish.

» **Crab Cay Crevasse** A very atmospheric blue hole, divable only at outgoing tide.

» **Angelfish Blue Hole** Has an O-shaped entryway in about 25ft. Look for the resident lobsters, grunts, angelfish and nurse sharks.

Grand Bahama

Grand Bahama boasts an exceptional diversity of underwater wonders. The island is world famous for its **Dolphin Experience** programs offered by the Underwater Explorers Society (UNEXSO; p77). Divers can interact with tame bottlenose dolphins in the open ocean, in a fascinating – though artificial – show conducted by dolphin trainers. Divers are positioned on the seafloor while two semicaptive dolphins glide over and play with them, under the guidance of the trainer. Divers can interact with tame bottlenose dolphins in the open ocean, swimming along the reef with the graceful cetaceans.

Mount Olympus and **Memory Rock** rank among the most spectacular sites, and for good reason. On the eastern edge of the Gulf Stream, far from the island, they boast a dramatic seascape. Memory Rock is a superb wall-dive, sporting a dazzling array of sponges, corals and gorgonians. The frequent occurrence of pelagics also spices up the diving. Mount Olympus is a very atmospheric site, featuring a series of prominent, mountain-like coral boulders laced with sand valleys and gullies. The area shelters an underwater Eden of lush coral growth and copious fish life. If you're lucky, you'll spot hammerheads.

Grand Bahama is also blessed with first-rate shipwrecks. Some of the best:

» **Theo's Wreck** A photogenic long-standing favorite. She rests on her port side at a depth of 110ft. Divers can penetrate the engine rooms and cargo holes.

» ***Sea Star II*** This large vessel was scuttled in 2002. She is starting to be encrusted by invertebrates, and can be entered as well.

» **Sugar Wrecks** In less than 20ft, these scattered remains are not exactly impressive but they host a profusion of fish life, including nurse sharks, moray eels, turtles, groupers and barracuda.

Inland, experienced divers can brave **Ben's Cavern**, which sits within the boundaries of Lucayan National Park. The vast cave is decorated with huge stalactites and stalagmites.

In the mood for a thrill-packed dive? Try **Shark Junction**, another shark dive. Here, the feeders wear chain mail shark suits and lead an exceptional show. They place sharks in a trance-like state, stroking their snouts and holding the predators' heads in their laps for several seconds. Visiting divers are thus given a chance to approach a shark very closely.

Southern Bahamas

Relaxed, unhurried Long Island has superb dive sites off its northwestern tip. There are some outstanding reefs with thriving fish life.

» **MV *Comberbach*** This steel freighter, scuttled in 1986 and resting upright in 100ft, is a not-to-be-missed wreck. Over the years, it has become nicely encrusted and has attracted a host of colorful species, including amberjacks, groupers and parrotfish. Inside you'll find a broken van.

» **Barracuda Heads** This perennial Long Island favorite is a vast, sandy expanse studded with a

RESPONSIBLE DIVING

The Bahamas islands are ecologically vulnerable. By following these guidelines while diving, you can help preserve the ecology and beauty of the reefs:

» Encourage dive operators in their efforts to establish permanent moorings at appropriate dive sites.

» Practice and maintain proper buoyancy control.

» Avoid touching living marine organisms with your body and equipment.

» Take great care in underwater caves, as your air bubbles can damage fragile organisms.

» Minimize your disturbance of marine animals.

» Take home all your trash and any litter you may find as well.

» Never stand on corals, even if they look solid and robust.

TOP DIVE CENTERS

Abacos Brendal's Dive Center (☎242-365-4411; www.brendal.com) See p129.

Andros Small Hope Bay Lodge (☎242-368-2014, 800-223-6961; www.smallhope.com) See p108.

Biminis Bill & Nowdla Keefe's Bimini Undersea (☎242-347-3089, 800-348-4644; www.biminiundersea.com) See p98.

Cat Island Hawk's Nest Resort & Marina (☎242-342-7050, 800-688-4752; www.hawksnest.com) See p175.

Eleuthera Valentine's Dive Center (☎242-333-2080; www.valentinesdive.com) See p142.

Exumas Dive Exuma (☎242-336-2893; www.dive-exuma.com) See p159.

Grand Bahama Underwater Explorers Society (UNEXSO; ☎242-373-1244, 800-992-3483; www.unexso.com) See p77.

Southern Bahamas Stella Maris Resort Club & Marina (☎242-338-2051, 800-426-0466; www.stellamarisresort.com) See p185.

New Providence Stuart Cove's Dive & Snorkel Bahamas (☎242-362-4171; www.stuartcove.com) See p52.

San Salvador Riding Rock Resort & Marina (☎242-331-2631, 800-272-1492; www.ridingrock.com) See p179.

jumble of large coral heads, with the usual species of multicolored reef fish fluttering about. Big barracuda also patrol the area.

» **Shark Reef** Thrill-seekers dig this very special shark feed. Divers kneel on the sandy seabed in about 40ft, then a bucket of chum is released from the stern of the dive boat. A gang of Caribbean reef sharks will immediately dart to the scene, vying for the free meal.

» **Dean's Blue Hole** On Long Island, the deepest undersea blue hole in the world is accessible from shore.

New Providence

The strength of New Providence is the sheer variety of attractions, including superb shipwrecks, breathtaking walls along the Tongue of the Ocean, a varied topography and healthy coral gardens. But what makes it so unique is the shark diving. Divers from all over the world come here to experience a fantastic adrenaline rush at **Shark Wall** and **Shark Arena**, two feeding spots south of the island. On a coral rubble patch, in less than 65ft, the divers form a semicircle a few meters away from the feeders to watch the show. And what a show! A dense cloud of Caribbean reef sharks tear hunks off the a bait pole, ripping it away with a shake of the head. After 15 minutes of intense activity, the remains are tossed aside and the dive continues at a calmer pace.

Less, uh, adrenaline-pumping dive sites:

» **Bond Wreck** A tugboat and the remains of a mock fighter plane were used in the James Bond films *Thunderball* and *Never Say Never Again*. Swim around and inside the ribs of the mock-up, festooned with soft and hard corals, all with vivid hues.

» ***Wil Laurie*** A massive wreck draped with corals and glowing sponges; in about 60ft.

» ***Bahama Mama*** A 110ft-long pleasure vessel which was scuttled in 1995.

» ***Sea Viking*** A vessel still in good shape, on the edge of the drop-off. The abundant fish life is a bonus.

San Salvador

'San Sal' boasts world-class wall-diving. The island is an exposed seamount, surrounded by walls that tumble vertically to several thousand feet. Its isolation and the depth of the water make it a magnet for both pelagic and reef species, including big numbers of groupers and hammerheads. There are also big cave and tunnel formations. Most dive sites are scattered along the west coast, sheltered from the prevailing winds. Don't think this is all challenging diving, however. You don't need to go deep – the wall starts at just 50ft or so. The local dive center, Riding Rock Resort & Marina (p179) uses at least 20 dive sites. Don't miss **Devil's Claw**, **Telephone Pole**, **Doolittle's Grotto**, **North Pole Cave**, **Black Forest** and **French Bay**.

Travel With Children

Best Regions for Kids

Nassau

Pirate history, horse-drawn carriage rides and colorful Junkanoo displays make downtown an eye-popping treat for the junior set.

Paradise Island

Atlantis' wet and wild adventureland of waterslides, dolphin lagoons, faux ruins and shark-filled aquariums appeal to the kid in all of us.

Grand Bahama

This clean and peaceful island is one of the most family-friendly in the country, its busy beaches abounding with kid-oriented water sports and activities.

Abacos

Renting a sailboat to ferry your family around the cays is a favorite activity for seaworthy vacationers.

Exuma

Kids will love exploring the fish-filled shallows of the Exuma Cays, followed by hearty island suppers of local specialties like mac 'n' cheese.

The Bahamas for Kids

Attractions

Family-oriented Bahamians love kids (babies especially will be fawned over!), and fun-oriented kids love the Bahamas. I mean, what part of 'petting dolphins, riding waterslides, and eating mac 'n' cheese for dinner every night' isn't to like? Resorts, especially in Nassau and Grand Bahama, aim to woo the family traveler with perks like babysitting, kid menus and on-site playgrounds. Family travel in the Out Islands takes a bit more planning (buy diapers ahead of time!), but you'll be well-rewarded watching your children run merrily around secluded beaches, splashing in bathtub-warm waters.

Nassau, Paradise Island and Grand Bahama are your best bets for young children, attractions-wise. Nassau has a kid-friendly pirate museum, horse-drawn carriage rides, beaches with parasailing and banana boat rides, and a fun zoo, while Paradise Island's water park will blow Junior's mind. Grand Bahama offers lots of family-oriented snorkel and nature trips, and has a famous shallow-water dolphin experience perfect for those too young to dive. Older kids will love the nature of the Out Islands – snorkeling amid giant eagle rays, swimming with the infamous pigs of Exuma.

Entertainment

Vibrant rake 'n' scrape music, Junkanoo dancing and impromptu drum circles

A PIRATE'S LIFE FOR ME

Yo ho ho and a bottle of rum! Though pirates haven't been seen in these waters in several hundred years, their scallywag legacy remains. Pirate-loving kids will adore the **Pirates of Nassau** (p41) museum, complete with a replica pirate ship. A few miles away, **Blackbeard's Tower** (p47) is said to be the handiwork of the dastardly villain himself – you'll have to use your imagination on the pile of stones. More vivid are the dungeons at **Fort Charlotte** (p49), where costumed local teens offer tours of the dank depths. Parts of *Pirates of the Caribbean* II and III were filmed in Grand Bahama – ask locals about their Johnny Depp sightings.

entertain kids of all ages. Many restaurants feature live music on weekends and the atmosphere stays family-friendly until 10pm or 11pm. Local Fish Fries are also a great place for kids to bop their heads to the beat and maybe even make a few local pals.

Dining

Bahamian cuisine – heavy on starches like rice, sweet potatoes and mac 'n' cheese – tends to suit young palates just fine. Local restaurants are very casual and family-friendly. Just watch out for desserts like guava duff (boiled jellyroll pastries filled with sweetened guava paste), which sometimes contain a healthy slug of rum!

Most tourist-heavy areas have plenty of casual family-friendly dining. With the exception of a handful of very high-end establishments in Nassau, Paradise Island and Harbour Island, kids are welcome almost anywhere.

Children's Highlights

Accommodations

» **Atlantis Royal Towers, Paradise Island** Atlantis' biggest property is its theme park-iest, with a lobby aquarium, a faux archaeological dig, and pools and grottoes galore.

» **Reef Atlantis, Paradise Island** Atlantis's all-condo hotel is perfect for long-term stays, with full-kitchens and ample space.

» **Wyndham Nassau Resort, Cable Beach** Has a kids' club, children's pools and a bustling family atmosphere.

» **Our Lucaya Beach & Golf Resort, Reef Village** This massive resort has a giant family pool and a full-service kids' club, as well as multiple on-site family restaurants.

» **Bahama Beach Club, Treasury Cay** This condo-style resort is popular with families for longer-term stays.

» **Bimini Sands Resort & Marina, South Bimini** One- and two-bedroom apartments are perfect for families, and the on-site recreation department has tons of fun activities.

» **Coral Sands Hotel, Harbour Island** This large resort is less precious than some, with large villas and apartments, and kid-friendly perks like free boogie boards and a games room.

Dining

» **Mosaic, Paradise Island** An all-you-can-eat buffet that both kids and adults can love, with endless tables of pizza, create-you-own pasta, sushi, waffles and way more.

» **Carmine's, Paradise Island** This boisterous Italian joint serves family-style heaps of red-sauce classics like spaghetti and meatballs.

» **Arawak Cay, Nassau** Treat your kids to conch fritters and Junkanoo music at this vibrant Fish Fry. Things get less family-friendly late at night.

» **Billy Joe's on the Beach, Lucaya** Young'uns will love eating at sandy beachfront picnic tables at this classic Grand Bahama conch shack.

» **Cap'n Jack's, Hope Town** Deckside dining and killer key lime pie make this town staple a kid favorite.

» **Beach Bungalow, Long Island** This friendly spot is well loved for its delicious pizzas.

» **Ma Ruby's, Harbour Island** Cure your kids of Big Mac obsession at this patio cafe, home to the fabulous Cheeseburger in Paradise.

Water Adventures

» **UNEXSO Dolphin Encounter, Grand Bahama** Kids stand on a shallow water platform to pet and kiss tame dolphins at this wildly popular encounter.

» **Stuart Cove's Dive & Snorkel Bahamas, New Providence** Older kids who aren't quite ready for scuba diving can hop into these personal mini 'submarine suits' for an underwater ride.

» **Seaworld Explorer, Nassau** This semi-submarine gives a thrilling ride over the reef.

» **Aquaventure, Paradise Island** This gargantuan water park has rides for kids of all ages, from a gentle lazy river to a stomach-knotting 200ft-long slide.

» **Exuma Cays** Older children and teens love snorkeling in the calm, gin-clear waters of the cays. Go solo or join a tour.

» **Lucaya Beach** Ride bouncing banana boats, fly high in a parasail, snorkel in the shallows – Grand Bahama's most popular beach has kid-friendly water sports galore.

Planning

Babies & Toddlers

If visiting the Out Islands, be sure to pack plenty of diapers, formula or other necessities, as grocery stores are few and ill-stocked. Many larger hotels and resorts offer babysitting services, but infants may not be eligible. Be aware that Bahamian women rarely breastfeed or change diapers in public.

Kids Six to 12

Check ahead to make sure your accommodations are kid-friendly – some smaller hotels and resorts only allow children 12 or 14 and up. Look for resorts offering kids' clubs – minicamps full of video games, toys and art supplies to keep Junior busy while you get some quality grown-up time. Kids 12 and under are generally allowed to sleep in their parents' rooms for free. If you have multiple kids, rental apartments and villas are often a good bet.

Teens

Teens are generally treated as adults in the Bahamas, so you may have to pay extra to have them sleep in your room. While we're sure your kids would *never* attempt such a thing, be aware that the drinking age in the Bahamas is 18, but is rarely enforced – a mature-looking 15 or 16 year old could easily be served at a bar or nightclub.

regions at a glance

With 29 islands and nearly 700 cays spread across 100,000 sq miles of Atlantic ocean, the Bahamas feels more like many nations than one. The vibe ranges wildly from one island to the next – New Providence is a thrumming capital and megatourism destination, while a 15-minute flight away, Andros is a slumbering giant of unexplored pineyard forest and untouched beaches, with not a person in sight.

So whether you're looking for glitzy urban revelry or blissed-out solitude on a white-sand beach, the Bahamas has an island for you.

Nassau & New Providence

History ✓✓✓
Resorts ✓✓✓
Nightlife ✓✓✓

Resorts the size of small European nations. Bikini-clad Spring Breakers lying elbow-to-elbow on white-sand beaches. A chaotic downtown of honking cabbies, historical buildings and duty-free diamond shops. This is the Bahamas' throbbing heart. **p38**

Grand Bahama

Family-friendly ✓✓✓
Shopping ✓✓✓
Resorts ✓✓✓

The Bahamas' oft-overlooked second fiddle of an island steps into the spotlight with affordable, family-friendly resorts, wide golden beaches and excellent duty-free shopping. If you're lucky, maybe you'll even meet a friendly dolphin or two. **p73**

Biminis, Andros & Berry Islands

Fishing ✓✓✓
Diving ✓✓✓
Seclusion ✓✓✓

Anglers, divers and adventurers delight in these three little-developed island groups. Explore hidden blue holes on Andros, cast your reel for marlin on fishing-crazed Bimini, or drift amid the unpopulated cays of the Berry Islands. **p93**

Abacos

Sailing ✓✓✓
History ✓✓
Fishing ✓✓

Yachties flock to the 'sailing capital of the world,' though you don't have to have your own boat to explore the history-filled Loyalist Cays, fish the Marls or lie for hours on splendiferous Treasure Cay Beach. **p114**

Eleuthera

Beaches ✓✓✓
Shopping ✓✓
Dining ✓✓

Jetsetter-types dig the resorts, boutiques and pink sands of chichi Harbour Island, while independent travelers love to explore the skinny stretch of mainland Eleuthera, with its hidden rock grottoes, jaw-dropping coves and funky little hotels. **p137**

The Exumas

Beaches ✓✓✓
Yachting ✓✓✓
Kayaking ✓✓

Some of the Bahamas' most perfect beaches can be found in this string of 365 islands, dominated by Great Exuma, the yachting capital of the country. Take your pick of the cays: you won't be disappointed. **p156**

Cat & San Salvador Islands

Beaches ✓✓✓
Diving ✓✓✓
Caribbean Culture ✓✓

San Salvador is *the* wall diving destination in the Bahamas, and is also a fascinating step back in time, while Cat Island excels in white-sand beaches and is a great spot to avoid the crowds. **p169**

Southern Bahamas

Beaches ✓✓
Wildlife ✓✓
Fishing ✓✓✓

The undeveloped Southern Bahamas are a place to come for total escape. Bonefishing is superb on Crooked and Acklins Islands, while remote Inagua boasts excellent birdwatching. Long Island has some stunning beaches and dive sites. **p181**

Turks & Caicos

Beaches ✓✓✓
Diving ✓✓✓
Caribbean Culture ✓✓

With the Turks & Caicos you have the choice of the resort-heavy, dazzling beaches of Provo, or the old-Caribbean atmosphere on Grand Turk, Salt Cay or the other Caicos Islands. **p196**

Look out for these icons:

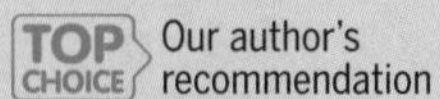

Our author's recommendation

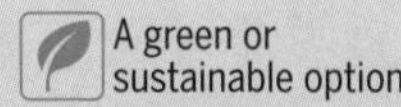
A green or sustainable option

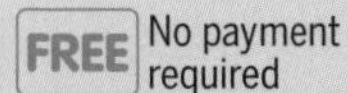

No payment required

On the Road

The Bahamas

RICHARD CUMMINS/LONELY PLANET IMAGES ©

Nassau & New Providence

TELEPHONE CODE: 242 / POPULATION: 249,000 / AREA: 80 SQ MILES

Includes »

Best Places to Stay

» British Colonial Hilton Nassau (p56)
» Cove Atlantis (p59)
» Atlantis Royal Towers (p58)
» A Stone's Throw Away (p57)
» Compass Point Beach Resort (p58)
» One & Only Ocean Club (p59)

Best Places to Eat

» Graycliff Restaurant (p60)
» Arawak Cay (p62)
» Nobu (p63)
» Mesa Grill (p63)
» Goodfellow Farms (p62)

Why Go?

What New Providence lacks in size, it more than makes up for in energy, attitude and devil-may-care spirit. In fact, this 21-mile-long powerhouse of an island is a perfect fit for the Type-A tourist with money to burn. Plummet down a 50ft-long waterslide, puff on a hand-rolled stogie, place your bets on a high-stakes hand and party like a pirate into the wee hours – it's all there for the grabbing.

But all is not lost for value-minded Type B's, who can escape the go-go party track with minimal effort. In Nassau, just a few blocks off Bay St, there are engaging museums, historic buildings and locally owned restaurants that are crowd-free and personality-full. Scenery hounds can head to the island's western shores and hilltops. Those really wanting to disappear should beeline for the ferry terminals where sailing jaunts, fishing trips and snorkeling cruises are only an impulse away.

When to Go

Nassau

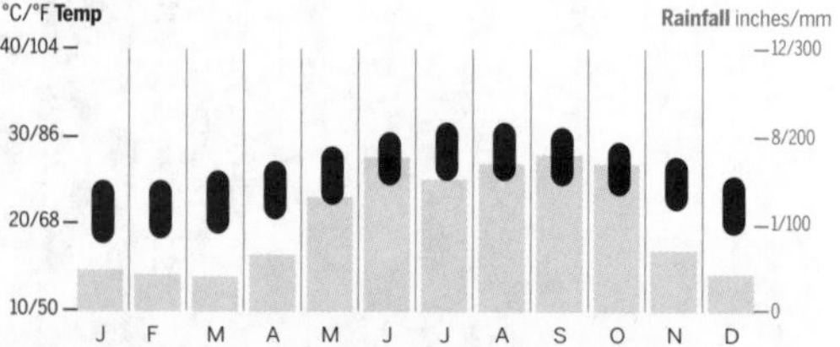

March College Spring Break means Nassau is crawling with Jell-O shot-fueled partiers. Dream or nightmare?

September–November Low season brings great rates on hotels, including the ever-pricy Atlantis. It also brings rain.

December Junkanoo bands and masked dance troops turn the island into a giant carnival.

History

The island's colorful early history is steeped in rum-running and roguery. Nassau (initially known as Charles Town) was established in 1666, its dirt streets pounded by pirates and wreckers, and lined with brothels and taverns. Fed up with relentless attacks by Charles Town's pirates on their ships, the Spaniards attacked the town in 1684, followed by an assault by a combined Spanish and French force in 1703, which didn't help the city's development much either.

Fifteen years later the pirates were ousted by the British but by the middle of the 18th century Nassau still simply consisted of a church, jail, courthouse plus an Assembly House on Bay St. In the 1760s Governor William Shirley, who had been a governor of Massachusetts, brought a Yankee sense of order and ingenuity: the swamps were drained, the land was surveyed and tidy new streets were laid.

The American Revolution boosted the city's fortunes, as citizens took to running the English blockade and a flood of entrepreneurial loyalist refugees arrived. In 1787 the haughty and inept Earl of Dunmore arrived as governor of the Bahamas in a state of disgrace, having failed to halt the American colonist rebellions as governor of Virginia. Dunmore's legacy is evident today in several fine buildings. These include Fort Charlotte and Fort Fincastle. The governor was saved from the axe for his extravagance by the outbreak of Britain's war with France in 1793.

By the late 18th century Nassau had settled into a slow-paced, glamorous era in which the well-to-do lived graciously and were served by slaves who resided in Over-the-Hill shanties. Following the abolition of

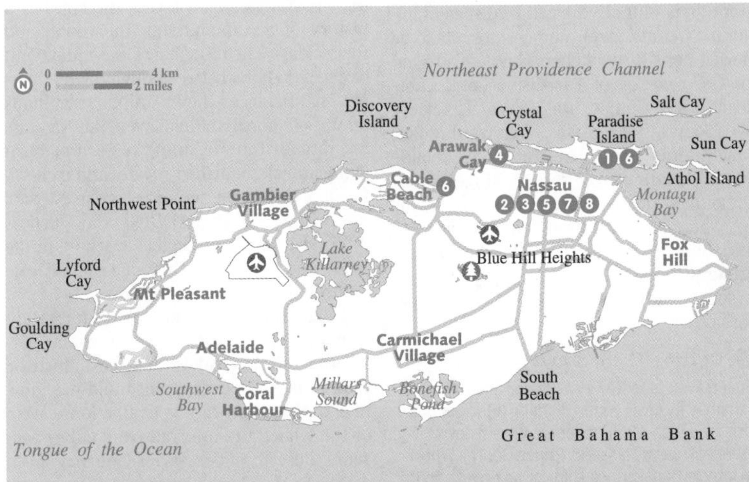

Nassau & New Providence Highlights

1 Hurtling down a 200ft-long waterslide at Atlantis' high-octane **Aquaventure water park** (p49)

2 Chatting with the real-deal Cuban cigar rollers at the **Graycliff Cigar Co** (p45), then buying a stogie or three to take home

3 Learning about the original *Pirates of the Caribbean* at the interactive **Pirates of Nassau museum** (p41)

4 Munching cracked conch, sipping on Sky Juice and shaking your bootie with the locals at the **Arawak Cay Fish Fry** (p62)

5 Sun-worshipping at **Cable Beach** (p51)

6 Praying to Lady Luck at the blackjack tables at the **Atlantis Resort & Casino** (p66)

7 Strolling the photogenic pink-and-white colonial **downtown Nassau** (p41)

8 Shopping til you drop at the duty-free palaces of **Bay St** (p67)

the slave trade by the Brits in 1807, numerous public edifices and sites, such as the Queen's Staircase, were constructed using the manual labor of former slaves.

The American Civil War and Prohibition further enhanced Nassau's fortunes; many fine hotels and homes were erected on the proceeds from blockade- and rum-running. The 'winter season' of visiting socialites set the pattern for the Bahamian peak tourism season.

National Parks

The **Retreat** (p47) is tucked away in the center of Nassau and has a vast collection of palms and tropical plants plus the **Bahamas National Trust** (BNT; p243). Enjoy a stroll through the garden's 11 acres and collect some detailed information on regional sites of interest.

Harrold and **Wilson Ponds** are perfect for a spot of hiking or birdwatching, with more than a hundred listed bird species, including herons, egrets and cormorants to be viewed here. Birdwatchers should also head for the reserves of Paradise Island, Cable Beach Golf Course, the Caves, Lakeview, Red Sound, Twin Lakes, Westward Villas, Lake Cunningham, Lake Waterloo, Adelaide Creek, Goulding Cay, Prospect Ridge, Waterworks and Skyline Heights. For the details on where to find these and other Wild Bird Reserves contact the **Department of Agriculture** (p243).

See p243 for details of other national parks.

Getting There & Away

Most travelers to New Providence and the Bahamas fly into Lynden Pindling International Airport, which lies 10 miles west from downtown. Others arrive at Nassau's Prince George Wharf on international cruise ships or on private boats.

Getting Around

You can easily navigate your way around downtown Nassau and Cable Beach by foot. They are joined by a regular stream of jitney buses (private minibuses), which also run around the island, making exploration pretty easy. Pedestrians can either take the regular ferries between Prince George Wharf and Paradise Island or walk across the Paradise Island bridges to/from downtown. Keep in mind that there is a walk of almost a mile from the bridges into Nassau's tourism center.

Car-rental agencies are located at the airport and in all tourism areas, as are scooter-hire operators.

There are tons of tourism and dive operators who visit surrounding cays and other Bahamian islands, as do mail boats and Bahamas Ferries services.

See p71 for information on getting to/from the airport.

Nassau

Who needs Red Bull when there's downtown Nassau? This cacophonous blur of bouncing jitney buses, hustling cabbies, bargaining vendors, trash-talking pirates and elbow-knocking shoppers is a guaranteed pick-me-up for even the sleepiest of cruise-ship day-trippers.

And it's been luring high-energy hustlers for centuries. From the 17th-century pirates who blew their doubloons on women and wine to the dashing blockade runners who smuggled cargo from the Confederacy during the American Civil War, the city has a history of accommodating the young and the reckless. The trend continues today, with bankers dodging between downtown's international banks as they manipulate millions on this offshore banking haven. But Nassau's not just for those wanting to earn or burn a quick buck. Banished royalty and camera-fleeing celebs have found refuge in Nassau, too, with the disgraced Duke and Duchess of Windsor keeping tongues wagging in the 1940s and the ultimately tragic Anna Nicole Smith hiding out here in 2006.

Today, duty-free shops jostle for attention on Bay St with jewelry, coins, perfumes and rum cakes. Just east, historic Georgian-style government buildings glow like pink cotton-candy confections. West of the wharf, the informative Pompey Museum describes the slaves' journey from Africa to the Caribbean while faux buccaneers set a rowdier mood at the Pirates of Nassau museum a few steps south.

Nassau has a grittier vibe than you might expect from a cruise-ship destination, but don't be put off by the initial hustle. Slow down, look around, then embrace its unabashed verve – it might be the perfect high-energy antidote to your lingering case of cabin fever.

Sights

History buffs can get an eyeful of Nassau's past in a few short hours, as most historical sights are found in a small area of downtown around West Hill St and East Hill St.

Art fans should also head to these locations and to Village Rd for the galleries, while those itching for sand and sea should go to Cable Beach, the southern beaches and Paradise Island. On the way to Cable Beach, families may want to stop downtown and west of downtown for fun museums and some wildlife, but don't miss Atlantis on Paradise Island!

DOWNTOWN NASSAU

For those stepping off a quiet cruise ship, Bay St may seem to teeter on the verge of absolute chaos. Scooters, trucks and jitneys hurtle through the center of town on this narrow artery, dodging throngs of tourists looking for duty-free deals. But there's more to downtown than liquor stores and T-shirt shops.

TOP CHOICE **Pirates of Nassau** MUSEUM

(Map p48; www.pirates-of-nassau.com; King St; adult/child $12/6; ⌚9am-6pm Mon-Fri, 9am-12:30pm Sat; 👪) Don't even try to ignore the pirate pacing outside the museum. Like any seafaring ruffian worth his parrot and peg-leg, he had you in his sights the moment you turned the corner. But that's OK – with its partial recreation of a 130ft-long sailing ship, animatronic pirates and accessible exhibits on everything from marooning to pirate hall-of-famers, this museum provides the right mix of entertainment and history for kids, parents and students of piratology. Great gift shop, Plunder, next door.

It may be blasphemous to mention in this piratical context, but a dashing statue of pirate menace **Woodes Rogers** stands guard just across the street.

Rawson Square MONUMENT

(Map p48; Bay St) The heart of town for tourists is Rawson Sq, on the south side of Bay St. It's a natural place to begin a tour of downtown Nassau. Nearby is a life-size bronze statue, **Bahamian Woman**, which honors the role of women during 'years of adversity.' She holds a small child. In the center of the square is a **bust of Sir Milo Butler**, the first governor-general of the independent nation, and a fountain pool with leaping bronze dolphins.

Parliament Square MONUMENT

(Map p48; Bay St) The area immediately south of Rawson Sq on Bay St is known as Parliament Sq. On three sides of the square nestle three pink-and-white Georgian neoclassical buildings (1805–13) that house the offices of the leader of the opposition (on the left, due west), the Assembly House (right), and the Senate (facing Bay St). In their midst sits the 1905 **Queen Victoria statue**.

You can peek inside the House of Assembly to watch proceedings when it's in session. Make such arrangements at the

NASSAU IN...

Two Days

Start your day with a Bahamian breakfast at **Café Skan's** followed by a stroll through historic downtown before getting your 'arrg' on at the **Pirates of Nassau** museum, then jumping on the **jitney bus 10** to explore the island.

Then laze on **Cable Beach**, sipping a rum cocktail at sunset before treating yourself to fine dining and even finer wine and cigars at the **Graycliff Restaurant**.

The next day, shop for duty-free goodies along **Bay St**. Salute the marching flamingos and snoozing iguanas of **Ardastra Gardens, Zoo & Conservation Center** before jumping on the ferry to Paradise Island for an afternoon of splashes and thrills at Atlantis' massive **Aquaventure** water park.

Fuel up on avant-garde sushi and sake at Atlantis' celebrity chef–run **Nobu**, followed by bootie shaking at the hotel's ultrahip **Aura**.

Four Days

Go scuba diving or have a fun day trip **snorkeling** at Rose Island, take a walk around the leafy **Retreat** and have a look at the vibrant artworks found in Nassau's studios and elegant **National Art Gallery of the Bahamas**.

One Week

Add a **fast ferry ride** to Eleuthera's pink-sand beaches, an **island adventure trip** to the Exuma Cays and a **diving** or **fishing expedition** to the Abacos or Biminis.

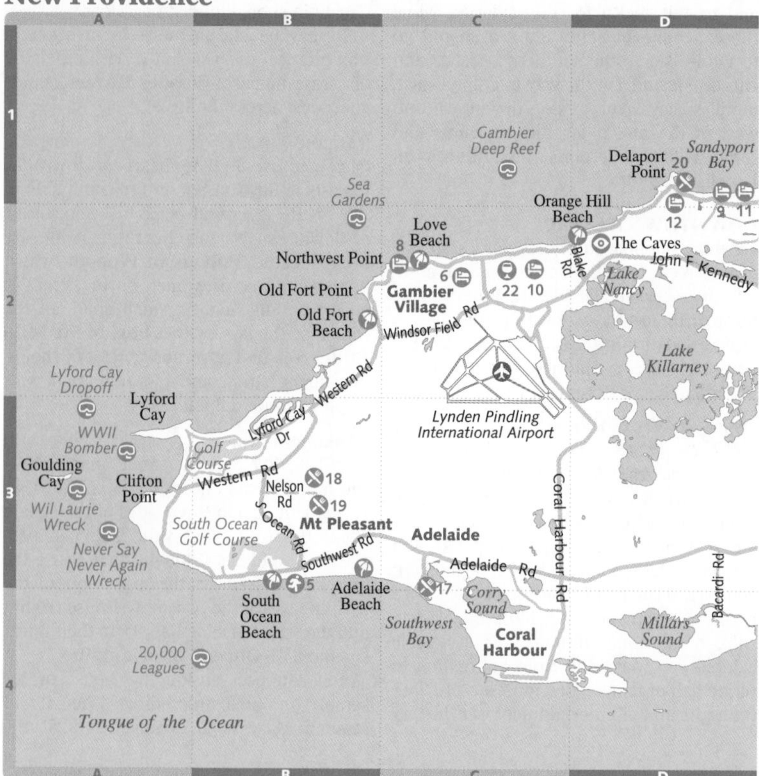

House Office of the Clerk of Courts (☎ 242-322-7500). Note its green carpet, symbolizing the English meadow (3 miles southeast of Windsor, England) where King John and his barons signed the Magna Carta in 1215. The Senate also has a visitors' gallery, with tickets given out free on a first-come, first-served basis.

Immediately south of Parliament Sq, between Parliament St and Bank Lane, is the **Supreme Court**. Each January, April, July and October pageantry marks the Opening of the Supreme Court Sessions. Lawyers and judges in full regalia march to Christ Church Anglican Cathedral for a service, followed by an inspection of the guard of honor. And a few yards further north is the small Garden of Remembrance, with a **cenotaph** honoring Bahamian soldiers who died in the two world wars. Also note the plaque to four members of the Royal Bahamas Defence Force killed in 1980 when their patrol vessel, *Flamingo,* was attacked by Cuban MiGs.

Prince George Wharf WHARF DISTRICT

The historic cruise-ship wharf, north of Rawson Sq and Bay St, is the gateway to Nassau for more than a million visitors a year. The wharf is fronted by bustling **Woodes Rogers Walk**, lined with souvenir stalls, fast-food outlets, the **Junkanoo Expo** ($2) with displays of masks and costumes, and a canopied stand where **horse-drawn surreys** await customers. The drivers will take you around the historical landmarks of the Bay St area. The rides begin and end at the Welcome Centre on Woodes Rogers Walk. A 30-minute ride costs approximately $10/5 per adult/child. Ferries to Paradise Island also leave from Woodes Rogers Walk.

Fort Fincastle FORT

(Map p48; Elizabeth Ave; admission $1; ⏰8am-4pm) Shaped like a paddle-wheel steamer (why? No one knows), this hilltop fort was built by Lord Dunmore in 1793 to guard the harbor against invaders. Never used, it

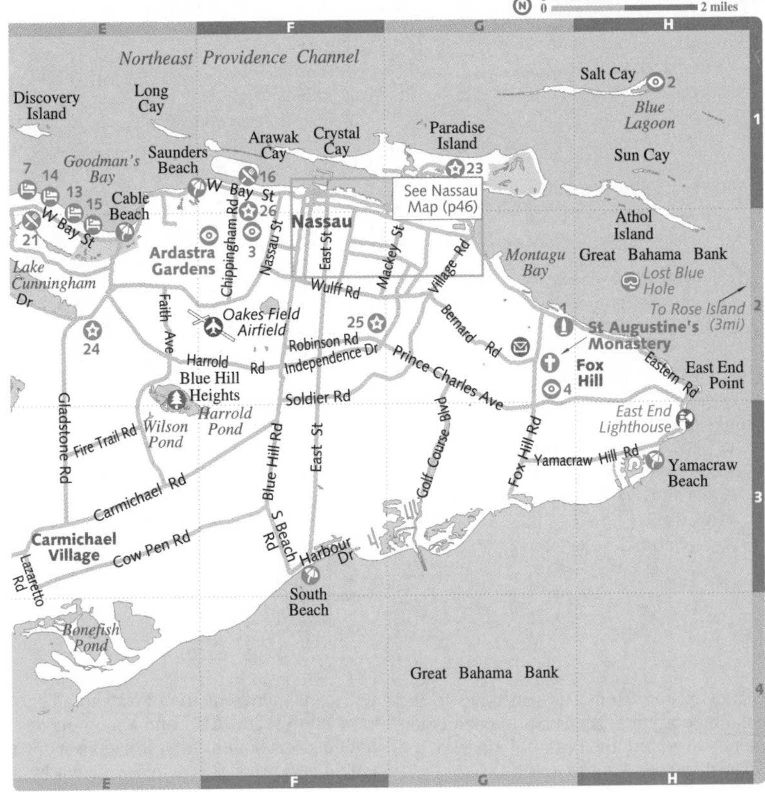

was eventually converted into a lighthouse. The fort itself is not particularly fascinating, but it's worth the trip for the sweeping panoramic views from the top. Young 'tour guides' will try to offer their services – you won't need them. The **Queen's Staircase** leads the way up. Carved by slaves from solid limestone, it's one of the island's most enduring landmarks.

Nassau Public Library — LIBRARY

(Map p48; Shirley Ave; admission free; ⏲10am-8pm Mon-Thu, to 5pm Fri, to 2pm Sat) For chills with your historical thrills, stop by this pink octagon, the oldest government building downtown. Built in 1797, it served as a jail in the 1800s but its cells are now crammed with books and dusty periodicals. Ask the librarian for the key to the tiny but creepy dungeon underneath the building. The dank walls bear scratches carved on their surface – a somber marking of days by prisoners long dead?

Pompey Museum — MUSEUM

(Map p48; Bay St; adult/child/senior $3/1/2; ⏲9:30am-4:30pm Mon-Wed, Fri & Sat, 9:30am-1pm Thu) Named after a Bahamian slave who led an unsuccessful rebellion, this spare but moving museum traces the harrowing 'Middle Passage' slave voyages from Africa to the Caribbean and Americas. Stark exhibits – a 45lb ball-and-chain, a branding iron and slave collars – reinforce the horrors inflicted on millions of Africans between the 1500s and 1860s. The building is located on a former slave auction site. Hours have been irregular in recent years, so check before planning a trip.

Bahamas Historical Society Museum — MUSEUM

(Map p48; www.bahamashistoricalsociety.com; cnr Shirley St & Elizabeth Ave; adult/child $1/0.50; ⏲10am-4pm Mon, Tue, Thu, Fri, to noon Sat) This pink corner building has a modest miscellany of artifacts and documents tracing the

New Providence

Sights

1 Blackbeard's Tower G2
2 Dolphin Encounters H1
3 Fort Charlotte F2
4 Freedom Park G2

Activities, Courses & Tours

5 Stuart Cove's Dive & Snorkel Bahamas B3

Sleeping

6 A Stone's Throw Away' C2
7 Blue Water Resort E1
8 Compass Point Beach Resort C2
9 Marley Resort D1
10 Orange Hill Beach Inn C2
11 Sandals Royal Bahamian D1
12 Sandyport Beaches Resort D1
13 Sheraton Nassau Beach E1
14 Westwind II E1
15 Wyndham Nassau Resort & Crystal Palace Casino E2

Eating

Amici .... (see 13)
16 Arawak Cay F1
17 Avery's Restaurant & Bar C3
Black Angus Grille .... (see 15)
18 Goodfellow Farms B3
19 La Hipica B3
20 Poop Deck D1
21 Swiss Pastry Shop E2

Drinking

22 Above .... (see 15)
Compass Point .... (see 8)
22 Traveller's Rest C2

Entertainment

23 Atlantis Resort & Casino G1
24 Galleria 6 .... E2
25 Galleria Cinema 11 .... F2
26 Haynes Oval F1
Wyndham Nassau Resort & Crystal Palace Casino .... (see 15)

Shopping

Marley Boutique .... (see 9)

islands' history from Lucayan times to the contemporary era. It's worth the admission merely to admire the beautiful model of the Spanish galleon *Santa Luceno*.

Straw Market MARKET
(Map p48; Bay St; ⏲7am-7pm) Currently undergoing renovation, this frenetic stall market has long been the go-to place for knock-off purses, cheap souvenir t-shirts, and cheap, made-in-China straw goods. Tacky as can be, but fun for a browse. For Bahamian-made products and straw goods, stay in Festival Place at the wharf.

Christ Church Anglican Cathedral CHURCH
(Map p48; King St; www.christchurchcathedralbahamas.com) This striking 1841 cathedral has a splendid wood-beamed roof, stained glass and pendulous Spanish-style chandeliers. The current structure is the fifth version. The original church was destroyed in 1684 by the Spaniards. Its successors were leveled during the French-Spanish invasion in 1703 and by the ravages of weather and termites.

Trinity Methodist Church CHURCH
(Map p48) At the west end of Shirley St, this delightful church was originally planned for a congregation of 800 people. Alas, the four carpenters sent from Scotland all succumbed to yellow fever and a more modest building was built in 1861. It had been open only a year when it was blown down by a hurricane. The current church dates from 1869 and was significantly repaired following damage in the 1928 hurricane.

WEST HILL STREET AREA

As you head uphill from Bay St, the neighborhood grows quieter and more regal before crumbling into the chaos of the Over-the-Hill area.

TOP CHOICE **National Art Gallery of the Bahamas** MUSEUM
(Map p48; www.nagb.org.bs; W Hill St; admission adult/child $5/free; ⏲10am-4pm Tue-Sat) Inside the stately 1860s-era Villa Doyle, this grand art museum is one of the gems in the Bahamas' crown. The permanent collection focuses on modern and contemporary Bahamian artists, from renowned sculptor Antonius Roberts to folk painter Wellington Bridgewater. Temporary exhibits cover hot topics like global warming or the Haitian earthquake. If you're jangled by the chaos of Bay St, the peaceful gallery is a welcome oasis.

TOP CHOICE **Graycliff Cigar Co** CIGAR FACTORY

(Map p48; W Hill St; admission free; ⏲9am-5pm Mon-Fri) Wandering into the back room of the Graycliff Hotel's steakhouse is like falling from 2010s Bahamas into 1920s Cuba. In a narrow, smoke-yellowed room with old-fashioned mosaic floors, a dozen *torcedores* (cigar rollers) are busy at work, their hands a blur as they roll hand-dried tobacco leaves into premium stogies. Until his recent death, the company's head *torcedor* was Avelino Lara, the former personal cigar roller to Fidel Castro. If you speak Spanish, the rollers will be happy to chat with you about their craft.

Government House GOVERNMENT BUILDING

(Map p48; W Hill St) This splendid Georgian mansion, residence to the Bahamas' Governor-General, sits atop W Hill St like a pink candied topping. Below, the **statue of Christopher Columbus** has maintained a jaunty pose on the steps overlooking Duke St since 1830. The original home was built in 1737 by Governor Fitzwilliam but was destroyed by a hurricane in 1929. The current building was completed in 1932, and the lavish decorations date from the Duke of Windsor's time as governor in the 1940s. Visitors can walk the grounds for a close look at the building, but must be accompanied by the guards. Between 4pm and 5pm on the last Friday of the month, you can 'have a cuppa' with the governor-general's wife, complete with high-tea sandwiches and live music from local bands.

St Andrews Presbyterian Kirk CHURCH

(Map p48; Prince's & Market Sts) Below Government House, this handsome church owes its existence to a Loyalist who settled in Nassau at the end of the American Revolution. In 1798 he established the St Andrew's Society, comprising 55 Scots, to 'cultivate good understanding and social intercourse.' The Freemasons laid the cornerstone in 1810, and the church has since undergone many architectural changes.

Gregory Arch MONUMENT

(Map p48; Market St) Informally delineating the border between downtown Nassau and Over-the-Hill, this stone tunnel topped with iron railings spans Market St at the east end of Government House grounds.

St Francis Xavier Cathedral CHURCH

(Map p48; cnr W Hill & West Sts) This 1885 cathedral has a long, slender nave topped by a bell tower, illuminated within at night. Many prominent Protestants of the time resented the incursion of the Catholics and ascribed to the hands of God the bolt of lightning that struck the church during construction, killing a workman and doing significant damage.

EAST OF DOWNTOWN

Potter's Cay Market MARKET

(Map p46; Bay St) The liveliest market in town sits beneath the Paradise Island Exit Bridge, where fishing boats from the Family Islands arrive daily carrying the sea's harvest,

BAHAMIAN ELOPEMENT

OK, who hasn't dreamt of mother-in-law- and hassle-free nuptials, where you and your beloved are alone on an idyllic island beach with a backdrop of astonishing turquoise seas? Where simple white cotton clothes and a garland of wild flowers mark the occasion, and the celebrant blesses you with a smile and a reasonable invoice?

The Bahamas is a popular destination for honeymooners, many of whom also tie the knot in these gorgeous islands. The Bahamians make it easy for non-nationals to meet their requirements and it is possible to marry with just a 24-hour wait.

Marriage licenses cost $100 and can be obtained from the **Registrar General's Office** (☎242-326-5371, 242-328-7810; Rodney E Bain Bldg, Parliament St). You'll need photo identification, proof of citizenship, proof of status if divorced or widowed, and to swear an oath of eligibility before a notary of the Bahamas. No blood test is required. Anyone under 18 years of age requires notarized parental consent.

If you want help with the event, contact the **Bahamas Ministry of Tourism** (☎242-302-2034; www.bahamas.com), who have a division specifically for all the dewy-eyed romantics out there. It can put you in touch with local wedding consultants, photographers and ministers. Most major hotels and tour operators can also make arrangements; they usually ask couples to send notarized copies of required documents at least one month in advance. Major resorts also have special honeymoon packages and can make wedding arrangements at your behest.

Nassau

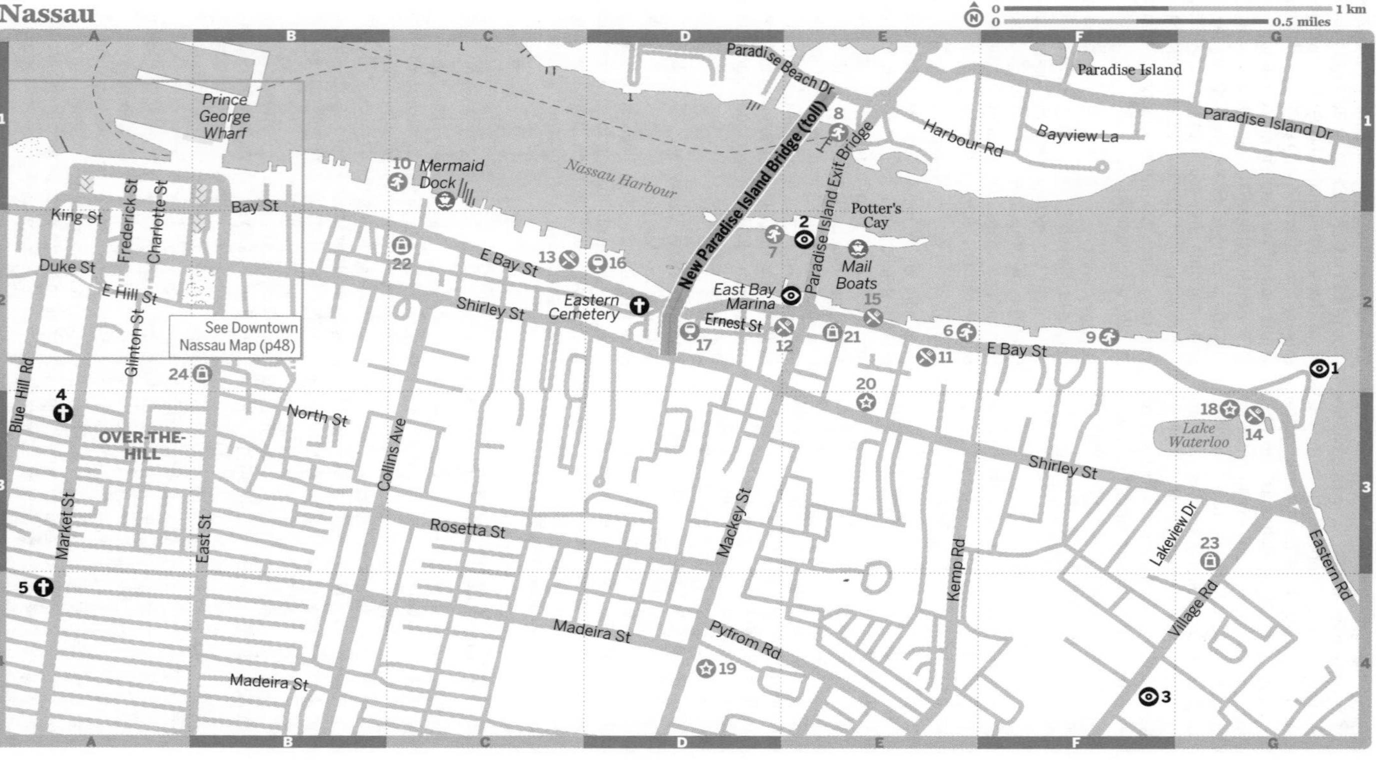
0
1 km
0
0.5 miles
Paradise Island
Paradise Island Dr
Bayview La
Harbour Rd
Paradise Beach Dr
New Paradise Island Bridge (toll)
Paradise Island Exit Bridge
Nassau Harbour
Potter's Cay
Mail Boats
East Bay Marina
Ernest St
10 Mermaid Dock
Prince George Wharf
Eastern Cemetery
E Bay St
Bay St
King St
Duke St
E Hill St
Frederick St
Charlotte St
Glinton St
See Downtown Nassau Map (p48)
Shirley St
Blue Hill Rd
OVER-THE-HILL
North St
Collins Ave
Market St
East St
Rosetta St
Madeira St
Mackey St
Pyfrom Rd
Kemp Rd
Lake Waterloo
Lakeview Dr
Village Rd
Eastern Rd

Nassau

Sights

1 Fort Montagu G2
2 Potter's Cay Market E2
3 Retreat F4
4 St Agnes Anglican Church A3
5 Wesley Methodist Church A4

Activities, Courses & Tours

6 Bahama Divers E2
7 Bahamas Ferries D2
8 Flying Cloud Catamaran Cruises & Snorkeling Trips E1
9 Powerboat Adventures F2
10 Seaworld Explorer C1

Eating

11 Balduccino Fine Foods E2
12 Double D's E2
13 Luciano's of Chicago C2
14 Montague Gardens G3
15 Poop Deck E2

Drinking

16 Green Parrot D2
17 Hammerhead Bar & Grill D2

Entertainment

18 Club Waterloo G3
19 Dundas Centre for the Performing Arts D4
20 National Centre for the Performing Arts E3

Shopping

21 Bahama Handprints E2
22 Bahamas Rum Cake Factory C2
23 Doongalik Studios G3
24 Mortimer Candies B2

as well as fruit, herbs, biting pepper sauces and vegetables. Piles of glistening conch, crab, jack, mackerel and spiny lobster are sold alive, dead, dried or filleted. It's a great place to hang out and watch the pandemonium whenever a boat returns, or to grab a cheap meal of conch salad or souse at one of the wooden food stalls. The offices and docks for Bahamas Ferries and mail boats are just northwest and northeast of the market respectively. The area can be dodgy at night.

Retreat GARDEN

(Map opposite; www.bnt.bs/parks_retreat.php; Village Rd; admission $2; ⏲9am-5pm Mon-Fri) Just southeast of downtown but a universe away from the hustle and bustle of Bay St, this 11-acre urban garden has one of the largest private collections of palms in the world. Wander the shady pathways admiring some of the 176 species on display, from the frilly Cuban petticoat palm to the aggressively spiny Zombie palm. Native orchids grace the trunks and splendid ferns nestle in the limestone holes in which the palms are planted.

FREE **Fort Montagu** FORT

(Map opposite; Eastern Rd) There's not much to draw you to this diminutive fort, though the place is intact and the cannon in situ. The oldest of Nassau's remaining strongholds, it was built in 1741 to guard the eastern approach to Nassau Harbour. It never fired its cannon in anger. The surrounding park is enjoyed by football-playing Bahamians and occasional market stalls.

FREE **Blackbeard's Tower** HISTORIC BUILDING

(Map p42; Eastern Rd) According to local lore, this semiderelict stone tower, a few miles east of Fort Montagu, was built by Edward Teach – AKA the dreaded pirate Blackbeard. It's probably just a myth, but hardcore pirate history buffs will be undeterred.

OVER-THE-HILL

Just south of downtown Nassau on the other side of a steep rise, the Over-the-Hill neighborhood is home to many of the island's working people. The Gregory Arch, a stone-cut tunnel on Market St, was blasted through the hill in the mid 1800s to allow workers a shortcut home; it now marks the dividing line between downtown and Over-the-Hill. During the daytime, feel free to explore this vibrant neighborhood, stopping at takeout chicken shacks or small local bars. The historic 1847 **Wesley Methodist Church** (Market St) and the 1846 **St Agnes Anglican Church** (Cockburn St) are both worth a visit. At night, it's probably best to stay away – Over-the-Hill is the nexus of the disturbing rise in drug violence that's plagued the Bahamas in recent years.

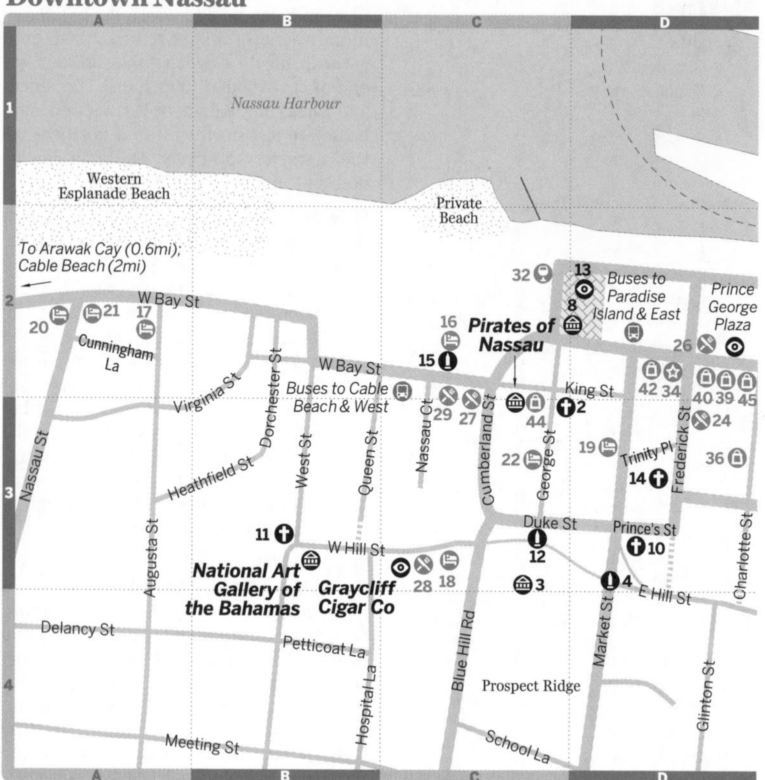

FOX HILL

This settlement for freed slaves began life in the 18th century as Creek Village. During the 1900s, Robert Sandilands, chief justice of the Bahamas, bought much of the area and distributed land grants to black people for $10 or the equivalent in labor. The recipients named their settlement after their benefactor.

St Augustine's Monastery MONASTERY

(Map p42; ☎242-364-1331; admission by donation) Atop a rocky perch on Bernard Rd is this fortresslike working monastery. It was designed by Father Jerome, the itinerant architect-cleric who blessed Cat and Long Islands with beautiful Gothic churches (see boxed text, p174). The imposing building dates from 1947 and is still used by Benedictine monks, who give guided tours of the gardens that offer a fascinating glimpse of monastic life. A college run by the monks is attached. Phone ahead to enquire about tour hours.

Freedom Park PARK

At the juncture of Fox Hill Rd and Bernard Rd, this park is the center of town and the setting each year for Emancipation Day celebrations in the first week of August.

WEST OF DOWNTOWN

TOP CHOICE **Ardastra Gardens, Zoo & Conservation Center** GARDEN, ZOO

(Map p42; www.ardastra.com; Chippingham Rd; adult/child/under 4yr $15/7.50/free; ⏲9am-5pm, last admittance at 4:15pm; 👪) A hit with the kids, this sunny minizoo is home to nearly 300 species of animals from around the world. Crowd-pleasers include the Madagascar lemurs, a pair of jaguar siblings and a small herd of African pygmy goats. The undisputed highlight, however, is the small regiment of marching West Indian flamingos, who strut their stuff at 10:30am,

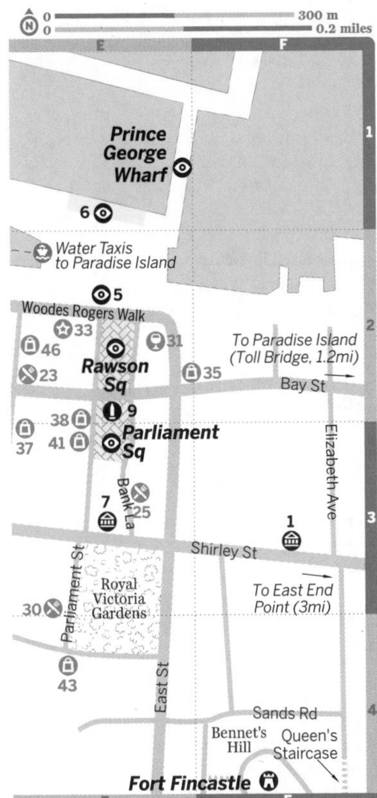

2:10pm and 4:10pm daily. Pint-sized visitors will thrill at feeding the lory parrots by hand at 11am, 1:30pm and 3:30pm.

FREE **Fort Charlotte** FORT
(Map p42; W Bay St; 8am-4pm;) Built between 1787 and 1790 to guard the west entrance to Nassau Harbour, this massive fort was the pet project of Lord Dunmore, who named it after King George III's wife. Ill-designed (the troop's barracks were built directly in the line of fire!) and hugely over-budget, it quickly took on the name 'Dunmore's Folly.' What's more, it was never even used. Today its moat, dungeon and underground tunnels make an intriguing excursion. Kids will especially enjoy the re-creation of a torture chamber. Tours are free, but guides expect a tip.

PARADISE ISLAND

Shimmering Paradise Island, linked to Nassau by two great arcing bridges, is built for one thing and one thing only: pleasure. Its landscape seems entirely artificial: glittering hotel towers, hangar-sized casinos, prefab shopping villages, impeccably manicured lawns.

It wasn't always this way. Back in the day, Paradise was a muddy plot of farmland known by the far less melodious moniker of 'Hog Island.' All that changed with the 1959 arrival of A&P supermarket heir Huntington Hartford II, who renamed the place Paradise Island with an eye towards turning it into the next Monte Carlo. In 1998 South African billionaire Sol Kerzner opened Atlantis, a vast and ever-expanding resort, shopping complex and water park which now dominates the island's landscape.

Today Paradise Island caters to every sector of fun-seeker: families with children, honeymooners, high-stakes gamblers, bachelor partiers. This isn't a place for budget or off-the-beaten-path travel: long lines, noisy crowds and inflated prices are the name of the game here. But if you know what you're getting into, it's hard to imagine a better place to have a wild good time.

Atlantis' central hotel, the **Atlantis Royal Towers**, is a sight in and of itself, with shopping, a casino, and a faux archaeological excavation and giant aquarium windows in its lower lobby. The adjacent **Marina Village** is a popular shopping and eating destination.

TOP CHOICE **Aquaventure** WATER PARK
(www.atlantis.com; adult/child/hotel guests $110/90/free;) Kids and adults alike will hyperventilate at the sight of this astonishing 141-acre water park, an Indiana Jones–style vision of the ruins of the Lost City of Atlantis. The vast park – one of the largest in the hemisphere – is centered on a five-story Mayan temple, with multiple waterslides shooting guests into a variety of grottoes and caves. The most insane of them all, the Leap of Faith, sends brave vacationers through a Plexiglas tube that plummets down through a lagoon full of sharks. The nearby Power Tower has a 200ft drop through total darkness into an underground cavern full of fish. Non-adrenaline junkie types can meander along the artificial rapids of a mile-long river ride, swim in various grotto-style pools, and kayak or snorkel in a peaceful artificial lagoon. For the littlest guests, there's a Mayan-themed minipark, with small slides, rope bridges and water cannons. You can purchase tickets at Guest Services inside

Downtown Nassau

Top Sights

Fort Fincastle ... F4
Graycliff Cigar Co ... C3
National Art Gallery of the Bahamas ... B3
Parliament Sq ... E3
Pirates of Nassau ... C3
Prince George Wharf ... E1
Rawson Sq ... E2

Sights

1 Bahamas Historical Society Museum ... F3
2 Christ Church Anglican Cathedral ... C3
3 Government House ... C3
4 Gregory Arch ... D3
5 Horse-Drawn Surreys ... E2
6 Junkanoo Expo ... E1
7 Nassau Public Library ... E3
8 Pompey Museum ... D2
9 Queen Victoria Statue ... E2
10 St Andrews Presbyterian Kirk ... D3
11 St Francis Xavier Cathedral ... B3
12 Statue of Christopher Columbus ... C3
13 Straw Market ... D2
14 Trinity Methodist Church ... D3
15 Woodes Rogers Statue ... C2

Sleeping

16 British Colonial Hilton Nassau ... C2
17 El Greco ... A2
18 Graycliff Hotel ... C3
19 Mignon Guest House ... D3
20 Nassau Palm Resort ... A2
21 Quality Inn Junkanoo Beach ... A2
22 Towne Hotel ... C3

Eating

23 Athena Cafe ... E2
24 Brussels Bistro ... D3
25 Café Matisse ... E3
26 Café Skan's ... D2
27 Conch Fritters Bar & Grill ... C2
Graycliff Restaurant ... (see 18)
28 Humidor Churrascaria ... C3
29 Imperial Cafeteria & Take-Away ... C2
30 Taj Mahal ... E3

Drinking

Bullion Bar ... (see 16)
31 Green Parrot ... E2
32 Señor Frog's ... C2

Entertainment

33 Bambu ... E2
34 Club Fluid ... D2

Shopping

35 Bacardi ... E2
Balmain Antiques ... (see 45)
Balmain Art Gallery ... (see 45)
36 Brass & Leather Shops ... D3
37 Coin of the Realm ... E3
38 Coles of Nassau ... E2
39 Colombian Emeralds ... D2
40 John Bull ... D2
41 Kennedy Gallery ... E3
42 Perfume Shop & Beauty Spot ... D2
43 Philatelic Bureau ... E4
44 Plunder ... C3
45 Solomon's Mines ... D2
46 Tortuga Rum Cake ... E2

Royal Towers. If you're not having fun, you're doing something wrong!

Discover Atlantis Tour AQUARIUM
(www.atlantis.com; adult/child/hotel guest $35/25/free; 9am-5pm;) Strolling through a clear glass tunnel while sharks glide overhead is, simply put, awesome. This underwater thrill is found in the Predator's Lagoon, one of the exhibits on this popular walking tour of Atlantis' aquariums and faux archaeological sites. Look for manta rays, spiny lobsters, striped Nemos, translucent jellyfish and thousands of other sea creatures in the underground Great Hall of Waters, noting the fake hieroglyphics and ersatz artifacts along the way. Buy tickets outside the Dig, an 'archaeological site' on the lower level of the Royal Towers lobby. Some parts of the Dig are free – you're welcome to watch the fish swim past the giant windows in the lobby, but you have to pay for the tour if you want to enter the more elaborate aquarium areas and shark tanks.

Versailles Gardens GARDENS
This hushed, intimate garden is the last thing you expect to find on bling-lovin' Paradise Island. The formal, multi-tiered landscape is lined with classical statues

BEST BEACHES

New Providence

» **Cable Beach** New Providence's biggest and most popular beach is three curving miles of white sand and sparkling turquoise sea just west of downtown Nassau. Named for the undersea telegraphic cable that came ashore here in 1892, Cable Beach has for years been populated with nondescript beach resorts. Currently, these resorts and the casino are in the midst of a massive redevelopment project overseen by Baha Mar Resorts. Construction is set to begin any minute, though locals say they'll believe it when they see it. Currently the beach is vibrant with vacationing families, Spring Breakers, water-sports operators, hair braiders and roving souvenir vendors. If you want a beach chair, pay a day-use fee at one of the hotels for use of their facilities.

» **Delaporte Beach** Adjoining Cable Beach on the west, this is a quiet spot with soft sand, gin-clear water and few crowds.

» **Orange Hill Beach** Another quiet spot beloved by locals, it's just west of Caves Point.

» **Saunders Beach** A mile east of Cable Beach, this tiny spot is popular with locals at lunchtime, who munch cracked conch in their cars and listen to reggae.

» **Junkanoo Beach** The closest beach to downtown, this smallish stretch is crowded with locals and budget travelers from nearby hotels. It ain't fancy, but the water's just as clear and aqua as anywhere else on the island.

Paradise Island

» **Cabbage Beach** This powder-sand stunner stretches 2 miles along the north shore, with plenty of activities and water sports. Look out for banana boats, jet ski rental, parasailing and more. Several resorts have facilities at the west end.

» **Pirate's Cove** Nestled in its own cove west of Atlantis, it has no facilities.

» **Paradise Beach** Another beauty, Paradise Beach curves gently along the northwest shore of the island; it is very lonesome to the west. The resorts have their own facilities, but nonguests pay for privileges.

» **Snorkeler's Cove Beach** East of Cabbage Beach, it's favored by day-trippers on picnicking and snorkeling excursions from Nassau.

depicting notable men throughout the ages: Hercules, Napoleon Bonaparte and Franklin D Roosevelt to name a few. The garden's big photo op is the **Cloister**, a rectangular stone colonnade built by Augustinian monks in 12th-century France. Huntington Hartford purchased the cloister from newspaper magnate William Randolph Hearst and had it shipped piece by piece to the Bahamas. Another don't-miss is the waterfront **gazebo**, a popular wedding spot. As the property is part of the One & Only Ocean Club hotel, some parts are off-limits to nonguests – signs will tell you where you can and cannot go.

Dolphin Cay DOLPHIN ENCOUNTER
(☎242-363-3000; www.atlantis.com; 👪) Atlantis' artificial lagoon is home to 31 dolphins, 16 of which are refugees taken in from a New Orleans aquarium after Hurricane Katrina. Shallow water encounters ($150) let visitors greet and hug the slippery mammals, or swim alongside them using special water scooters ($185). These book up way in advance. If you just want to watch the dolphins dive and play, hang out at the snack bar or the beach surrounding the lagoon.

BEACH FACILITIES

Cable Beach and Cabbage Beach on Paradise Island are both lined with operators offering water-sports activities and equipment for hire. Beachside resorts usually have their own facilities which are open to nonguests upon the purchase of a day ticket.

Water Adventures WATER ACTIVITIES

(☎242-363-3000; www.atlantis.com;) Atlantis offers guests a huge variety of snorkel, scuba and 'snuba' (a snorkel and scuba combo using long tubes to the surface) adventures, both in the ocean and in the hotel's endless pools, lagoons and tanks. Thrill-seekers should try the Shark Adventure, an underwater walk through the Predator Lagoon using diving bell helmets.

Activities

Look out for the free monthly *What's On* guide, which can be found in most hotel lobbies and outside many retail outlets. The guide details a lot of upcoming events and sporting matches as well as containing discount coupons for plenty of tourist activities.

Diving & Snorkeling

New Providence has excellent diving close to its shores, including fantastic wall and wreck dives. The most noted sites lie off the southwest coast between Coral Harbour and Lyford Cay, as well as north of Paradise Island.

The most famous Nassau dives are definitely **Shark Wall** and **Shark Arena**, where divers watch clouds of hungry sharks descend for feedings just feet away.

At **Anchor Reef** a coral head pokes out of a wall 60ft below the surface, and teems with fish life. At **School House**, another favorite snorkeling and diving spot, there are endless varieties of coral at depths that rarely exceed 20ft. Fish life ranges from blennies and gobies to schooling yellowtail.

Divers love the **Lost Blue Hole**. This vertical cavern gapes in 30ft of water on a sand bottom and is frequented by nurse sharks and stingrays. The cave bells out to 200ft and deeper. There's a lobster-filled cavern at 80ft. **Oasis Wall**, a deep dive just off Old Fort Beach, is known for reef corals all the way down to 200ft. There's plenty of lobster and pelagics, too.

The spectacular **Razorback** is named for the arcing ridge of coral-covered limestone that rises from a sand bottom before plummeting into the bottomless Tongue of the Ocean. The reef is a menagerie of fish and the wall attracts hammerhead sharks. Equally spectacular is the **Valley**, a path leads you through a labyrinth of coral and marine life to the Tongue of the Ocean, just over the ridge.

TOP CHOICE **Stuart Cove's Dive & Snorkel Bahamas** SUBMARINE TOUR

(Map p42; ☎242-362-4171; www.stuartcove.com; Southwest Rd) One of the Bahamas' best and largest dive operators, Stuart Cove's offers a mass of diving, PADI certification and snorkeling choices, including a bone-rattling shark wall and shark-feeding dive ($150); a two-tank dive trip ($109); and a three-dive 'Seafari' trip to the blue holes and plunging walls of Andros island ($225). Non-divers can snorkel (adult/child $65/30) or – better yet! – pilot their own SUB (Scenic Underwater Bubble), a scooter with air wheels and a giant plastic bubble that envelops your shoulders and head ($119).

Bahama Divers DIVING, SNORKELING

(Map p46; ☎242-393-5644; www.bahamadivers.com; E Bay St) The pros at this well-regarded dive shop run a variety of trips, including some to the Lost Blue Hole (famous for its

NASSAU FOR CHILDREN

From pirate history museums to massive water parks to dolphin-filled lagoons, Nassau is basically one big playground.

» Plunge down waterslides and float through shark tanks at the 141-acre Aquaventure water park (p49) at the Atlantis resort. The littlest kids will love the Mayan-themed shallow water playground.

» Sit and wave at people from your horse-drawn surrey (p42).

» Salute a marching flamingo, yawn at a dozing iguana, cluck at a Bahama parrot and smile at a big cat at Ardastra Gardens, Zoo & Conservation Center (p48).

» Walk past a bunch of wicked and wanton buccaneers and their pirate ship at the brilliant interactive Pirates of Nassau museum (p41).

» Ride in a glass-hulled semi-submarine with Seaworld Explorer (opposite).

» Frolic with tame dolphins and romp in the sand at the Blue Lagoon (opposite), a fantasy desert island.

For more information on traveling with children in the Bahamas, see p29.

sharks and schools of stingrays) and wrecks. A three-hour learn-to-dive course can be taken prior to PADI certification courses (PADI course $549). A two-tank dive trip costs $109 and half-day snorkeling trips are $50.

Sportfishing & Boat Charters

For general information about sailing and chartering boats see p252. Nassau is a great base for sportfishing, with superb sites just 20 minutes away. Game species include blue marlin, sailfish, yellowfin tuna, mahi-mahi and wahoo. Charters can be arranged at most major hotels or by calling a charter company. The following recommended companies mainly offer sportfishing, but will also happily take you exploring, diving and snorkeling. They charge two to six people from $500 to $700 per half-day, and from $900 to $1400 per full day.

Born Free Charter Service SPORTFISHING
(☎242-393-4144; www.bornfreefishing.com)

Chubasco Charters SPORTFISHING
(☎242-324-3474; www.chubascocharters.com)

Hunter Charters SPORTFISHING
(☎242-364-1546; www.huntercharters.com)

Paradise Island Charters SPORTFISHING
(☎242-363-4458; www.paradise-island-charters.com)

Boat Excursions

There's a jaunt for every type of adventurer in New Providence. Dozens of operators run snorkel trips, island jaunts, party boats and sunset and dinner cruises. Most vessels depart from the Woodes Rogers Walk area or the Paradise Island Ferry Terminal between the Paradise Island bridges.

TOP CHOICE **Seaworld Explorer** SUBMARINE TOURS
(Map p46; ☎242-356-2548; www.seaworldtours.com; Paradise Island Ferry Terminal; adult/child $45/25; 👪) It's not every day you get to ride in a semi-submarine, is it? One of the island's more unique experiences, this window-lined 45-passenger semi-submarine has an ultracool 90-minute excursion above the fish-filled coral reefs of the Sea Gardens Marine Park off the north shore of Paradise Island.

TOP CHOICE **Powerboat Adventures** BOAT TRIP
(Map p46; ☎242-363-1466; www.powerboatadventures.com; Paradise Island Ferry Terminal; adult/child $199/140; 👪) Takes you on a thrilling powerboat trip which zips you from Nassau to the Exuma Cays in an hour. The first stop is Allan's Cays to say hi to some iguana families, then it's time for drift snorkeling before heading to Ship Channel Cay for a nature hike. The excursion also includes shark feeding, snorkeling with stingrays, a barbecue lunch and plenty of rum swizzles.

Bahamas Ferries BOAT TRIP
(Map p46; ☎242-323-2166; www.bahamasferries.com; adult/child $184/124) Hop on one of these sleek passenger ferries for a 'Harbour Island Day Away' excursion to shimmering Harbour Island just off the coast of northern Eleuthera. It departs from Potter's Cay, takes two hours each way and includes a history-oriented island tour, a restaurant lunch and lounging on the famous pink sand beach. A great way to squeeze one of the Out Islands into your Nassau vacation.

Flying Cloud Catamaran Cruises & Snorkeling Tours SNORKELING, CRUISE
(Map p46; ☎242-363-4430; www.flyingcloud.info; Paradise Island Ferry Terminal) These fast-flying catamarans whisk you away for half-day snorkel adventures on a secluded beach (adult/child $70/35), or for romantic rum-fueled sunset cruises ($70/35). Sunday trips are five hours and include reef snorkeling and a BBQ on low-key Rose Island ($85/42.50).

Island World Adventures SNORKELING, CRUISE
(☎242-363-3333; www.islandworldadventures.com; Paradise Island Ferry Terminal; adult/child $200/150) Has daylong excursions on a

WORTH A TRIP

BLUE LAGOON

Just 3 miles from Nassau, the **Blue Lagoon** (☎242-363-1003; www.bahamasbluelagoon.com) is a horseshoe of sugar-white sand fringed with coconut palms surrounding a shallow turquoise lagoon. The island has been developed as a choose-your-own adventure ecopark, with nature trails, snorkeling beaches, volleyball courts and hundreds of hammocks, making it one of Nassau's most popular and family-friendly day-trips. Sign up for an all-day beach adventure (adult/child $45/35), with add-on extras like kayaking ($10 per person), paddle-boating ($15) or snorkel tours ($40). Encounters with wildlife are also available, see p54.

DOLPHIN ENCOUNTERS

While dolphin encounters are undeniably a huge attraction, the practice is not without controversy (see p246). A more ecofriendly alternative to visits with captive or semicaptive dolphins is to visit wild dolphins in their own habitat, where they can choose whether or not to interact with the humans in their midst. The best places to do this are **Bill & Nowdla Keefe's Bimini Undersea** (p98) and **Underwater Explorers Society** (UNEXSO; p77).

high-powered speedboat to Saddleback Cay, in the Exumas. There's great snorkeling and seven private beaches to wander. Trips include lunch, an open bar, snorkeling gear and a stop at lovely Leaf Cay to commune with iguanas.

Wildlife Encounters

Dolphin Encounters (☎242-363-1003; www.dolphinencounters.com; Paradise Island Ferry Terminal) offers a boat ride to the Blue Lagoon (p53), where visitors can swim, kiss and play with tame dolphins in the enclosed lagoon, where such films as *Flipper* and *Splash* were shot. A 30-minute swim is $185, while a waist-deep standing encounter is $98. Up-close encounters with the island's newest attraction – sea lions – are $80. All trips include boat transportation from Paradise Island and several hours of free-range sun and fun on the island, which has a cafe and changing facilities. Boats depart four times daily, at 8:30am, 10:30am, 1:30pm and 3:30pm. Trips fill up fast; so book well in advance.

For more dolphin action, see also Dolphin Cay (p51) on Paradise Island.

Water Sports

Most resort hotels either include water sports in their rates or offer them as optional extras. Just wander any one of the more populated beaches and look for kiosks offering nearly every kind of water activity, including parasailing ($60, about 10 to 15 minutes), banana boat rides ($15, about 10 to 15 minutes) and wave runners ($60 per 30 minutes). Aussie AJ Watson will teach your to catch some gnarly air at **Cross-Shore** (☎242-362-4702; www.cross-shore.com; South Beach), a high-octane kiteboarding school on New Providence's southern shore. Options start with a two-hour intro course ($150) and range all the way to a 10-day all-you-can-surf orgy for $2200.

Golf

The **Cable Beach Golf Club** (☎242-677-4175; Cable Beach; guests/nonguests per nine holes $75/130) at the Sheraton Cable Beach is the only course currently open to the public; it's soon to undergo a redesign by Jack Nicklaus's firm.

Horseback Riding

Take a trot on a trail with the horses of **Happy Trails Stables** (☎242-362-1820; Coral Harbour, Southern Beaches; per 1½hr $90; ⏲Mon-Sat). Rides take in the woodland and beach scenery of the southern coastlands, and transfers are also provided.

Tours

Nearly all hotels have tour desks that will offer a selection of choices and make all bookings on your behalf. Also refer to the recommended boat excursions, p53. Nassau's quaint horse-drawn surreys (p42) are also a great way to explore downtown Nassau at an easy pace. Many taxi drivers will offer tours of the island and/or Nassau. Negotiate prices carefully prior to commencing any trips. It may well be cheaper to hire a car and take yourself to any spots of interest.

Bahamas Outdoors NATURE TOURS
(☎242-457-0329; www.bahamasoutdoors.com) Get down and dirty with these eco-adventures, including an all-terrain bike trip through woodlands, beach and mangrove swamps ($79), a summer-only kayak trip, and an expert-led birding tour of area wetlands and seashore ($69/109 per half-/full day).

Bahamas Segway Tours SEGWAY TOURS
(☎242-376-9016; www.bahamassegwaytours.com; tours $65; 👪) It's hard not to feel a little bit goofy zipping along on a Segway 'personal transporter,' but try to lose your inhibitions! After a quick bus tour of downtown, you'll be whisked to a private beachfront property to get the hang of the equipment. Then off you go on an all-terrain nature tour, bumping across sand, mud and shallow water.

Majestic Holidays HISTORY TOURS (☎242-457-0329; www.majesticholidays.com) Offers a variety of history- and culture-oriented bus tours, including a popular 2½-hour City and Country tour (adult/child $45/22.50).

Festivals & Events

Snipe Winter Sailing Championship Draws homemade boats in April to race one another in Montagu Bay.

Opening of Parliament A colorful, formal occasion in April, featuring the Royal Bahamas Police Force Band marching in pith helmets, starched white tunics and leopard-skin shawls. The governor-general delivers a speech on behalf of Her Majesty, to whom the gathered officials swear allegiance.

Great Bahamian Seafood & Wine Festival This weeklong food orgy in May includes a gala, and all-day beach party, and special seafood menus at restaurants around town.

Fox Hill Day Celebration Held a week after Emancipation Day, in August, this celebration recalls the day on which residents of Fox Hill learned of emancipation.

Summer Madness Revue A satirical review in September at the Dundas Centre for the Performing Arts looks at local politics.

Bahamas National Trust Art & Wine Festival Sip a glass of red and peruse local art in the palm tree gardens of The Retreat (p47), held in October.

Thanksgiving Ball This black-tie do at the British Colonial Hilton Nassau (p56) is a long-established traditional fund-raiser in November for the Bahamas Humane Society. Anyone who is anyone is seen here.

Bahamas International Film Festival Local and foreign glitterati screen international indie films at venues around the island during December. You never know who you'll spot – past honorees include Johnny Depp, Laurence Fishburne and Nicholas Cage.

Sleeping

Hotel pricing in Nassau is a tricky business. Some tatty, bare-bones establishments charge shockingly high prices, while plush modern resorts may offer quite reasonable internet rates or last-minute deals. Prices zip up and down depending on the season and the current economic climate. It definitely pays to shop around. There are ways to find reduced rates (up to 60%), at all budget levels, with a bit of easy planning. Many hotel websites offer lower rates not available through tour operators, or have room plus airfare deals. See p250 for more information.

SAND & SPA

As if lounging on powder-white sand or floating in the warm aqua ocean wasn't relaxing enough, Nassau spas offer a full menu of beach-inspired pampering services.

» At Paradise Island's Atlantis (p49), the **Mandara Spa** (www.mandaraspa.com) is as opulent as the hotel itself, with a marble-and-mahogany lobby and orchids everywhere. Choose Eastern- or Western-style massages, Bahamian-flavored body treatments (try the divine lime and ginger salt rubdown) or an array of salon services. A second location, in the exclusive One & Only Ocean Club (p59), has private Balinese-style villas, each with its own garden sitting area. Experience the signature One & Only massage, where two therapists blend five different styles of massage (Shiatsu, Thai, Hawaiian, Swedish and Balinese) until you're reduced to a quivering jelly.

» In the Marley Resort (p57), Bob Marley's former Bahamian getaway, the **Natural Mystic Spa** (www.marleyresort.com) offers Afro-Caribbean–inflected treatments inspired by Marley's wife Rita. Try the Jamaican Coffee Scrub or the Royal Rita Bath of orange blossoms, red clay and roses.

» The trendy Compass Point Beach Resort's **Barefoot Retreat** (www.compasspointbeachresort.com) has a long list of reflexology, wrap and rubdown treatments, including a couple's-only twilight massage.

» For the nonspa types, various operators on Cable Beach and Cabbage Beach offer ocean-front massages on the spot!

Downtown Nassau

In general, downtown Nassau hotels tend to be smaller and cheaper than those in Cable Beach. Paradise Island resorts top the scale, both in terms of luxury and rates. It is likely that many Cable Beach hotels and adjacent businesses are to be demolished to make room for the Baha Mar megaresort and casino complex, which probably means a price hike in Cable Beach, so get there while the gettin's good.

TOP CHOICE Graycliff Hotel BOUTIQUE HOTEL **$$$**
(Map p48; ☎242-322-2796/97; www.graycliff.com; 8-12 W Hill St; r/ste $325/450; ❄@📶🏊) Nassau's most discreet and character-laden hotel is this slightly spooky 260-year-old home built by a wealthy pirate. Hidden above town on W Hill St, the Georgian-style main house is filled with high-ceilinged rooms, musty antiques, mismatched oriental rugs, and intriguing nooks and corners begging further exploration. Huge gardenside cottages are equally alluring. There's an extraordinary Spanish-tiled pool surrounded by mossy masonry walls trailing hibiscus and bougainvillea; a smoking room and a library resplendent with the rich aroma of Cuban cigars; an astonishing wine cellar and a five-star restaurant beloved by deep-pocketed gourmands. Former guests include Sir Winston Churchill, the Beatles and LL Cool J.

TOP CHOICE British Colonial Hilton Nassau HOTEL **$$$**
(Map p48; ☎242-322-9036; www.hiltoncaribbean.com/nassau; 1 Bay St; r $195-450; ❄📶🏊) Built in 1922, this seven-story grande dame is a downtown Nassau institution. The hotel was a location for two James Bond movies, and it's easy to see why – with its gleaming marble lobby and sleek graphite-and-mahogany common spaces, it has the timeless international elegance of 007 himself. The 288 rooms and suites have tastefully muted contemporary decor, with marble-lined bathrooms and crisp white linens. Several on-site restaurants and bars offer excellent people-watching – this is where Bahamian bigshots wheel and deal. The small private beach doesn't get washed by the sea, but it does have interesting views of the cruise ship docks.

El Greco HOTEL **$$**
(Map p48; ☎242-325-1121; www.hotels-nassau-bahamas.com; cnr W Bay & Augusta Sts; r $125-275; ❄📶🏊) Choose your room wisely and this Spanish-style hotel can be a sweet deal. What to pick: a sunny end room with gracefully arched entranceways and a view over the bougainvillea-draped balconies. What to avoid: a dim, gloomy interior room with motel-style beds. The tiny lobby has an Old World European feel, as does the statue-filled pool deck. Walking distance from downtown.

Nassau Palm Resort HOTEL **$$**
(Map p48; ☎242-356-0000; www.nassau-hotel.com; cnr W Bay & Nassau Sts; r $99-199; ❄📶🏊) At the western corner of downtown, this bustling 183-room property works best for on-the-go travelers looking for a simple home base at the end of a busy day. Bright tropical colors splash across bedspreads, brightening otherwise standard rooms. Junkanoo Beach, a small but pretty stretch of sand, is right across the street.

Mignon Guest House GUESTHOUSE **$**
(Map p48; ☎ 242-322-4771; 12 Market St; s/d $55/60; ❄📶) Run by a very sweet (though slightly hard-of-hearing!) elderly Greek couple, this 2nd-floor guesthouse is a bargain in the heart of downtown. Six guestrooms are bare-bones but clean, with personal air-conditioning units and cable TVs. Shared bathrooms are in the hallway. Two locked iron gates will make you feel safe.

Towne Hotel HOTEL **$**
(Map p48; ☎242-322-8450; www.townehotel.com; 40 George St; r $70; ❄📶🏊) Friendly management and a kitschy Junkanoo-themed bar make this otherwise ordinary 46-room hotel feel more cheerful than it might otherwise. Motel-style rooms have tile floors and small, but clean, bathrooms; the nicer rooms have balconies, too. Spice things up by trying to make the resident lobby parrot say 'Hello.'

Quality Inn Junkanoo Beach HOTEL **$**
(Map p48; ☎242-322-1515; www.qualityinn.com; cnr W Bay & Nassau Sts; r $95; ❄🏊) Currently the cheapest but least appealing of the western downtown options, this aging tower was undergoing renovations when we visited. Hopefully the dingy, motel-style rooms will be dramatically updated.

Cable Beach

West of downtown, Cable Beach is New Providence's most popular stretch of sand, lined with dozens of beachfront resorts and time-share complexes. Changes are afoot in the area as the $2.6 billion Baha Mar megaresort, which hopes to rival Atlantis, inches further towards reality. Two of the beach's biggest hotels – the Sheraton and the Wyndham – are already transitioning towards becoming part of the Baha Mar complex, which means some newly renovated rooms and slick new restaurants.

Wyndham Nassau Resort & Crystal Palace Casino RESORT **$$**
(Map p42; 242-327-6200; www.wyndhamnassauresort.com; W Bay St; r $199;) With its retro-futuristic peach and turquoise towers, this gaudy behemoth resort dominates the Cable Beach scene. Rooms are more tasteful than the exterior might suggest, with slick modern furniture and private balconies. Fun-lovers will revel in the Crystal Palace Casino, a cabaret nightclub, golf course, tennis and squash courts, shopping plaza and several bars and restaurants. The hotel also has a kids' club, with supervised activities and theme days. The landscaped beachfront courtyard has a 100ft-long waterslide, Jacuzzi and swim-up bar – what else do you need?

Sheraton Nassau Beach RESORT **$$**
(Map p42; 242-327-6000; www.starwoodhotels.com; W Bay St; r $179-249;) The Wyndham's lower-key sister is slated to become a Baha Mar property, and its 694 rooms have already been upgraded accordingly. Style is crisp and nautical, with lots of white, khaki and navy blue. The property is chockablock with resort activities and amenities: three pools with flowing waterfalls, a swim-up bar, several restaurants, a fitness center, a kids' camp (ages 4 to 12) and an interior walkway to the Wyndham's casino.

Marley Resort BOUTIQUE HOTEL **$$$**
(Map p42; 242-702-2800; www.marleyresort.com; W Bay St, Cable Beach; r $295-495m/ste $495-900;) Bob Marley's old Bahamian getaway is now an intimate 16-room boutique hotel run by his wife and daughter (though they spend most of their time in Jamaica). Rooms, each named after a Marley song, are spare-no-expense luxurious – hand-carved mahogany furniture, rich linens, original Africana art. The place does have a bit of a fan club feel, with a room dedicated to Marley photos and a boutique hawking rasta wear. Cable Beach is a short walk away.

Westwind II VILLAS **$$$**
(Map p42; 242-327-7211; www.westwindii.com; W Bay St; villas s/d/tr/q $290/315/340/365;) Popular with families and retirees on long vacations, these rental villas have a ski chalet vibe – beamed roofs, slope-ceilinged sleeping lofts. Grounds are neatly trimmed, management is friendly, and the two pools are always hopping with guests sipping icy cocktails from the on-site bar.

A couple of other options:

Sandals Royal Bahamian RESORT **$$$**
(Map p42; 242-327-6400; www.sandals.com; W Bay St; d $475-925;) Doric columns and marble sculptures evoke a Greco-Roman bacchanalia at this swanky couples-only resort, part of the Sandals chain. Everything's included – food, booze, trips to the resort's private island – so you can focus on gettin' romantic.

Blue Water Resort VILLAS **$$**
(Map p42; 242-327-7568; www.bluewaterresort.com; villas $149-499;) Resembling a pleasant suburban condominium development, this colony of beachfront villas is a bit out-of-date (lots of pink, aqua and mauve decor) but friendly and good for families.

West of Downtown

TOP CHOICE **A Stone's Throw Away** B&B **$$$**
(Map p42; 242-327-7030; www.astonesthrowaway.com; W Bay St; r $175-290;) Talk about dramatic entrances: getting to this extraordinary B&B requires climbing steep stone stairs through a cliff-side tunnel to emerge into a tropical garden like something out of a Merchant Ivory film. The plantation-style house has an airy globetrotting glamour: burnished wood, whitewashed walls, vintage Orientals. Guests take breakfast on the spacious deck overlooking the ocean, lounge on outdoor daybeds, or swim in the lagoon-style pool with its rock grotto. The restaurant, which is open to the public, reflects the German owner's international flair – duck breast with brandied fruits, salmon in vodka cream.

TOP CHOICE **Orange Hill Beach Inn** GUESTHOUSE **$$**
(Map p42; 242-327-7157; www.orangehill.com; W Bay St, Orange Hill Beach; r $120-170;) Divers and international backpackers adore this homey hillside guesthouse, with its Fawlty Towers sign and jokey, just-like-family staff. The sprawling property has a wide range of rooms, from basic motel units (upper rooms are nicer)

NASSAU FOR COUPLES

Nassau is a hotspot for destination weddings and honeymoons, with plenty of opportunities for (non-cheesy) romance. Try the following:

» Luxuriate in a beachfront massage *a deux* at Atlantis' **Mandara Spa** (www.mandara.com), followed by a shared bath and champagne lunch, part of the spa's Couples Ritual Retreat.

» Wander the hushed classical landscape of **Versailles Gardens** (p50). The garden's waterfront gazebo is a popular spot for weddings – and proposals!

» Book a room at the **Cove Atlantis** (opposite), Paradise Island's most adult hotel. The private Cain at the Cove pool area is a veritable bacchanalia of cocktail-sipping couples and wandering masseuses. For even more privacy, rent a poolside cabana.

» Dress up for dinner at one of Nassau's quieter, more intimate restaurants (no Jell-O shots here!). Good picks include the low-lit, antique-filled **Graycliff Restaurant** (p60) and the elegantly minimalist **Dune** (p63), floating above the sand of Cabbage Beach.

» Pack a picnic of prosciutto, fresh mozzarella, organic chocolate and other gourmet dainties at **Balduccino Fine Foods** (p61), then zip across town to the uncrowded western end of Cable Beach to eat.

» Sip lychee-infused martinis at **Nobu** (p63), then head upstairs to dance the night away at **Aura** (p66), Paradise Island's swankest nightclub.

» Ride a horse along the beach at sunset with **Happy Trails Stables** (p54). Yeah, we know it's a cliché. But it's the good kind of cliché.

to cottages with kitchenettes to a lovely full apartment. At night, everyone congregates in the funky main house, with its self-serve bar and shelves full of used books. Great for solo travelers looking to get away from the resort scene, or for island-hoppers on overnight layovers – the airport's only a few minutes away.

TOP CHOICE Compass Point Beach Resort HOTEL $$$
(Map p42; ☎242-327-4500; www.compasspointbeachresort.com; W Bay St, Gambier Village; r $150-400; ❄@🛜🏊) With a color scheme best described as jellybean Junkanoo, this jumble of crayon-bright luxury huts is an automatic mood enhancer. The huts are on the small side, but hip furniture, cute porches and astounding views make up for tight quarters. And who's staying inside when Love Beach and a sweet poolside bar are steps away? Monthly house parties draw local and international hipsters, as does the daily happy hour. On Friday nights, keep an ear out for karaoke-singing Sean Connery, who's been known to drop in from Lyford Cay.

Sandyport Beaches Resort HOTEL $$$
(Map p42; ☎242-327-4279; www.sandyport.com; W Bay St; r $200, condos $300-600; ❄🏊) Town houses are airy and modern at this resort/residential home complex, but ongoing construction and an un-scenic suburban location detract from the ambiance. The beach is across the street.

Paradise Island

Those who choose to stay within Paradise Island's magic bubble do so at a price – rooms are at least 50% more here than in downtown Nassau or Cable Beach. But for those craving all-inclusive, nonstop vacation fun, this is your place. Streets are safe and walkable, and free buses make the loop from hotel to hotel. Atlantis dominates the scene, both literally and figuratively, but several other properties offer rooms that are more budget friendly but still have access to Atlantis' amenities.

TOP CHOICE Atlantis Royal Towers RESORT $$$
(☎242-363-3000; www.atlantis.com; r $350-700; ❄@🛜🏊👪) If Disneyland, Vegas and Sea World birthed a lovechild, this watery wonderland would be its overpriced but irresistible spawn. Atlantis' signature property, the Royal Towers is the 23-story pink palace with the enormous central arch you see on the front of all the brochures. It's the most heavily invested in the 'Lost World of Atlantis' mythology – even the lobby bathrooms are designed to look like ancient

underwater ruins. As the nexus of all activity on Paradise Island, the Royal Towers draws gawkers from hither and yon. They stand in the cathedral-like marble lobby, snapping pictures of the mermaid mosaics in the ceiling dome. They watch sharks and rays swim past the aquarium windows of the lobby's lower level. They wander gilded shopping corridors lined with luxe retailers like Versace and Cartier. They gamble in the casino, watch movies in the theater, eat at celebrity chef–run restaurants like Nobu. Unsurprisingly, the 1200 rooms are rather less exciting than the common areas. But with crisp white linens, beachy art prints and private balconies, they're plenty nice. Got an inheritance to burn? Book the Bridge Suite, which, at $25,000, has been called one of the world's most expensive hotel rooms.

TOP CHOICE **Cove Atlantis** RESORT **$$$**
(242-363-3000; www.atlantis.com; r $800-1100;) Set at a tasteful distance from the madness of the Royal Towers, this is Atlantis' most adult property. Almost painfully chic, its open-air lobby is a zen fantasy of koi ponds and minimalist chandeliers, while its lobby bar offers international-caliber people-watching (Saudi princes, American starlets). Rooms are also super-slick, all white with contemporary orange and lime accents. Bathrooms have massive soaking tubs bigger than many city apartments. The adults-only pool area, Cain at the Cove, is an all-day bacchanalia of ambient techno and wandering masseuses. Not exclusive enough? Rent a poolside cabana ($750 per day), with couches, plasma TV and your very own butler.

TOP CHOICE **One & Only Ocean Club** RESORT **$$$**
(242-363-2501; oceanclub.oneandonlyresorts.com; r $600-1300;) Paradise Island's most elite hotel, this is the kind of place where people with marquee names come to get away from it all (paparazzi and other hoi polloi are kept out by a guarded gate). Though it's owned by Atlantis, the intimate pink plantation house feels a world apart from the glitter and noise of greater Paradise Island. Guests putter around in spa robes, drinking scotch or flipping through art books in the seaside sitting area. Rooms come with personal butlers, who will sprinkle rose petals on your bed or bring you your afternoon champagne. After your champers, lounge on the private beach, have a massage at the Balinese-style spa, or stroll through the 12th century cloister at the adjoining Versailles Gardens (p50).

Reef Atlantis RESORT **$$$**
(242-363-3000; www.atlantis.com; r $450-700;) Atlantis' condo-style hotel is designed for those who want a family vacation without the theme park atmosphere. Studios and suites are stylish and contemporary, all crisp white linens and bold blocks of color, all with views over Paradise Beach. All have kitchen areas and laundry facilities, making this a good pick for long-term stays. When you're ready for action, walk or hop the shuttle to the Royal Towers.

A short distance from the Royal Towers hustle and bustle, the following three properties are family-friendly and have full Atlantis privileges.

Beach Towers at Atlantis RESORT **$$$**
(242-363-3000; www.atlantis.com; r $300-450;) Atlantis' most affordable (relatively speaking!) property, this boxy pink building doesn't have any noteworthy amenities or sights, but it's just steps from the hustle and bustle of Royal Towers and Marina Village. Carpeted rooms are beachy and pleasant and the pool is large and lovely.

Coral Towers at Atlantis RESORT **$$$**
(242-363-3000; www.atlantis.com; r $350-600;) Like the Beach Towers, this is another undistinguished but (relatively) affordable option walking distance from the Royal Towers and Marina Village. Rooms are sunny, carpeted and comfortable.

Comfort Suites RESORT **$$$**
(242-363-3680; www.comfortsuitespi.com; Casino Dr; r incl breakfast $270-450;) Though not part of Atlantis, guests at this above-average beach hotel get full pool and water-park privileges at the neighboring megaresort. The 200-plus rooms are newly renovated with bright tropical appeal, and several on-site restaurants and bars are good for lazy days.

Eating

Dining in Nassau can be a demoralizing experience: with high prices, huge crowds and low quality. But don't despair – with a little extra patience and forethought, you can find anything from cheap and authentic Bahamian home cooking to sublime sushi to the kind of haute cuisine that would feel

JUST SAY OM

In the backyard of the Atlantis megaresort is something quite unexpected: a yoga ashram. On a heavily forested 5.5-acre patch of Paradise Island, **Sivananda Yoga Ashram** (☎242-363-3783; www.sivananda.org) has been attracting both hardcore yoga devotees and spandex-clad chippers for 40 years. Staying at Sivananda means following the rules: eight daily hours of outdoor yoga and meditation, and no meat, booze or cigarettes. Accommodations range from tent camping (sites $60) to barebones dorms ($70) to nicely furnished private huts ($130). There's an Ayurveda clinic with Thai massage and healing oil treatments, and nightly lectures from experts in spirituality and natural health. Keep in mind that this ain't no luxury retreat – facilities are shared, meals are vegetarian buffets, and long-term guests are super-serious about their discipline (as in, 'I've been living here for three years' serious). If that's not your idea of a vacation, you can drop in on yoga classes or meals for $10. The only way to get here is by boat, which leaves regularly from the Mermaid Dock on E Bay St in Nassau.

at home in Paris or New York. In these listings, places with phone details indicate that reservations are recommended.

Downtown Nassau

Too many downtown Nassau eateries are high-volume food factories for the cruise ship hordes. But look carefully and you'll find plenty of places that are serious about good cooking. The further away from the wharf, the better.

TOP CHOICE **Café Matisse** ITALIAN, INTERNATIONAL **$$**
(Map p48; ☎242-356-7012; www.café-matisse.com; Bank Lane; mains $15-26; ⊙lunch & dinner Tue-Sat) Tucked in the shadows of historic buildings and leafy palms, this casually elegant bistro just off Parliament Sq is a delightful escape from the cruise-ship-and-Bay-St-mob scene. Savor top-notch pastas, pizzas and seafood dishes on the inviting back patio where you'll be served by crisp-shirted waiters to the sounds of cool world beats. If you don't opt for wine, try the refreshing ginger lemonade.

Graycliff Restaurant CONTINENTAL **$$$**
(Map p48; ☎242-322-2796; www.graycliff.com; 8-12 W Hill St; mains $35-68; ⊙lunch Mon-Fri, dinner daily) Make like a colonial-era dignitary at this hushed restaurant, in the atmospherically creaky parlor of the 18th-century Graycliff Hotel. French-style dishes take inspiration from the tropics – think crispy duck with Bahamian citrus sauce, lobster in puff pastry. The wine cellar is legendary, with such extraordinarily precious vintages as an 1865 Château Lafite among its 250,000 bottles. Finish up with one of the 9000 cognacs, ports and Armagnacs from the Graycliff's 'Cognateque,' and a hand-rolled cigar from the factory next door.

Humidor Churrascaria BRAZILIAN, STEAKHOUSE **$$$**
(Map p48; ☎242-322-2796 ext 301; www.graycliff.com; W Hill St; mains $40; ⊙dinner Mon-Sat) Machismo hangs in the smoky air at this tropical mansion turned Brazilian steakhouse, where hunks of dripping meat are delivered tableside on wicked-looking metal skewers. The *prix-fixe* menu includes a salad bar stuffed with seafood appetizers, veggies and pastas. Conclude with a fine Graycliff stogie, hand rolled at the on-site cigar factory.

Brussels Bistro BELGIAN **$$**
(Map p48; www.brusselsbistro.biz; Frederick St; mains $15-29; ⊙lunch & dinner) You'd swear you were in Old World Belgium at this intimate side-street cafe, with its dim interior of burnished wood, brass and chalkboard menus. Delicate crepes, baguette sandwiches and old-fashioned salads full of ham and boiled eggs make this a long-luncher's paradise. Dinner means continental classics like steak *au poivre* (pepper steak) and lamb chops in mustard sauce; don't miss the Friday night *moules frites* (mussels and French fries), a Belgian standard.

Taj Mahal INDIAN **$$**
(Map p48; ☎242-356-3004; 48 Parliament St; mains $16-38; ⊙lunch & dinner) British expats claim that wood-paneled Taj Mahal serves the city's best Indian food. Lucky they didn't have to move from their bar stools to find it – the restaurant assumed the dark, clubby space formerly known as Green Shutters

Restaurant & Pub, a very English watering hole. Look for tandoori dishes, curries and rice specialties.

Athena Cafe GREEK $$
(Map p48; cnr Bay & Charlotte Sts; mains $15-35; breakfast & lunch 8:30am-6pm Mon-Fri, to 4pm Sun) Locals have a love-hate affair with this cozy Greek cafe perched tightly over the bustling Bay and Charlotte Sts intersection. The authentic Greek food may be scrumptious (try the grilled octopus!), but $15 for a gyro? Pass the ouzo, take another bite and blame the just-off-the-boat cruise-ship crowd. Enter through the jewelry store.

Café Skan's BAHAMIAN, AMERICAN $$
(Map p48; cnr Bay & Frederick Sts; mains $7-23; breakfast, lunch & dinner) Typically stretched to its deep-fried seams, this down-home diner bustles with office workers, vacationing families and the occasional hungry cop. If the happy hordes and friendly service don't pull you in, the tiered dessert case by the door should close the deal. Fried daily specials look to be most popular.

Imperial Cafeteria & Take-Away BAHAMIAN $
(Map p48; Marlborough St; mains $5-10; breakfast, lunch & dinner) Ignore the yellow Formica, this is consistently the best-value takeout food in Nassau, beloved of many Bahamians and guests of the lordly British Colonial Hilton Nassau opposite. Simple fast-food cooked well; the fish is fresh, light and crispy, the burgers are tasty and the $3 breakfasts are filling.

Conch Fritters Bar & Grill BAHAMIAN $
(Map p48; Marlborough St; mains $9-16; lunch & dinner) Clean, shiny fast food-style place specializing in conch, barbeque ribs, wings and other local snacks.

East of Downtown

Under the Paradise Island Exit Bridge, Potter's Cay market (p45) has straight-from-the-sea conch dishes and an exuberant Bahamian atmosphere. Open til late, but be careful at night. Heading further east, ritzy marinas and residential subdivisions mean restaurants catering to an upscale yachtie/expat clientele.

Balduccino Fine Foods GOURMET MARKET $
(Map p46; www.balduccino.com; Cotton Tree Trader's Plaza, E Bay St; mains $8-14; 8am-7pm Mon-Sat) Nassau's best gourmet market brims with hard-to-find international foods like Swiss yogurt, boneless quail, artichokes, gluten-free flour and organic chocolate, making it popular with yachties looking to stock up for their next island hop. The espresso counter and pre-prepared baguette sandwiches draw homesick European expats for miles around.

DON'T MISS

NASSAU MEALS

» Fried turbot, Sky Juice (gin, coconut water, nutmeg...whoa) and dancing at the weekend Fish Fry at **Arawak Cay** (p62)

» Tender grilled octopus dripping with herby olive oil, served by the chatty Greek waiters at **Athena Cafe** (left)

» French-style lobster and your choice of 250,000 wines at the gothic **Graycliff Restaurant** (opposite), followed by a Cuban-rolled stogie from the onsite cigar factory

» Just-off-the-boat fresh conch salad from a wooden shack at vibrantly gritty **Potters Cay market** (p45)

» Avant-garde sushi and sashimi (try the 'live conch') and celebrity chef Nobu Matsuhisa's signature black cod at ultra-slick **Nobu** (p63), in Atlantis' Royal Towers

» Spice-rubbed pork loin and a flight of fine tequilas at Bobby Flay's cow hide-and-stone palace, Mesa Grill (p63)

Luciano's of Chicago ITALIAN $$$
(Map p46; 242-323-7770; www.lucianosnassau.com; 701 E Bay St; dinner mains $23-46; lunch Mon-Fri, dinner daily) This handsome Italian restaurant, with its warmly lit dining rooms and romantic harbor-side balconies, is a perennial favorite with expats and yachties. The huge menu runs the gamut of northern Italian dishes, from osso bucco to tortellini with pesto, with a few nods to its Bahamian location (think hog snapper alla Romana).

Poop Deck SEAFOOD $$$
(Map p46; 242-393-8175; www.thepoopdeckrestaurants.com; E Bay St; mains $18-50; lunch & dinner) It's a pick-your-lobster kind of place where old salts ogle fresh snappers at the been-there-forever front bar. On the back deck, locals and tourists select from a

seafood menu heavy on Bahamian favorites – conch, grouper, mahi-mahi – that's complemented by scenic views of the harbor. Second location in **Sandyport** (☎242-327-3325; W Bay St).

Montagu Gardens CONTINENTAL **$$**
(Map p46; ☎242-394-6347; E Bay St; mains $13-29; ⏱lunch & dinner Mon-Sat) Though the Roman villa decor (faux stone walls, headless statues) is kitschy, this garden restaurant has a reasonably priced and appealing menu of continental and Bahamian favorites like grouper almandine and fettuccine with blackened shrimp.

Double D's BAHAMIAN **$**
(Map p46; E Bay St; mains $5-10; ⏱24hr) Adventuresome eaters can try waaaay down-home Bahamian dishes like pig feet souse (stew) at this 24-hour stripmall joint, across from the Paradise Island Exit Bridge.

Cable Beach

All the hotels on Cable Beach have their own restaurants, cafes and beach bars, so you're never far from a snack. If you're looking for a bargain, mobile lunch vendors sometimes set up in the parking lot across from the Wyndham and Sheraton.

TOP CHOICE **Arawak Cay** BAHAMIAN **$**
(Map p42; mains $8-20; ⏱breakfast, lunch & dinner; 👪) There's always a party on at this colorful village of seafood shacks, known to locals as 'the Fish Fry.' No Nassau vacation is complete without a pilgrimage here – it's a mile or so west of downtown. Come for conch fritters, fried snapper, and Sky Juice. Stay for rake 'n' scrape bands, Junkanoo dances and friendly chatter. Tourists tend to gravitate towards Twin Brothers and Goldie's, two of the bigger sit-down establishments, but we suggest following locals' leads and queuing up at whatever takeout stand has the longest line.

Black Angus Grille STEAKHOUSE **$$$**
(Map p42; ☎242-327-6200; www.wyndhamnassauresort.com; Wyndham Nassau Resort & Crystal Palace Casino, W Bay St; mains $28-48; ⏱lunch & dinner) The Wyndham's clubby steakhouse sticks to the basics: dripping hunks of sirloin, filet mignon or prime rib, dunked in your choice of sauces (try the Bahamian-flavored Goombay curry). Lobster tails, iceberg wedge salads and fat steakhouse fries keep things classic. Atmosphere is very 'let's make a deal,' with leather banquettes and a wood coffered ceiling.

Amici ITALIAN **$$$**
(Map p42; ☎242-327-6000; www.sheratonnassau.com; Sheraton Nassau Beach, W Bay St; mains $22-32; ⏱dinner) In the Sheraton, this neo-trattoria is less cozy and more corporate than one might wish, but its menu of Italian classics – calamari, chicken Florentine, veal scaloppini and more – is well-received, and it's a nice change of pace from the greasy beach bars that populate Cable Beach.

Swiss Pastry Shop BAKERY **$**
(Map p42; W Bay St, Cable Beach; pastries $3-6; ⏱9am-6pm Mon-Sat) Caribbean meat patties, guava duff and glossy fruit tarts make this Euro-Bahamian bakery a great stop for a quick bite. No seating.

Western New Providence

TOP CHOICE **Goodfellow Farms** GOURMET MARKET **$**
(Map p42; ☎242-377-5000; www.goodfellowfarms.com; Nelson Rd, Mt Pleasant; mains $6-14; ⏱lunch 11am-2pm Mon-Sat, 10am-3pm Sun, market 9am-4pm Mon-Sat, 10am-3pm Sun) As far off the beaten path as you can get in New Providence, this rustic-chic farmstand and cafe is a fave of yachties, picnickers and Lyford Cayers who lunch. Grab a pork tenderloin wrap or a cranberry chicken salad sandwich and relax on the patio overlooking the fields. The greens and herbs are all home-grown; the owner's husband, a pilot, flies in regularly with fresh berries and meats from the US. Everyone stops by on weekends for herb-roasted ribs or special pizza nights. Don't be scared off by the winding dirt road to the farm – just keep going straight, you'll get there.

La Hipica GOURMET MARKET **$**
(Map p42; ☎242-376-5554; Nelson Rd, Mt Pleasant; mains $6-14; ⏱lunch Tue-Sat, dinner Thu-Sat) Across the field from Goodfellow Farms, this working horse stable runs an intimate little tapas bar in the garden. Expats gossip and nibble chorizo, fried chickpeas and shrimp *al ajillo* (with garlic) while downing glass after glass of Spanish red. The Saturday night suckling pig roast is an all-evening social affair.

Paradise Island

Expect major sticker shock on Paradise Island, as most restaurants are contained within the Atlantis monopoly. That said, there's some truly fine dining on the island, mostly of the 'bigger-is-better' celebrity chef variety. Those wishing to DIY it can

PARADISE ISLAND BUDGET TIPS

The words 'budget' and 'Paradise Island' go together about as well as 'pacifist' and 'grenade launcher.' There's simply no way to enjoy the island without spending a pretty penny, but these tips may help keep you from having to take out a second mortgage:

» Stay at Comfort Suites instead of one of the Atlantis hotels. You'll get a cheaper room, but retain full privileges at Aquaventure and the rest of the sights.

» Stock up on groceries. This means a) taking a taxi to Nassau to stock up at City Market supermarket chain (one on Village Rd, one in Cable Beach), or b) scrounging what you can at the overpriced, under-stocked convenience stores on Paradise Island. Either way, a few boxes of cereal and peanut butter sandwiches will save big bucks to put towards fancy dinners or blackjack.

» By the same token, buy your own liquor and mixers for cocktails on your balcony.

» Look out for promotional deals on bars and nightclubs (free appetizers at Nobu, $20 admission to Aura nightclub etc).

» If you want to go into downtown Nassau, just walk across the bridge and catch the $1 jitney rather than take a pricey taxi.

» Enjoy what's free – wandering Marina Village, watching Hollywood hits in the Atlantis Theater (complimentary for guests), strolling Versailles Gardens, lounging on Cabbage Beach, watching the dolphin shows from the snack bar at Dolphin Cay. Atlantis also offers free-for-guests activities like tennis clinics, as well as regular 'free slots' days at the casino.

try the ill-stocked grocery store in the Paradise Island Shopping Center on Casino Dr.

TOP CHOICE **Mesa Grill** SOUTHWESTERN **$$$**
(☎242-363-3000; Cove Atlantis; mains $32-49; ⊙dinner) Southwestern style gets the Atlantis treatment at Bobby Flay's latest, in the ever-so-chic Cove. Think cow-print chairs, undulating stone walls, a stadium-sized open kitchen with enough hammered copper to keep the Bahamas in pennies for a decade. Clientele are moneyed and glam, dining on New Mexican spice-rubbed pork tenderloin and sipping top-drawer margaritas. The menu makes a few nods to the Bahamas - crispy conch with pepper-mango relish, curried halibut, a to-die-for pineapple upside-down cake with caramelized rum sauce.

TOP CHOICE **Nobu** JAPANESE **$$$**
(☎242-363-3000; www.atlantis.com; Atlantis Royal Towers; mains $18-48; ⊙dinner) Dot-com bubble? Recession? What? The carefree, flashy 1990s are still alive and sipping saketinis at Nobu - think investment bankers in Armani suits, models in stilettos, lots of neon-green lighting. One of celebrity chef Nobu Matsuhisa's many international outposts, this is one of Nassau's hottest tickets. Choose from a range of designer sushi rolls or noodle dishes, or go with Matsuhisa's signature black cod with miso. 'Live conch' sashimi is not for the faint of heart. Decor might be described as 'Zen on steroids' - towering ceilings, avant-garde light fixtures, glowing stone sushi bar.

Dune FUSION **$$$**
(☎242-363-2501; oceanclub.oneandonlyresorts.com; One & Only Ocean Club; mains $22-60; ⊙breakfast, lunch & dinner) International celebrity chef Jean-Georges Vongerichten created the menu at this ultrachic (and ultrapricey) fusion restaurant, on the beach in front of the genteel One & Only Ocean Club hotel. The menu globe hops with impunity: Asian fish dishes, French-inflected lamb, Caribbean-flavored calamari. Don't miss Jean-Georges' signature molten chocolate cake (he's said to have invented the now-ubiquitous dessert). The minimalist black-painted dining room seems to float above the dune; on balmy nights when all the shutters are thrown open, you'll feel like you're on a ship at sea.

Café Martinique FRENCH **$$$**
(☎242-363-3000; www.atlantis.com; Marina Village; mains $42-63; ⊙dinner) The original Café Martinique was made famous for its appearance in the 1965 James Bond movie, *Thunderball*. This recreation, in Atlantis' Marina Village, goes over-the-top on the Old World

opulence – mahogany staircase, wrought iron birdcage elevator, antiques everywhere – to luscious results. The French colonial menu (think foie gras with mango, Nassau grouper with sauce Béarnaise), created by megachef Jean-Georges Vongerichten, gets mixed reviews from diners.

Carmine's ITALIAN **$$$**
(www.atlantis.com; Marina Village; mains $34-46; ⏲dinner; 👪) Waits for dinner at this theme park-y Italian joint routinely top an hour or more, which speaks to its popularity among vacationing families. All the classics are here: spaghetti with meatballs, chicken parmigiana, tiramisu, all big enough to feed a crowd. Be aware that 'family friendly' does not mean 'budget friendly' – a plate of spaghetti with garlic and oil will cost you upwards of $30, which is not much less than an entrée at one of the island's truly fine dining spots.

Mosaic BUFFET **$$$**
(Cove Atlantis; breakfast/lunch/dinner buffet $32/35/60; ⏲breakfast, lunch & dinner; 👪) Any anti-buffet prejudices will evaporate at this luxe all-you-can-eat spot, with endless tables of sushi, pizza, made-to-order pasta and waaaaay more, in an airy open dining room graced with contemporary glass fountains.

Anthony's Grill AMERICAN **$$**
(www.anthonysgrillparadiseisland.com; Casino Dr, Paradise Island Shopping Center; mains $14-32; ⏲breakfast, lunch & dinner) One of Paradise Island's few nonhotel restaurants, this Caribbean-bright diner is a favorite with families for its big menu of burgers, pizzas, pastas and big American-style breakfasts.

Murray's Deli AMERICAN, DELI **$**
(www.atlantis.com; Marina Village; mains $10-16; ⏲breakfast, lunch & dinner) Grab a bagel with a *schmear* of cream cheese at this retro-themed Jewish deli, in the Marina Village.

Drinking

Most bars in Nassau bill themselves either as English-style pubs or US-style sports bars (or 'satellite lounges,' so named for their satellite TVs). Many resort hotels have at least one such bar, as well as more sophisticated lounge bars where music plays in the background to the low-key chatter of groups of groomed cocktail drinkers.

You will not experience the local color by playing the tourist, however. For that, you need to hang out at satellite lounges. Although middle-class locals tend toward the same places as out-of-towners, there are plenty of funky watering holes where the activities center on downing beers and playing dominoes. Most have a TV and pool table.

Downtown Nassau

Though downtown seems to drop dead after 5pm when the stores close and the cruise ships depart, there are a few bright spots. Plan on taking a taxi rather than walking.

Señor Frog's PUB
(Map p48; www.senorfrogs.com; Woodes Rogers Walk; ⏲11am-1pm) Snubbed by locals, this raucous tourist trap is actually, er, kind of fun if your mood's right. Down-and-dirty Mexican grub (mains $11 to $18), cheesy pop tunes, bad frog puns and colorful tropical cocktails – it's tacky, it's wacky and don't tell anyone we sent you.

Bullion Bar BAR
(Map p48; www.hiltoncaribbean.com; British Colonial Hilton Nassau, 1 Bay St) This swank new lounge is very Wall St, all leather and wood and angular gray furniture. Try the signature Rumbullion cocktail – dark rum, fresh lime, pineapple homemade ginger infusion.

Green Parrot PUB
(Map p46; www.greenparrotbar.com; Prince George Wharf) Right on the wharf, this lively tropical-themed pub ropes in cruise shippers with cheap, tasty sandwiches and enough rum to drown a pirate. There are two other outposts, one overlooking **Nassau Harbour** (Map p46) west of the Paradise Island entrance bridge, and another in Paradise Island's Hurricane Hole.

East of Downtown

Hammerhead Bar & Grill BAR
(Map p46; E Bay St; ⏲noon-late) 'Get hammered at Hammerheads' is the oh-so-subtle motto of this funky little bar, between the two Paradise Island Bridges. A three-hour Happy 'Hour' starts at 4pm, and there's live music on weekends. Mixed crowds include locals, Spring Breakers, yachties.

West of Downtown

Arawak Cay FISH FRY
(Map p42; 👪) Weekends at Arawak Cay mean 'Fish Fry' – an island-wide

TOP 5 BAHAMIAN COCKTAILS

» **Bahama Mama** Sure, it's strictly for the tourist crowd, but this icy, coral-colored mixture of multiple rums, coffee liqueur, pineapple and lemon juices and grenadine sure does go down easy.

» **Goombay Smash** Invented on Abaco's Green Turtle Cay, this Bahamian classic is a mix of spiced rum, coconut rum, apricot brandy, pineapple juice and orange juice.

» **Sky Juice** The favored tipple at Fish Fries across the islands, this stomach-burning rocket fuel is gin (sometimes rum), coconut water and nutmeg.

» **Daiquiri** These smoothie-like blends of fruit, ice and rum are sold at roadside stands across the island; kids and teetotalers can ask for a virgin.

» **Rum Punch** A sweetened blend of rum and lime juice, watered-down versions of this punch are frequently the beverage on offer at all-you-can-drink cruises and buffets.

neighborhood party with food, music and rockin' reggae and Junkanoo music at the various seafood shacks and daiquiri bars. The area can get a bit wild later on, but the early evenings here are lively with all age groups, and the police do keep an eye on things. See also p62.

TOP CHOICE **Compass Point** BAR
(Map p42; www.compasspointbeachresort.com; W Bay St, Gambier Village) You're three times cooler than you used to be the moment you step onto the resort's thatched deck. Here, a stylish crowd sips potent cocktails with the deep blue sea as a backdrop. Monthly house parties are major events.

Travellers Rest BAR, CAFE
(Map p42; www.bahamastravellersrest.com; W Bay St, Gambier Village; ⏲11am-11pm Mon-Sat) For laid-back ocean views framed by palm trees, head west to this roadside bar and cafe, popular with locals and visitors alike for its down-home cooking and potent daiquiris.

22 Above BAR
(Map p42; www.wyndhamnassauresort.com; Wyndham Nassau Resort & Crystal Palace Casino, W Bay St, Cable Beach) On top of the Wyndham resort, this glam lounge is all about low lights and fancy cocktails. Live music on weekends.

Paradise Island

Many of Atlantis' restaurants, including Mesa Grill and Nobu, have separate bar areas perfect for sipping high-end cocktails and people-watching. The One & Only Ocean Club's Dune restaurant is another hotspot. For daytime drinking, there are plenty of casual tiki-style bars.

Sea Glass BAR
(www.atlantis.com; Cove Atlantis) Jet-setters sip Scotch and try their luck at roulette and blackjack at Sea Glass, in the lobby of the ultraswank Cove Atlantis hotel.

Bimini Road BAR
(www.atlantis.com; Marina Village Atlantis) This casual bar and restaurant attracts a slightly older crowd of drinkers, who enjoy fruity cocktails, tapas and outdoor seating.

Green Parrot Bar & Grill PUB
(www.greenparrotbar.com; Hurricane Hole Marina; ⏲noon-midnight) This fun-loving tropical pub is one of the few bars on the island outside the hotel complexes. Live music, cheap food, and plenty of rum draw party crowds nightly.

☆ Entertainment

Downtown Nassau is strangely dead at night, once the day's business is put to bed. Cruise-ship passengers return to their ships and the Christian community, including the Bahamas Christian Council, have influenced the decision to centralize nightspots in a couple of areas. Anyone who wants to party should head for the tourist nightspots of Cable Beach and Paradise Island. Here you can party and swill at will!

Nightclubs

There are numerous clubs that come and go, but the following are staunch favorites. Some clubs only open at weekends in quieter periods but then party nightly during the peak times of Spring Break, Easter, Christmas and New Year. Admission prices vary wildly, usually anywhere from $5 to $30 (or more, in the case of Atlantis).

Aura NIGHTCLUB
(www.atlantis.com; Atlantis, Paradise Island; ⌚9:30pm-4am Thu-Sat) Designed to recreate the exclusive feel of a trendy New York nightclub, Atlantis' premier dance spot is one VIP lounge after another. DJs spin as couture-clad partiers gyrate in their stilettos and investment banker types sip top-drawer vodka and stare from the surrounding banquettes. When young celebrities visit Atlantis, this is where they get wild. Cover charges vary wildly – try to snag a cheap promotional pass.

Club Waterloo NIGHTCLUB
(Map p46; www.clubwaterloo.com; E Bay St; ⌚9pm-4am) In an old lakeside mansion near Fort Montagu, the Waterloo has been getting Spring Breakers drunk and dancing for 30 years. With various indoor and outdoor dance floors and multiple bars, it's got something for everyone (provided you're between 18 and, oh, 25). Music ranges from techno to calypso, with a heavy emphasis on bootie-shaking beats. Thursday night is Ladies' Night; weekends bring live bands and big crowds.

Other options:

Bambu NIGHTCLUB
(Map p48; www.bambunassau.com; upstairs at Prince George Plaza, Prince George Wharf; ⌚9am-5am Thu-Sat) This sexy new rooftop dance club promises an Ibiza vibe: throbbing house music, skin-to-skin crowds, shoooooort skirts. Things don't really get pumping until after midnight. Then watch out!

Club Fluid NIGHTCLUB
(Map p48; W Bay St) Hidden in plain sight in a downtown basement, this locals' favorite gets sweaty to hip-hop and reggae beats. Hottest after midnight.

Casinos & Shows

Atlantis Resort & Casino CASINO
(Map p42; www.atlantis.com; Royal Towers Atlantis, Paradise Island; admission free; ⌚10am-4am) The nerve center of the entire Atlantis complex, this 7-acre casino has 90 game tables and 850 slot machines surrounding a multistory Dale Chihuly glass sculpture of the sun. Even if you don't gamble, it's worth a walk-through just to get a sense of its vast size. If you're lucky, maybe you'll spot a celebrity high roller – Michael Jordan is said to be a regular, among others.

Wyndham Nassau Resort & Crystal Palace Casino CASINO
(Map p42; ☎242-327-6200; www.wyndhamnassauresort.com; Wyndham Nassau Resort & Crystal Palace Casino, W Bay St, Cable Beach) Spend enough time in this vast, 24-hour black and gold casino, and you may forget whether it's night

GAY & LESBIAN NASSAU

The pink dollar is not welcomed by many Bahamians and there are few public illustrations of support for a Bahamian gay and lesbian population across the islands, unless individuals openly support the political pressure group Rainbow Alliance. Sadly, although Bahamians are generally an extremely tolerant and friendly people, the pervasiveness of fundamentalist religious beliefs has fostered intolerance of progressive lifestyles, particularly towards gays and lesbians.

Most Bahamian gays are still deeply in the closet, and the nation has draconian laws against homosexual activity, which is punishable by prison terms. Laws are strictly enforced and public expressions of affection between gays will bring trouble.

In 1998 a group called Save the Bahamas made waves when it protested against the arrival of a gay charter-cruise. The group compounded the negative press by also protesting against the arrival of the company Holland America's *Veendam*, which they mistakenly believed was chartered by a gay group, causing Bahamian Prime Minister Hubert Ingraham to issue a public apology.

This remonstration was then followed up by a preemptive protest against the docking of the *Norwegian Dawn*, a gay family cruise backed by American comedian and actor Rosie O'Donnell, in July 2004. By the actual date of the cruise ship's arrival, the previously vocal protestors were greatly reduced in number, but among them were the Bahamian gay rights group Rainbow Alliance, who met and welcomed the cruise ship's gay and lesbian passengers.

Rainbow Alliance (www.bahamianglad.tripod.com), the aforementioned political pressure group, is a good point of contact for assistance and advice in planning a trip.

PIRATE-HUNTING

'It was a short life, but a merry one,' said Captain Bart Roberts about life as a wayfaring pirate. In downtown Nassau you can easily imagine pirates striding the gritty, narrow streets, looking for two-bit grog and a one-night girlfriend after a long few months at sea. Spend the night at gothic **Graycliff Hotel** (see p56), the hillside former home of Captain Graysmith, who plundered ships off the Spanish Main. Learn about marooning, parrots and peg-legs at the **Pirates of Nassau** (p41) museum then walk to the British Colonial Hilton Nassau to gaze upon the statue of pirate hunter **Woodes Rogers**, who restored order to the city in 1718 and inspired the motto 'Expulsis Piratis, Commercia Restituta' (Pirates Expelled, Commerce Restored).

or day outside. The continuous tinkling sound from 400 slot machines enhances the otherworldly feel. This is where visitors throw their money to the fates at the poker tables, blackjack, craps, roulette and more, or play the ponies in the sports lounge.

Joker's Wild COMEDY CLUB
(www.atlantis.com; Royal Towers Atlantis, Paradise Island; admission price varies; ⏲from 9:30pm Tue-Sun) International comedians take the stage at this high-end comedy club.

Atlantis Live CONCERTS
(www.atlantis.com; Paradise Island) Atlantis' concert series brings top pop stars – Justin Bieber, the Jonas Brothers, Katy Perry – to play at various venues throughout the resort, including stages set directly on the beach. Check out the website for schedules.

Cinemas

Galleria Cinemas 11 CINEMA
(Map p42; Mall at Marathon, cnr Prince Charles Ave & Marathon Rd; tickets adult/child $10/5) An 11-screen theater with super-surround sound that has day and evening shows.

Galleria 6 CINEMA
(Map p42; RND Plaza, John F Kennedy Dr; tickets adult/child $10/5) This six-screen multiplex also has matinees and evening shows.

Theater

National Centre for the Performing Arts THEATER
(Map p46; ☎242-301-0600; Shirley St) This 600-seat center hosts large-scale performances and international productions. Look out for 'Summer Madness,' when popular local theatrical troupes address contemporary issues in Bahamian society. The excellent National Youth Choir, who have recorded eight CDs, hold an annual concert here in late April or early May. Performances by the National Dance Company, Nassau Amateur Operatic Society, Chamber Singers, and Diocesan Chorale are also a fabulous treat.

Dundas Centre for the Performing Arts THEATER
(Map p46; ☎242-393-3728; Mackey St; admission $10-20) This is Nassau's most valued venue, hosting plays, dances, revues, musicals and (occasionally) ballets.

Spectator Sports

Haynes Oval CRICKET
(Map p42; W Bay St, Nassau; admission free) On weekends, the Bahamas' British roots show when cricket teams in dress whites come to bowl and bat at Haynes Oval. The on-site Cricket Club serves English pub grub and has balcony seating; you can hang out in the bleachers or on the grass for free.

Shopping

Bay St is lined with arcades and duty-free stores selling everything from Swiss watches and nugget-sized Colombian emeralds to Milanese fashions and spicy rums. The side streets are favored by stores selling leather goods, artwork and collectibles. Upscale resorts also have duty-free jewelry and gift stores. By far the largest is the **Crystal Court Shops** at Atlantis, with its gleaming marble halls and international couture shops.

If you're planning on buying any big-ticket items, be sure to research prices beforehand to make sure you're getting a good deal. Bargaining is only acceptable at the Straw Market (p44).

Antiques & Collectibles

Balmain Antiques ANTIQUES
(Map p48; 2nd fl, Mason's Bldg, cnr Bay & Charlotte Sts) In the old Masonic Lodge, this diminutive shop specializes in Masonic items, as well as antique maps and etchings.

PORT OF CALL: NASSAU

Only have a few hours in Nassau? Here are a few quickie activity ideas to make the most of your limited time in town. Cruise ships dock at Prince George Wharf downtown, which is walking distance from many of the city's best sights, shopping and eating options.

» Shopping for duty-free diamonds on Bay St (opposite)

» Riding horse-drawn surreys in historic downtown Nassau (p42)

» Saying 'arrrg' at the Pirates of Nassau museum (p41)

» Sipping cocktails at the swanky Bullion Bar (p64) at the British Colonial Hilton Nassau

» Munching cracked conch and listening to Junkanoo beats at Arawak Cay (p62)

» Playing your luck at the casinos (p66)

» Going under with the Seaworld Explorer semi-submarine (p53)

» Puffing a hand-rolled stogie at the Graycliff Cigar Co (p45)

» Picking up a rum cake to eat back in your cabin at the Bahamas Rum Cake Factory (opposite)

Coin of the Realm COINS
(Map p48; Charlotte St) Salvaged Spanish doubloons are the coolest find at this busy coin and jewelry shop.

Philatelic Bureau STAMPS
(Map p48; E Hill St at Parliament St) The main post office sells collectible stamps.

Arts & Crafts

Galleries abound, as do souvenir shops selling cheap original or hand-copied oil and acrylic Haitian paintings from as little as $15. For made-in-China trinkets, the Straw Market (p44) on Bay St is hard to miss (even if you want to). Vendors expect you to bargain the price down by about 10%.

Doongalik Studios ART GALLERY
(Map p46; www.doongalik.com; 18 Village Rd) The best gallery for modern Bahamian art, including painting, sculpture, mixed media installations, Junkanoo masks and more. One location southeast of downtown Nassau, and another in Paradise Island's Marina Village.

Balmain Art Gallery SOUVENIRS
(Map p48; 2nd fl, Mason's Bldg, Bay & Charlotte Sts) Good-quality Bahamian gift items like guava jam, tea, shell earrings and art prints.

Kennedy Gallery ART GALLERY
(Map p48; http://mymurphys.com/kennedy/; Parliament St) Paintings, sculptures, ceramics, wind chimes and other works from both established and emerging artists, includes children's art.

Cigars

Premium Cuban cigars can be bought for a song in Nassau, but remember, Uncle Sam prohibits US citizens from importing them. The good news is that Graycliff's cigars are not made with Cuban tobacco so *are* permitted into the US by customs.

Graycliff Cigar Co CIGARS
(Map p48; www.graycliff.com; 8-12 W Hill St) A team of Cuban *torcedores* (cigar rollers) hunker down at antique desks to hand-roll these gorgeous stogies; see also p45.

Havana Humidor CIGARS
(www.havanahumidor.net; Crystal Court, Atlantis, Paradise Island) A sizeable collection of Cuban cigars; includes rolling demonstrations. Americans: you better smoke these here!

Clothing & Fabric

You'll find T-shirts and resort wear at all the resort boutiques and in dozens of stores downtown. Look out for clothes and home goods of Androsia batik, handmade on the Bahamian island of Andros. International designers like Gucci and Versace are well represented on Bay St and at Atlantis.

Bahama Handprints CLOTHING
(Map p46; www.bahamahandprints.com; Island Trader's Bldg, Ernest St) Bolts of its handmade interior design fabric, in tropical seashell or fish prints, sell at a premium abroad. Buy raw fabric, home furnishings, or women's clothes, or ask to tour the factory.

Marley Boutique CLOTHING, SOUVENIRS
(Map p42; www.marleyresort.com; Marley Resort, Cable Beach) Get your Bob Marley T-shirts and Rasta wear at this boutique, in the hotel that was once Marley's Bahamian getaway.

Brass & Leather Shops LEATHER
(Map p48; Charlotte & Bay Sts) All-leather goods and clothes.

Coles of Nassau WOMEN'S CLOTHING
(Map p48; cnr Parliament & Bay Sts) Selling clothes and swimsuits since 1956 to ladies who lunch.

Food & Liquor

Bahamas Rum Cake Factory BAKERY
(Map p46; 602 E Bay St) Made from Grand Bahama's Don Lorenzo rum, these buttery little Bundt cakes sell for about $16 in a decorative tin. Buy and eat a warm one right now, or take some home for gifts – they keep well.

Mortimer Candies CANDY
(Map p46; www.mortimercandies.com; East St) A Nassau tradition since 1928, this old-fashioned candy kitchen sells humble sweets like bennie (sesame seed) cakes and soft mints in the colors of the Bahamian flag.

Tortuga Rum Cake BAKERY
(Map p48; Charlotte St) Tasty yes, local no. Tortuga's treats are made in the Cayman Islands. But the samples are delish.

Bacardi LIQUOR
(Map p48; cnr Bay & East Sts) Get your duty-free Bacardi rum (including the rare 16-year-old Reserva Limitada) and Bacardi themed hats, towels, shot glasses and more at this two-story retail outlet.

Gifts

Plunder PIRATE GEAR
(Map p48; www.pirates-of-nassau.com; cnr King & George Sts) Eye patches, black flags, pirate tees and a good selection of pirate lit for buccaneering bookworms.

My Ocean SOAPS, CRAFTS
(Airport) Hand-rolled glycerin soaps, bath salts and scents, all made with Bahamian botanicals. Also sells locally made home accessories and wooden crafts.

Jewelry, Perfume & Duty-Free

Bay St is lined with palatial duty-free shops selling diamonds, Swiss watches, French perfumes, Japanese cameras and more. Sometimes you can get a bargain, but you have to know the market.

Colombian Emeralds JEWELRY
(Map p48; www.colombianemeralds.com; Bay St) Grass-green emeralds as big as your thumb, and much more at this Caribbean-wide chain store.

John Bull DUTY-FREE
(Map p48; www.johnbull.com, Bay St) This ubiquitous chain, with locations throughout New Providence, has a jaw-dropping variety of luxury goods, including watches, jewelry, leather goods and cosmetics.

Solomon's Mines DUTY-FREE
(Map p48; Bay St) A massive trove of jewels and watches.

Perfume Shop & Beauty Spot PERFUME, COSMETICS
(Map p48; cnr Bay & Frederick Sts) A vast collection of designer sniffs and international cosmetics.

Information

Dangers & Annoyances

Crime has been a hot topic: local papers have kept a close tally on the Bahamas' record high number of murders – 98 in 2010 – most of which took place in Nassau. Although most criminal activity occurred in the 'Over-the-Hill' neighborhood outside of tourist-filled downtown, travelers should avoid this neighborhood at night; this area suffers from violence. Also use caution by day, as the area's down-at-the-heels quality is aggravated by the presence of 'Joneses' (drug users). You should also avoid walking alone downtown at night; stick to well-lit main streets.

Watch for scams by taxi drivers. Rates are regulated and posted at the larger hotels, but the occasional driver will try to overcharge you. Avoid unlicensed drivers offering to give you a lift. All licensed taxi drivers should have a government ID badge.

Emergency

Air Sea Rescue Association (242-325-8864)
Ambulance (242-323-2597, 911)
Fire (911)
Med-Evac (242-322-2881)
Police (242-322-3335, 911; E Hill St)

Internet Access

There's free wi-fi along downtown Nassau's Woodes Rogers Walk, in Paradise Island's Marina Village, at the Wyndham casino, and in all Starbucks. All hotels have wi-fi, sometimes free, sometimes not.

Bahamas Internet Café (Bay St; 9am-6pm)

NASSAU OFF THE BEATEN PATH

When the cruise ships are in town and the hotels of Paradise Island are fully booked, sometimes hanging out in Nassau can feel like being at a shopping mall the week before Christmas. But getting off the beaten path is easy, with or without a rental car. If you're going to be here for more than a few days, why not do a little exploring and check out these underrated gems:

» Do as in-the-know celeb and fashion types do, and swig evening cocktails by the oceanfront pool at **Compass Point Beach Resort** (p58), a swank collection of beach villas on the island's far west side.

» Brave the winding dirt road to **Goodfellow Farms** (p62) in the island's little-visited interior for home-grown salads and sandwiches overlooking the horse pasture.

» Say 'om' at a drop-in yoga class at Paradise Island's rustic **Sivananda Yoga Ashram** (p60), accessible only by boat.

» Swim and sun yourself far from the maddening crowds at quiet **Delaporte** or **Orange Hill Beaches** (p51).

» Sleep in a cliff-top colonial-style mansion at **A Stone's Throw Away** (p57), a luxe European-run B&B in quiet western New Providence.

Media

Apart from the daily and weekly newspapers listed in the boxed text, p253, there's a monthly tourist paper, *What's On*, available free in hotel lobbies, stores and tourist information booths. They include feature articles, a calendar of events, and discount coupons. *What to-do: Where to shop, dine, stay, play, invest* is available free at tourist bureaus and most hotel lobbies. It has a good shopping section.

Medical Services

Pharmacies exist in all shopping malls, but mainly keep standard shop hours.

Doctor's Hospital (☎242-322-8411, 242-302-4600; www.doctorshosp.com; cnr Shirley St & Collins Ave) Privately owned full-service hospital east of Princess Margaret Hospital; provides emergency services and acute care.

Princess Margaret Hospital (☎242-322-2861; cnr Elizabeth Ave & Sands Rd) This government-run, full-service hospital is the island's main facility, providing emergency services and acute care.

Money

There are plenty of banks clustered around Rawson Sq and Bay St. ATMs dispensing US and Bahamian dollars can be easily found throughout Nassau. The Rawson Sq branch of Scotiabank has an ATM.

Commonwealth Bank (☎242-327-8441; W Bay St, Cable Beach)

Destinations (☎242-322-2931; 303 Shirley St) Represents American Express.

First Caribbean International Bank (W Bay St, Cable Beach) Opposite Sandals Royal Bahamian.

Royal Bank of Canada Cable Beach (☎242-327-6077; W Bay St); Downtown Nassau (☎242-322-8700; E Hill St; ☎242-356-8500; W Bay St)

Scotiabank Cable Beach (☎242-327-7380; Cecil Wallace Whitfield Centre, W Bay St); Downtown Nassau (☎242-356-1400; Rawson Sq) The Cable Beach branch is opposite Nassau Beach Hotel.

Western Union (☎242-394-1429; W Bay St, Cable Beach)

Post

DHL Worldwide Express (www.dhl.com.bs; Out Island Traders Bldg, E Bay St)

FedEx (www.fedex.com; EE McKay Plaza, Thompson Blvd)

Main post office (cnr E Hill & Parliament Sts)

Telephone

BaTelCo East St (☎242-323-6414; ⌚7am-10pm); John F Kennedy Dr (☎242-323-4911; ⌚7am-10pm) Has public phone booths for international calls. The East St branch is a half-block south of Bay St.

Toilets

There are public toilets on Bay St (on the west side of the Straw Market) and on the north side of Rawson Sq. Apart from those two, public toilets are as rare as hen's teeth. Just pop in and use the facilities at big hotels as everyone else does!

Tourist Information

Bahamas Ministry of Tourism (www.bahamas.com); Welcome Centre (☎242-323-3182, 242-322-7680; Prince George Wharf); Airport Arrivals Terminal (☎242-377-6806)

Getting There & Away

For information on international flights to the Bahamas and Nassau please refer to p260. For travel information between Nassau and other Bahamian islands, please refer to those destinations.

Getting Around

Historic downtown Nassau is 10 blocks long and four blocks wide and faces north toward Paradise Island and Nassau Harbour. The Paradise Island bridge is about a mile east of downtown, while Cable Beach begins about 3 miles west of downtown. The island's main drag, Bay St, traverses the entire north shore of the island, passing right through downtown Nassau.

To/From the Airport

Lynden Pindling International Airport (242-377-7281) lies 10 miles west of downtown.

There are no buses to or from the airport, as the taxi-drivers' union has things sewn up. Bus 12 does come to the airport's outskirts, but not to the terminals – if you're hell-bent on taking the bus, ask a local where to stand. A few hotels do provide shuttle services, and taxis also line the forecourts of hotels and the area outside the arrivals lounge of the airport. Call the day ahead to book a **taxi** (242-323-5111/4555). Rates are fixed by the government and displayed at the airport on the wall by the taxi-rank; all destination rates are for two people with standard luggage (each additional person costs $3).

One-way rates to/from the airport are as follows: Cable Beach $18; downtown Nassau and Prince George Wharf $27; and Paradise Island $32.

Taxi sightseeing rates are usually in the vicinity of $50 per hour, which makes car hire a very attractive option!

Bicycle

Biking in traffic-clogged Nassau is not recommended, while East and West Bay Sts are death-traps of blind curves and speeding minibuses. Paradise Island is safer but has no bike rental shops; if you're keen on biking, ask if your hotel can arrange a rental.

Boat

Small ferries or water taxis (round trip $6, every 15 minutes or when full, from 8am to 6pm) ply the route between the downtown Nassau cruise ship dock and Paradise Island. You'll see the signs or be hustled aboard by touts.

Car & Scooter

You really don't need a car to explore Nassau, Cable Beach and Paradise Island or to get to their beaches. However if you intend to explore New Providence, it's worth saving the taxi fare to and from Nassau by hiring a car at the airport. Rates start at about $80, per day, with an extra $15 for collision damage insurance. For information on road rules, see p265.

The following companies have rental booths at the airport:

Avis (242-377-7121)

Budget (242-377-9000)

Dollar (242-377-8300)

Hertz (242-377-8684)

Several local companies also rent cars that are cheaper, from about $50 daily. Ask your hotel to suggest a company or try **Orange Creek Rentals** (242-325-0005; Bougainvillea Dr).

Scooters (from about $60 per day) are widely available and can be found outside most major hotels. The same warnings we gave about biking apply to scooting! Try **Bowcar Scooter Rentals** (242-328-7300; www.bahamasscooterrentals.com; Welcome Centre, Prince George Wharf), which has pick-up at this location, on Cable Beach, or will deliver the scooters to hotels island-wide.

Public Transportation

Nassau and New Providence are well served by jitney buses, which run constantly from 6am to 8pm, although there are no fixed schedules. No buses run to Paradise Island. All jitney buses depart downtown from the corner of Frederick St and Bay Sts and at designated bus stops. Destinations are clearly marked on the buses, which can be waved down. Likewise to request a stop anywhere when you're onboard, simply ask the driver.

The standard fare is between $1 and $1.50, paid to the driver upon exiting the bus.

BUS NUMBER	DESTINATION
6	South New Providence
10 or 10A	Cable Beach & Sandy Point
38	Cable Beach & Prince George Wharf via Over-the-Hill
24 or 30	New Paradise Island Bridge

If you're car-less in Nassau, bus 10 will be your best friend. It plies the stretch of Bay St between downtown and the island's west end, stopping in Cable Beach.

While there's no bus service to Paradise Island, you can catch bus 24 or 30 from Frederick St in downtown Nassau to the New Paradise Island Bridge, and then walk over to the island.

The 'Casino Express,' operated by Atlantis, runs a clockwise route throughout the day and early evening on Paradise Island, picking up and dropping off passengers at major hotels; the fare is $1/free for nonguests/guests of Atlantis.

Western Transportation runs hourly buses from downtown Nassau (opposite the British Colonial Hilton Nassau) to Lyford, South Ocean and Compass Point ($2 one way). In the evenings buses only depart from town at 9pm and midnight.

Free shuttle buses run between the Cable Beach hotels from 6pm to 2am.

AROUND NASSAU

West New Providence

Running west from downtown to Cable Beach on the island's north shore, W Bay St is a gorgeously curving seaside drive. One-and-a-half miles west of Delaport Point you'll pass the **Caves**, just east of Blake Rd. This large cavern system once sheltered Lucayan Indians. Just west is **Orange Hill Beach**, shaded by sea grapes and palms. It is undeveloped, except for the Orange Hill Beach Inn (p57) hidden on the bluff overlooking the beach, and very popular with Bahamian families.

West of Compass Point is **Love Beach**, a small, little-used beach near Gambier Village. It's known for its snorkeling. Beyond Love Beach, the road turns inland and curls past the small settlement of Mt Pleasant and around **Lyford Cay**, a sprawling walled estate of manicured, tree-lined streets and canals framed by glorious multimillion dollar mansions. Here billionaires and celebrities – Sean Connery for one – protect themselves from the world.

South New Providence

Most of this region is backed by mangroves, swampy wetlands and brine pools, parts of which have been used for years as rubbish dumps. Curiously, dozens of minor Christian denominations have erected interesting little churches along these roads.

On the southwest side of the island, **South Ocean Beach** is narrow, secluded, several miles long, and trodden by very few people. You'll find great scuba-diving offshore.

ADELAIDE

Adelaide is a quiet village whose nostalgic lifestyle revolves around fishing. Visually it isn't noteworthy, but it is about as close as you can get to traditional life on the island. Seventeen miles southwest of Nassau on a spit of land jutting into a navigable creek rich in conch, fish and lobster, the village dates back to 1832 when it was founded for slaves freed from a Portuguese slave trader.

A hurricane in 1926 wrecked the harbor. An army of volunteers helped the Bahamas National Trust restore Adelaide Creek's causeways with bridges and the tidal creek was reopened. It now teems with marine life. Today, baby tiger sharks, barracudas, snappers, lobsters and vast armadas of other young fish journey in and out.

The village is fronted by narrow, white-sand **Adelaide Beach**, extending between South Ocean and the village. Fishing boats are drawn up on the beach, and the wharf is lively at sunset when the day's work is done.

For yummy seafood and rum drinks, loiterat **Avery's Restaurant & Bar** (Map p42; ☎242-362-1547; Adelaide Village; mains $10-20; ⏰lunch & dinner), a very popular little restaurant and bar.

Grand Bahama

TELEPHONE CODE: 242 / POPULATION: 51,800 / AREA: 530 SQ MILES

Includes »

Best Places to Eat

» Billy Joe's on the Beach (p85)

» Sabor (p85)

» Miss Zelma's Conch Stand (p91)

» Smith's Point Fish Fry (p86)

» Churchill's Chophouse (p85)

Best Places to Stay

» Pelican Bay (p83)

» Our Lucaya Beach & Golf Resort (p83)

» Seagrape Bed & Breakfast (p83)

» Old Bahama Bay Resort & Marina (p92)

» Paradise Cove (p92)

Why Go?

After years of playing second banana to bigger, more glamorous Nassau, Grand Bahama is finally coming into its own. If you're looking for a laid-back, affordable getaway with a minimum of fuss, this is your place. The streets of its main city Freeport and Lucaya, are clean and calm. Its golden beaches and aquamarine waters are rarely overcrowded, even in high season. All the amenities of a perfect vacation – dive shops, restaurants, pubs, boutiques – are at your fingertips within a few blocks' radius. No wonder then, that Grand Bahama has become so popular with cruise-ship tourists and families on quickie weekend breaks.

Outside the city, the 85-mile-long island is an unexplored playground of mangrove swamps, sea caves and uninhabited sandy cays. There's world-class diving and snorkeling, great kayaking and world-famous bonefishing. All this, just a hop, skip and a 55-mile jump from the US.

When to Go

Freeport

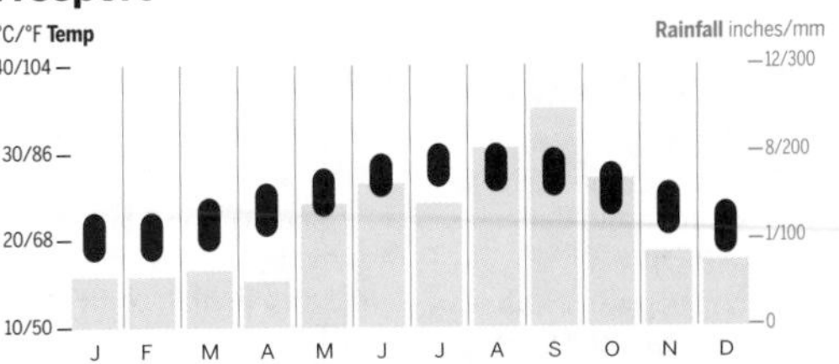

March–May Balmy weather and blooming hibiscus equal high season, with crowds lasting through April's Spring Break.

July Summer Junkanoo festival brings color and flair. Weather is hot, and crowds are thinning.

September–December Low season means killer deals but chilly weather, with Junkanoo parades in December.

History

Juan Ponce de León visited Grand Bahama in 1513 while searching for the Fountain of Youth, and pirates marauded their way around the island during the 17th and 18th centuries. The islanders benefited from the pirates' spoils, and briefly from acting as a supply depot for the Confederacy during the US Civil War. Another prosperous time came when Grand Bahama acted as a staging post for rumrunners during Prohibition.

For many decades the islanders then lived meagerly from the proceeds of lumbering, fishing and diving for sponges, until the 1950s when American Wallace Groves and Brit Sir Charles Hayward developed the area. This turned a vast, uninhabited area into a town known as Freeport, complete with an airport and a port with an oil-bunkering storage complex that would prove a bonanza for the Bahamas. (Oil is still purchased, stored and resold to the US at a handsome profit.)

The British crown then granted permission for these men to buy and develop a further 150,000 acres of the island's middle section, which led to the destruction of the remaining West Indian and British architecture. Initial plans for tourism floundered, and Freeport was then (optimistically) promoted as an offshore financial and high-technology industrial center.

The city is still overseen by the Grand Bahama Port Authority, which maintains strict zoning laws and governs which cars can drive in which areas, depending on their tax status.

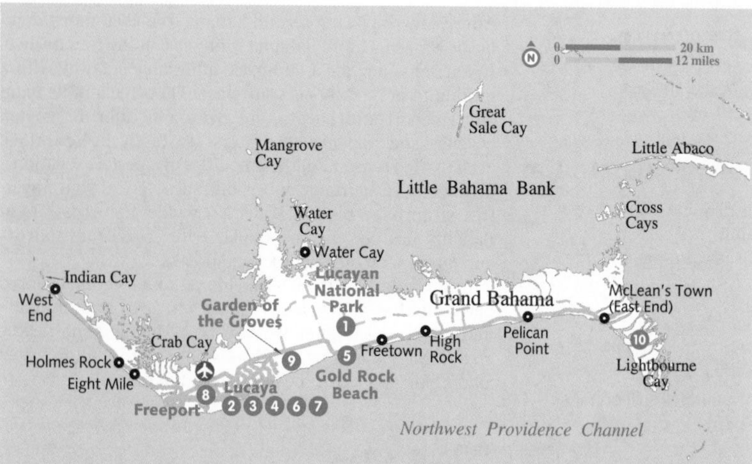

Grand Bahama Highlights

1. Paddling a kayak through Lucayan National Park with **Grand Bahamas Nature Tours** (p80)
2. Vegging out on the powdery sands of **Lucaya Beach** (p79)
3. Shopping for duty-free diamonds, fancy French perfumes and local straw work at the **Port Lucaya Marketplace** (opposite)
4. Snorkeling, paddle-boating and sunning at **Junkanoo Beach Club** (p80) on Taino Beach
5. Spending an afternoon swimming and wading at secluded **Gold Rock Beach** (p79)
6. Splashing and playing with a pod of friendly dolphins with UNEXSO's famous **Dolphin Experience** (p77)
7. Listening to Junkanoo bands rock out on weekends at **Count Basie Sq** (p85), daiquiri in hand
8. Mixing up your very own perfume blend at the **Perfume Factory** (p76)
9. Strolling past waterfalls, tropical birds, labyrinths and historical chapels at **Garden of the Groves** (opposite)
10. Bonefishing the vodka-clear shallows of the **East End** (p78)

In 1996 a development group, Sun & Sea Estates, began a major redevelopment project in Lucaya. The five-year, $290 million multiresort project has integrated existing hotels with new hotels, vacation clubs, restaurants, shops, theme parks, a new golf course and golf school and a marina.

Many hoped that this massive investment would do for Grand Bahama what the Atlantis resort did for Paradise Island. It is certainly successful. However, hurricanes such as Frances and Jeanne in 2004 badly damaged residential communities, nature reserves and woodlands, as well as many hotels, and certainly dampened the island's hopes. Grand Bahama is now attempting a modest rebound as an affordable family getaway and cruise ship destination.

National Parks

Grand Bahama has some of the country's best and most accessible parks, which are perfect for those interested in hiking, biking and kayaking, as well as those wanting to sunbathe, stroll and lounge in the shallows. For more information see p243.

Lucayan National Park (p90) contains one of the world's longest known underwater cave and cavern system, with caves that are habitats for rare underground crustaceans and migratory bats, and mangrove wetlands. It's also home to Gold Rock Beach, one of the island's most stunning and secluded stretches of sand.

In town, the 100-acre **Rand Nature Centre** (right) has distinctive flora and fauna.

Peterson Cay National Park (p90) is a small cay that has a striking coral garden.

Freeport & Lucaya

POP 27,000

Freeport, Grand Bahama's only urban settlement, was built seemingly overnight in the 1950s to serve as a duty-free tourism destination for Rat Pack–era pleasure-seekers. Half a century and several major hurricanes later, it's now an uninspiring grid of banks, strip malls and government buildings, with little appeal for travelers.

Lucaya, a modern coastal suburb of Freeport, is where most of the vacation action takes place. Its tidy – some might say antiseptic – strip of shops and restaurants appeals to a largely cruise ship–based tourist contingent, who appreciate its safety and walkability. On warm nights when the music's thumping at the Port Lucaya Marketplace bandstand, this is the place to be.

Sights

TOP CHOICE Garden of the Groves BOTANICAL GARDENS

(Map p76; ☎242-373-5668; www.thegardenofthegroves.com; Midshipman Rd & Magellan Dr, Freeport; adult/child $15/10; 9am-5pm;) This recently renovated 12-acre botanical garden is a lush tropical refuge on an island that's otherwise more about scrub pine and asphalt. A walking trail meanders through groves of tamarind and java plum trees, past cascading (artificial) waterfalls, a placid lagoon, and a tiny 19th-century hilltop chapel. The spiritually minded will enjoy a meditative stroll through the limestone labyrinth, a replica of the one at Cathédrale Notre Dame de Chartres in France. Birders will be in hog heaven here, and kids will definitely dig the raccoon habitat, where trapped specimens of the invasive critter come to retire. The garden's small 'arts and crafts village' sells high-quality local souvenirs like handmade soaps and shell work; it's a good place to avoid the cheap Chinese-made goods that pervades much of the city. Throw in lunch at the on-site cafe, and you can make a day of it. Hour-long walking tours are scheduled twice-daily at no extra charge; just book ahead.

Port Lucaya Marketplace MARKET

(Map p82) At Lucaya's heart, this tidied-up pastel version of a traditional Bahamian marketplace has the majority of the area's shopping, dining and entertainment options. Haggle for tote bags and batik cloth at the **straw market**, peruse duty-free emeralds at one of the many jewelry shops, or have a cocktail overlooking the Bell Channel waterway. At the market's center is Count Basie Sq, which hops with goombay bands, church choirs and karaoke parties on weekends.

Rand Nature Centre BOTANICAL GARDEN

(Map p76; ☎242-352-5438; East Settlers Way, Freeport; adult/child $5/3; 9am-4:30pm) This headquarters of the Bahamas National Trust is a low-key 100-acre retreat. There are more than 130 native plant species, including a number of weird and wonderful orchids and a native coppice that has grown here since before the time of Columbus. Highlights of the park's half-mile nature trail include a variety of bush medicine plants, a wooden

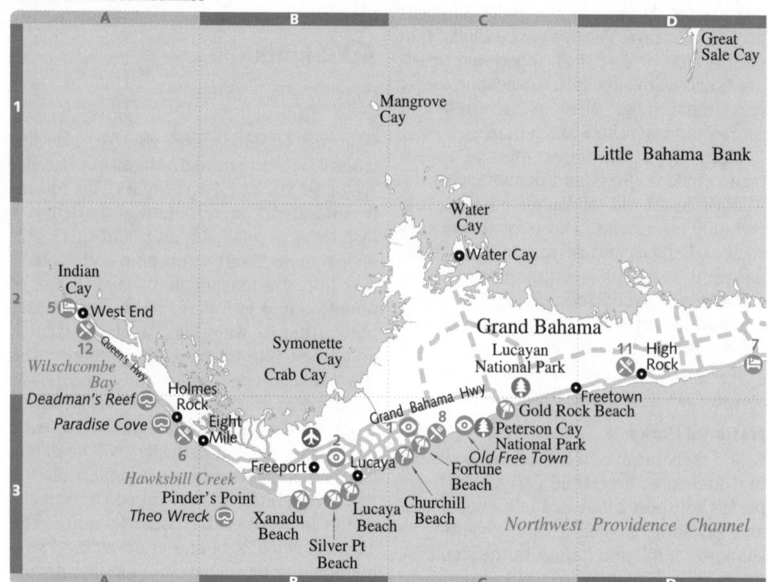

boardwalk overlooking a lily pad-choked pond, and a flock of high-stepping West Indian flamingos. On the first Saturday of every month, bird-lovers can join a guided tour in hope of spotting red-tailed hawks, egrets, kingfishers, Cuban emerald hummingbirds and Antillean peewees.

Perfume Factory FACTORY
(Map p78; ☎242-352-9391; behind the International Bazaar, Freeport; ⌚9am-5:30pm) Have you ever wanted a perfume named after you, a la J Lo? Now's your chance. Inside this pink-and-white mock colonial mansion, lab coat-wearing technicians mix, strain and bottle perfumes and colognes for Fragrances of the Bahamas. Top sellers include Sand for Men, with a pinch of Bahamian sand at the bottom of the bottle, and women's Pink Pearl, a frangipani-tinged scent with a pink conch pearl inside. For $30, you can choose three essential oils to blend with 190-proof alcohol to create your very own signature fragrance ($30). See also p88.

International Bazaar MARKET
(Map p78; Freeport; ⌚some shops open daily, others only for cruise ship tours) Back in the 1960s, this warren of international-themed shops and restaurants was a cutting-edge attraction, with faux European alleys, mock Chinese temples and simulated Middle Eastern souks. Today it's a half-abandoned curiosity, notable mostly for its decay. Despite the ghost town vibe, a handful of interesting shops remain – check out glassblower Sidney Pratt, or Bahamian bath and beauty product shop Jubulee. Or just bring your camera and snap some eerie pics of the cracked Parisian facades or mildewed Chinese Buddha statues.

Activities

Diving & Snorkeling

The diving here is considered some of the best in the Bahamas. In addition to dolphin, shark and cave dives, wreck-dive fans will love the thrill of swimming through Theo's Wreck, a 240ft-long sunken freighter, where you can safely wiggle through the hold and engine room, and visit the friendly resident moray eels. Other super-cool wrecks include two Spanish galleons, the *Santa Gertrude* and *San Ignacio,* which ran aground in 1682 off the south shore near present-day Lucaya.

All dive operators offer half-day snorkel trips that include transportation (adult/child $45/30). A popular and established dive and snorkel operator:

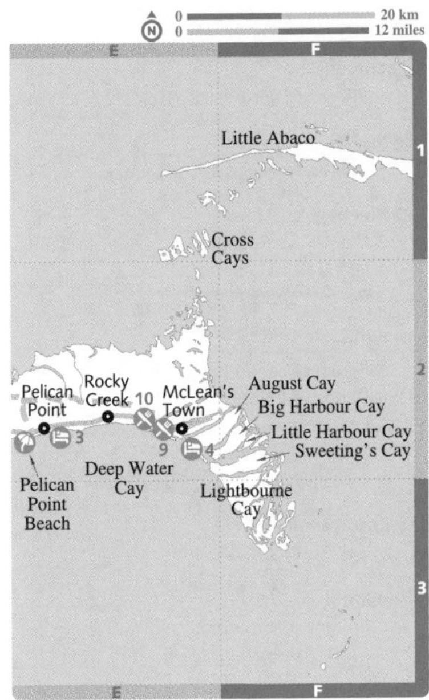

Grand Bahama

Sights

Sleeping

Eating

Underwater Explorers Society (UNEXSO) DIVING

(Map p82; ☎242-373-1244, 800-992-3483; www.unexso.com; Port Lucaya Marina, Lucaya; 2-tank dives $99, dolphin dive $219, equipment rental $40) One of the world's premiere diving centers, PADI five-star certified UNEXSO offers the full range of scuba activities. Choose from one of multiple daily reef and wreck dives, or check out one of UNEXSO's specialty trips. The shark dive with shark expert Cristina Zenato will earn you bragging rights for years to come, as will the spooky subterranean cave dives. For the less adventurous (or more prudent), the center's popular dolphin dive gives you the chance to socialize with Flipper and friends (see right). Sign up early. For student divers, a four-hour intro to diving course is $109, while three-day open water certification courses start at $449.

Other options:

Pat & Diane Fantasia Tours SNORKELING

(☎242-373-8681; www.snorkelingbahamas.com; adult/child $40/25) Offers two-hour snorkeling and fish-feeding trips to shallow coral reefs on their Snorkeling Sea Safari. The trip on its 72ft catamaran, which has an in-built 30ft-long waterslide and a 20ft-high rock-climbing wall is great fun.

Caribbean Divers DIVING

(Map p82; ☎242-373-9111; Bell Channel Inn, Port Lucaya Marina; 2-tank dive $80) In the Bell Channel Inn across the waterway from Port Lucaya Marketplace, this outfit runs NAUI certification courses ($399) and has a full menu of reef, wreck and night dives.

Dolphin Encounters

TOP CHOICE **Underwater Explorers Society (UNEXSO)** DOLPHIN ENCOUNTERS

(Map p82; ☎242-373-1244; www.unexso.com; Port Lucaya Marina; 👪) There's a reason 'swimming with dolphins' rates high on many people's bucket lists – a face-to-face encounter with these gentle sea mammals is the kind of mind-blowing 'whoa' experience you'll remember for the rest of your days. Lucky for you, UNEXSO, Grand Bahama's highly rated dive shop, has a variety of Dolphin Experiences designed to appeal to all ages and swimming abilities.

The Close Encounter (adult/child $75/50) trip is great for nondivers and children, who receive an educational lecture and then stand waist-deep in a sheltered lagoon, where they meet dolphins well-accustomed to humans. Take the experience up a notch by diving in for a quick swim ($169) alongside the frolicking pod. Or opt for the Open Ocean Experience ($199), where you can interact with the dolphins using hand signals while swimming in the outer ocean. For the true dolphin fanatic, the Assistant Trainer Program ($359) is a hands-on day

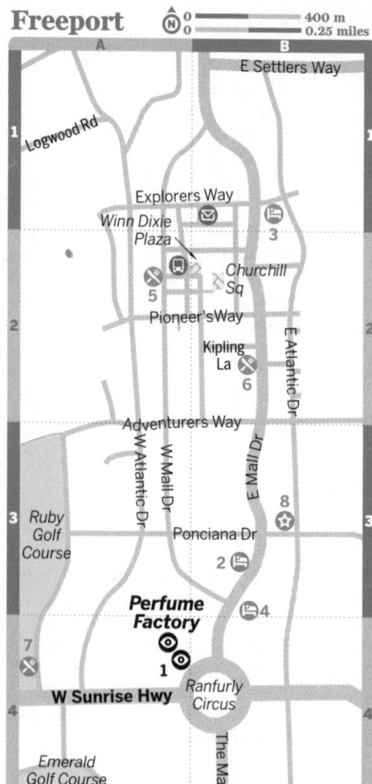

Freeport

Top Sights

Perfume Factory....A4

Sights

1 International Bazaar....A4

Sleeping

2 Castaways Resort....B3
3 Island Palm Resort....B1
4 Royal Islander Hotel....B3

Eating

5 Freeport Vendor's Market....A2
6 Geneva's Place....B2
Le Rendezvous....(see 1)
7 Ruby Swiss European Restaurant....A4

Entertainment

8 Galleria Cinemas....B3

Shopping

Columbian Emeralds International....(see 1)

of learning about dolphin care, feeding and habitats. A Dolphin Dive trip ($219) involves enjoying these creatures' company in the outer ocean. All of these are hugely popular activities and require major advanced booking.

Bonefishing & Sportfishing

The Gulf Stream, off the west coast of Grand Bahama, teems with game fish. The Northwest Providence Channel drops to 2000ft just 400yd off the south shore, where snapper and barracuda glide through the depths. On the north and east sides of the island, the flats of the Little Bahama Bank are fertile grounds for spotting the elusive bonefish.

Most hotels and resorts have their own fishing guides on tour. Deep-sea fishing per person costs around $70 to $130 per half-day. And bonefishing will generally run to $350/450 per half-/full day. Popular independent operators:

Captain Phil & Mel's BONEFISHING
(☎242-353-3023; bahamasbonefishing.net; McLean's Town) Runs half- and full-day charters out of McLean's Town, with free transportation from Freeport.

Reef Tours SPORTFISHING
(Map p82; ☎242-373-5880; www.bahamasvg.com/reeftours; Port Lucaya Marketplace) Offers both bottom fishing and deep-sea trolling for tuna, wahoo, marlin and more.

Exotic Adventures SPORTFISHING
(☎242-374-2278; www.exoticadventuresbahamas.com) Captain AJ runs rum-fueled deep-sea and bottom fishing trips.

Boat Excursions

Grand Bahama has no dearth of trips offering underwater sightseeing, beach parties, on-board dining, dancing and partying. Most hotels have booking desks for these tours. If your hotel doesn't, walk into the nearest one and book from there. Transfers are usually provided. If your time on the island is limited, see Tours, p80, as some operators combine land and water excursions.

Superior Watersports SNORKELING, CRUISE
(☎242-373-7863; www.superiorwatersport.com) Runs two very popular party tours on board the *Bahama Mama*. The Robinson Crusoe Beach Party includes a 1½-hour snorkeling

GRAND BAHAMA'S BEST BEACHES

» **Lucaya Beach** Dominated by the Our Lucaya resort, this is far and away Grand Bahama's most crowded beach. You won't lack for action here – go parasailing, snorkel, get your hair braided, or order a bowl of conch salad at Billy Joe's. If you seek solitude, walk west. Crowds thin and views expand as you approach Silver Point, which is especially nice at sunset.

» **Taino Beach** The island's second most popular beach, this postcard-perfect stretch of white sand has ample parking and a handful of seafood shacks. Shoot the breeze with conch stand proprietor Tony Macaroni, or spend a day lounging and snorkeling at Junkanoo Beach Club (p80). Taino's just across the Bell Channel from Port Lucaya Marketplace; to get here, either drive or take the ferry from behind Pelican Bay.

» **Churchill Beach/Fortune Beach** East of Taino, Churchill and Fortune Beaches are equally glorious, but far less crowded. The patch of sand directly in front of the Wyndham is guests-only, but everyone's welcome at the nearby Margaritaville Sandbar.

» **Xanadu Beach** Dominated by the decaying Xanadu Resort, where eccentric millionaire Howard Hughes spent the last years of his life holed up in the penthouse, Xanadu Beach is far enough from Port Lucaya to keep the crowds thin, but close enough for an easy afternoon trip. Sands are powdery, water's warm and blue. What more could you want? It's a few miles west of Port Lucaya, so you'll have to drive or take a cab here.

» **William's Town Beach** Also known as Island Seas Beach, this narrow strip of sand is not known for its beauty, but for its nightlife. After dark, locals and tourists alike pack in to tiny wooden beachfront bars like Bikini Bottom and the Two-Dollar Bar (yep, all drinks are $2) to drink rum and shake their booties. It's just west of Lucaya and Silver Point Beaches, though separated by a concrete channel.

» **Gold Rock Beach** You'll see more raccoons and sea birds than people at this gloriously empty stretch of golden sand, part of Lucayan National Park. Many people call Gold Rock the island's most beautiful beach, and we wouldn't dispute the claim. Park across the highway, pay your $3 entrance fee, and hike the short trail down to the sand. Don't forget a towel, some bug spray and a picnic – you'll want to stay a while. If you don't have your own wheels to get here, many tour operators in town offer group excursions.

trip followed by a Bahamian buffet, unlimited rum punch and beach games on a deserted beach (adult/child $59/39) and the Bahama Mama Booze Cruise, which is a drink and dance party (hot and cold hors d'oeuvres, and all the Bahama Mama cocktails and wine you can drink) on Tuesday, Thursday and Saturday ($39). Dinner cruises with limbo dancing (adult/child $79/45) and sunset dinner cruises ($45) are also on offer.

Pat & Diane Fantasia Tours SNORKELING, CRUISE
(☎242-373-8681; www.snorkelingbahamas.com) Runs snorkeling trips as well as a Steak & Lobster Cruise (adult/child $79/45) and a Deserted Island & Beach Party trip (adult/child $75/45) where you head off to the marine park at Peterson Cay for snorkeling and then on to private beaches for swimming, sunning, lunch and drinks.

Bahamas EcoVentures SNORKELING, CRUISE
(☎242-352-9323; www.bahamasecoventures.com; tours Wed, Fri & Sun) A yellow airboat zips you through the shallows as a guide points out blue holes (underwater sea caves), turtles, sharks and bonefish, before depositing you on an uninhabited island for a nature walk, lunch and splashing.

Reef Tours CRUISE
(☎242-373-5880; www.bahamasvg.com/reeftours) Has a wine- and cheese-fueled Enchanted Evening Sailing Cruise, a glass-bottomed boat tour (adult/child $30/18), and a snorkel and fish-feeding trip (adult/child $40/20), among others.

Water Sports

Most resort hotels rent snorkel gear ($15 per day), sea kayaks ($20 per hour), Sunfish dinghies ($20 per hour) and equipment for other water sports. Independent concessions on most beaches offer parasailing ($70 per ride), banana boat rides ($15), wave runners ($75 per 30 minutes), waterskiing ($40 per 30 minutes) and windsurfing ($30 per ride).

WORTH A TRIP

DIY SNORKEL ADVENTURES

Not a 'joiner'? You don't have to take a tour to get in some great snorkeling on Grand Bahama. DIY-ers have two good options for solo snorkeling day-trips. West of Freeport, **Paradise Cove** (☎242-349-2677; www.deadmansreef.com) is a mini-resort with a vibrant reef in the shallows just off the beach (see p92). Rent snorkel gear at the restaurant ($15) and hop right in. Closer to town is Taino Beach's new **Junkanoo Beach Club** (Map p82; ☎242-373-8018; www.junkanoobeachfreeport.com;), with a beachfront restaurant, bar and changing facilities. You can use the club's pedal boats and kayaks for free, or pay $19 and jump in a boat for an hour-long snorkel tour on the nearby reef. Possibly the island's best-value, most-fun day-trip.

Ocean Motion WATER SPORTS
(☎242-374-2425; www.oceanmotionbahamas.com; Lucaya) On the beach in front of Our Lucaya Beach & Golf Resort, the island's largest outfitter has virtually every water sport under the sun, including water trampolines ($10 per half-day), and also rents out Hobie Cat sailboats (14ft/16ft per hour $50/75).

Lucaya Watersports WATER SPORTS
(☎242-373-6375; www.lucayawatersports.com; Lucaya) Rents wave runners, kayaks and paddleboats, and does banana boat rides from two locations, one at Port Lucaya, one at the Taino Beach Resort & Club.

Golf

Golf's a popular pastime on the island, home to four championship courses. All clubs are open to the public and rent equipment and carts.

Fortune Hills Golf & Country Club GOLF COURSE
(☎242-373-4500; E Sunrise Hwy, Freeport) Popular with beginners.

Our Lucayan Golf Course GOLF COURSE
(☎242-373-2004; Balao & Midshipman Rds, Lucaya) The island's first golf course features 6800yd of tight doglegs and elevated greens.

Reef Golf Course GOLF COURSE
(☎242-373-2004; Seahorse Rd, Port Lucaya) This is the island's largest course at 6920yd.

Ruby GOLF COURSE
(☎242-352-1851; West Sunrise Hwy, Freeport) Newly redesigned and considered relatively easy.

Horseback Riding

There are some grand places on the island to take a horse for a gallop, and both experienced and amateur riders are welcomed by operators.

Pinetree Stables HORSEBACK RIDING
(☎242-373-3600; www.pinetree-stables.com; rides 2hr $99) Takes horseback rides twice daily, where you gallop through pine forests, along the southern shore and through the shallows.

Trikk Pony Adventures HORSEBACK RIDING
(☎242-374-4449; www.trikkpony.com; rides 1½hr $95) Everyone harbors a secret desire to ride a horse along a deserted beach – now's your chance! These 90-minute tours run twice daily Monday to Friday and guarantee a wet, sandy good time.

Spas

Senses Spa & Fitness Center SPA
(☎242-373-1333; Our Lucaya Beach & Golf Resort, Seahorse Rd, Port Lucaya) From lime-and-rum body wraps to beachside massages, Our Lucaya's capacious spa specializes in Bahamian-themed treatments. The fitness facility has Pilates and yoga classes for both guests and nonguests. In the Radisson.

Tours

All the hotels can book you onto rather uninspiring city bus tours (adult/child $25/18). These will generally take you to Freeport's International Bazaar (p76), liquor stores, as well as the Garden of the Groves (p75). Entry fees are included in the price and tours take generally half a day.

TOP CHOICE **Grand Bahamas Nature Tours** NATURE TOURS
(☎242-373-2485; www.grandbahamanaturetours.com) One of the island's top operators has a number of high-quality trips. Top among them include the kayak and snorkel trip ($79) to uninhabited Peterson's Cay, and a kayak journey through the jade-colored waterways of Lucayan National Park ($79). These trips relish the natural quiet and

splendor of the park and its many scaled, furry and feathered inhabitants. The certified and trainee guides really know their stuff.

Smiling Pat's Adventures CULTURAL TOURS
(☎242-359-2921; www.smilingpat.com) The ever-cheerful Pat earns top ratings for her high-energy bus tours, which include a culture-oriented West End Tour ($40), which ends in a sweet trip to her grandmother's bakery, and a beach tour ($40) that hits Lucayan National Park and the location of the filming of *Pirates of the Caribbean* II and III.

Grand Bahamas Nature Tours CULTURAL TOURS
(☎242-373-2485; www.grandbahamasnaturetours.com) Best known for its nature trips, this especially well-regarded outfit also offers a more history-oriented West End Tour ($79) that also includes beach and snorkel time, as well as city-center bike and Jeep trips ($79).

HG Forbes Charter & Tours CITY TOURS
(☎242-352-9311; www.forbescharter.com) Offers a Super Combination City Tour ($35/25 per adult/child) of the standard sights (International Bazaar, Garden of the Groves, Millionaire's Row) and a nature-oriented East End Extravaganza ($40/30) of Lucayan National Park and Gold Rock Beach.

Festivals & Events

New Year's Day Junkanoo Parade The flamboyant music, dancing and costumes of Boxing Day's Junkanoo are publicly judged and awarded, with much crowd support and hollering.

Bahamas Wahoo Challenge Season-opening tournament for this celebrated national competition starts in January from Port Lucaya Marina.

Bacardi Rum Billfish Tournament This long-running fishing tourney brings the world's biggest big game hunters to town. Held in March.

Sailing Regatta In June, a huge three days full of self-made boats, racing, and much hollering and onshore partying.

Junkanoo Summer Festival Held at Taino Beach in July, where Junkanoo shacks compete for the Best Music title.

McLean's Town Conch Cracking Festival Watch the conch shells fly at this don't-miss October event, which includes a category for tourists.

Grand Bahama Conchman Triathlon (www.conchman.com) November sees amateur athletes tested to the limit with a ½-mile swim, 20-mile bike ride, and 3½-mile run. Exhausted just reading about this one? Then just watch with a coconut ice cream and put your feet up.

Junkanoo Boxing Day Parade A highlight of the December social calendar, the parade kicks off at 5am with costumed revelers and a cacophony of sounds. The build up to this starts the January before, with practices downtown near the post office.

Sleeping

Grand Bahama has long been one of the country's most affordable islands, and great deals are always easy to come by, especially online. Condo or cottage rentals can be a good budget option, especially for families and long-term stays. Units generally rent from $85/450 per night/week from mid-December to mid-April, and drop even lower in summer and fall. Many condos are part of resort complexes, so renters get full use of the facilities.

Try contacting **Thompsons Real Estate** (☎242-373-9050; www.thompsonsrealestate.com; Freeport) which rents out a range of apartments from studios to two-bed units (mainly around Lucaya).

Freeport

Downtown Freeport hotels are a bargain, but the savings may quickly diminish once you factor in bus and taxi trips to the beaches and restaurants of Lucaya. Other than price and convenience to the airport, there's little reason for visitors to sleep here.

Royal Islander Hotel HOTEL **$$**
(☎242-351-6000; www.royalislanderhotel.com; East Mall Dr, Freeport; r $90; ❄@📶🏊) Bold floral-print bedspreads, colorful pictures and faux rattan furniture keep things bright at this well-traveled property. Mid-sized rooms surround a courtyard pool and come with in-room safe, cable TV and phone.

Castaways Resort HOTEL **$$**
(Map p78; ☎242-352-6682; www.castaways-resort.com; E Mall Dr; r $105; ❄@📶🏊) Popular with Bahamian business travelers, this pink stucco rectangle is so clean it smells like an explosion at the Lysol factory. Carpeted

Lucaya

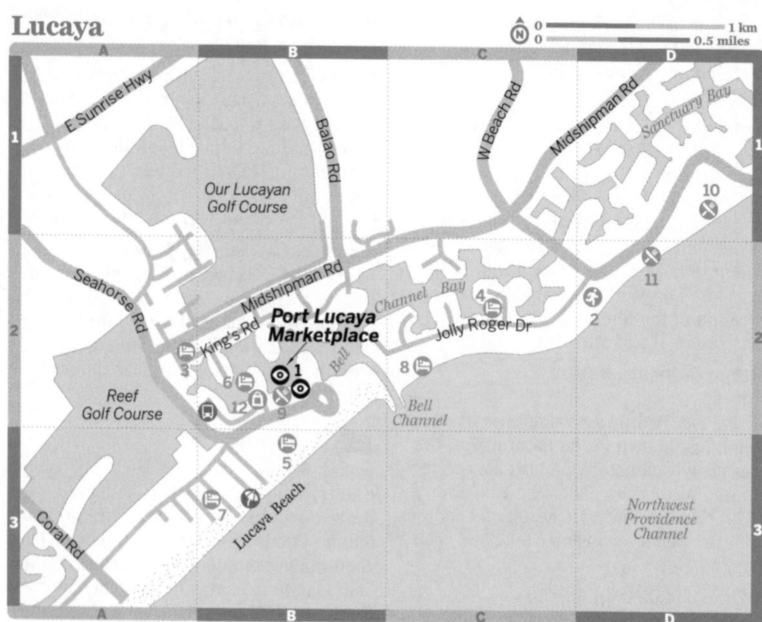

Lucaya

Top Sights

Port Lucaya Marketplace........ B2

Sights

1 Underwater Explorers Society (UNEXSO)........ B2

Activities, Courses & Tours

Caribbean Divers........ (see 3)
Dolphin Experience........ (see 4)
2 Junkanoo Beach Club........ D2
Reef Tours........ (see 9)

Sleeping

3 Bell Channel Inn........ A2
4 Flamingo Bay Hotel & Marina........ C2
5 Our Lucaya Beach & Golf Resort........ B3
6 Pelican Bay........ B2
7 Seagrape Bed & Breakfast........ B3
8 Taino Beach Resort & Marina........ C2

Eating

9 Agave........ B2
Billy Joe's on the Beach........ (see 5)
China Beach........ (see 5)
Churchill's Chophouse........ (see 5)
Dive-In Bar & Grill........ (see 1)
Iries........ (see 5)
Island Java........ (see 9)
Sabor........ (see 6)
10 Smith's Point Fish Fry........ D1
11 Tony Macaroni's Conch Experience........ D2
Zorba's........ (see 9)

Entertainment

Androsia........ (see 9)
Havana Cay Cigar Bar........ (see 5)
Prop Club Beach Bar & Restaurant........ (see 5)
Shenanigan's Irish Pub........ (see 9)
Treasure Bay Casino........ (see 5)

Shopping

Bandolera........ (see 9)
Colombian Emeralds International........ (see 9)
Freeport Jewellers........ (see 9)
Havana Cay Cigar Bar........ (see 5)
Leo's Art Gallery........ (see 9)
Les Parisiennes........ (see 9)
12 Straw Market........ B2
Underwater Explorers Society (UNEXSO)........ (see 1)

QUICKIE CRUISES

Just 55 miles east of Florida, Grand Bahama is close enough for day-trip or overnight cruises. Two operators ply the 'quickie cruise' territory: **Discovery Cruise Line** (☎800-259-1579; www.discoverycruiseline.com; trips from $99) does a popular one-day party cruise from Fort Lauderdale, with all-you-can-eat breakfast and dinner buffets, free booze and casino gambling. The trip is about four hours each way, which leaves time for an afternoon of shopping and sun in Freeport and Lucaya. You can also elect to stay overnight and cruise back a day or two later. **Bahamas Celebration** (☎800-314-7735; www.bahamascelebration.com; trips from $99) leaves Palm Beach in the afternoon, spends the night at sea, then docks in Grand Bahama the following morning for a day of island activities before returning that evening. More upscale and family-friendly than the party-hearty Discovery, it's got a spa and a kid's club onboard and cabins ranging from bare-bones to luxe. For a longer stay, choose a two- or four-night add-on at Our Lucaya Beach & Golf Resort.

suites, some overlooking the manicured lawn and pool, have sleeper couches.

Island Palm Resort MOTEL $
(☎242-352-6648; www.islandpalm.com; cnr Explorers Way & E Mall Dr; r $79; ❄🏊) There's nothing remotely resort-like about this character-free downtown motel, but it's cheap, clean and convenient to the airport. A free daily bus takes guests, mostly young, party-happy Spring Breakers on internet package trips, to the beach.

Lucaya

TOP CHOICE **Our Lucaya Beach & Golf Resort** RESORT $$
(Map opposite; ☎ 242-373-1333; www.ourlucaya.com; Seahorse Rd, Port Lucaya; Radisson r from $176, Reef Village r $159; ❄@📶🏊👪) Incorporating two hotels, the Radisson and the Reef Village, this perfectly coiffed beachfront complex hogs the best views of stunning Lucaya Beach. The resort sits on 7.5 acres and incorporates numerous restaurants, bars, spas, a casino, and multiple swimming pools of every style and variety, all directly across the street from the action of Port Lucaya Marketplace. The ambience at the pricier Radisson is a bit more sophisticated and low-key; check out the 'Manor House' lobby with its tall potted palms, rattan armchairs and cigar lounge. The Reef Village is unabashedly family-friendly, with a sand playground, massive wading pool, and kids' camp. Price at both hotels fluctuate wildly; the best deals can usually be found online.

TOP CHOICE **Pelican Bay** BOUTIQUE HOTEL $$$
(Map opposite; ☎242-373-9550; www.pelicanbayhotel.com; Port Lucaya Marina; r from $190; ❄📶🏊) Lucaya's chicest property rocks an upscale British colonial vibe, with a series of interconnected villas decked out with punchy tropical colors and white shutters. Rooms continue the theme, with lots of dark wood, canopy beds and private balconies. Though the hotel's not oceanfront, the views of Bell Channel from the pool deck are lovely at sunset. The beach itself is right across the road. The hotel's open-air restaurant, Sabor, is one of the island's slickest, attracting a nightly crowd of see-and-be-seen types.

Seagrape Bed & Breakfast B&B $$
(Map opposite; ☎242-373-1769; www.seagrapehouse.com; Sea Spray Ln; r incl breakfast $95; ❄📶) Run by a friendly Canadian-American couple, this low-key B&B is just a 10-minute walk to the heart of Port Lucaya, but feels a million miles away. The two simple guestrooms have cable TV and shelves of used novels; you'll feel like you're staying at a friend's suburban house. The owners, both ex-divers, are always at the ready with restaurant suggestions or offers to borrow a bike. If big resorts are not your thing, this is your best bet.

Bell Channel Inn MOTEL $
(Map opposite; ☎242-373-1053; www.bellchannelinn.com; King's Rd, Port Lucaya Marina; r from $85; ❄🏊) On the far side of Bell Channel from the Port Lucaya Marketplace, this aging pink hotel is popular with divers, who can book package room-and-scuba deals with the on-site dive center.

The Beaches

Taino Beach Resort & Clubs HOTEL $$
(Map opposite; ☎242-373-4682; www.tainobeach.com; Jolly Roger Dr, Taino Beach; r from $150;

ROMANTIC GRAND BAHAMA

Just a 25-minute flight from the US, Grand Bahama is a popular pick for couples on quickie weekend getaways. Make the most of your alone time with the following suggestions.

Stay at **Pelican Bay** (p83), an upscale boutique property with intimate villas and a swanky pool lounge and restaurant, on the quiet side of Port Lucaya Marketplace. Head across the street to unwind with a Sense of Togetherness couples massage at the **Senses Spa & Fitness Center** (p80) in the Our Lucaya Beach & Golf Resort, then stay on for the classic romantic dinner combo of steak, wine and dim lighting at the resort's **Churchill's Chophouse** (p85). Get away from the crowds at **Gold Rock Beach** (p91) in Lucayan National Park, where you'll often have the sands entirely to yourselves. If hanky panky ensues, well, the pelicans won't tell anyone! Before you leave, buy each other a little memento of your island time – how does a bottle of customized, named-after-you perfume from the **Perfume Factory** (p76) sound?

) On the far end of Taino Beach, this low-key complex encompasses three buildings: the upscale Marlin, the midrange Coral, and the dated but budget-friendly Ocean. The all-suite setup is good for families and longer-term visitors, with one-bedrooms and studios. The nicer units have sleek, contemporary kitchens with granite counters and in-room tubs (romantic!). A huge, grotto-style pool with waterslides will keep the kids occupied, and grownups can nip over on the hourly ferry to Port Lucaya Marketplace for cocktails or dinner.

Viva Wyndham Fortuna Beach RESORT **$$**
(242-373-4000; www.wyndham.com; Fortune Beach; r from $140;) The island's only all-inclusive resort bustles with groups of largely Spanish-, Italian- and German-speaking tourists, who come here to veg out on the white sand or snooze poolside, cocktail in hand. A techno-pulsing bar keeps partiers happy, while kids can take trapeze lessons or hang out in the Kids Klub. The property's relatively small and isolated, so those on long vacations may get bored with the limited options. And rooms, while adequate, are older and motel-basic.

Island Seas Resort HOTEL **$$$**
(242-373-1271; www.islandseas.com; 123 Silver Point Dr, Silver Point Beach; r $179-359;) Tucked away on its own small patch of beach, this friendly, modest resort is highly popular with families. Tidy, tiled one- and two-bedroom units surround a circular pool and outdoor bar; other amenities include a tennis court, shuffleboard court and water sports. A complimentary bus runs into town. To get here, take East Sunrise Hwy west, then turn left on East Beach Dr, then left again at Silver Point Dr.

Flamingo Bay Hotel & Marina MOTEL **$**
(Map p82; 242-373-5640; www.tainobeach.com/flamingo.html; Jolly Roger Dr, Taino Beach; r $99;) The sibling to Taino Beach Resort & Club, this old-fashioned stucco motel has beachy little tiled efficiencies overlooking a not-so-scenic marina.

Eating

Hotels tend to have at least one in-house cafe or restaurant, while resorts offer a choice of casual and formal dining rooms and bars, which are always open to nonguests. There are a heap of both formal and informal places to eat in the Port Lucaya Marketplace; on weekends the atmosphere is enlivened by the live music or DJs in Count Basie Sq.

Freeport

Geneva's Place BAHAMIAN **$$**
(Map p78; 242-352-5085; cnr E Mall Dr & Kipling Lane; mains $5-26; breakfast, lunch & dinner) You'll hardly spot a non-Bahamian face in this huge, fluorescent-lit dining room, popular with locals for traditional breakfasts, such as pig's feet souse and sardines and grits. Lunch means cracked conch or fish sandwiches, while dinner features massive portions of fish, chicken or steak.

Simply Native BAHAMIAN **$**
(242-352-5003; East Beach Dr; mains $6-12; breakfast, lunch & dinner) Hands-down best grits we have had in ages. If you want to try chicken souse, johnnycakes and other traditional Bahamian dishes – and eat where locals eat – ditch Port Lucaya and come here. Hanging baskets of flowers don't go

far in sprucing up the dim, wood-railed dining room but who cares, just pass the grits. It's just east of Ranfurly Circus off East Sunrise Hwy.

Le Rendezvous INTERNATIONAL **$$**
(Map p78; ☎242-352-9610; International Bazaar; mains $8-22; ⏰breakfast, lunch & dinner) This frilly little pink-and-turquoise trooper of a restaurant has clung to life while the International Bazaar crumbled around it. New owners, a peppy Scottish-Bahamian couple, have revived the menu with a long list of international favorites, from boil fish (a kind of breakfast stew) to tacos to lasagna. Lunch specials, usually a Bahamian classic like barbecue ribs with mac 'n' cheese, are a big draw.

Freeport Vendor's Market BAHAMIAN **$**
(Map p78; West Mall Dr, across from Winn Dixie Plaza; mains $8-10; ⏰breakfast, lunch & dinner) This scrappy outdoor market has some of the city's best seafood stalls – locals recommend McBane's for grilled conch. Also look for exotic fruit like custard apples, plantains, avocados.

Ruby Swiss European Restaurant FRENCH, ITALIAN **$$$**
(Map p78; ☎242-352-8507; Atlantic Way off West Sunrise Hwy; mains $25-45; ⏰lunch & dinner) A perennial favorite for stodgy, but delicious, Continental classics like steak Diane and lobster Thermidor. Has one of the island's better wine lists.

Lucaya

The majority of Lucaya's eateries are in or around the Port Lucaya Marketplace or the Our Lucaya resort complex. Choices range from faux Irish pubs to American fast food to sanitized Bahamian cuisine to upscale steakhouses. Expect high prices and a lively, party-happy atmosphere, especially on weekends when the bands crank up in Count Basie Sq.

TOP CHOICE **Sabor** FUSION **$$**
(Map p82; ☎242-373-5588; Pelican Bay; mains $17-28; ⏰breakfast, lunch & dinner) With a hip young Icelandic chef and a prime location on the pool deck of the chic Pelican Bay hotel, Sabor is Lucaya's most buzzed-about new restaurant. Mojito-sipping Beautiful People crowd the small outdoor tables, nibbling Asian- and Latin-tinged treats like ginger calamari, curry mussels and guava cheesecake. A long list of burgers keeps things casual. At night, salsa music and free-flowing cocktails lend a nightclub vibe. Breakfast hours are really brunch.

TOP CHOICE **Billy Joe's on the Beach** BAHAMIAN, SEAFOOD **$**
(Map p82; ☎305-735-8267; Lucaya Beach; mains $8-13; ⏰lunch & dinner Mon-Sat; 👪) Tucking into a bowl of Billy Joe's conch salad as you wiggle your bare feet in the sand is a quintessential Grand Bahama experience. This venerable waterfront conch shack was here long before the Our Lucaya complex took over the beach – when the resort came to town, Billy Joe had to fight to keep his territory. Lucky for you, he won, and his humble wooden beach hut is still the place to go for cold Kalik and conch cooked any way you like it. Non-conch-eaters can chow on chicken fingers and other snacks.

China Beach ASIAN **$$**
(Map p82; ☎242-373-1333; Our Lucaya Beach & Golf Resort; mains $20-28; ⏰dinner Mon-Sat) One of Our Lucaya's more popular dinner spots, this mod Asian bistro is heavy on the atmosphere: pagoda-style bar, Buddha statues, stone lions. The menu leans toward old-school Chinese classics like sweet and sour chicken, though hand-rolled sushi adds a fresh touch. Killer views over the water.

Dive-In Bar & Grill GRILL **$**
(Map p82; ☎242-373-5183; behind UNEXSO; mains $8-14; ⏰breakfast, lunch & dinner) Divers, bonefishers and locals gather to brag about the day's conquests at this ultracasual outdoor grill, on the patio behind the UNEXSO building. Order a blackened fish burger and chat up whoever's sitting next to you at the bar – if you're lucky you'll get some sweet tips on diving/fishing/boating/local parties. Salads, pizzas and burgers round out the simple but tasty menu.

Some other selections:

Zorba's GREEK **$$**
(Map p82; ☎242-373-6137; www.zorbasbahamas.com; Port Lucaya Marketplace; mains $7-26; ⏰breakfast, lunch & dinner; 👪) Savor souvlaki and *spanakopita* (spinach pie) beneath a canopy of grapevines and pink bougainvillea at this reasonably priced and commonly recommended Greek diner in the heart of the Port Lucaya Marketplace.

Churchill's Chophouse STEAKHOUSE **$$$**
(Map p82; ☎242-373-1333; Our Lucaya Beach & Golf Resort; mains $25-68; ⏰dinner) Swill martinis and slice into truly excellent dry-aged beef at this clubby, opulent

steakhouse. For special occasions, you can't go wrong here.

Iries CARIBBEAN $$
(Map p82; ☎242-373-1333; Our Lucaya Beach & Golf Resort; mains $21-30; ⊙dinner) Bahamian and Jamaican dishes get dressed up at Iries, in a mahogany-shuttered faux 19th-century sugar baron's mansion. Think coconut milk–braised oxtail, guava tiramisu.

Agave LATIN $$
(Map p82; ☎242-374-4887; www.agavelucaya.com; Port Lucaya Marketplace; mains $21-30; ⊙lunch & dinner) Latin-fusion tapas and hefty margaritas keep the crowds happy at this new hotspot. Devour an arm-sized burrito or try something more ambitious, like the Cuban-style pork with mojo sauce.

Island Java COFFEE SHOP $
(Map p82; Port Lucaya Marketplace; items $3-12; ⊙breakfast & lunch) Lucaya's go-to spot for your caffeine fix, this sweet little cafe has a range of pastries, salads and sandwiches, as well as free wi-fi.

The Beaches

The beachside hotels and resorts all have bars, most of them beachside, that will happily indulge you with fruity rum cocktails or an icy, golden beer. Most of these bars also serve snacks.

TOP CHOICE **Smith's Point Fish Fry** BAHAMIAN, SEAFOOD $
(Map p82; Taino Beach; mains $7-15; ⊙from 6pm Wed & Sat) Wednesday night at the Fish Fry is like a giant neighborhood party. Several beachfront shacks fire up oil drum cookers and fry turbot, lobster and conch fritters for crowds of locals, who gossip the night away eating and drinking cold Kaliks and rum punch. Everyone comes – schoolteachers, hotel clerks, wealthy expats – and everyone seems to know each other. The scene heats up after 9pm when the live music gets rolling. Saturday nights are lower-key and attract more tourists, but are still good fun.

Tony Macaroni's Conch Experience BAHAMIAN, SEAFOOD $$
(Map p82; ☎242-533-6766; www.tonybahamas.com; Taino Beach; mains $10-22; ⊙lunch & dinner Wed-Sun) Tony Macaroni, the self-proclaimed 'most unique man in the Bahamas' and the proprietor of this famed Taino Beach conch shack, is as well-known for his joke-a-minute personality and flirtatious reputation as he is for his delectable conch salad and roast conch – the island's best, by many accounts. Fortify yourself with a gully wash (a high-octane mix of coconut water and rum) and watch the sun set over the sand as Tony yuks it up behind the bar.

Banana Bay BAHAMIAN $
(Map p76; ☎242-373-2960; Fortune Beach; mains $8-14; ⊙breakfast & lunch) 'World-famous' banana bread and colorful cocktails are the big draws at this isolated rainbow-colored beach shack. Have a leisurely lunch (soups, sandwiches) on the waterfront patio then wander the white sands of Fortune Beach, returning later to slurp down a 'Wacky Frozen Banana.'

☆ Entertainment

The resorts offer in-house entertainment and shows as well as live music and plenty of opportunities to trip the light fantastic. Hotels also host frequent beach parties, which include bonfires and barbecues (remember your mosquito repellent). The Port Lucaya Marketplace is always good for drinks and fun, especially on Thursday through Sunday when live music throbs in Count Basie Sq.

Many of the evening boat excursions (see p78) are tremendous fun, providing liberal drinks, liberating music and lithe limbo dancers; a great way to spend an evening or two.

Prop Club Beach Bar & Restaurant BAR
(Map p82; Our Lucaya Beach & Golf Resort, Seahorse Rd, Port Lucaya; ⊙till late) The TV screens attract fans of the big American sports games, but the dance floor takes pride of place for either nights of entertainment or live music. Karaoke nights are *de rigueur* for the more extroverted, and the glass walls lift up to expose a sand volleyball court.

Club XS NIGHTCLUB
(Les Fountains Plaza, Sunrise Hwy, Freeport; ⊙9pm-late Wed-Sat) Local partiers swear by this capacious new nightclub, where DJs spin techno and reggae beats inside while music videos flash on a big screen on the patio. Crowds are young, fun and dressed to shake their booties. If all that grinding makes you hungry, there's an on-site grill. East of Ranfurly Circus.

TOP CHOICE **Margaritaville Sandbar** BAR
(Churchill Beach, Mather Town) It's tricky to find (ask a local), but this funky little beach shack is an under-the-radar classic. Sand on the floor, cold Kalik, friendly patrons, waves crashing a few yards away. Perfect.

GRAND BAHAMA FOR KIDS

Clean, orderly, laid-back Grand Bahama is one of the most family-friendly islands in the Bahamas. **Our Lucaya Reef Village** (Our Lucaya Beach & Golf Resort; p83) has a kids' club to entertain your little ones while you get some 'mommy and daddy time,' as well as plenty of junior-sized pools and playgrounds. Petting dolphins at UNEXSO's **Dolphin Experience** (p77) will give school-age kids bragging rights among their friends for years to come. **Garden of the Groves** (p75) is also fun – little kids will love the raccoon habitat. For slightly older kids, a day of snorkeling, paddle-boating and chowing down on burgers at **Junkanoo Beach Club** (p80) or **Paradise Cove** (p92) is hard to beat. Closer to town, **Lucaya Beach** (p79) has tons of kid-friendly water sports, from parasailing to banana boat rides. For food, try feeding 'em cracked conch at **Billy Joe's on the Beach** (p85) – whether or not you tell them they're eating snail is up to you!

Havana Cay Cigar Bar CIGAR BAR
(Map p82; Our Lucaya Beach & Golf Resort, Seahorse Rd, Port Lucaya) A beamed ceiling and wrought iron light fixtures create an Old World ambiance at this clubby cigar bar, in the 'Manor House' lobby of the Radisson Our Lucaya.

Shenanigan's Irish Pub PUB
(Map p82; Port Lucaya Marketplace; www.irishpubbahamas.com) If you're craving a Guinness or a plate of bangers and mash, this dimly lit Irish pub is your place. Daily happy hours pack in the (mostly foreign) crowds.

Treasure Bay Casino CASINO
(Map p82; ☎242-373-2396; www.ourlucaya.com; Our Lucaya Beach & Golf Resort, Seahorse Rd, Port Lucaya) This 35,000 sq ft casino has 400 slot machines and 21 tables of baccarat, Caribbean stud poker, blackjack and roulette. There's a Thursday night dinner show in the theater, plus regular cheesy-but-fun 'spectaculars' involving plenty of glitter and skimpy costumes.

Galleria Cinemas CINEMA
(Map p78; RND Plaza, E Atlantic Dr, Freeport; tickets $10) This five-screen cinema shows mainstream hits.

Shopping

The duty-free shopping fans head to the International Bazaar (p76) and Port Lucaya Marketplace (p75) for their jewelry and perfume. It is worth bringing a price-comparison list from home when considering purchasing these goods.

The **straw markets** of the International Bazaar and Port Lucaya Marketplace hawk straw purses, hats and placemats as well as batik items, Africana jewelry and painted carvings. Most of it is made in China.

Some of the resort wear and batik prints are worth a look, too, but you will find that prices can vary quite considerably between the Freeport and Port Lucaya markets, where it is acceptable to haggle the prices down by about 10% to 15%.

Art & Crafts

African-style wooden carvings, driftwood art and bright, folksy oil paintings are all popular take-home items. Be aware that most of the stuff sold in the local straw markets is more likely to have been made overseas.

Leo's Art Gallery ART GALLERY
(Map p82; Port Lucaya Marketplace) Leo paints vibrant and rich portrayals of Caribbean living in Haitian style.

Grand Bahama Arts & Crafts Centre CRAFTS
(East Sunrise Hwy; Freeport) Slated to open in early 2011, this 5,000-sq ft government-sponsored center will offer visitors a chance to see local artisans at work and to buy directly from the craftsperson. East of Ranfurly Circus.

Garden of the Groves CRAFTS
(Map p76; Midshipman Rd & Magellan Dr, Freeport) The 'arts and crafts village' at this popular botanical garden sells good quality shell crafts, straw work and other local items. See also p75.

Cigars

Havana Cay Cigar Bar CIGARS
(Map p82; Our Lucaya Beach & Golf Resort, Seahorse Rd, Port Lucaya) Classy cigar bar has a solid selection of both Cuban and non-Cuban stogies.

Clothing & Cloth

Androsia, a type of batik fabric native to the Bahamian island of Andros, is a popular item.

Androsia CLOTHING, CLOTH
(Map p82; Port Lucaya Marketplace) Sells batik clothing and cloth.

Bandolera BOUTIQUE
(Map p82; Port Lucaya Marketplace) Chic boutique with a good range of women's resort wear and swimsuits.

Diving Gear

Underwater Explorers Society (UNEXSO) DIVE SHOP
(Map p82; ☎242-373-1244, 800-992-3483; www.unexso.com; Port Lucaya Marina) The two-story shop at the UNEXSO dive center has a vast array of dive gear, from watches to wetsuits to flippers. There's also an excellent range of swimwear and sunhats. See also p77.

Jewelry

Watches and gems are top of most visitors' shopping lists. Yes, it's possible to get good deals here, but you have to know your gemology and have a good understanding of market prices.

Colombian Emeralds International JEWELRY
(Map p82; Port Lucaya Marketplace) With outposts throughout the Bahamas and Caribbean, this corporate chain specializes in the green stuff: emeralds.

Freeport Jewellers JEWELRY
(Map p82; Port Lucaya Marketplace) In addition to the standard diamonds 'n' emeralds, this shop sells unique contemporary Bahamian conch shell jewelry and a rare sea-blue gem called larimar, found only in the Caribbean.

Perfume

Perfume Factory PERFUME
(Map p78; International Bazaar, Freeport) Snag a bottle of Bahamian-themed scents like Sand, Pink Pearl, Goombay or Guanahani at this fragrance factory, in a faux pink mansion (p76). Or mix your own scent for $30.

Les Parisiennes PERFUME
(Map p82; Port Lucaya Marketplace) Another good choice for an international array of duty-free scents.

Information

Emergency

Ambulance (☎242-352-2689)

Internet Access

Many restaurants and nearly all hotels offer free wi-fi access for guests. There's free wi-fi at the Port Lucaya Marketplace, as evidenced by park benches full of people hunched over laptops.

Medical Services

Health Enhancing Pharmacy (☎242-352-7327; 1 W Mall Dr, Freeport; ⊗8am-9pm Mon-Sat)

Lucayan Medical Centre (☎242-373-7400; www.lucayanmedical.com; E Sunrise Hwy, Lucaya; ⊗8:30am-5:30pm Mon-Fri, 8:30am-1pm Sat) Has six full-time doctors and two dentists on staff.

Rand Memorial Hospital (☎242-352-6735; www.phabahamas.org; E Atlantic Dr, Freeport) This public hospital has the island's only emergency room.

Money

There's no shortage of banks with ATMs in Freeport. The ATM at the Treasure Bay Casino dispenses American dollars, useful for those on short-term stays.

Bank of the Bahamas (cnr Bank Lane & Woodstock St, Freeport)

British American Bank (East Mall Dr, Freeport)

First Caribbean International Bank (E Mall Dr, Freeport)

Royal Bank of Canada (cnr E Mall Dr & Explorers Way, Freeport)

Scotiabank (Regent Centre, Freeport)

Western Union (British American Bank; East Mall Dr, Freeport)

Post

Post office (Explorers Way, Freeport)

FedEx (Seventeen Plaza, cnr Bank Lane & Explorers Way, Freeport)

Telephone

BaTelCo (Pioneer's Way, Freeport) Offers telephone and fax services.

Tourist Information

The daily *Freeport News* (www.freeport.nassauguardian.net) is worth checking out for arts and entertainment information as well as any upcoming sporting events. The free tourism brochure, *What-to-do in Freeport/Lucaya & Grand Bahama* is full of handy information and discount coupons, while *Bahamas Weekly* (www.thebahamasweekly.com) provides information on shopping, dining, and entertainment.

Also visit the following for information on local events and activities.

Grand Bahama Island Tourism Board (☎242-350-8600; www.grandbahama.com)

Grand Bahama Ministry of Tourism (☎242-352-2052, 242-352-8044; www.bahamas.com) The ministry's 'People to People' program puts you in touch with locals who share their visitors' interests or professions.

Getting There & Away

Air

Freeport International Airport (FPO; ☎242-352-6020) lies 2 miles north of Freeport. For international flights to Grand Bahama and the Bahamas see p260.

The following airlines fly between Grand Bahama and other Bahamian islands.

Bahamasair (UP; www2.bahamasair.com) Freeport (☎242-352-8346); George Town, Exuma (☎242-345-0040); Nassau (☎242-702-4140) Direct flights from Freeport to Florida. Most Out Island flights involve a stop in Nassau, its hub.

Regional Air (☎242-351-5614; www.goregionalair.com) Grand Bahama–based, connects Freeport to Abaco, Bimini, Eleuthera.

Sky Bahamas (☎242-351-5614; skybahamas.net) Direct flights to Nassau and Turks and Caicos.

Western Air (☎242-351-3804; www.westernairbahamas.com) Flies to Nassau, then on to Abaco, Andros, Bimini and Exuma.

Quoted airline fares are one-way:

ROUTE	COST	FREQUENCY
Freeport-Nassau	$85	6 daily
Freeport-Marsh Harbour, Abaco	$85	1 daily
Freeport-Bimini	$65	1 daily
Freeport-Governors Harbour (Eleuthera)	$135	2 weekly
Freeport-North Eleuthera	$135	2 weekly

Boat

MAIL BOAT Contact the **Dockmaster's Office** (☎242-393-1064) located at Potter's Cay in Nassau or **Freeport Harbour** (☎242-352-9651) to confirm departure schedules.

MailBoat (www.mailboatbahamas.com) A privately owned cargo boat goes to/from Nassau thrice weekly (one way $50, six hours), leaving Freeport Tuesday at 9pm, Thursday at 8pm and Friday at 9pm.

Marcella III Sails for Nassau (one way $45, 12 hours) at 8am on Saturday, returning on Wednesday at 4pm.

MARINAS If traveling in your own boat, you must call ahead to arrange clearance with **Customs** (☎242-352-7361) and **Immigration** (☎242-352-9338).

All marinas provide electricity and freshwater hookups.

Grand Bahama Yacht Club (☎242-373-8888; www.grandbahamayc.com; Midshipman Rd, Lucaya) Located on the north side of Port Lucaya, with facilities for mega yachts.

Ocean Reef Yacht Club (☎242-272-4661; www.oryc.com; Silver Point Beach) Has accommodations, more than 55 slips, and free buses to town.

Old Bahama Bay Resort & Marina (☎242-346-6500; www.oldbahamabay.com; Bayshore Rd, West End) Has 70 slips and fuel, shower and laundry facilities.

Port Lucaya Marina (☎242-373-9090; www.portlucaya.com) Has more than 100 slips. The marina is in the area around the Port Lucaya Marketplace.

Getting Around

Air

Freeport International Airport (☎242-352-6020) lies 2 miles north of Freeport. There's no bus service to/from the airport. However, car rental booths are based in the arrivals hall and taxis meet each flight. Taxi rides for two people to/from the airports: $15/22 Freeport/Lucaya. Each additional passenger costs $3. Displayed fares are set by the government.

Boat

Cruise ships dock at Freeport Harbour, west of town. Taxis meet all cruise ships and charge $20/27 to Freeport/Lucaya.

In McLeans Town (East End), a free government ferry runs daily to Sweeting's Cay. Also in McLean's Town, **Pinder's Ferry Service** (☎242-353-3093; one way $50; ⏲ferry leaves 8:30am & 4:30pm) runs twice-daily 45-minute trips to Crown Haven, Abaco. This is not generally a convenient way to travel to Abaco, as land transportation is sketchy to nonexistent from Freeport to McLean's Town and from Crown Haven to Marsh Harbour, 2½ hours south. If you go this route, ask the Pinder's people to hook you up with a rental car on the other side.

Bus

A handful of private minibuses operate as 'public buses' on assigned routes from the bus depot downtown at Winn Dixie Plaza, Freeport, traveling as far afield as West End and McLean's Town. Buses are frequent and depart when the driver decides there are enough passengers. In Lucaya, the main bus stop is on Seahorse Dr, 400yd west of the Port Lucaya Marketplace.

One-way fares from Freetown include Port Lucaya Marketplace ($1.25), East End ($8, twice daily) and West End ($4, twice daily). Though drivers are meant to stick to their circuit, they'll often function as impromptu taxis, taking you wherever you want to go for a fee. Just ask.

Free shuttles also run between most downtown hotels, the beach and town.

Car & Scooter Hire

The following companies have car-rental agencies at the airport. The local companies are cheaper than the internationals, and daily car rental is from $50. Collision waiver insurance is about $15 a day.

Avis (☎242-352-7666)

Brad's (☎242-352-7930)

Dollar (☎242-352-9325)

KSR Rent A Car (☎242-351-5737)

Millie's (☎242-351-3486)

You can rent a scooter in the parking lot of the Port Lucaya Marketplace for about $40 a day, plus a hefty cash deposit.

Taxi

You'll find taxis at the airport and major hotels. Fares are fixed by the government for short distances (eg the fare from the airport to Lucaya is about $15). Bonded taxis (with white license plates) can't go outside the tax-free zone. You can call for a radio-dispatched taxi from **Freeport Taxi** (☎242-352-6666) or **Grand Bahama Taxi Union** (☎242-352-7101).

East of Freeport

East of the Grand Lucayan Waterway (a 7½-mile canal), the Grand Bahama Hwy runs parallel to the shore to East End. Side roads lead to the south shore's talcum-powder soft beaches.

PETERSON CAY NATIONAL PARK

This 1.5-acre park is the only cay on Grand Bahama's south shore. It's a popular getaway, busy with locals' boats on weekends. Coral reefs provide splendid snorkeling and diving. You can hire a boat from any marina in Freeport and Lucaya. Take snorkel gear and a picnic. Also try Grand Bahamas Nature Tours (p80).

OLD FREE TOWN

The settlement of Old Free Town, 3 miles east of the Grand Lucayan Waterway, was forcibly abandoned in the 1960s when the Port Authority acquired the land. There are several blue holes (subaqueous caves) in the surrounding swamp, notably Mermaid's Lair and **Owl Hole**. Stalactites dangle from the roof of the bowl. And owls have nested on the sill as long as residents can remember – the blue holes are well hidden, so ask a local for directions!

LUCAYAN NATIONAL PARK

With bottomless sea caves, acres of dense forest and one of the prettiest stretches of beach on the island, this tiny (40 acre) **national park** (☎242-352-5438; www.bnt.bs/parks_lucayan.php; admission $3; ⏲8:30am-4:30pm) packs a big wallop.

If visiting by car, park in the parking lot on the north side of the highway, which divides the park in two, then pay the entrance fee to the attendant before continuing on. On the north side, trails lead from the parking lot onto a limestone plateau riddled with caves that open to one of the longest known underwater cave system in the world, with over six charted miles of tunnels. From here you can follow steps down to viewing platforms in **Ben's Cave** and **Burial Mound Cave**, which have formed blue holes. Colonies of bats use Ben's Cave as a nursery in summer, where a unique class of opaque blind crustacean, *Speleonectes lucayensis* – resembles a swimming centipede – also resides. In 1986 four skeletons of indigenous Lucayans were found in what appeared to be an ancient cemetery on the floor of one cave.

Creek Trail (330yd) and **Mangrove Swamp Trail** (480yd) form a loop on the southern side of the park and pass through three signed shoreline ecosystems. The trails head first through miniature woodlands with ming, cedar, mahogany and poisonwood, cinnecord, cabbage palms and agaves, which produce towering yellow flowers favored by insects and hummingbirds. Their low branches are festooned with orchids and bromeliads.

Between this area and the shore lie mangroves, where raccoons and land crabs roam under the watchful eyes of ospreys, herons and waterfowl. **Gold Rock Creek** is the home to snapper, barracuda, manta ray and crabs. Passages lead underground between the creek and the Lucayan Caves so that ocean fish are often seen in the blue holes north of the road.

Trails are marked through the beachside whiteland coppice of giant poisonwood and pigeon plum trees, frequented by woodpeckers ('peckerwoods' in local parlance).

Both trails spill out onto the secluded and beautiful white-rippled sands of **Gold Rock Beach**, fringed by dunes fixed by coco plum, sea grape, spider lily and casuarina trees. Named for the small rock that lies 200yd offshore, this is one of the island's most stunning beaches.

Bring all water and food with you and don't forget your bug spray. The park is open daily year-round, although Ben's Cave is closed in June and July to protect the birthing bats.

The best way to visit the park is by car, scooter, or organized tour.

Cave diving is allowed only by special permit under the supervision of UNEXSO (p77) in Port Lucaya.

LUCAYAN NATIONAL PARK TO MCLEAN'S TOWN

The route to **McLean's Town** (population 3740) is normally taken by those seeking a boat ride to Sweeting's Cay, Lightbourne and Deep Water Cays for snorkeling or the excellent bonefishing. On the way you will pass sleepy Freetown and High Rock settlements. About 10 miles east, beyond the Burma Oil Depot (with a harbor facility for the world's largest supertankers), is Pelican Point Beach and Rocky Creek, which harbors another blue hole.

McLean's Town residents live off their conch and lobster fishing, and some also act as bonefishing guides.

Deep Water Cay attracts fishing fans while **Sweeting's Cay** (population 480) holds a small fishing village and some visitors' accommodations. Lightbourne Cay has a lovely beach and shallows that are a snorkeler's dream.

Captain Phil & Mel's Bonefishing Guide Service (☎242-353-3960; www.bahamasbonefishing.net; half-/full-day $350/450) provides customers with transportation to/from Freeport.

Sleeping & Eating

Bishop's Bonefish Resort, Restaurant & Bar MOTEL $$
(Map p76; ☎242-353-5485; High Rock Beach; r $100; ❄) Seven bright beachfront motel rooms cater to hardcore bonefishers. An on-site bar and popular local restaurant serve Bahamian dishes and burgers; when the weather's nice, the beachfront gazebo bar is the place to be.

TOP CHOICE **Miss Zelma's Conch Stand** BAHAMIAN, SEAFOOD $
(Map p76; Pink house on the right as you enter McLean's Town) Freeport-dwellers will often plan an entire weekend trip out to McLean's Town for the sole purpose of dining on Miss Zelma's cracked conch. It may take a while – Zelma cooks everything from scratch in her freestanding home kitchen, so take a drive around town while you wait. Be sure to come on Saturday for her famous crab rice. Outdoor seating only, cash-only.

Smitty's One Stop Shop FAST FOOD $
(Map p76; ☎242-353-4242; Bevans Town; mains $6-10) About 5 miles east of Lucayan National Park, Smitty's serves burgers and basic fare; sells gasoline and has a general store.

Deep Water Cay LODGE $$$
(Map p76; ☎888-420-6202; www.deepwatercay.com; Deep Water Cay; package rates incl fishing per 3 nights from $1700, to $4000 per 7 nights; ❄📶) On a private island with its own airstrip, this ultra-luxe bonefishing club caters to Master of the Universe types, who revel in the airy private cabanas and Happy Hour at the clubhouse.

Sandy Beach Villas COTTAGES $$
(Map p76; ☎242-442-9555; www.sandybeachvillas.com; cottages weekly $900-1400; ❄) On a delightfully isolated stretch of Pelican Point beach, these cute furnished cottages cater to those looking to get away from it all (and we mean ALL).

You can buy groceries at the Cooper's Convenience Store (Map p76), a tiny hut in the middle of McLean's Town.

Getting There & Around

A minibus operates twice daily from Winn Dixie Plaza in downtown Freeport. Water taxis operate between McLean's Town and the cays. Rates are negotiable. A ferry also runs twice-daily to Crown Harbour, Abaco (see p89).

West of Freeport

This peninsula is separated from the 'mainland' by Freeport Harbour Channel and the surrounding industry. Already pretty poor, the area was further devastated by the 2004 hurricanes and is in the process of recovering.

The highlight here is Paradise Cove and the pristine Deadman's Reef, which can be reached by simply walking off the beach.

HAWKSBILL CREEK TO WEST END

The channel opens to Hawksbill Creek, named for the once-common marine turtles that now infrequently come ashore. Fishermen bring their catch ashore here to the Conch Wharf; and huge shell mounds line the road.

The rough and poorer suburb of Eight Mile lies west of the channel and should be avoided after dark, along with the area that stretches west to Holmes Rock. Nearby are several 'boiling holes' (subterranean water-filled holes that bubble under the tides' pressure).

Down a sandy side road, the outpost **Paradise Cove** (242-349-2677; www.deadmansreef.com; Paradise Cove; 1/2-bedroom cottages $175/225;) is one of the island's best day-trip destinations. This friendly beach club has clusters of psychedelic-colored reef just offshore, so rent snorkel gear ($15) and wade right in. Not a snorkeler? Lounging on the beach, kayaking, playing volleyball and enjoying a grouper sandwich and a Kalik at the resort's tiny Red Bar are also on tap. Overnighters can snag one of two modern, beachy cottages on stilts.

Jitney buses run several times a day from Winn Dixie Plaza in Freeport to Eight Mile and Holmes Rock ($4), but don't count on getting a ride back. Better to rent a car or join a group excursion (see p80).

WEST END

A rum-runners' haven during the Prohibition years, Grand Bahama's westernmost settlement once played host to marquee names like Al Capone. These days, West End is a sleepy collection of tumbledown shacks, half-sunken boats and piles of sun-bleached conch shells.

Sleeping & Eating

Old Bahama Bay Resort & Marina RESORT $$$

(Map p76; 242-346-6500; www.oldbahamabay.com; Bayshore Rd; r from $249;) On the island's isolated westernmost tip, this unfinished 150-acre luxury resort feels a little lonely. But the completed parts of the resort have some of the island's swankest facilities. Pink stucco cottages, all outfitted in airy whites and colonial dark woods, dot manicured grounds of hibiscus and coconut palms. The marina has its own customs and immigration facility, making it popular with well-heeled yachties in from Florida, just 55 miles west. Facilities include walking and snorkeling trails, a vast heated swimming pool with massage jets, a gym, spa, restaurant, bar and helipad.

West End Bakery BAKERY $

(Map p76; West End; items $4-6; 7am-6pm daily) Drop in to this spic-n-span bakery for a massive slab of guava duff (boiled pastry filled with sweet guava paste) or a turmeric-spiked meat patty.

Getting There & Away

A jitney bus (one way $4) runs several times daily from Freeport's International Bazaar and Port Lucaya Marketplace. Return times can be iffy – visitors are better off renting a car or joining a tour group.

Biminis, Andros & Berry Islands

TELEPHONE CODE: 242 / POPULATION: 10,200 / AREA: 2321 SQ MILES

Includes »

Best Places to Stay

» Bimini Big Game Club (p99)

» Pineville Motel (p105)

» Kamalame Cay (p106)

» Small Hope Bay Lodge (p108)

» Tiamo (p111)

Best Beaches

» Bimini Bay Beach, Bimini (p95)

» Tiki Hut Beach, Bimini (p97)

» Morgan's Bluff beach, Andros (p105)

» Congo Town Beach, Andros (p110)

» Sugar Beach, Berry Islands (p112)

Why Go?

No casinos. No nightclubs. No fancy cocktails. These three relatively undeveloped island groups on the western side of the Bahamas may not be glitzy, but they're absolute heaven for anglers, divers and explorers.

The Biminis, just 50 miles east of Miami along the edge of the Gulf Stream, are a world-famous big-game fishing destination. Come to commune with the ghost of Hemingway, who immortalized the Biminis in his novel *Islands in the Stream*, or to explore the famed Bimini Road – is it really the lost city of Atlantis? Andros, the Bahamas' largest but least densely populated island, has the world's third-largest barrier reef, vast bonefishing flats and miles of dense interior forest filled with mythical man-bird creatures. The tiny Berry Islands, barely more than specks on the map, are a playground for yachties. Spend days sailing from cay to cay without ever encountering a fellow human.

When to Go

AliceTown

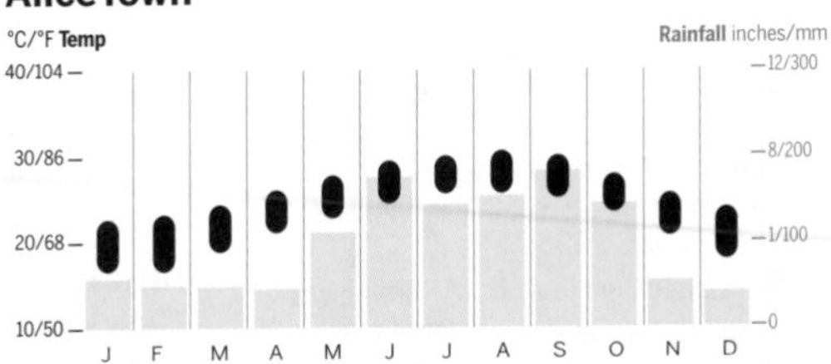

March & April Prime bonefishing season in Andros, so book your guides early.

June–August Gulf Stream waters are calmest, making this Bimini's busiest time of year.

December–February While the rest of the Bahamas crawls with tourists, Bimini, Andros and the Berries slumber.

BIMINIS

POP 2000

Itty-bitty Bimini has an outsized reputation. Its proximity to the Gulf Stream makes it one of the world's premier big-game fishing spots, attracting heavyweights like Ernest Hemingway and Howard Hughes since the early 20th century. During Prohibition, Bimini was a base for rum-runners heading to Florida, only 53 miles east. The combination of macho fishermen and lawless bootleggers gave Bimini a gritty, slightly Wild West feel, which it retains to this day. That may be changing though, as the new Bimini Bay Resort plans to turn the top half of North Bimini into luxury resorts and golf courses in the coming years – stay tuned.

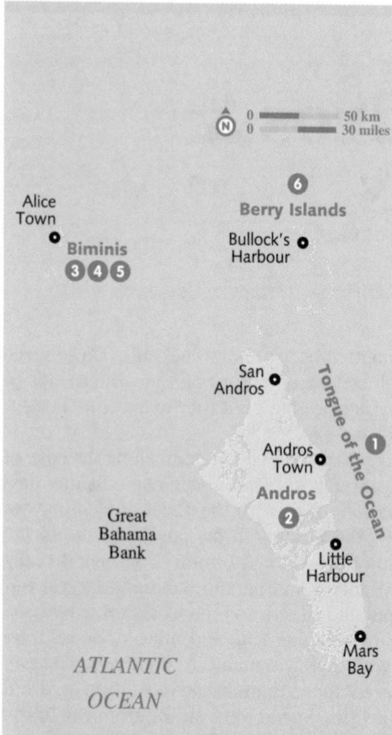

Biminis, Andros & Berry Islands Highlights

1. Diving into the dizzying abyss of the **Tongue of the Ocean** off Andros (p107)
2. Hiking through the vast, unspoiled **Androsian forests**, searching for blue holes while avoiding the mythical chickcharnies (p108)
3. Channeling the spirit of Hemingway by angling for marlin off **Bimini** (p98)
4. Splashing and playing with wild dolphins in the Bimini seas at **Bill & Nowdla Keefe's Bimini Undersea** (p98)
5. Snorkeling above the **Bimini Road**, an underwater limestone formation claimed to be the lost city of Atlantis (p99)
6. Sailing from secluded cay to secluded cay in the tiny **Berry Islands** (p111)

The Biminis (as the islands are formally known) are composed of two main islands. The skinny island of North Bimini stretches for almost 7 miles before fanning out into a quilt of mangrove swamps and fishing flats. The western side is edged with silver-white sand, which becomes whiter and lovelier the further north you go. The main settlement is ragtag Alice Town, at the south end of the island. The King's Hwy, the only real road, runs straight north through the shabby hamlets of Bailey Town and Porgy Bay, all the way to the Bimini Bay Resort.

A five-minute water taxi ride away, less-developed South Bimini is home to the airport and a number of expat-owned homes. Here, wide swaths of scrub forest are fringed by glorious, nearly untouched beaches. South of South Bimini, a number of small cays dot the continental shelf, accessible only by private boat.

Although Bimini's still mainly a fisherman and yachtie spot, it's also one of the best (and most economical places) to dive. In recent years the island has attracted scores of divers to explore its reefs, sunken wrecks and dizzying drop-offs.

Don't come here expecting anything fancy – you won't find any Nassau-style megaresorts or flashy nightclubs. But if your idea of a good time is swapping big fish stories with the locals over a cold Kalik, Bimini's your place.

History

Pirates like Henry Morgan thought the Biminis a splendid lair from which to pounce on treasure fleets, while the five founding families here in 1835 were licensed wreckers – 'rescuing' ships and their cargoes. Later Biminites tried the more honest occupation of sponging, which thrived until a decimating blight in the 1930s. Prohibition in the 1920s boosted the Biminis' economy (if not reputation) when Alice Town became the export capital for illegal Scotch whisky runs into the US.

Ernest Hemingway (see the boxed text, p97) briefly made the Biminis his summer home. Other infamous visitors included Howard Hughes, Richard Nixon and Adam Clayton Powell Jr (New York congressman and Harlem preacher), who arrived with his mistress. Back in 1987 US presidential contender Gary Hart's aspirations were sunk when he was spotted here cavorting with a woman who was not his wife – on a yacht appropriately named *Monkey Business*!

In ensuing decades the Biminis became a major stopover for drug shipments. The work of the US and Bahamian authorities continues; in June 2004 the US attorney general announced the smashing of an international cocaine-trafficking network, in which Bahamians were arrested in the Biminis, New Providence and Eleuthera.

The Biminis have been featured in films such as *Cocoon* and *Silence of the Lambs*.

Getting There & Around

Most visitors fly into the Biminis, while others arrive by mail boat or private yacht. The **Bimini International Airport** (BIM; ☎242-347-3101) is on South Bimini. **Continental Airlines** (www.continental.com) offers the only major commercial service between the Biminis and the US, flying daily to and from Fort Lauderdale.

The following airlines fly between the Biminis and other Bahamian islands:

Regional Air (☎242-347-4115; www.goregionalair.com) Flies between Freeport and Bimini three times daily.

Western Air (☎242-347-4100; www.westernairbahamas.com) Flies between Nassau and Bimini twice daily.

One-way fares include flights to Nassau ($65, twice daily) and Bimini International Airport flights to Freeport ($70, once daily).

A minibus meets all commercial flights into the airport. Pay the driver $5, which includes the ride to the ferry dock and the ferry fare to North Bimini.

With only one compact settlement on North Bimini, feet are the main transportation for getting around, although bicycles and golf carts are easily hired for longer excursions.

Sights

NORTH BIMINI

Narrow but exquisite beaches line the west side of North Bimini – the wonderfully named **Radio Beach**, **Blister Beach** and **Spook Hill Beach** are among the most popular, though only Radio Beach has public facilities. Further north, the wide white **Bimini Bay Beach** is the hands-down beauty queen of the bunch.

Bimini Museum MUSEUM
(King's Hwy, Alice Town; admission $2; ⌚9am-9pm Mon-Sat, noon-9pm Sun) Up a rickety staircase just across the street from the ferry dock, this one-room museum tells the island's history through sun-bleached, water-stained newspaper clippings and Xeroxed photos. Check out the pics of Hemingway standing proudly in front of a row of just-caught gleaming marlin, and learn about legendary Bimini rum-runner Bill McCoy, whose name is said to have given rise to the phrase 'the real McCoy.'

Dolphin House MUSEUM
(Alice Town; admission $2; ⌚10am-6pm Mon-Sat) 'A dolphin looked me right in the eye and I ain't never been the same since,' says Ashley Saunders, Bimini's poet laureate and the mad genius behind this enchantingly bizarre building. Saunders has spent the past decade building the two-story edifice from found objects – shells, bottles, coral, bits of tile from destroyed hotels. Check out the mermaid shrine and the glowing pink conch shell lamps. There's a small museum and gift shop, but the real point of your visit is talking to the voluble Saunders, who describes his work as 'a poem in stone.' If you're an 'artist, poet, humanitarian or dolphin swimmer,' you can rent the two-bedroom upstairs apartment.

Healing Hole NATURAL SPRING
Local lore attributes the inspiration for Martin Luther King Jr's 'I Have a Dream' speech to the mystical effect of the so-called Healing Hole, hidden in the middle of the North Bimini mangrove swamps. The great man bathed in this freshwater sulfur spring shortly before speaking those memorable words. Many visitors here claim an enigmatic calming sensation after visiting the hole, though others report nothing but a sulfur stench and mosquito bites. You'll need help from a local to find the place – plenty will be happy to show you the way for a fee.

SOUTH BIMINI

Less-developed South Bimini has long been a weekend hideaway for wealthy ex-pats, but has also maintained large areas of mangroves, tropical hardwood forest and saltwater pools. This tiny 5-mile-long isle is therefore still popular with waterfowl, who

North & South Bimini

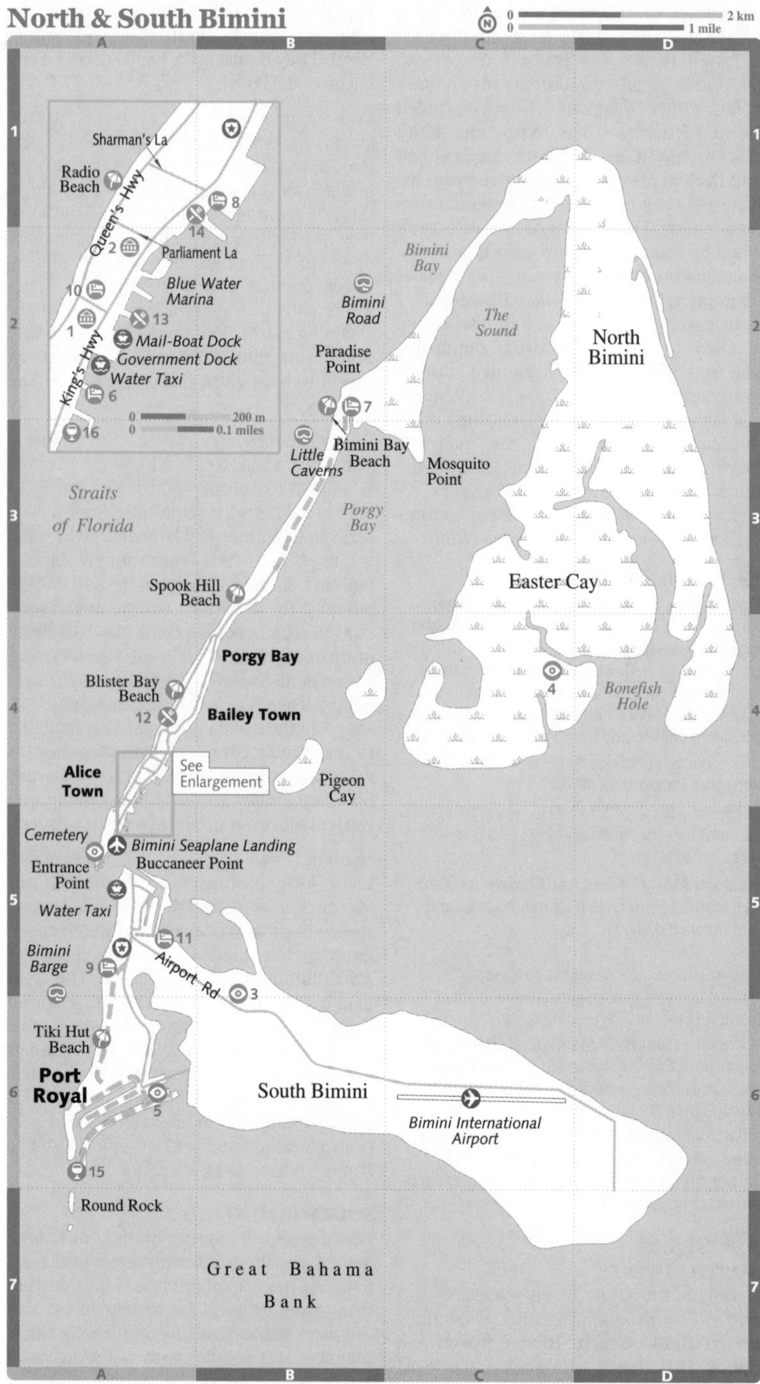

North & South Bimini

head for Duck Lake, their winter getaway. The sweetest spot for sand and sun is **Tiki Hut Beach**, on the west shore.

Shark Lab RESEARCH STATION
(305-274-0628; www.miami.edu/sharklab/index.html) Sharks adore Bimini, with its easy Gulf Stream access and mangrove swamps perfect for spawning babies. Meet some at the 'Bimini Biological Field Station,' AKA 'Shark Lab,' a working research station run by prominent American shark biologist Dr Samuel Gruber. Come at low tide and a rotating staff of enthusiastic young volunteers will show you around the lab, then take you out back to the mudflats to visit the captive baby lemon sharks.

Bimini Nature Trail WALKING TRAIL
On the grounds of the Bimini Sands Resort & Marina, this well-tended, well-marked 1-mile nature trail passes through forests of palm and poisonwood. Stop and say hi to the caged green iguana and the Bimini boa, a subspecies of the endemic Bahamian boa.

Fountain of Youth FOUNTAIN
Local legend places Ponce de Leon's Fountain of Youth some 2 miles south of the ferry dock on Airport Rd. Seek out the dry limestone hole and see for yourself.

Activities

Diving, Snorkeling & Water Sports

Bimini's most unique dive sites include the wreck of the ***Sapona***, a WWI-era cargo steamer sank by rum-runners in the 1920s, now lying half in, half out of 20ft of water.

HEMINGWAY & THE BIMINIS

The cigar-chomping, rum-swilling, marlin-reeling ghost of Ernest Hemingway looms large in Bimini. 'Papa,' as the ultimate man's man was known, made the island his summer home during the mid-1930s. He docked his boat, the *Pilar*, at Brown's Marina, and spent much of his days indulging his love of big-game fishing.

Hemingway wrote several of his later works in Room 1 of North Bimini's **Compleat Angler Hotel**, including the 'Bimini' chapter of his posthumously published novel, *Islands in the Stream*, and several sections of *To Have and Have Not*. At night Hemingway would take on all comers in a boxing ring he built in the hotel bar, promising $200 for any islander who could take him for three rounds. No one ever won. The hotel burned to the ground in 2006, killing the owner and destroying a trove of Hemingway photos and other memorabilia. The hotel's chimney and foundation still bear their grim testimony on the Queen's Hwy just north of the ferry dock.

The **Bimini Museum** (p95) has a number of Hemingway photos and news clippings, and the lobby of the **Bimini Big Game Club** has a framed letter from Hemingway to Michael Lerner, founder of the International Game Fishing Association. The **Marlin Cottage** at the Bimini Blue Water Resort was another one of Hemingway's temporary homes – literary pilgrims can still rent it today.

NORTH CAT CAY

Ten miles south of South Bimini, North Cat Cay is a private island run as an exclusive, members-only club, beloved by magnates, Hollywood stars, and the Duke of Windsor and late former US president Richard Nixon. Nonmembers are restricted to the marina area. For information on membership, call the **Cat Cay Yacht Club & Marina** (242-347-3565; www.catcayclub.com).

A more advanced wreck dive, the ***Bimini Barge*** is a 270ft metal carcass lying in 90ft of water. Just offshore, the **continental shelf** plummets 2000ft into the blue-black depths. Divers can ride the rushing Gulf Stream over the abyss.

There are plenty of excellent shallow reef sites for diving and snorkeling – look out for stingrays, turtles and even the occasional whale shark. For good DIY snorkeling, try the beaches off South Bimini's southwestern tip.

Bill & Nowdla Keefe's Bimini Undersea DIVING, DOLPHINS
(242-347-3089, in US 1-800-348-4644; www.biminiundersea.com; Bimini Bay Resort & Marina) Two of Bimini's longest-standing dive operators, the Keefes run dive (two-tank dive $99) and snorkel trips (adult/child $39/29) to more than two dozen sites. All are memorable, especially the adrenaline-pumping continental shelf drift dive. But perhaps the most memorable of all is the Wild Dolphin Adventure ($129), where you get the chance to swim and play alongside a pod of wild Spotted Atlantic Dolphins in the open ocean.

Bimini Sands Recreation & Activities Center SNORKELING, WATER SPORTS
(242-347-3500; www.biminisands.com; Bimini Sands Resort;) Former Shark Lab workers Grant and Katie offer a full menu of excellent adventures, from snorkel excursions (adult/child $21/10) to kayak trips (half-/full day $20/35) to shark encounters (adult/child $21/10) to all manner of boat charter trips. Botany buffs should join their guided nature tours (adult/child $12/6) – they really know their stuff.

Bimini Kiteboarding WATER SPORTS
(242-473-4585; www.biminikiteboarding.com; per hour $70; Bimini Sands Beach Club;) Kiteboarding, stand-up paddleboarding, windsurfing and wakeboarding lessons, run from a stand in front of the Bimini Sands Beach Club.

Bonefishing & Sportfishing

What drew Hemingway more than half a century ago still draws people today – the famous big fish. The catch of the day in winter months is wahoo. All manner of other game fish – tuna, sailfish, mako shark, barracuda and, above all, blue marlin and other billfish that put up a bruising battle – are caught year-round. The hot spots are Bimini Road, off Paradise Point; just off Bimini Bay's Three Sisters Rock; and off Great Isaac, 15 miles north.

Typical fishing charter fees are $350 to $650 for half a day and $600 to $1200 per full day. Any of the island's hotels or marinas can set you up with a guide and a boat. The **Bimini Big Game Club** (opposite) is the nexus of fishing tournament activity.

Also contact these excellent guides:

Bonefish Ansil Saunders BONEFISHING
(242-347-2178) The world champ, once guided Richard Nixon.

Bonefish Ebbie David BONEFISHING
(242-347-2053; shannyshome@msn.com) Also runs a small bonefishing lodge, with package deals.

Bonefish Tommy BONEFISHING
(242-347-3234) Two decades of experience in Bimini waters.

Captain Jerome's Deep Sea Fishing SPORTFISHING
(242-347-2081; www.biminifishing.com) Fishing for 25 years, specializing in shark-hunting trips.

Tours

Bonefish Ansil Saunders NATURE TOURS
(242-347-2178) Runs tours that take in the Bonefish Hole, Healing Hole, East Point, Creeks (mangroves) and Bimini Bay.

Bimini Boat Tours NATURE TOURS
(242-347-2240; www.biminihealingarts.com) Does half-day trips to the Healing Hole and the mangrove swamps, as well as free-diving and spearfishing adventures.

BIMINIS FISHING TOURNAMENTS

MONTH	TOURNAMENT
Feb	Midwinter Wahoo
Mar	Bacardi Billfish Tournament
	Bimini Wahoo Championship
May	Billfish Invitational
	Memorial Day Weekend Tournament
Jul	Fourth of July Tournament
Aug	Native Fishing Tournament
Nov	Bahamas Wahoo Challenge

Bimini Sands Recreation & Activities Center NATURE TOURS
(242-347-3500; www.biminisands.com; Bimini Sands Resort;) Guided botany tours, boat charters, as well as the snorkel and water sports trips listed on p97.

Festivals & Events

The Biminis' party-hearty islanders put on a **Junkanoo** extraordinaire each Boxing Day and New Year's Day, and on July 10 in celebration of **Bahamian Independence**. There's also a festive, despite being early, 5am **Christmas Day parade**.

The **Bimini Regatta Blast** at the end of March features live reggae and other bands. The **Bimini Festival** in mid-May features a sportfishing tourney and cookouts.

The Biminis welcome yachters in the annual **Bahamas Boating Flings** each June through mid-August, when first-time boaters arrive en masse from Fort Lauderdale.

Sleeping

All the hotels in Alice Town are strung along King's Hwy. Hotel rooms are usually sold out during big fishing tournaments.

Bimini Big Game Club HOTEL $$
(242-347-3391; www.biggameclubbimini.com; King's Hwy, Alice Town; r $149-179, cottages $199-229, penthouses $225-350;) Newly renovated by famed marine life painter Guy Harvey, whose macho images of sharks and marlins adorn basement rec rooms worldwide, this is by far the nicest place to stay in Alice Town. Huge rooms have plush beds with shipshape white linens, flat panel TVs and mosaic stone shower stalls. There's a lovely pool and a two-story restaurant and bar, which gets hopping at night even in the low season. For fishing tournaments, the resort books up years in advance.

Bimini Bay Resort & Marina RESORT $$$
(242-347-2900; www.biminibayresort.com; studios from $250, villas from $350-1200;) Rapidly expanding across the top half of North Bimini, this ambitious resort complex was still in its early phases when we visited. But if things continue as planned, Bimini Bay will change the face of this low-key island, turning mangrove swamp into Florida-style condos and golf courses (see the boxed text, p100). There's even a Dubai-style fake island in the works! As of now, it has 370 pastel luxury condos, with plantation shutters, multiple patios and shiny new granite kitchens, scattered across acres of manicured lawns. A small pedestrian shopping zone has luxuries heretofore unknown on Bimini – a John Bull duty-free store and an espresso bar.

Bimini Sands Resort & Marina RESORT $$$
(242-347-3500; www.biminisands.com; units $260-400;) On South Bimini, these beachy, modern one- and two-bedroom condos attract yachties, retired Floridians and families with kids. Feels more like an upscale apartment complex than a resort – take the free shuttle bus to the nearby **Beach Club** for drinks and socializing.

Big John's MOTEL $$
(242-347-3117; www.bigjohnshotel.com; King's Hwy, Alice Town; r $150-175;) Although its

ATLANTIS FOUND?

In the shallows off North Bimini lies a mysterious sight: a half-mile-long underwater 'road' of massive limestone blocks, some as big as 15ft across. Is the so-called **Bimini Road** simply an unusual geometric rock formation? Or were these stones hewn by an ancient race of men, citizens of the lost city of Atlantis? While a passionate group of 'Atlantologists' hew to the latter theory, scientists say the formation is merely naturally occurring beachrock. Take a snorkeling trip to the road, and decide for yourself!

MANGROVES IN DANGER?

The Bimini Bay Resort & Marina on North Bimini, currently in its first phase of development, is by far the biggest resort complex in the Biminis. Some say it's also the biggest threat to the island's ecosystem. The resort's planned expansion will destroy some of North Bimini's mangrove swamps, which are crucial fish and shark spawning grounds, as well as an important bulwark against hurricane damage. International groups like the Mangrove Action Project as well as national environmental organizations like the Bahamas National Trust have spoken out against the resort's expansion.Fabien Cousteau, grandson of legendary ocean explorer Jacques Cousteau, has made a short video about the mangrove threat, which you can watch on YouTube.

claims of being a 'boutique hotel' are puzzling, this friendly blue motel is plenty nice, with seven sunny white rooms above a popular bar by the ferry dock.

Seacrest Hotel & Marina MOTEL **$$**
(☎242-347-3071; www.seacrestbimini.com; King's Hwy, Alice Town; r standard/dockside $100/135, ste $225-320; ❄) Take a 3rd-floor room for views over the marina at this pleasant yellow motel. Room facilities include cable TV and a fridge. The beach is a five-minute walk away.

Thirsty Turtle HOTEL **$**
(☎242-347-4444; South Bimini; r with/without kitchen $80/120; ❄) This South Bimini cheapie has clean motel-style rooms, some with kitchenettes, overlooking an unscenic inland waterway. Popular bar and restaurant downstairs.

Eating

Most hotels and pubs around town offer basic meals. Think fried fish, peas 'n' rice, hamburgers.

Sabor INTERNATIONAL **$$$**
(☎242-347-3500; Bimini Bay Resort; mains $18-48; ⏰lunch & dinner) A touch of South Beach in Bimini, this swanky white-and-slate bistro serves what might be termed 'jetsetter comfort food' – steak frites, paella, herb-grilled lobster tail. Poolside lunches of Cuban sandwiches and coconut ice cream are divine, as are tropical cocktails at the long hammered copper bar. The location, deep within the grounds of the Bimini Bay Resort, is worlds away from scrappy Alice Town.

Captain Bob's BAHAMIAN **$$**
(King's Hwy, Alice Town; mains $8-26; ⏰breakfast, lunch & dinner) This frills-free cafe is a long-time local favorite, with walls papered in fading 'big fish' pictures and a menu of sandwiches and deep-fried Bahamian fare. A top pick for big, hearty breakfasts before along day of bonefishing.

Bimini Twist BAHAMIAN, SUSHI **$$**
(Bimini Sands Beach Club; mains $12-25; ⏰dinner) Panoramic ocean views and an upscale Mediterranean ambiance make this isolated South Bimini bistro an expat hotspot. Fresh-rolled sushi is a rare treat on this otherwise fried-fish-obsessed island. On busy nights, live bands turn the Twist into a big dance party.

Bimini Big Game Bar & Grill BAHAMIAN, AMERICAN **$$**
(Bimini Big Game Club; mains $10-25; ⏰breakfast, lunch & dinner) Poolside at the Bimini Big Game Club, it has the macho vibe appropriate to its name – wood-paneled walls, American sports on TV, and sunburned fishermen devouring drippy burgers, blackened fish and BBQ ribs.

Amicci's ITALIAN, BAKERY **$$**
(Bimini Bay Resort; mains $8-16; ⏰breakfast & lunch) In Bimini Bay's ritzy shopping area, this minimalist cafe offers an unexpected whiff of Milan – panini, fancy coffee drinks, pizza, gelato.

Head to **Jontra's Grocery Supply** (Alice Town) or **Bimini Food Supply** (Bailey Town) for groceries.

Drinking

Mackey's Sand Bar BAR
(Bimini Sands Beach Club; ⏰3pm to late Mon-Fri, from 11am Sat & Sun) Sandy floors and a loooooong polished wood bar make this casual sports pub the island's primo drinking destination for locals and visitors alike. There's football on Sundays and a very popular karaoke night on Wednesdays.

End of the World BAR
(Alice Town; ⏰to 3am) The health authorities had the original shack condemned, and it's been replaced with a modern wooden unit.

But the floor is still covered in sand, dogs wander in and out, and you can add your scrawl to the graffiti-covered walls.

Information

There are public telephone booths all along King's Hwy. A small library is opposite the customs building at the mail-boat dock.

Bahamas Ministry of Tourism (242-347-3529; Government Bldg, King's Hwy, Alice Town; 9am-5:30pm Mon-Fri)

Government Medical Clinic (242-347-2040; King's Hwy, Porgy Bay)

Police (242-347-3144; King's Hwy, Alice Town)

Post office (Government Bldg, King's Hwy, Alice Town)

Royal Bank of Canada (King's Hwy, Alice Town; 9am-3pm Mon, Wed & Fri) Has an ATM.

Getting There & Away

Air

Refer to p260 for information on international flights to the Bahamas and p95 for information on getting to the Biminis.

Boat

Call the **Dockmaster's Office** (242-394-1237) in Nassau and check the website of the **Bahamas Ministry of Tourism** (www.bahamas.com) for the latest schedules and prices.

MAIL BOAT MV *Bimini Mack* mail boat ($45, 12 hours) departs Nassau for Bimini, Cat Cay and Chubb Cay on Thursday, returning on Monday.

MARINAS Boaters and pilots arriving from abroad must clear **Customs** (242-347-3100; by the mail-boat dock) in Alice Town.

Bimini Bay Resort & Marina (242-347-2900; www.biminibayresort.com) On North Bimini's northern end, with nearly 200 slips, with on-site customs and immigration.

Bimini Sands Resort & Marina (242-347-3500; www.biminisands.com) Located on South Bimini, with a full-service marina with on-site customs and immigration.

Brown's Marina (242-347-3117; Alice Town) In central Alice Town, with 17 slips and full facilities.

TIMES THEY ARE A-CHANGIN'

Take note! The peak holiday time in Andros (February 20 to April 23) is different to the rest of the Bahamas. This coincides with the peak bonefishing season through March and April.

Getting Around

Most places are within walking distance. The exception is the Bimini Bay Resort & Marina, which is a bit of a hike. Rent a golf cart by the docks for about $50 a day.

Water taxis between North and South Bimini depart near the Bimini mail-boat dock; the trip costs $3 one way, or $5 if you include the minibus trip to the airport.

ANDROS

POP 7400

Known to Bahamians as 'the Big Yard,' Andros is the country's unexplored backcountry – a whopping 2300 sq miles of mangrove swamps, palm savannas and eerie primal forests full of wild boar and (as legend has it) an evil man-bird known as the chickcharnie. By far the biggest island in the Bahamas, it's the least densely populated – its eastern shores are dotted with ramshackle, blink-and-you'll-miss-'em hamlets, while the entire western side is an uninhabited patchwork of swampland known, appropriately, as 'The Mud.'

Diving and bonefishing are the two main draws for most visitors. A 140-mile-long coral reef, the world's third largest, lies a few hundred yards off the east shore. Beyond it, the continental shelf drops into the blackness of the 6000ft deep Tongue of the Ocean. The island's bizarre blue holes – water-filled vertical caves occurring both inland and offshore – attract advanced divers and National Geographic crews alike.

Travel in Andros is not easy. Just getting from point to point can be harrowing, as the island is divided into three chunks by wide ocean sounds, with little transportation between them. Getting a meal can be a challenge, as most 'restaurants' are nothing more than a shack in someone's front yard, only open when they happen to have a fresh shipment of food. Unless you're staying in one of Andros' small handful of all-inclusive resorts, travel on the island is very, very DIY.

OK, clearly Andros is not for everyone. But if you're eager for off-the-grid adventure, Andros offers a glimpse of the Bahamas the way it was 50 years ago – unpaved roads, starry skies, empty beaches, curious locals.

A word of warning, especially for hikers and birdwatchers; the gargantuan forests, marshlands and scrublands are also used by Bahamians hunting wild boar and birds, so be careful.

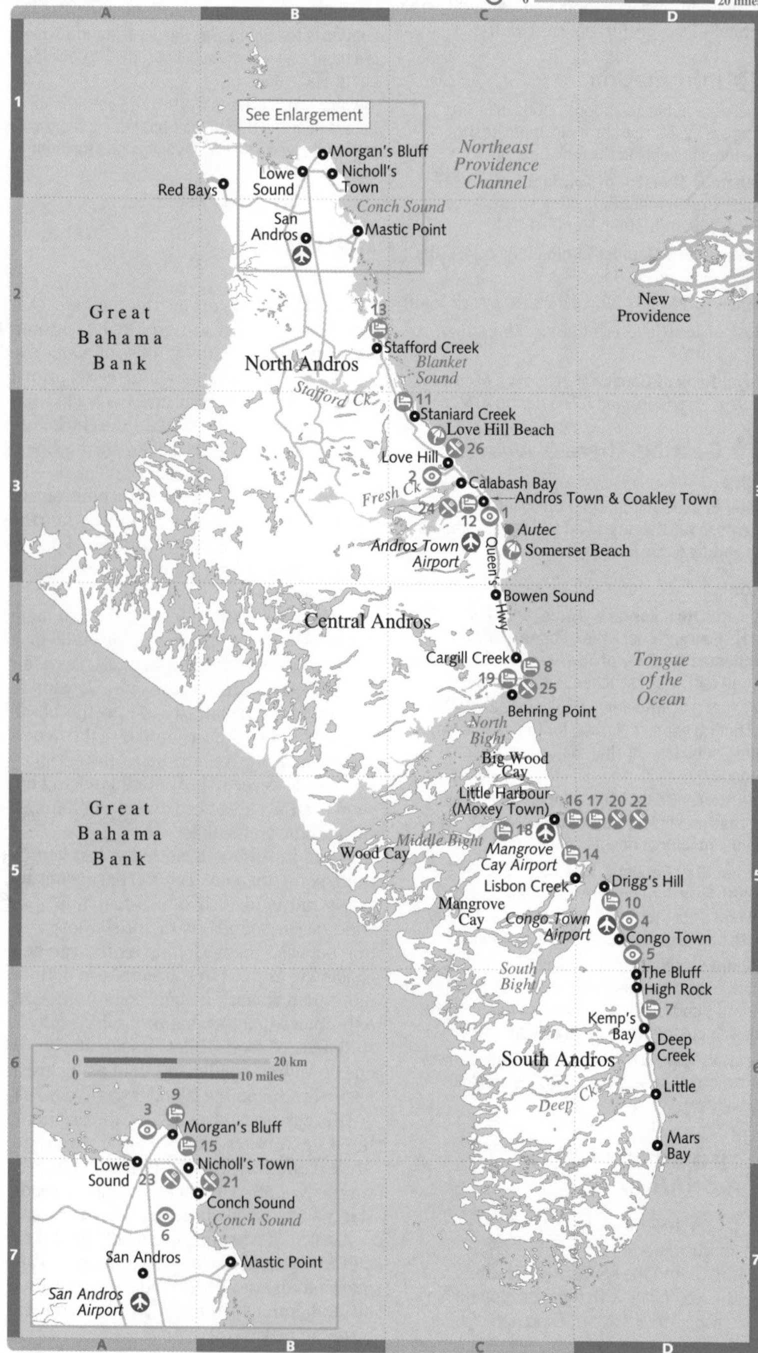

Great Bahama Bank
North Andros
Central Andros
South Andros
See Enlargement
Morgan's Bluff
Lowe Sound
Nicholl's Town
Red Bays
Conch Sound
San Andros
Mastic Point
Northeast Providence Channel
New Providence
Stafford Creek
Blanket Sound
Stafford Ck
Staniard Creek
Love Hill Beach
Love Hill
Calabash Bay
Fresh Ck
Andros Town & Coakley Town
Autec
Andros Town Airport
Somerset Beach
Queen's Hwy
Bowen Sound
Cargill Creek
Behring Point
Tongue of the Ocean
North Bight
Big Wood Cay
Little Harbour (Moxey Town)
Middle Bight
Mangrove Cay Airport
Wood Cay
Lisbon Creek
Drigg's Hill
Mangrove Cay
Congo Town Airport
Congo Town
South Bight
The Bluff
High Rock
Kemp's Bay
Deep Creek
Deep Ck
Little
Mars Bay
San Andros Airport

Andros

Sights

1	Androsia LTD	C3
2	Captain Bill's Blue Hole	C3
3	Henry Morgan's Cave	A6
4	Jerry Davis	D5
5	Stargate Blue Hole	D5
6	Uncle Charlie's Blue Hole	A7

Sleeping

7	Andros Beach Club	D6
8	Andros Island Bonefishing Club	C4
9	Conch Sound Resort Inn	A6
10	Emerald Palms Resort	D5
11	Kamalame Cay	C3
12	Lighthouse Yacht Club & Marina	C3
13	Love at First Sight	B2
14	Mangrove Cay Inn	C5
15	Pineville Motel	A6
16	Seascape Inn	C5
17	Swain's Cay Lodge	D5
18	Tiamo	C5
19	Tranquility Hill Fishing Lodge	C4

Eating

	Adderley's Bargain Mart	(see 24)
20	Dianne Cash	D5
21	Fish Fry	B7
	Food Store	(see 15)
22	Four Kids Bakery	D5
23	Grizzly's	A7
24	Hank's Place	C3
25	Sea View Restaurant & Bar	C4
26	Taste & See	C3

Also come well prepared for the aggressive horsefly (or 'doctor fly,' because its bite hurts like a syringe) and clouds of mosquitoes and sand flies.

History

The wild island became a refuge for both Seminole Indians and runaway slaves fleeing Florida during colonial days. A community of their descendants still exists in Red Bay on the northwest coast.

Andros' renowned sponge beds, west of the island, supported much of the population in the late 19th and early 20th centuries, until a mysterious blight in 1938. Some believe that the island was named by Greek spongers for the Mediterranean island of Andros. A few locals still make a living sponging (see the boxed text, p106), but most earn a living from fishing. The famous Androsian sloops, however, have been replaced by fiberglass outboards.

Getting There & Away

AIR

Refer to p261 for information on international flights to the Bahamas.

Many visitors arrive in Andros by plane. Andros is served by four airports (be sure to fly to the correct airport for wherever you intend to stay!):

Andros Town Airport (ASD; ☎242-368-2030) Serves Central Andros; 3 miles south of Fresh Creek.

Congo Town Airport (TZN; ☎242-369-2640) Serves South Andros.

Mangrove Cay Airport (MAY; ☎242-369-0083) On Mangrove Cay.

San Andros Airport (SAQ; ☎242-329-4224) Serves North Andros; 10 miles south of Nicholl's Town.

The following airlines fly between Andros and other Bahamian islands:

LeAir (☎242-377-2356; www.leaircharters.com) Has two daily flights from Nassau to Andros Town, and charter service to all the airports.

Regional Air (☎242-329-7108; www.goregionalair.com) Flies twice weekly between Freeport and San Andros.

Western Air (☎242-329-4000; www.westernairbahamas.com) Flies twice daily between Nassau and San Andros, and Nassau and Congo Town. Sometimes, the airline combines the flight, meaning you can hop on during the stopover in San Andros and travel on to Congo Town, or vice-versa.

The following fares are one way.

ROUTE	COST	FREQUENCY
Andros Town–Nassau	$90	2 daily
Congo Town–Nassau	$70	2 daily
San Andros–Freeport	$150	2 weekly
San Andros–Nassau	$70	2 daily
South Andros-Nassau	$60	2 daily

BOAT

You can also catch a fast ferry (car and passenger) or mail boat to the islands. Call the **Dockmaster's Office** (☎242-394-1237) and check the website of the **Bahamas Ministry of Tourism** (www.bahamas.com) for the latest schedules and prices.

FERRY **Bahamas Ferries** (☎242-323-2166, 242-323-2168; www.bahamasferries.com; adult/child $90/55) operates a car-and-passenger ferry service from Nassau to Morgan's Bluff (2½ hours) on Saturdays from April to December, and to Fresh Creek on Wednesday, Friday and Sunday year-round.

MAIL BOAT The following mail boats are available for travel:

MV *Captain Moxey* Departs Nassau for Kemp's Bay, Long Bay and the Bluff ($35, 7½ hours) on Monday, returning Wednesday.

MV *Lady D* Departs Nassau for Fresh Creek ($35, 5½ hours) on Tuesday, returning Sunday.

MV *Lisa JIII* Departs Nassau for Morgan's Bluff and Nicholl's Town ($30, six hours) on Wednesday, returning Tuesday.

MV *Mangrove Cay Express* Departs Nassau for Drigg's Hill, Mangrove Cay and Cargill Creek ($30, 5½ hours) on Thursday, returning Tuesday.

Getting Around

Saying this is a tough place to get around would be an understatement. Car rentals are mainly organized on an informal basis – ask ahead when you book your hotel; someone will manage to scrounge up something. Taxis also run on an informal basis, and can be very expensive. A privately owned minibus runs the length of North and Central Andros each morning (p106).

Getting between the islands that make up Andros is seriously tricky. There is no official interisland air service, though it's sometimes possible to jump on Western Air's twice-daily flight from Nassau to Congo Town when it makes a pit stop in San Andros (though sometimes the flight goes reverse, from Nassau to Congo Town to San Andros. Your best bet is to call ahead the day of the flight). Chartering your own flight on a tiny plane is sometimes your only option.

There is no ferry service between Central Andros and Mangrove Cay, though you can sometimes shell out to charter your own ride. A small ferry runs between Mangrove Cay and South Andros.

You can rent a car for $80 to $90 per day from several places – your hotel will set something up. There are gas stations in Nicholl's Town and Calabash Bay. There are taxi services on all the islands of Andros, rates are not set and can be quite pricey.

For more information, see the Getting There & Around section for each region.

North & Central Andros

Technically one island, North and Central Andros are the largest of the three islands that make up Andros (North Andros lies north of Stafford Creek and Central Andros lies to the south). Much of the island is smothered in pine forests that have twice been logged – first to provide pit props for English coal mines and later for Chicago newspapers. The island's exotic hardwoods, mahogany and lignum vitae (sometimes called 'sailor's cure' because its sap provided a cure for syphilis in the 19th century), for example, are long gone, but the logging tracks remain. It's the most popular of the Andros islands, and visitors here enjoy great diving, fine beaches and bonefishing.

NICHOLL'S TOWN AREA

Sleepy Nicholl's Town (population 500) is the closest settlement to the San Andros airport and the center of activity for all of North Andros. It has small stores, a supermarket, a gas station, a Georgian-style government building and not a heck of a lot more.

North of town lies the hamlet of Morgan's Bluff, with some extraordinary beaches hidden down dirt roads. Ask a local to draw you a map. You'll still get lost.

To head south, follow the road via the little fishing village of Lowe Sound, and then pass Conch Sound to Mastic Point. This small commercial harbor dates from 1781, and is the place to hunt down *goombay* music. Much of the land inland around San Andros is intensively farmed for citrus, potatoes, tomatoes and other produce. If you see a woman in a prairie dress and bonnet, she's a member of the island's Mennonite community, who moved down from the US to start a farming operation.

Sights

Scuba divers who first explored **Uncle Charlie's Blue Hole** were quite astonished to find sharks swimming in the narrow caverns. The bottomless sinkhole, hidden deep in the pine forest, was made famous by Jacques Cousteau, who dumped dye in the water to prove that it connected to the ocean via underwater channels. Today local kids use a dangling rope swing to splash their way into the hole's black waters. To get

BUSH MEDICINE

Traditional folk healing is still alive, especially in the Family Islands, where locals have a suspicion of doctors and cling to folk remedies. Bush-medicine healers, often respected obeah practitioners, rely on native herbs, which they mix into concoctions, or potents, using recipes that have been handed down through many generations.

The sovereign ingredient is *cerasee* (Momordica charantia), an orange-fruited vine credited with resolving every imaginable human ailment. Aloe is also used for curing many ills, from sunburn to insect bites, while breadfruit leaves are said to cure high blood pressure.

However, not all cures use berries and leaves. For example, 'goat nanny' (goat droppings) is said to cure whooping cough, while congested air passages are cured by pouring 'chamber lye' on the head. This golden liquid is named for the pot into which a person relieves himself at night when not blessed with an indoor toilet.

here, follow the signs from Queen's Hwy and drive down a short dirt road.

At **Conch Sound**, just south of Nicholl's Town, there's a small blue hole just offshore at the public beach – bring your snorkel gear and explore.

There's a nice beach west of **Morgan's Bluff**, and an eerie, shipwreck-filled harbor.

If you believe local lore, Henry Morgan, the wily Welsh pirate, hid his treasure in a cave – **Henry Morgan's Cave** – about 30yd from the road (it's well signed). Bring a flashlight.

At the island's northwestern tip, **Red Bays** is the only west-coast settlement in Andros. The rundown, isolated village is inhabited by descendants of the Seminole Indians and runaway slaves who fled Florida in the 17th and 18th centuries. A few locals earn an income from straw weaving, using practices passed down from Seminole forebears – keep your eyes peeled for women selling baskets from their front lawn.

Activities

Rates are around $250/375 per half-/full day for bonefishing, $250/420 per half-/full day for reef fishing and $300/500 for deep-sea fishing. The following are recommended bonefishing guides:

Phillip Rolle BONEFISHING
(☎242-329-2661)

Elias Griffin BONEFISHING
(☎242-329-7624)

Rodney Miller BONEFISHING
(☎242-329-2039)

Sleeping & Eating

Credit cards may not be accepted at some lodgings, so check when booking. Food can be hard to find, as restaurants are usually home-based and fairly casual (read: completely irregular) in their opening hours. Always ask a local, who will likely direct you toward a roadside BBQ shack or his own granny's kitchen.

TOP CHOICE **Pineville Motel** MOTEL $
(☎242-329-2788; www.pinevillemotel.com; Nicholl's Town; r from $70;) Independent travelers couldn't ask for a better base than this eclectic motel complex. Rooms, each eccentrically decorated with murals and bits of seashells, surround a manmade forest garden and petting zoo – say hi to the Androsian land crabs and the tetchy wild boar. There's a homemade indoor movie theater, small lending library and a handbuilt outdoor tiki bar. It's all the creation of Pineville's owner, the ebullient Eugene, who bubbles over with information about Andros – the best conch stand, the bus driver's home phone number, the route to a hidden beach (complete with hand-drawn map).

Conch Sound Resort Inn HOTEL $
(☎242-329-2060; conchsoundresort@yahoo.com; Conch Sound; r from $85;) This cheerful, though rather isolated, orange hotel has clean, bright-painted rooms on manicured lawns. There's a restaurant and bar, open sporadically.

Fish Fry BAHAMIAN, SEAFOOD $
(Nicholl's Town; mains $8-14; lunch & dinner) In Nicholl's Town's Sea View Park, a handful of bright-painted seafood shacks sell cheap and tasty local food, mostly of the fried variety. Smitty's is tops for cracked conch, while locals swear by Sky Fox for conch salad. Wash it all down with a plastic cup of homemade wine while you shoot the breeze with *tout le monde* of North Andros.

SPONGERS

Sponging in the Bahamas began in earnest in 1841 after a Frenchman, Gustave Renouard, was shipwrecked here and discovered superior sponges to the Mediterranean varieties. Greek deep-sea sponge divers left their homeland to make their money from the Bahamian seabed, using glass-bottom buckets and a hooked pole. (Today spongers dive with snorkel or scuba gear. They also slice the sponges at the base, leaving the root to regenerate.) Ashore, the sponges were beaten to death and put in shallow-water 'kraals' to allow the flesh to rot and decompose. Then they were rinsed, pounded to a pleasing fluffiness, and strung up to dry before being shipped for sale at the Greek Sponge Exchange in Nassau.

At the close of the 19th century, 500 schooners and sloops and 2800 smaller vessels were working the sponge beds, and in the peak year of 1917, 1½ million lb of sponges were exported. 'The Mud,' an extensive 140-mile-long, 40-mile-wide shoal off Andros, was a major source of income for sponge divers. Sponging was the chief source of livelihood on all the Bahamian islands until 1938, when a fungal blight killed the sponges overnight.

To see a sponger in action, head to the isolated North Andros village of Red Bays and ask for Sponge Pete, an elderly Greek man who loves to show visitors the drying process.

Grizzly's BAHAMIAN $
(Queen's Hwy; mains $8-12; lunch & dinner) A relatively reliable source of grub, this highway-side restaurant has sandwiches and fried snackies.

You can stock up at the **Food Store** behind the gas station on the Queen's Hwy outside Nicholl's Town.

Information

Banks open Monday and Wednesday, but the hours across the whole island are erratic.

North Andros Medical Clinic (242-329-2055; Queen's Hwy, Nicholl's Town)

Police (242-329-2353)

Post office (Nicholl's Town)

Scotiabank (Queen's Hwy, Nicholl's Town)

Tourist office (242-368-2286; Andros Town Airport, Fresh Creek)

Getting There & Around

The San Andros Airport serves North Andros. From April through December, the Fast Ferry travels once weekly from Nassau to Morgan's Bluff. For more information on flights, boats and ferries, see p103.

The Mastic Point harbor is clogged by sunken boats and is not recommended for private boaters.

Barry runs a **private bus** (242-471-3276) from the top of North Andros to the bottom of Central Andros and back daily ($5). Call ahead to request pick-up.

You can rent cars from around $70 per day and there's a gas station at the entrance to Nicholl's Town. Ask a local for a hookup. For a taxi, call **North Andros Taxi** (242-329-2273).

STAFFORD CREEK AREA

The southern road from Nicholl's Town cuts inland through a very lonely stretch of pine forest before heading south. It then turns east and leaps over the mouth of Stafford Creek. On the northern side of the bridge is the disheveled village of **Staniard Creek**, which sits on the southern end of a cay. A really lovely 2-mile-long beach forms the eastern shore, with swaying palm trees and enticing tranquility.

Sleeping

TOP CHOICE **Kamalame Cay** RESORT $$$
(242-368-6281; www.kamalame.com; villas $840-1500;) A barge whisks lucky guests across the water to a 97-acre private island, home to this exquisite luxury resort. Ultra-private villas are tucked away down paths lined with kamalame trees, wild dilly, casuarina and love vine. Decor is the height of Merchant Ivory chic, all whitewashed walls and carved wood furniture and worn oriental rugs, with showers big enough for two. Guests dine at the open-air Great House, wander the 3-mile-long beach, or take guided diving or bonefishing trips. But the highlight is really the resort's extraordinary spa. It's perched on stilts above the ocean, with plexiglass holes in the floor beneath the massage tables for views down on the aqua water!

Love at First Sight MOTEL $$
(242-368-6082; Stafford Creek; loveatfirstsights.homestead.com; r incl breakfast $110;) On a quiet ridge overlooking the creek (more like a river), this tidy and pleasant motel has 10 rooms decorated with the owner's handmade shell crafts. The hotel restaurant serves three daily meals.

FRESH CREEK AREA

Andros Town and Coakley Town make up the Fresh Creek township and are the crossroads of Central Andros, lying about 30 miles south of Nicholl's Town. A giant plastic crab greets visitors at Coakley Town on the north side of the creek; the hamlet of Andros Town is on the south side. Fresh Creek itself extends from the inland depths of Andros. This is an area popular with divers and anglers, many of whom head here for the facilities at Small Hope Bay Lodge.

Sights

The jointly run US-UK navies' **Atlantic Undersea Test & Evaluation Center** (Autec) antisubmarine warfare testing facility is a mile south of town and strictly off-limits; the same goes for the waters up to 2 miles offshore.

Somerset Beach is 2 miles south of town, and when the tide recedes, the miles-long beach is extremely deep and splendid. Wading birds patrol the shore, and you can admire the sand dollars at low tide.

The famous Androsia batiks of **Androsia Ltd** (www.androsia.com; 9am-4pm Mon-Fri, 8am-1pm Sat) are sold throughout the Bahamas. Melding age-old wax techniques and island motifs, workers create a wide range of clothing out of four types of natural fabrics. A guide will show you around and there's a factory outlet.

Calabash Bay is a small coastal settlement, which gains a certain charm from its several churches and the flats that are picked at by herons when the tide is out. An apocryphal story has Henry Morgan and Blackbeard together here with a cache of treasure. The two rogues rowed ashore with six sailors, buried the loot and then killed the witnesses. As they were rowing back, one of the two supposedly said, 'There's small hope that'll ever be found.' Hence the bay's alternative name, **Small Hope Bay**.

The Small Hope Bay settlement merges into the **Love Hill** settlement, where a side road just north of the gas station reaches pleasant **Love Hill Beach**. Nearby, **Captain Bill's Blue Hole**, amid pine forests, is popular with divers. There's a ladder and a rope swing for would-be Tarzans.

Activities

DIVING & SNORKELING

For some fabulous dive sites, try the following: the Barge, where a wreck lies 70ft below the surface and is now a home to large groupers; the Black Forest, with its crop of three-dozen black coral trees; the deep Blue Hole, where large rays and sharks often gather; and the *Potomac,* a 345ft British tanker that sank in 1929.

Expert divers may venture to Alex & Cara Caverns, descending 90ft on the edge of the Tongue of the Ocean, and to Over the Wall, which begins at 80ft and plunges another 100ft at the edge of the Tongue of the Ocean. The Tongue itself drops another 6000ft.

Snorkelers should seek out the Solarium, shallow flats favored by lobsters and stingrays; Red Shoal, for schooling grunts and elkhorn reef; and China Point, where blue tangs and sergeant majors frolic. Also try the Compressor, where, yes, a compressor has metamorphosed into a reef; Central Park, with acres of corals; and Trumpet Reef, home to brittle stars and spiny urchins.

The only operator is **Small Hope Bay Lodge** (p108), highly acclaimed by divers, which offers a whole range of specialist and basic one-/two-tank dives ($80/100) and night and shark dives ($80/85), as well as snorkeling trips ($35). Divers should ask about blue hole dives and ultra-deep continental shelf dives.

BONEFISHING & SPORTFISHING

At least a dozen expert bonefishing guides operate out of Central Andros.

A couple of recommended guides:

Charlie Neymour SPORTFISHING
(242-368-4297)

Andy Smith BONEFISHING
(242-368-4261)

Tours

The Small Hope Bay Lodge (below) offers some great birdwatching treks with ornithologists. Check what is planned closer to the time of your visit.

Sleeping & Eating

Credit cards may not be accepted by guesthouses or some smaller lodgings; check when booking.

BEWARE THE CHICKCHARNIES & LUSCA'S LAIR

If you're walking in the deep Androsian forest and you spot a pair of red eyes glowing at you through the trees, chances are you've run into the dastardly chickcharnie.

Chickcharnies are a strange hybrid of man and bird – red-eyed, three-fingered, owl-like elves with beards and feathered scalps, who live atop cotton or pine trees and hang by their tails. They wreak mayhem on whoever disturbs them, screech like the damned and are quite vain despite their freaky looks.

Some say the chickcharnie legend may have actually sprung from sightings of a real-life creature, the now-extinct Tyto pollens, a 3ft-tall barn owl that lived in the Androsian pineyards until the 16th century.

But don't think you're safe in the water, either! The monstrous octopus Lusca prowls the offshore blue holes of Andros, pulling boats and swimmers into her tentacled clutches. Scuba divers have not yet discovered this vile leggy monster, or maybe we just didn't hear them scream...

Small Hope Bay Lodge RESORT **$$$**
(242-368-2014; www.smallhope.com; Calabash Bay; r $260 per person;) This laid-back eco resort is small enough and isolated enough that everyone gets to know each other – stay a week, and you'll surely come away with new friends. Guests wander around barefoot in the chalet-like main lodge, chatting with the owner or watching movies on a rec room TV. Kids play on the small private beach, while their diver parents clean their scuba rigs nearby. Most people are here on dive packages, though the lodge is also popular with anglers. Everything, from bikes to kayaks to dinners, is included in the daily rate. The lodge takes a genuine interest in sustainability, composing food and making drinking glasses from old wine bottles. Only half of the rustic stone and wood rooms have air conditioning – request your preference at booking.

Lighthouse Yacht Club & Marina MOTEL **$**
(242-368-2305; www.androslighthouse.com; Fresh Creek; r $85;) Large and somewhat institutional-feeling, this pink motel has clean tiled rooms with minifridge set on manicured rolling lawns. There's a restaurant, a pool and a tiki bar open on the weekends.

TOP CHOICE **Taste & See** BAHAMIAN **$$**
(Love Hill; mains $10-20; lunch & dinner) Expect to be embraced when you walk into this homey cafe – literally! Owner Cinderella Hinsey hugs all her guests, whether or not she's met them before. Her love overflows into the food – delectable cracked conch, sautéed lobster, BBQ turkey. The sunny, spotless dining room, perched on stilts above a marsh, is one of Andros' most pleasant lunch spots.

Hank's Place BAHAMIAN **$$**
(Fresh Creek; mains $10-25; lunch & dinner) On concrete pylons overhanging the water, this brown wooden beach bar is a prime spot to munch conch fritters, pork chops or lobster, all washed down with the lethal house cocktail, the Hanky Panky. Look out for weekend fish fries and roasts.

For groceries, try **Adderley's Bargain Mart** or the small store at the **Chickcharnie Hotel**, both in Fresh Creek.

Information

Bahamas Ministry of Tourism (242-368-2286; Andros Town)

Government Medical Clinic (242-368-2038) On the north side of the Fresh Creek Bridge.

Police (242-368-2626; Coakley Town)

Post office (Coakley Town)

Royal Bank of Canada (Calabash Bay; 9:30am-3:30pm Wed) Has an ATM.

Getting There & Around

The Andros Town Airport serves Central Andros. The Bahamas Fast Ferry travels between Nassau and Fresh Creek two or three times weekly. For specific information on flights, boats and ferries, see p103.

The **Lighthouse Yacht Club & Marina** (242-368-2305; www.androslighthouse.com; Fresh Creek) has 18 slips for vessels.

You can rent cars from around $80 per day. Ask a local for a hookup. For a taxi, call **Central Andros Taxi** (242-368-2333).

CARGILL CREEK AREA

South of Fresh Creek, the Queen's Hwy becomes a lonely, pitted track traveling through marshlands and mudflats. This is Andros' prime bonefishing territory; what precious little tourism infrastructure there is exists to cater to anglers on frills-free fishing trips. The two main hamlets are **Cargill Creek**, which opens westward into the expansive flats of both the North and Middle Bights. Two miles further south, **Behring Point** is the literal end of the road. Across the water is Mangrove Cay, but there's no transportation to get there.

Sleeping & Eating

The lodgings are designed for anglers seeking bonefishing packages, not romantic beachy getaways. If you happen to be in the area and just want a room for a night, they can likely accommodate you. Dining options are slim pickin's – if you're just down here for a day-trip, you might want to pack a picnic.

Andros Island Bonefishing Club BONEFISHING LODGE **$$$**
(242-368-5167; www.androsbonefishing.com; Cargill Creek; packages from $1235 per person for 3 nights;) On a scrubby patch of land that was once a sisal plantation, this frills-free collection of bungalows caters to – you guessed it – bonefishers, who wander around the bar area wearing safari hats and carrying rods.

Tranquility Hill Fishing Lodge MOTEL **$$$**
(242-368-4132; www.tranquilityhill.com; Behring Point; packages from $1185 per person for 3 nights;) At the literal end of the Queen's Hwy, this blocky motel sits on a ridge overlooking the bight. Rooms are clean, bright and nothin' fancy.

GET CRABBY

During late spring and early summer, football-sized land crabs cross the road en masse for a paroxysm of mating and egg laying – though many will wind up in Androsian cooking pots instead. Crab hunting is an island-wide sport, done at night with flashlights, net bags and quick reflexes (those suckers can pinch!). The captured crustaceans are usually kept in cages for weeks or months, fed a diet of coconut and mango to fatten them and sweeten their meat. In June taste the results at the **All Andros Crab Fest** in Fresh Creek, a rollicking party and island-wide feast featuring crab soup, baked crab, crab rice, crab patties and 'crab cultural events.'

Sea View Restaurant & Bar BAHAMIAN **$**
(Behring's Point) Locals frequent this place, 100yd south of the Cargill Creek Bridge.

Mangrove Cay

If you're looking to drop off the grid for a while, this is the place. The most rural and isolated chunk of Andros, Mangrove Cay was only blessed with electricity in 1989. The island hasn't changed much in the past century – kids ride rusty bikes on dirt roads, women carry banana bundles on their heads, dogs run wild through the underbrush. The island's one settlement, Moxey Town, is a mere handful of wooden houses overlooking the Middle Bight. So grab a hammock, crack an icy Kalik and let the waves hypnotize you into tranquility.

Sights & Activities

Activities on Mangrove Cay mainly run to lounging on the beach and eating bananas. Ask locals about where to find some of the island's two dozen or so **blue holes**, some hidden in the underbrush, others just offshore (hint: there's one just off the beach at Seascape Inn; you can walk there at low tide). Bonefishers should ask at their hotel about guides, who will charge around $500 per day for two people. Or try **Eddie Bannister** (242-369-0025) or **Leslie Greene** (242-369-0721).

Sleeping & Eating

Be warned – credit card machines are a rarity here. Most visitors to Mangrove Cay eat at their accommodations, which are also happy to serve food to nonguests. There's a small **Fish Fry** with wooden conch shacks in Dorset Park.

TOP CHOICE **Seascape Inn** CABANA RESORT **$**
(242-369-0342; www.seascapeinn.com; cabanas incl breakfast $159;) New Yorkers Mickey and Joan McGowan escaped city life to run this *Swiss Family Robinson*-like colony of beach cabanas, and their friendliness has earned them a loyal following of repeat guests. A small wooden restaurant, perched on stilts above the sand, is the Seascape's heart, where visitors shoot the breeze, play pub games and read battered paperbacks from the book exchange. Outside, you can play with the dogs, borrow kayaks, bikes and snorkel gear, or simply lounge on the silvery sand. The five blue

cabanas are cheery and rustic, with tiled floors and ceiling fans.

Mangrove Cay Inn MOTEL **$$**
(242-369-0069; www.mangrovecayinn.net; r $110;) The closest thing on Mangrove Cay to a traditional motel, with 12 rooms and two cottages done up in homey, floral fabrics and wood-paneled walls. The owners, a friendly Bahamian-American couple, run a casual on-site restaurant serving cheeseburgers, fried fish fingers and the like. The beach is a short walk away. No credit cards.

Swain's Cay Lodge BONEFISHING LODGE **$$**
(242-369-0296; www.swainscaylodge.com; r $199;) Nicer than the average bonefishing lodge, Swain's has eight clean, well-appointed rooms and a restaurant on a quiet stretch of sand.

Dianne Cash BAHAMIAN, SEAFOOD **$$**
(242-369-0430) South of the Seascape Inn, Mangrove native Dianne Cash cooks up legendary stuffed Androsian crab and other local delights, all made to order – call ahead.

Four Kids Bakery BAKERY **$**
(Moxey Town) Stop in for yummy, hot-from-the-oven cassava bread, banana cake or muffins.

Information

Bank of the Bahamas International (242-369-1787; 10am-2pm Mon & Fri)

Police (242-369-0083)

Saunder's Drugs & Notions (242-369-0312)

South Andros

Virtually bypassed by tourists, South Andros has superb bonefishing and some extraordinary silver-and-pink beaches. Look out for Androsian iguanas, which can grow to 5ft in length and dwell in scattered coppices.

Poverty is highly visible here, as there's little industry besides lobstering, crabbing and sponging.

The Queen's Hwy runs from Drigg's Hill, a scrawny hamlet at the island's north tip, through the scrappy settlements of Congo Town, High Rock and The Bluff, petering out in Mars Bay, some 25 miles south.

A small government-run passenger ferry runs from Lisbon Creek to Drigg's Hill.

Sights & Activities

Stretching from Drigg's Hill to Congo Town and beyond, **Congo Town Beach** is a heavenly strip of silver sand fronting gin-clear shallows.

There are a number of semi-defunct straw markets along the Queen's Hwy, and sometimes you'll be lucky enough to catch an elderly South Andros woman selling baskets in front of her house. But your best bet for island art is the studio of **Jerry Davis** (Congo Town, turn at the wooden sign), a local artisan who makes truly wonderful driftwood carvings of groupers, bonefish and Androsian iguanas. Starting at around $30, his work is a fraction of the price you'd pay in Nassau. If he's not around when you stop by, ask a neighbor to give him a call.

In The Bluff, you'll find the trailhead to **Stargate Blue Hole** midway down the road that leads to the water tower; the hole itself is a short walk through the underbrush. Beneath the eerie black surface lie hundreds of feet of caves filled with Ice Age stalactites, a wonderland for brave divers.

Jesse, a young American transplant, runs **Andros Diving** (242-369-1454; www.androsdiving.com; 2-tank dive $125, snorkeling $90), the only dive operation around. His specialty is exploring the bottomless blue hole caves that dot the South Andros shallows, and he knows all the best reefs for elkhead coral and ginormous groupers. Snorkel trips are pricey but take in multiple locations in a half day.

Captain Roggie of **Reel Tight Charters** (242-369-2638; www.androsbahamasfishing.com) is the island's main fishing guide, offering deep sea and reef trips, as well as snorkeling and nature excursions.

Sleeping & Eating

As mentioned earlier, South Andros sees precious little tourism. Almost all visitors are here to stay at Tiamo or the Emerald Palms. Beyond the resorts, food choices are limited to a handful of sometimes-open-sometimes-not conch stands and roadside BBQ stalls.

TOP CHOICE **Emerald Palms Resort** RESORT **$$**
(242-369-2713; www.emerald-palms.com; r $159-245, villas $395-645;) This luxury beach resort would be nice anywhere; on rural South Andros it's a genuine oasis. Airy poolside rooms have four-post beds, crisp white linens

and fresh hibiscus blossoms on the bedside table. Villas pull out all the stops – high ceilings, marble floors, in-room Jacuzzis, gauzy white bed canopies. The lovely pool deck opens directly onto a miles-long stretch of beach. The restaurant's no great shakes, but at the time of writing we heard management was looking for a new chef.

Tiamo RESORT **$$$**
(242-369-2330; www.tiamoresorts.com; all-incl from $895 per night per couple;) Only accessible by boat, this all-inclusive resort caters to couples seeking intimacy and exclusivity. Ten cottages have a luxe ecochic vibe, all pale wood, slate tile and textured linens. Guests lounge on their private porches, swim in the placid, protected beach or sip cocktails on the tiered terraces overlooking the infinity pool. The Michelin-trained chef at the open-air restaurant serves highly rated Caribbean-fusion cuisine. Everything but liquor is included. No kids under 14.

Andros Beach Club GUESTHOUSE **$$$**
(242-369-1454; www.androsbeachclub.com; r from $250;) Jesse of Andros Diving rents out two nice rooms and a villa on his property, a deal popular with laid-back diver types.

Getting There & Around

Refer to p260 for information on international flights to the Bahamas and p103 for information on getting to Andros.

BERRY ISLANDS

POP 800

Just north of Nassau, 30 mostly uninhabited islands freckle the turquoise shallows. Although a popular stop for passing yachties, these islands have virtually no tourism infrastructure and attract precious few traditional vacationers. But if you have your own boat or are willing to shell out for charter flights, the Berries are an ideal place to kick off your shoes and go native. Spend long days cruising from secluded cay to secluded cay, bonefishing in the gin-clear flats, beachcombing the starfish-spangled sands, snorkeling in isolated coves.

Although the Berry Islands only make up 12 sq miles of land, they span a distance of about 30 miles across the ocean. The largest and most important island is Great Harbour Cay, a 10-mile-long, mile-wide stretch of scrub-covered rolling terrain. Chub Cay, a favorite of mid-20th-century jetsetters, now attracts yachties and big game fishermen. Several other cays are privately owned, such as Bond's Cay, a private bird sanctuary, Coco Cay, owned by Royal Caribbean cruise lines for their guests' exclusive use, and Great Stirrup Cay, owned by Norwegian Cruise Line for the same purpose.

History

In the 1960s Douglas Fairbanks Jr and others among the US social elite took Great Harbour Cay to their hearts. The Great Harbour Cay Club was formed, nine rippling fairways were sculpted on the rises falling down to the sea, and marinas were built and lined with luxury waterfront homes. Jet-setters flocked to these shores, including Brigitte Bardot, Cary Grant and members of the Rockefeller clan (mobster Meyer Lansky also had a stake). However, the troubled club was closed and ransacked in the 1970s.

Since then the island has mostly kept its own counsel. Occasional visitors arrive to restock their boats and join the locals in fishing expeditions.

Getting There & Around

AIR

The Berry Islands are served by two airports: Great Harbour Cay Airport, based on Great Harbour Cay; and Chub Cay Airport, at Chub Cay.

The following airlines fly to the Berry Islands:

Cat Island Air (242-377-3318; www.flycatislandair.com) Flies into Great Harbour Cay from Nassau twice daily.

Gulf Stream Connection (954-985-5241; www.gulfstreamconnection.com) Flies from Fort Lauderdale, Florida, to Great Harbour Cay and Chub Cay three times a week.

BOAT

Call the **Dockmaster's Office** (242-394-1237) in Nassau and check the website of the **Bahamas Ministry of Tourism** (www.bahamas.com) for the latest schedules and prices.

The following mail boats are available:

MV *Bimini Mack* Departs Nassau for Chub Cay, Bimini and Cat Cay on Thursday ($45, 12 hours), returning Monday.

MV *Captain Gurth Deane* Departs Nassau for Bullock's Harbour ($45, seven hours) on Friday, returning Sunday.

MARINAS Boaters and pilots arriving from abroad must clear **Immigration**

Berry Islands

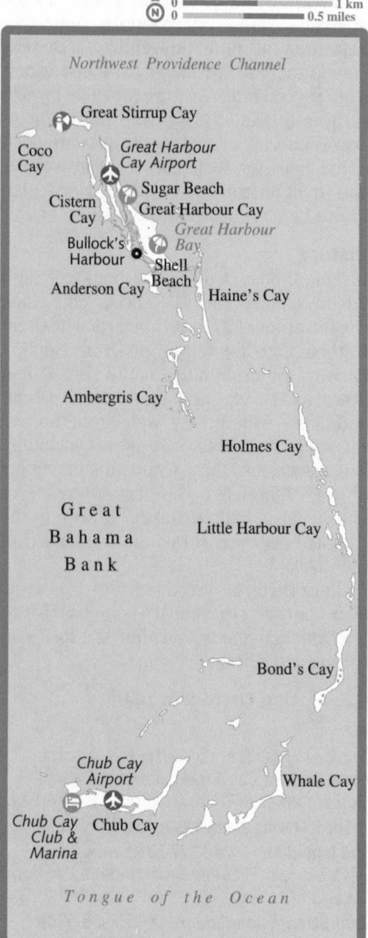

(242-367-8112) and **Customs** (242-367-8566) at Great Harbour Cay.

Great Harbour Cay Yacht Club & Marina (242-367-8005; VHF Channels 16 & 68) Has 86 slips and full services.

Great Harbour Cay

POP 370

This is the main center of the islands, where most islanders live and where most visitors will find company, lodgings and food. **Great Harbour Marina** (242-367-8005) is built on a narrow channel south of the island's main settlement, **Bullock's Harbour**, and is entered via a slender cut with cliffs to each side.

The island's main attraction is the 8-mile-long white-sand beach along the eastern shore, where the warm shallows are every shade of green. The beach is formed by two great scallops: **Sugar Beach** to the north and **Great Harbour Bay** to the south. A few dozen expats have houses along the shore. Great Harbour Bay runs south to **Shell Beach** and a reef (exposed at low tide) that is good for finding sand dollars.

Birds prefer the mangroves, flats and salt pools on the west of the island, where herons and egrets hunch and watch for their lunch. Most of the interior is smothered in thatch palm, scrub and casuarinas, and snakes and butterflies abound. There are vast flats for bonefishing. Great Harbour Dr runs the length of the east coast.

The island's annual Homecoming Regatta is held each August, with plenty of home cooking, live music and fun.

Happy People (242-367-8117; Great Harbour Marina; 8am-5pm) rents boats, cars, bikes and snorkel and fishing gear.

Bonefishing guides can be hired through the marinas. Try **Percy Darville** (242-461-4149; www.bonefish.cbt.cc; Great Harbour Yacht Club & Marina; half-/full day $400/600). Sport-fishing boats need permits.

There are no hotels on the island – most visitors rent a villa or a town house by the marina. For rental info, contact realtor **Lauren Higgs** (242-67-8135; www.coldwellbanker bahamas.com; villas per night from $100; ❄).

For food, try the casual **Beach Club** by the airport or **Coolie Mae's**, serving up Bahamian-style fried seafood by the Marina. There are a handful of small grocery stores in Bullock's Harbour.

Information

Medical clinic (242-367-8400; Bullock's Harbour; 9am-2pm Mon-Fri)

Police (242-367-8344; Bullock's Harbour)

Post office (Bullock's Harbour; 9am-5:30pm Mon-Fri) Has a public telephone kiosk.

Getting There & Around

Most visitors arrive at Great Harbour Cay either by charter plane, private boat or mail boat. You can get around mainly on foot, or rent a bicycle or scooter. For more information, see p111.

Chub Cay

The southernmost isle in the chain, this little place has been popular over the years with all sorts of moneyed folk who like to fish, from Texan businessmen to musician Quincy Jones and comedian Bill Cosby.

The 4-mile-long Chub Cay sits at the edge of the Tongue of the Ocean and offers fabulous wall-diving. One of the best sites is **Mama Rhoda Rock**, protected by the Bahamas National Trust and known for its moray eels, lobsters and yellow trumpetfish, as well as healthy staghorn and elkhorn coral. There's a shipwreck with a cannon nearby. Divers will require their own gear.

Refer to p111 for information on travel to the Berry Islands.

Abacos

TELEPHONE CODE: 242 / POPULATION: 16,700 / AREA: 650 SQ MILES

Includes »

Best Beaches

» Tahiti Beach, Elbow Cay (p123)

» Treasure Cay Beach, Treasure Cay (p134)

» Coco Bay, Green Turtle Cay (p128)

» Gillam Bay Beach, Green Turtle Cay (p128)

Best Places to Stay

» Lofty Fig Villas, Marsh Harbour (p119)

» Hope Town Harbour Lodge, Elbow Cay (p124)

» Abaco Inn, Elbow Cay (p124)

» Dolphin Beach Resort, Great Guana Cay (p127)

Why Go?

Yachting and the Abacos go together like wind and sail: this glittering crescent of islands and cays is known as the 'Sailing Capital of the World.'

The main island is 130-mile-long Abaco, whose main city, Marsh Harbour, is the prime launch pad for exploring the surrounding cays and reefs. The Loyalist Cays – Elbow, Great Guana, Man O' War and Green Turtle – beckon offshore just a short ferry ride away. Named after the 18th-century settlers who came here to avoid prosecution during the American Revolution, they're an inviting collection of clapboard homes, narrow streets and chock-a-block museums.

But it's not all fish and history. The Abacos may be most fondly known for their fantastic island bars, which make this lovely chain the best Bahamian spot for a yacht crawl.

When to Go

Green Turtle Cay

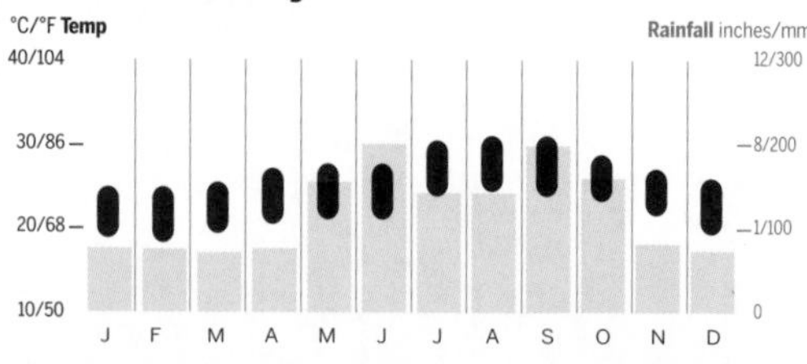

December–February High season means balmy weather and better nightlife, but higher prices.

July Regatta Week brings hundreds of yachties to the islands. Party time!

August–November Hurricane season brings things to a slowdown, with some hotels closing while others slash their prices.

History

After decimating the Lucayan Indian population on 'Habacoa,' early Spanish explorers moved on to more fruitful lands. It was not until the American Revolution, when numerous Loyalists left the newly independent USA in the 1700s and settled in the Abacos, that a thriving population began.

Their names linger on today in quaint communities whose residents cherish their past and independence. On the eve of independence in 1972, Loyalist Abaconians petitioned the Queen to be made a British crown colony, separate from the Bahamas. Upon refusal, some even contemplated a revolution. Each cay still follows its own Protestant church, but the islanders share a strong Christian ethic.

The Loyalist settlers were mostly merchants and craftspeople involved in trading, boatbuilding and salvaging shipwrecks, and they became relatively wealthy.

This island group was severely affected by Hurricane Floyd in 1999 and Jeanne and Frances in 2004. However, rebuilding began immediately after the hurricanes passed, although roads remain potholed and many outlying villages still bear visible damage.

National Parks & Reserves

The Abacos has four national parks and reserves: Pelican Cays Land & Sea Park (p126), which preserves the barrier islands and coral reefs south of Tilloo Cay; Tilloo Cay National Reserve (p126) is an 11-acre shoreline area, popular with birdwatchers; the Abaco National Park (p133), which protects the native habitat of the endangered Bahama parrot and other wildlife; and Black Sound Cay National Reserve (p244), which has mangrove habitats loved by birds.

Getting There & Away

Most travelers to the Abacos fly into Marsh Harbour's International Airport, about 3 miles southeast of Marsh Harbour; others arrive on their own boats, or on the weekly mail boat from Nassau (see p121). For information on international flights to the Abacos, see p260. For information on flights from other islands in the Bahamas, see p263.

Getting Around

You'll need your own transportation if you want to explore the main island outside of Marsh Harbour, where a car-, bicycle- and motorbike-rental agency is fortunately based (see p122). An excellent ferry service links the mainland and the major cays, while boats can also be easily rented to explore further afield. Golf carts are used on all inhabited cays.

FERRY **Albury's Ferry Service** (☎242-367-3147; www.alburysferry.com) Operates scheduled daily water taxis from Marsh Harbour to Elbow Cay, Man O' War Cay and Great Guana Cay.

Bahamas Ferries (☎242-323-2166; www.bahamasferries.com; Nassau) Comfy passenger ferry makes the three-hour trip between Nassau and Sandy Point twice weekly; keep in mind that Sandy Point is 1½ hours from Marsh Harbour with no public transportation or rental car agencies.

Green Turtle Ferry (☎242-365-4166) Makes eight daily trips between the Treasure Cay dock (a few miles north of Treasure Cay town) and Green Turtle Cay, from 8:30am to 5pm.

Pinder's Ferry (☎242-365-2356) Sets off twice daily (one way $40, one hour) from McLean's Town, Grand Bahama, for Crown Haven, Abaco and back.

Marsh Harbour

POP 5300

Believe it or not, this one-stoplight town is the third-largest city in the Bahamas. Situated on a peninsula, quiet Marsh Harbour has worked to establish itself as a small tourism and boating center for visitors to the Abacos. It's a pleasant enough place, with most of the hotels and restaurants lining a small strip of road alongside the marina. Most visitors stop here to refuel, shop for groceries, get cash (seriously, DO take advantage of the ATM) or rest for a night or two before sailing on or hopping a ferry to the cays.

The ferry docks for Elbow Cay and Man O' War are at the eastern end of Bay St and the Great Guana Cay ferry stops beside the Conch Inn. For Treasure Cay, follow the Bootle Hwy 17 miles north from Marsh Harbour. The Green Turtle Cay ferry dock is a few miles further north off the Bootle.

Sights

Marsh Harbour is a little lacking in terms of sights.

Abaco Neem PLANTATION

(☎242-367-4117; www.abaconeem.com; McKay Blvd, Marsh Harbour; ⊙9am-5pm Mon-Sat) In Casuarina Point, 14 miles south of Marsh Harbour, a few enterprising Bahamians have coaxed the notoriously poor Abaconian soil into supporting a thriving organic neem plantation. The neem – a type of tree native to India – is then transported to the company's Marsh Harbour factory, where its leaves and fruits are transformed into a variety of medicinal and cosmetic products. Visitors can watch employees pound dried neem leaves into powder, or pick up bars of lavender-scented neem soap or bottles of neem oil bugspray (if you're headed for the cays, you'll need it!). If you're bound for Casuarina Point, call ahead to see about tours of the plantation.

Activities

Though most visitors use Marsh Harbour as a jumping-off point for visiting the cays, there are several dive operators,

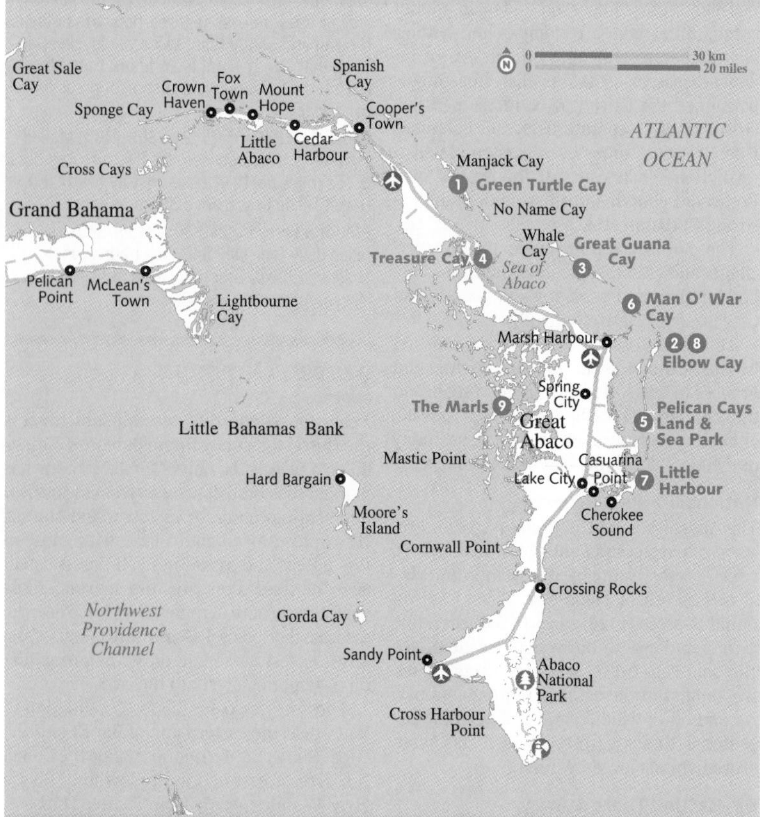

Abacos Highlights

1. Sipping a Goombay Smash at the source, **Miss Emily's Blue Bee Bar** (p132) on Green Turtle Cay
2. Renting a golf cart and zipping about on gorgeous, historic **Elbow Cay** (p122)
3. Partying at the famous Sunday pig roast at **Nipper's Beach Bar & Grill** (p127) on Great Guana Cay
4. Sunning on the fabulous talcum powder sands of **Treasure Cay Beach** (p134)
5. Diving among turtles, rays and crayon-colored fish in the **Abacos'** (p126) reefs and marine parks
6. Talking history with the Loyalists on **Man O' War Cay** (p125), where little has changed in 200 years
7. Making new friends at **Pete's Pub & Gallery** (p133) in Little Harbour – hard to get to, but so worth it
8. Climbing the iconic red-and-white **lighthouse** (p123) at Hope Town, Elbow Cay
9. Bonefishing the endless, uninhabited mangrove wetlands of **the Marls** (opposite)

fishing guides and tour companies operating right out of town. If you want a taste of the yachting life but lack your own vessel, several rental companies will set you up with a sailboat and (if you so desire) a captain for DIY cruising adventures.

Diving & Snorkeling

There are some tremendous and easy snorkeling sites to enjoy in the Abacos. Sandy Cay Reef in Pelican Cays Land & Sea Park is renowned for its population of spotted eagle rays and huge stingrays, Fowl Cay Reef in Fowl Cay Preserve for friendly groupers, and Pelican Park in Pelican Cays Land & Sea Park for eagle rays and sea turtles.

A huge variety of dive sites take in wrecks, walls, caverns and coral kingdoms, including Bonita Wreck, a WWII wreck populated by groupers that like to be hand-fed; Cathedral, a swim-through cavern with rays and parrotfish; and Tarpon Cave, a 50ft drop-off with smiling moray eels.

The thrilling prospect of blue-hole diving also draws many experienced divers to Abaco. These vertical caves can be found both inland and in the ocean shallows.

Many dive operators also offer snorkel trips for around $70.

Above and Below Abaco DIVING, SNORKELING
(☎242-367-0350; www.scuba-diving-abaco-bahamas.com; Bay St) Offers two-tank dives ($125), all-day island-hopping tours ($135, includes one dive) and full NAUI certification courses (from $550). Don't miss the Mystical Blue Hole, a stalactite-filled inland sinkhole where the water's as clear as air.

Dive Abaco DIVING, SNORKELING
(☎242-367-2787; www.diveabaco.com; Conch Inn Hotel & Marina, Bay St) Offers two-tank dives ($115) in the vibrant reef of Fowl Cay, night dives ($115) and NAUI and PADI cert courses ($635). Specialties include a shark-observation dive ($135), where Caribbean reef sharks gather to gnaw a frozen 'chumsicle' of fish while you watch, and an inland blue-hole dive ($135). Also runs a boozy sunset cruise ($50) and several fun snorkel/dive day-trips.

Bonefishing & Sportfishing

The Marls of Abaco, a 400-sq-mile stretch of mangrove flats on the island's uninhabited southwest side, is a bonefisher's Valhalla. The average price for bonefishing commences at around $400/500 per half-/full-day excursion. Sportfishing is also excellent, the warm seas teeming with marlin, wahoo and blackfin tuna.

JR's Bonefish BONEFISHING, SPORTFISHING
(☎242-366-3058; www.jrsbonefishabaco.com; Casuarina Point) Jr and his guides know the best secluded flats for spotting the elusive 'gray ghosts.' Also offers wild boar hunting.

Justin Sands Bonefishing BONEFISHING, SPORTFISHING
(☎242-367-3526; www.bahamasvg.com/justfish.html; Marsh Harbour) This is run by Captain Justin Sands, a past Abaco Bonefish Champion, which means he knows where to find the slippery critters you desire.

Danny Sawyer BONEFISHING, SPORTFISHING
(☎242-367-3577; fishsmiley@yahoo.com) Orvis-certified, Danny knows the top spots for finding bigger 'ocean bonefish.'

Jay Sawyer BONEFISHING, SPORTFISHING
(☎242-367-3941, 242-367-2089) Makes custom flys for Marls trips or shallow-water permit fishing.

Boat Rentals

Sailboats and motorboats can be rented at most marinas. Demand often exceeds supply, so make reservations early. These operators can be reached on VHF Channel 16. Rates do not include fuel and gas for cooking, but boats are provided with communication and safety equipment. Local weather reports can be heard on FM radio 93.5 and VHF marine channel 68.

Blue Wave Boat Rentals BOAT RENTAL
(☎242-367-3910; www.bluewaverentals.com; Harbour View Marina) Charges $200/500/1000 per day/three days/week for a 21ft Dusky, a favored family craft (rates are cheaper in low season). They also have 26ft Paramounts for $260/375/1350 per day/three days/week, as well as larger Duskys and Ocean Pros.

Seahorse Boat Rentals BOAT RENTAL
(☎242-367-5460; www.seahorseboatrentals.com; Abaco Beach Resort, Bay St) Rents a 17ft Boston Whaler for $165/735 per day/week or a 20-ft Albury Brothers for $210/1015 per day/week, among others.

Yacht Charters

Abaco is a sailor's paradise, so don't let the lack of a yacht keep you from enjoying the pleasure of island-hopping with the wind in your hair. Experienced yachties can opt for a 'bareboat charter,' which means you're on your own. For landlubbers, a

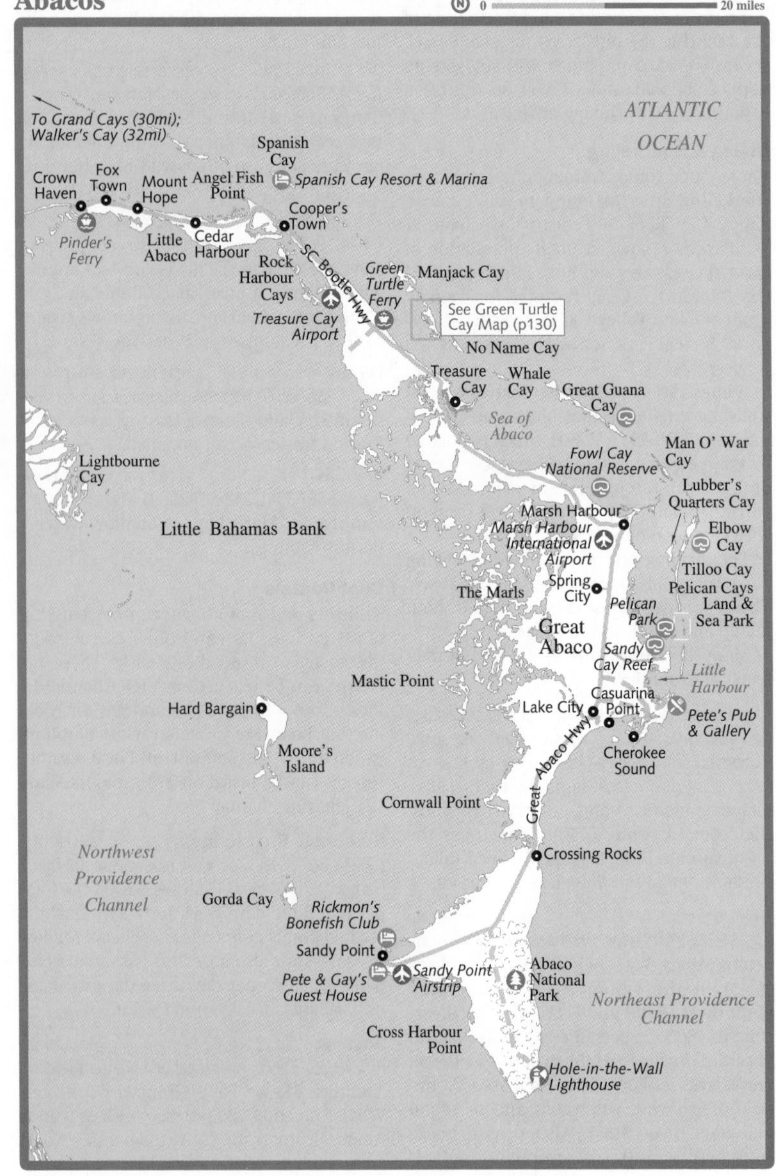

crewed charter comes with a captain and sometimes a cook.

Moorings YACHT CHARTERS
(☎242-367-4000; www.moorings.com; weekly from $3,300, Conch Inn Marina) This international outfitter has a dozen monohulls and catamarans on offer for custom-crewed or bareboat cruises.

Florida Yacht Charters YACHT CHARTERS
(☎242-367-4853; www.floridayacht.com; Mangoes Marina; weekly rates from $3,600) Luxury sloops sleep up to four.

THE BAHAMAS' MOST PHOTOGENIC LIGHTHOUSES

Though its seas are full of treacherous, barely submerged reefs, the Bahamas was rather late in building lighthouses. Why the hold-up? Well, its inhabitants were busy making a killing as 'wreckers,' salvaging goods and parts from the carcasses of reef-snagged shipwrecks – why build a lighthouse that would only take away your main source of income? Much to the wrecker's dismay, lighthouses were eventually called for, and Scot-Irish lighthouse builders arrived in the mid-1800s. These are some of their handiwork:

» **Elbow Cay Lighthouse** (p123) Built in 1864, this red-and-white striped beauty graces many a postcard; you can get here on the Elbow Cay ferry if you ask the captain nicely.

» **Hole-in-the-Wall Lighthouse** (p134) From 1836, this red stone tower is hidden deep within Abaco National Park.

» **Coakley Town Lighthouse** In Andros' Fresh Creek (p107), this 1892 gray stone turret looks like it's on loan from a medieval castle.

» **Hog Island Lighthouse** On Paradise Island ('Hog Island,' before its PR-motivated name change; p49), this 1817 white brick tower is the oldest lighthouse in the Bahamas and all of the West Indies.

» **Dixon Hill Lighthouse** (p180) On San Salvador, this 1887 round white tower is still in operation, with tours given by the working lightkeepers.

» **Great Inagua Lighthouse** (p193) From 1870, this 112ft-tall white tower still operates by hand-cranked kerosene motor.

Tours

Great Abaco Express NATURE, HISTORY
(☎242-367-0200; thegreatabacoexpress@yahoo.com) Tour guide Glender Knowles is a fountain of knowledge about Abaconian nature, history and culture. Join one of her customizable tours – birdwatching in Abaco National Park, Loyalist history in the cays, lighthouse trips – and get ready to be edified.

Festivals & Events

Check out the website www.destinationabaco.net or **Bahamas Ministry of Tourism** (☎242-367-3067; www.bahamas.com; Memorial Plaza, Queen Elizabeth Dr; ⏲9am-5:30pm Mon-Fri) for up-to-date information on these and many other events.

Arts for the Parks In February, local artists sell their crafts, jewelry and paintings to benefit local parks.

Marsh Harbour Wahoo Championship The first-ever big-game fishing competition kicks off in February, 2011.

Bahamas Billfish South Abaco Championship (www.bahamasbillfish.com) Five days in April chasing fish and a record or two.

Bahamas Billfish South Abaco Championship Stage 4 (www.bahamasbillfish.com) Six days in June chasing Stage 4's record at Treasure Cay.

Goombay Summer Festival Party, party, party at Marsh Harbour's Junkanoo Rush, which runs June through July.

Abaco Regatta (www.regattatimeinabaco.com) Held over a week in July, this great regatta commences with the 'cheeseburger in paradise' pre-race party; festivities really jump off after the final chew.

Sleeping

Midrange accommodations in Marsh Harbour book up quickly, even in low season. Most visitors only spend a night or two here before heading on to the cays, but if you're looking for a long-term stay try **Abaco Real Estate Agency** (☎242-367-2719; www.abacobahamas.com; Bay St).

TOP CHOICE **Lofty Fig Villas** VILLAS $$
(☎242-367-2681; loftyfig.com; Bay St; r from $120; ❄📶🏊👪) This mini-village of canary-bright duplexes works well for budget-minded travelers wanting to be close to the harborside action. Villas, which cluster around a small pool and outdoor grill area, are big, bright, airy and clean. Each has a small kitchen, flat panel TV and an open porch. Don't doubt any helpful tips provided by the Fig's friendly owner, Sid. The man knows Abaco and if he says it's cheaper to rent a car than hire a taxi to get to Treasure Cay, believe him.

Conch Inn Hotel & Marina HOTEL **$$**
(☎242-367-4000; www.conchinn.com; Bay St; r $120; ❄📶🏊) Yachties, divers and cay-hoppers inevitably buzz past this queen bee during extended Abaco vacations. Adjacent to a busy marina, Curly Tails restaurant, Dive Abaco and the Great Guana Cay dock, it's a well-situated gateway for exploring. Mid-sized rooms have white tile floors, wicker-style furniture, a fridge and a coffee-maker.

Abaco Beach Resort at Boat Harbour RESORT **$$$**
(☎242-367-2158; www.abacobeachresort.com; Bay St; r from $290; ❄📶🏊) Down a gated drive, Marsh Harbour's only resort sits on several fragrant acres of manicured hibiscus and casuarina palms set against a fat wedge of private beach. The 180-slip marina makes this a yachtie favorite. In high season, the swim-up pool bar is the place to be. Rooms, while beachy and pleasant, don't quite warrant the price tag (expect to spend an additional $100 or more per night on taxes and fees). The restaurant, Angler's, is a perennial favorite for upscale seafood.

Island Breezes Motel MOTEL **$$**
(☎242-367-3776; E Bay St; r $127; ❄📶) Nicer than its unassuming exterior suggests, this eight-room motel has airy tiled rooms with high ceilings and big bathrooms, and it's right in the center of town.

Eating & Drinking

Get your grub on while you're in town, as dining selection in the cays can be…limited. For groceries, stock up at the shining new **Maxwell's Supermarket** (Nathan Key Dr; ⏲8am-7pm Mon-Thu, to 8pm Fri & Sat, 9am-3pm Sun), with a standout selection of produce and imported goods.

TOP CHOICE **Conchy Joe's** SEAFOOD **$**
(Bay St; mains $5-10; ⏲11am-3pm & 5pm-late Tue-Sat) Stand on the gangway of this floating conch shack and watch Conchy Joe (AKA 'Brent') expertly flay live conch, tossing the shells into the water with a splash. If you're lucky, he'll let you sample the pissle (don't ask)! Inside the tiny kitchen, Brent's wife expertly fries the fresh conch or chops it into conch salad. The salad comes 'skin on' or 'skin off' – locals prefer it on. Sides vary, depending on what ingredients are available. No seating, but there are some benches on the shore nearby.

Snappa's SEAFOOD, PUB **$$**
(www.snappasbar.com; Bay St; mains $11-30; ⏲11am-late) We love Snappa's for its awesome grilled seafood – which can be darn hard to find on the Out Islands. The thick, grilled mahi mahi sandwich is superb and with a splash of Conchy Joe's Pepper Sauce you might just nibble into heaven. Live music is the evening draw at this marina-side mecca Wednesday through Saturday, with the biggest party crowds descending on Friday.

Jamie's Place BAHAMIAN, AMERICAN **$$**
(☎242-367-2880; Bay St; mains $7-18; ⏲breakfast, lunch & dinner) It's T-shirts, ball caps and flip flops at this sparely decorated diner where locals greet each other by name and Bahamian and American dishes are served up piping hot. For our money, the fried chicken is some of the best in the islands, served with a fat square of scrumptiously gooey baked macaroni 'n' cheese.

Angler's FUSION **$$$**
(☎242-367-2158; www.abacobeachresort.com; Abaco Beach Resort at Boat Harbour, Bay St; mains $16-34; ⏲breakfast, lunch & dinner Mon-Sat) At the Abaco Beach Resort, this waterfront restaurant is a favorite with yachties and wealthy expats. The Asian- and Caribbean-inflected menu runs from dumplings (pot stickers) to sesame-encrusted tuna steak with pickled ginger, as well as some local standbys like conch fritters. Steaks are also big. Orchids, white tablecloths and live music add a swank touch. Lunch is much more casual, with pizzas, salads and sandwiches.

Jib Room Restaurant & Bar SEAFOOD **$**
(☎242-367-2700; www.jibroom.com; Pelican Shores Rd; lunch $10-15, dinner $25; ⏲lunch Wed-Sat, dinner Wed & Sat) Got the post-snorkel munchies? After a morning at Mermaid Reef, order a salad or sandwich on the Jib's harborside deck and tell fish tales as the yacht's pull in. On Saturday nights, everyone's here for steaks, live music and dancing. Reserve ahead.

Bahamas Family Market BAHAMIAN, FAST FOOD **$**
(Queen Elizabeth Dr; mains $3-10; ⏲5:30am-8pm) This friendly convenience store is our pick for cheap breakfasts and snacks to go. Expect some cheerful banter or local tips along with your coconut breads, sandwiches and meat patties.

Mangoes BAHAMIAN, AMERICAN $$
(242-367-2366; www.mangoesmarina.com; Bay St; mains $18-49; lunch & dinner) Jack Daniel's-steeped BBQ ribs and potent house cocktails keep the international crowds happy at this bright and beachy harbor fave.

Java COFFEE SHOP $
(Bay St; mains $4-6; 8am-5pm Sun-Tue, to 9pm Wed-Sat) A morning must for java, pastries and local art.

Shopping

Conch Pearl Galleries JEWELRY
(Royal Harbour Village, Bay St) Bahamian art and jewelry, including items made from rare peachy-pink conch pearls.

Iggy Biggy SOUVENIRS
(Bay St) Across from the Conch Inn Hotel & Marina, this Bahamian chain sells resort clothing, T-shirts, gifts, jewelry and island music.

John Bull JEWELRY, PERFUME
(Bay St) This Bahamian chain hawks high-quality duty-free jewelry, perfume, watches, china and more.

Information

Emergency

Police (242-367-2560; Dundas Town Rd)

Fire Department (242-367-2000)

Internet Access

Most Marsh Harbour hotels and many restaurants have wi-fi for guests.

Media & Internet Resources

Abaconian (www.abaconian.com) The island's monthly newspaper.

Abaco Life (www.abacolife.com; $2) A quarterly island magazine with features and lifestyle stories.

Destination Abaco (destinationabaco.com) The Ministry of Tourism's useful dining, sights and accommodations brochure is available at most hotels and online.

Radio Abaco (www.radioabaco935.com) The station broadcasts on 93.5FM.

www.abacotoday.com Website with boat rental, accommodations and restaurant info.

Medical Services

Abaco Family Medicine (242-367-2295, after hr 242-359-6569; Don McKay Blvd; 9am-5pm Mon-Fri, to noon Sat)

Abaco Island Pharmacy (242-367-2544; Don McKay Blvd; 8:30am-6pm Mon-Sat, 9am-12pm Sun)

Agape Family Dental Centre (242-367-4355; Don McKay Blvd)

Marsh Harbour Government Clinic (242-367-0633; Don McKay Blvd)

Money

All the listed banks have ATMs.

Commonwealth Bank (Queen Elizabeth Dr; 8:30am-3pm Mon-Thu, to 4:30pm Fri)

First Caribbean International Bank (242-367-2166; fax 242-367-2156; Don McKay Blvd; 9:30am-3pm Mon-Thu, to 4:30pm Fri)

Royal Bank of Canada (242-367-2420; Don McKay Blvd; 9:30am-3pm Mon-Thu, to 4:30pm Fri)

Scotiabank (242-367-2142; fax 242-367-2565; Don McKay Blvd; 9:30am-3pm Mon-Thu, to 4:30pm Fri)

Post

Post office (Don McKay Blvd)

Tourist Information

Abaco Tourist Office (242-367-3067; fax 242-367-3068; Memorial Plaza, Queen Elizabeth Dr, Marsh Harbour; www.go-abacos.com; 9am-5:30pm Mon-Fri)

Getting There & Away

Air

Marsh Harbour International Airport (MHH; 242-367-3039) is on the southwest fringe of town. For information on international flights here, see p260. For details of airlines flying to Marsh Harbour from within the Bahamas, see p263.

Quoted fares are one way.

ROUTE	COST	FREQUENCY
Marsh Harbour–Freeport	$85	2 daily
Marsh Harbour–Moore's Island	$50	3 weekly
Marsh Harbour–Nassau	$90	several daily
Marsh Harbour–North Eleuthera	$75	2 weekly
Marsh Harbour–Treasure Cay	$39	2 daily
Treasure Cay–Freeport	$75	several daily

Boat

MAIL BOAT Contact the **Dockmaster's Office** (242-393-1064) at Potter's Cay in Nassau to confirm schedules, and for further contact and fare details. *Captain Gurth Dean* sails weekly from Nassau to Marsh Harbour

($45 one way, six hours). See p266 for more details.

FERRY Albury's Ferry Service (☎242-367-3147; www.alburysferry.com; one way/round trip $15/25, children half price) Operates scheduled daily water taxis to Elbow Cay (Hope Town, 20 min, seven times daily 7:15am-5:45pm), Man O' War Cay (20 minutes, five times daily, 10:30am-5:45pm) and Great Guana Cay (30 minutes, five times daily 6:45am-5:45pm). The dock for Elbow and Man O' War services is at the east end of Bay St; the dock for Great Guana Cay services is at the Conch Inn Hotel & Marina. Private charters are also available.

MARINAS All the following marinas can supply electricity and water.

Abaco Beach Resort and Boat Harbour (☎242-367-3910; www.abacobeachresort.com) Offers daily ($3.25 per foot) and long-term ($1.50 per foot for 90 days or more) dockage for vessels up to 200ft. The resort's full marina, accommodations and dining facilities are available with their 200 slips.

Conch Inn Hotel & Marina (☎242-367-4000; www.conchinn.com) Eighty slips accommodate boats up to 200ft. Costs $1.40 per foot for short-term stays.

Harbour View Marina (☎242-367-3910; www.harbourviewmarina.com) Centrally located, with slips from $0.85 per foot for long-term stays, $1.50 for short-term for vessels up to 120ft.

Mangoes Marina (☎242-376-4255; www.mangoesmarina.com) Adjacent to the Moorings, this marina has 29 slips at $1.50 per foot, and restaurant and bar facilities.

Getting Around

Car & Motorbike

Rental Wheels (☎242-367-4643; www.rentalwheels.com; Bay St; ⏲8am-5pm Mon-Fri, 9am-1pm Sat & Sun) Located in the tourist center, this is the only outfit open on Sundays. Bicycles are $10/45 per day/week, motorbikes are $45/200 and cars are $65/300.

Sea Star Rentals (☎242-367-4887; Marsh Harbour International Airport; ⏲8:30am-5pm Mon-Sat) Has handy premises at the airport, and rents cars from $65 per day.

A&P Auto Rentals (☎242-367-2655; Don McKay Blvd) Rents older-model cars from $70 per day.

Taxi

Taxi fares are pre-established. A ride between Marsh Harbour's airport and most hotels costs $15 for two people. Taxis run up and down Marsh Harbour and are easy to flag down.

LOYALIST CAYS

East of Marsh Harbour lie three Loyalist Cays: Elbow, Man O' War and Great Guana. The fourth Loyalist Cay, Green Turtle, lies miles to their northwest.

Elbow Cay

POP 310

Postcard-pretty Hope Town welcomes your arrival on Elbow Cay with its 120ft-high red-and-white-ringed lighthouse, set on the eastern slope of a splendid harbor. As you approach the docks, an entrancing toy-town collection of immaculate white and pastel-colored cottages will come into view. Tiny gardens full of bougainvillea and flowering shrubs spill their blossoms over picket fences and walls, and pedestrians stroll along the two narrow lanes that encircle the village.

Lying 6 miles east of Marsh Harbour, this 5-mile-long island mostly relies on low-key tourism for its income. Hope Town's council is responsible for the conservative but charming community by maintaining strict building and business codes, and banning cars in the village. The hamlet was founded in 1785 by Loyalists from South Carolina whose blond, blue-eyed descendants still live here, interacting, but not intermarrying, with African-Abaconians.

A blight in 1938 ruined the island's sponge-bed industry, but some locals still make a living from boat-building and fishing.

In July Hope Town hosts Regatta Week, a lively mix of sailing races and land-based festivities.

Sights

TOP CHOICE **Wyannie Malone Museum** MUSEUM (www.hopetownmuseum.com; Back St; adult/family $3/5; ⏲10am-3pm Mon-Sat, closed Aug-Oct) Wyannie Malone, a South Carolina Loyalist whose husband was killed during the American Revolution, fled to Elbow Cay with her four children and helped found Hope Town. Today, the Malone name is spread across the Bahamas, and Wyannie is considered the spiritual matriarch of Hope Town. Her story, and that of Elbow Cay, is told at this small but engaging museum. Downstairs, check out a 1783 *New York Post* article calling for a meeting for all Tories intending to move to the Abacos.

OUT ISLAND ARCHITECTURE

If you squint and ignore the palm trees, you might think you were in Cape Cod, not Elbow Cay. The Loyalist Cays have a unique architectural style thanks to the influence of the Loyalists, who built postcard-pretty villages on Elbow, Green Turtle and Man O' War Cays.

Loyalist houses are usually small clapboard cottages painted with paints derived from local pine and mixed with ochre, sienna and other mineral or organic pigments. Blue and white pigments were the most expensive, hence the classic white cottage with blue shutters was originally a Loyalist status symbol.

The Out Islands are also peppered with tiny square stone buildings, former slave homes that have survived decay and natural disaster. Many are still inhabited. Each is the size of a pillbox, with a steep-angled, four-sided roof and an open kitchen in back, but no toilet. Communal outhouses (they, too, still stand) were built along the shore, where one would make a deposit straight into the sea.

Upstairs, look for shipwreck artifacts and old island photos.

Elbow Cay Lighthouse LIGHTHOUSE
(8am-4pm Mon-Fri, 8am-noon Sat) The island's signature attraction, the candy-striped lighthouse, was an object of community-wide loathing when built in 1863. Many here supplemented their incomes by salvaging loot off ships that crashed against the cay's treacherous reefs – usually one a month. An 89ft lighthouse was the last thing these 'wreckers' needed. Today, you can check out views from the top. There's no admission, just follow the signs, walk up 101 steps and – if you dare – push your way through a small trap door to panoramic views from a scare-your-mother balcony. To get here, ask the ferry operator to drop you at the lighthouse, and catch the next mainland ferry by waving to the captain from the dock.

Tahiti Beach BEACH
South of Hope Town, the Queen's Highway continues along a narrow peninsula between the ocean and White Sound, a shallow, mangrove-lined bay with the Sea Spray Resort & Marina at its southern end. Follow the road through an upscale residential neighborhood to Tahiti Beach (you can ignore the 'Private Property' signs; this is the only way to get to this beach), which extends as a sandbar along the peninsula. Though small, its waters are warm and exquisitely clear. For the best views, round the peninsula on foot.

Cholera Cemetery CEMETERY
(Cemetery Rd) Decrepit graves recall the cholera epidemic that swept through Hope Town in 1850, claiming one-third of the population. Note the weathered Betrothal Bench at the crest of the hill. Cemetery Rd is off Back St.

Activities

The reefs off the Atlantic side of Elbow Cay are excellent for diving and snorkeling. The waters near Hope Town and the northern tip of the cay are calmer and are easily reached by swimming from shore. Staghorn, elkhorn, star and brain coral are abundant.

The offshore waters boast several good surfing breaks on the south Atlantic shore, especially in the winter. Try Rush Reef or the reef off Garbanzo Beach for some of the Bahamas' best surfing.

Elbow Cay's weeklong, family-oriented **Abaco Anglers Tournament** (242-366-0004) in mid-April requires little gear and welcomes all participants, children included.

Bonefishing guides will charge from $450/700 per half-/full-day.

Froggies Out Island Adventures DIVING, SNORKELING
(242-366-0431; www.froggiesabaco.com) Offers one-/two-tank dives for $110/145 and snorkeling excursions (adult/child $70/55) in the coral wonderlands of Fowl Cay Preserve and Sandy Cay Reef, as well as day-trip boat excursions.

Sundried T's CYCLING, SURFING
(242-366-0616) Located beside the Government Dock, rent bikes for $10 per day and surfboards for $30 per day.

A Salt Weapon BONEFISHING, SPORTFISHING
(242-366-0245; www.asaltweaponcharters.com) Offers a 31ft Bertram rigged and ready to go on deep-sea fishing charters.

Maitland Lowe BONEFISHING, SPORTFISHING
(☎242-366-0478; www.wildpigeoncharters.com) Lowe, the island's reigning bonefishing champion, knows exactly where the 'gray ghosts' hide.

Abaco Multihull Charters BOAT RENTALS
(☎242-366-0552; www.abacomultihull.com) Runs captained day charters for $350 and bareboat charters of its Maine Cat catamarans, starting at about $2,500 per week.

Seahorse Boat Rentals BOAT RENTALS
(☎242-366-0189; www.seahorseboatrentals.com) Rent a 17ft Boston Whaler for $165/735 per day/week or a 20-ft Albury Brothers for $210/1015 per day/week, among others.

Sleeping

Several agents rent out a number of properties in Hope Town and elsewhere on the cay. These rentals are great value for all sizes of wallet, and range in size and location. Try **Elbow Cay Properties** (☎242-366-0569; www.elbowcayrentals.com; Bay St), who list a variety of cottages and villas from $600 to $6000 per week. **Tanny Key's Vacation Rentals** (☎242-366-0053; www.tannykey.com; Back St, Hope Town) has houses all over the island from about $1100 to $3,000 per week. **Hope Town Hideaways** (☎242-366-0024; www.hopetown.com; Porpoise Pl, Hope Town) also has a huge selection of rentals to suit all budgets.

TOP CHOICE **Hope Town Harbour Lodge** BOUTIQUE HOTEL $$
(☎242-366-0095; www.hopetownlodge.com; Queens Hwy; r & cottages from $99-325;) With her white picket fence and frosting-blue balconies, this hilltop charm-cake will have you at hello; palm-framed harbor views will keep you from saying good-bye. Orange bedspreads, island prints and inviting balconies enhance smallish rooms in the main house. For more space and your own kitchenette, try one of the cottages tucked amid the hibiscus and jasmine on the bluff. Everyone's invited to chill by the tiled freshwater pool (non-guests just need to buy some food at the outdoor grill) or dine at the adjacent white tablecloth restaurant.

TOP CHOICE **Abaco Inn** HOTEL $$
(☎242-366-0133, US 1-800-468-8799; www.abacoinn.net; Queen's Hwy; r $160;) Talk about location! Straddling the bluff that forms the island's narrowest point, the Abaco Inn boasts killer views of two gorgeous, but very different beaches. The 20 rustic cottages have painted wood paneling, postage stamp–sized bathrooms and private hammocks. A lively tiki bar and dramatically situated oceanfront pool tie things together.

Turtle Hill Vacation Villas VILLAS $$$
(☎242-366-0557; www.turtlehill.com; Queen's Hwy; villas per day/week $275-600/1650-3500;) Perfect for families, these bright two- and three-bedroom villas have fully stocked kitchens and come with their own golf carts. Friendly management is happy to loan books or give dinner advice. Climb the stairs to the resort's On da Beach cafe for gasp-worthy views over the private beach.

Sea Spray Resort & Marina RESORT $$$
(☎242-366-0065; www.seasprayresort.com; White Sound; r $235-550;) On the island's southern tip, seven fresh and modern cottages sit serenely on a manicured lawn overlooking the water. A 60-slip marina draws the yachties, who wine and dine at the on-site Boat House restaurant. If that's not your thing, just hop the free shuttle to town.

Eating & Drinking

Dining options on Elbow Cay are relatively limited, especially on Sundays, though all the hotels have their own restaurants.

TOP CHOICE **Cap'n Jack's** PUB $$
(Hope Town; mains $8-17; breakfast, lunch & dinner Mon-Sat;) If *Cheers*' barflies Norm and Cliff drank beer in Abaco, this wood-planked watering hole is where you'd likely find them. Locals linger over burgers, salads and fish sandwiches at tight booths inside, while tourists opt for marina views on the waterside deck. Everyone heads here for live music on Wednesday and Friday nights. Try the bar's Jack Hammer (copious rum, vodka and Tia Maria), guaranteed to get you jiving.

Harbour's Edge BAHAMIAN, AMERICAN $$
(Queens Hwy; mains $8-25; lunch & dinner Wed-Mon) The deck here stretches out over the water with excellent views of the lighthouse and harbor, perfect for lingering sundowner drinks and meals. The Over the Edge cocktail (Matusalem rum, banana rum and fruit juices) was the result of a three-week taste testing.

Vernon's Grocery GROCERY STORES
(Bay St; ⏲8am-6pm Mon-Fri, to 7pm Sat) Whether or not you need groceries, be sure to pop into Vernon's, where the shelves are papered with handwritten note cards bearing quirky food-related wisdom like 'in a world of Cheerios, be a Fruit Loop.' Homemade jams and guava cake are also big draws.

Reef Bar & Grill BAHAMIAN, AMERICAN $$
(Hope Town Harbour Lodge, Queen's Hwy; mains $14-20; ⏲lunch & dinner) Lunch at the Reef is worth it for the accompanying pool privileges alone. Burgers and wraps keep things casual, while brunch, with its five different types of eggs Benedict, is a major event.

Abaco Inn Restaurant BAHAMIAN, CARIBBEAN $$
(Abaco Inn, Queen's Hwy; mains $18-30; ⏲breakfast, lunch & dinner) Dig into grilled seafood and key lime pie at this classy nouveau Bahamian restaurant, in a light-flooded sun porch overlooking the ocean.

Sugar Shack ICE CREAM $
(Hope Town; ice cream $4; ⏲11:30am-9pm) Ice cream at this bright blue Hope Town landmark is a classic afternoon outing.

Shopping

Ebb Tide ART, CRAFTS
(Back St, Hope Town) Original watercolors and prints by local artists make fun souvenirs. Also on offer are some Androsia batiks and locally made spices and preserves.

Iggy Biggy CLOTHING, ART
(Bay St, Hope Town) This clothing store sells some funky resort wear and handmade gifts.

Information

There's a meager visitors' information board in the peppermint green building facing the Government Dock on Bay St.

Public telephone booths can be found in central areas, including near the Government Dock, and public toilets are located opposite the Government Dock.

First Caribbean International Bank (☎242-366-0295; Fig Tree Lane; ⏲10am-2pm Tue)

Hope Town Clinic (☎242-366-0108; Queen's Hwy)

Post office (Queen's Hwy) Above tourist information opposite the dock.

Getting There & Away

FERRY **Albury's Ferry Service** (☎242-367-3147; www.alburysferry.com; Marsh Harbour; one way/round trip $15/25, children half price) operates water taxis from Marsh Harbour to Elbow Cay at 7:15am, 9am, 10:30am, 12:15pm, 2pm, 3:30pm, 4pm and 5:45pm daily. The boats depart Elbow Cay at 8am, 9:45am, 11:30am, 1:30pm, 3pm, 4pm, 5pm and 6:30pm daily. The ferry will stop at the lighthouse, and all docks and marinas on Elbow Cay, including many hotels. Albury's can also provide charters to Green Turtle Cay.

MAIL BOAT The mail boat *Captain Gurth Dean* sails to Hope Town from Nassau weekly. See p266 for more details.

MARINAS **Lighthouse Marina** (☎242-366-0154; VHF Channel 16; western harborfront) Has six slips, shower and laundry facilities.

Sea Spray Resort & Marina (opposite) Has a 60-slip, full-service marina exclusively for the use of guests at the Sea Spray Resort.

Getting Around

You can walk or bicycle everywhere in Hope Town. Cars and golf carts are banned along Bay St but can be rented at the ferry dock (Government Dock) to explore the rest of the island.

Island Cart Rentals (☎242-366-0448; www.islandcartrentals.com; Hope Town) Has gas and electric carts at $40/240 per day/week.

Hope Town Cart Rentals (☎242-366-0064; www.hopetowncartrentals.com; Hope Town) Offers carts at $40/240 per day/week. Ask about off-season rates.

Man O' War Cay

POP 300

This tiny ribbon of an island is home to a proud and insular 'Conchy Joe' Loyalist culture, whose origins are audible in their archaic British-tinged accents. Almost as powerful is the 200-year-old boat-building industry that still thrives today.

The island is undoubtedly one of the most conservative parts of the Bahamas. The village, with its tidy New England–style cottages, is clean and quiet, its residents polite but highly reserved. Churches abound, while bikinis and booze are frowned upon (liquor sale is prohibited on the island – bring your own).

The cay's boatyards have a long-held reputation of employing black laborers, mostly 'Bahaitians' (Haitians born in the Bahamas), who, until recently, were obligated to leave the island before nightfall.

The wreck of the USS *Adirondack*, which went down in 1862, lies offshore in 40ft of water and attracts many divers who head over for the day, as do most visitors.

OUTER OUT ISLANDS

Several smaller islands around Elbow Cay are worth exploring, especially if you have your own boat. **Lubber's Quarters Cay** is a 300-acre private island between Marsh Harbour and Elbow Cay. With no hotels, cars or stores, its perfect for secluded beaches and nature hikes. Spitting distance from Elbow Cay, 5-mile-long **Tilloo Cay** is renowned for its bonefishing flats. The 11 acres of pristine wilderness is a vital nesting site for sea birds, including the rare and beautiful tropicbird. South of Tilloo, **Pelican Cays Land & Sea Park** is a 2,100-acre wonderland of shallow coral gardens, underwater caves and tiny uninhabited islands. For the yacht-less, many tour operators and dive shops in Marsh Harbour and Elbow Cay can arrange trips or boat charters to these islands.

Sights

TOP CHOICE **Albury's Sail Shop** SHOPPING
(7am-5pm Mon-Sat) The stuttering sound of antique sewing machines dominates this waterfront shop, where multiple generations of Man O' War women are busy stitching items from cast-off sailcloth. Bright-colored canvas totes, shaving kits and duffles are high quality and have great retro-preppy charm. Chat with one of the women about their days sewing sails, which are now made from synthetic material.

Joe Albury's Studio ART, SHOPPING
(9am-3pm daily) A hand-carved sign points the way to the studio of Man O' War's finest boatbuilder. Joe crafted traditional Bahamian sailboats with a purist's passion, just as his great-great-great-uncle Billie Bo did 150 years ago. Beautiful model boats now dominate the studio, along with local artisans' works.

Sleeping & Eating

There's little in the way of tourist infrastructure here; the island is best visited as a day-trip or for a longer-term stay. For rental villas or cottages, try **Island Home Rentals** (242-365-6048) or **Waterways Rentals** (242-365-6143).

Albury's Harbour Store and Man O' War Grocery stock outrageously expensive canned goods and frozen fish and meat. Locals shop on the 'mainland' when they can. Don't plan on buying anything on a Sunday or during the (long) lunch hour.

Schooner's Landing RENTAL VILLAS $$
(242-365-6072; www.schoonerslanding.com; villas daily/weekly $275/1850;) Three fully-equipped town houses with full kitchen overlook the sea from their tranquil position northeast of town. The houses come with TV/VCR, private patio, dockage, plus laundry, bar and barbecue pit; a shared pool adds some sense of community. Beaches lie a stone's throw in either direction.

TOP CHOICE **Lola's Bakery** BAKERY $
(Cinnamon rolls $7; Cemetery Rd) Charming Lola, born on Man O' War in the 1930s, makes daily rounds of the island in her golf cart, hawking fresh cinnamon rolls and loaves of yeasty white bread. If you don't see her in town, head up to the Cemetery Rd and look for signs pointing to her house – she'll be happy to let you in to buy bread or guava jam.

Dock n' Dine BAHAMIAN, AMERICAN $$
(Mains $10-20; lunch & dinner Tue-Sat) The island's only sit-down restaurant serves up sandwiches, quesadillas and fish dishes on an open deck overlooking the marina.

Information

There are public phones and one bank, the **First Caribbean International Bank** (242-352-9365; 10am-2pm Wed).

Getting There & Around

FERRY **Albury's Ferry Service** (242-367-3147; www.alburysferry.com; one way/round-trip $15/25, children half-price) operates scheduled daily water taxis from Marsh Harbour to Man O' War Cay at 10:30am, 12:15pm, 2:30pm, 4pm and 5:45pm daily (the 2:30pm ferry doesn't operate on Sunday). Return service departs Man O' War at 8am, 11:30am, 1:30pm, 3:15pm and 5pm (no 3:15pm service on Sundays). Charters are available to outlying cays.

WATER TAXIS also run from Man O' War to Great Guana Cay at 7:30am and 3:30pm Friday; and from Man O' War to Elbow Cay at 7:30am, returning at 4:30pm. They leave from the same dock as the ferry to Marsh Harbour.

MARINAS Facilities for boaters include the 26-slip **Man O' War Marina** (242-365-6008), where you can ask about water sport and dive-gear rental.

Ask at businesses in Man O' War town about renting a golf cart.

Great Guana Cay

POP 100

'It's Better in the Bahamas, but...It's Gooder in Guana' reads a weathered old sign welcoming visitors to this undeveloped 6-mile-long cay. The sentiment captures Great Guana's laid-back vibe – this is unabashedly a party island. With few paved roads and only a tiny permanent population, Guana's main draws are its spectacular 5-mile-long Atlantic beach and its proximity to the underwater fairyland of Fowl Cay Preserve. Oh, and its bar scene. On the island's north side, Nipper's Beach Bar and Grill has gained an outsized reputation as one of the country's must-visit party spots, attracting a steady stream of yachties and locals from other cays.

Activities

Great Guana has superb snorkeling inside the reef along its windward shore and some excellent diving and bonefishing. Troy Albury is 'the main man' for many visitors' needs. He runs the friendly dive shop, and hires out a ton of gear for different activities, as well as looking after some decent accommodations.

Dive Guana DIVING, SNORKELING

(242-365-5178; www.diveguana.com; Fishers Bay) Offers two-tank dives ($120) and snorkeling trips (adult/child $50/30) to the fabulous Fowl Cay and the northern end of the island. Ask about visiting the divers' favorite 'pet' fish, Gilly the 70lb black grouper and Charlie the reef shark. Also call here for bikes ($12 per hour), kayaks ($12 per hour), fishing rods ($10 per day) and boat hire.

Henry Sands BONEFISHING, SPORTFISHING

(242-365-5133; www.grabbersatsunset.com) The folks at Grabber's will book you a trip with Sands, a bonefishing and sportfishing guide with his own 34ft Bertram.

Sleeping

TOP CHOICE **Dolphin Beach Resort** VILLAS $$$

(242-365-5137; www.dolphinbeachresort.com; r & cottages $220-430;) A true tropical dreamscape, these crayon-colored villas and cottages slumber sensuously beneath a lush tangle of hibiscus, trumpet vine and buttonwood plants. Borrow a book from the laid-back main lodge and climb to the roof for unbelievable ocean views. For the budget-minded, the lodge has three bedrooms with kitchenettes. The shady pool area has a secret-garden feel, with romantic bistro tables beneath towering palms.

Grabber's HOTEL $$

(242-365-5133; www.grabbersatsunset.com; s/d $100/125;) Run by a group of party-happy Floridians, this newly refinished mini-resort has nine rooms with a tiki vibe – wood paneling, stone accent walls, palm-frond decor. Drinking at the poolside bar starts early; sober up with a snooze in the hammock on the private beach. The casual outdoor restaurant is hugely popular with locals and day-trippers.

Flip Flops on the Beach VILLAS $$$

(242-365-5137; www.flipflopsonthebeach.com; one/two bedroom cottages $235-330/$330-400;) Just beyond town, self-contained putty-pink cabins cluster on a grassy hilltop. At the peak of the ridge, a wooden gazebo overlooking the crashing surf is a dream spot for reading and resting.

Eating & Drinking

For groceries, try Guana Harbour Grocery.

TOP CHOICE **Nipper's Beach Bar & Grill** BAR, BAHAMIAN $$

(242-365-5143; www.nippersbar.com; mains $10-30; lunch & dinner) Perched crookedly on stilts above the sand, this multi-level rainbow-painted tiki shack is like something from a Hollywood shipwreck movie. Sunday pig roasts at Nipper's are legendary, drawing party-hearty boaters from across the Abacos. The rest of the week, a chatty all-ages crowd downs rum drinks, chows on burgers or hops in the pool. For those itching to slip the crowds, there's 5½ miles of stunning white sand just out the back. On Thursday through Sunday, the air-conditioned Overso restaurant serves up pasta dishes and Bahamian-style seafood dinners. To get here, take a right off the ferry dock, walk a bit, then follow the signs, or just hop in the van that meets most ferries. The no-see-ums can be pesky so bring spray.

Orchid Bay Yacht Club & Marina BAHAMIAN, INTERNATIONAL $$$

(242-365-5175; www.orchidbay.net; mains $20-30; lunch & dinner Tue-Sun) Local hoteliers direct guests to the upscale dining room of the country club–like Orchid Bay Yacht

Club & Marina. Look for upscale Caribbean dishes and plenty of lobster tail.

Information

A post office with varied opening hours sits on the harborside. A part-time police office shares the same tiny cement building. A public phone box also sits on the waterfront.

Getting There & Around

Albury's Ferry Service (☎242-367-3147; www.alburysferry.com; Marsh Harbour; one way/round-trip $15/25) operates scheduled daily ferries from Marsh Harbour at 6:45am, 10:30am 1:30pm, 3:30pm and 5:45pm. The ferries depart Great Guana Cay at 8am, 11:30am, 2:30pm, 4:45pm and 6:30pm. Charters are available and the ferries will drop off or pick up at locations upon request.

Orchid Bay Yacht Club & Marina (☎242-365-5175; www.orchidbay.net) has 66 slips, a laundry, showers, telephone and internet service, pool, tennis court, restaurant and bar.

Donna's Golf Cart Rentals (☎242-365-5195) charges $40 per day for golf carts.

Green Turtle Cay

POP 450

The northernmost of the four Loyalist cays, Green Turtle takes a little more effort to get to, but only the most determined curmudgeons will leave unhappy.

This island wears its history on its sleeve. New Plymouth, the main town, looks much as it did in the early 1800s, with narrow lanes of New England-style cottages built by crown-loyal settlers fleeing the US after the Revolutionary War. Loyalist descendants won't sell property to non-islanders, and in low season the roosters easily outnumber the people.

Beyond New Plymouth, the island's roads become rutty as they snake into dense forests of Caribbean pine and casuarina. If you don't get lost (it's easy to do!), you'll find luxe resorts, magnificent empty beaches, and reefs just crying out for diving and snorkeling. At night, hop to the sounds of rake 'n' scrape at one of the island's tiny no-name bars, or down one of Green Turtle's most famous inventions, the Goombay Smash.

Sights

New Plymouth

New Plymouth is lined with interesting buildings of historical significance. Check out the **Loyalist Cemetery** (Parliament St), which has graves dating back two centuries. And don't miss the **Old Gaol**, a crumbling stone structure thought to be 150 to 200 years old.

TOP CHOICE **Albert Lowe Museum** MUSEUM
(cnr Parliament & King Sts, Loyalist Rd; admission $5; ⊙9am-noon & 1-4pm Mon-Sat) Every small town needs a musty, knick-knack-filled repository, and this 1825 house museum serves this purpose admirably. Once home to future British Prime Minister Neville Chamberlain, the museum now boasts a fine collection of locally crafted model ships and black-and-white photographs highlighting the cay's history. Ask to see the collection of old liquor bottles excavated from the outhouse. Museum director Ivy Roberts knows everything and more about the island, and loves to chat.

Vert's Model Ship Shoppe ART
(☎242-365-4170; Bay St; ⊙Mon-Fri) Vert Lowe picked up his genius for intricate model ship making from his father, a master boat builder. If he's around, you're welcome to watch him conjuring miniature sailing vessels from redwood, spruce and fir. If you want to make a purchase, prices begin at over $100. A 26-inch one-master costs about $600. For two- or three-masted ships up to 5ft long, expect to pay $1200 to $2500.

Loyalist Memorial Sculpture Garden SCULPTURE GARDEN
(Parliament St) Here, 24 busts of notable Bahamian loyalists and slaves all gaze in dead-eyed wonder at bronze statues of two girls, one holding a conch and the other a Union Jack. Historical, but kind of creepy.

Beaches

On the island's northern tip, **Coco Bay** is a sugar-white wedge of sand with calm turquoise waters protected by a horseshoe-shaped bay. Just half a mile east of town, handsome **Gillam Bay Beach** is heaven for shellers. On the island's west side, **White Sound** is a deep bay protected by a bluff-faced peninsula. Half an hour north of Green Turtle, uninhabited **Manjack Cay** is a desert island straight out of central casting. If you'd like to visit it but you don't have your own boat, ask around at the docks about charters.

Activities

Diving & Snorkeling

TOP CHOICE Brendal's Dive Center DIVING, SNORKELING
(242-365-4411; www.brendal.com; White Sound) This well-established and highly regarded diving outfit offers two-tank dives ($112), night dives ($95), open-water certification courses ($650) and snorkel trips ($70). Ask about meeting the divers' wild 'pets': groupers Junkanoo and Calypso, who cuddle up like dogs, and Goombay the grinning green moray eel. Specialty trips include diving and hand-feeding a family of wild stingrays ($105, including fresh seafood picnic). There's also a snorkel reef trip and wild dolphin encounter with lunch ($90) or a Great Guana Cay trip to Nipper's Beach Bar ($80). You can rent all kayaks, bicycles, diving and snorkeling equipment here, including underwater cameras and video gear.

Boat Excursions & Rentals

Brendal's Dive Center offers day-long sailing and snorkeling cruises with beach cookouts and punch on Manjack or No Name Cays, some complete with stingray-feeding, lobster-diving and shelling. Most hotels can arrange private boat tours with various operators.

Lincoln Jones FISHING, SNORKELING
(242-365-4223) Runs fishing and snorkel trips with beach picnics and cookouts.

Donnie's Boat Rentals BOAT RENTAL
(242-365-4119; www.donniesboatrentals.com) Rents Boston Whalers and other boats from $65 to $110 per day.

Reef Boat Rentals BOAT RENTAL
(242-365-4145; www.reefboatrentals.com) Has boats from 17ft to 26ft from $80 to $150 per day.

Bonefishing & Sportfishing

A 1035lb blue marlin was caught in 1998 in one of the Abaco tournaments held annually (the Green Turtle Club & Marina hosts the annual billfishing tournament in May). Typical bonefishing rates are $250/400 per half-/full-day.

Joe Sawyer FISHING
(242-365-4173) Has 45 years of bonefishing experience.

Rick Sawyer FISHING
(242-365-4270) A reef and bonefishing guide.

Eddie Bodie FISHING
(242-357-6784) Deep sea fishing.

Festivals & Events

Island Roots Heritage Festival Celebrated in May with maypole dancing, traditional music and conch-cracking competitions.

Abaco Regatta (www.regattatimeinabaco.com) The Abaco Regatta, held each July, begins with sailing races and festivities at Green Turtle Cay.

Guy Fawkes Day In November the Loyalists burn the notorious British plotter Guy Fawkes in effigy during this annual celebration.

Christmas Festival of Lights During December, New Plymouth turns into a twinkling fairy village, complete with a nighttime boat parade.

Sleeping

For rental cottages and villas contact **Island Property Management** (242-365-4047; www.abacoislandrentals.com) or **Green Turtle Real Estate** (242-365-4695; www.greenturtlerealestate.com)

TOP CHOICE Green Turtle Club & Marina RESORT $$$
(242-365-4271; www.greenturtleclub.com; White Sound; r per day/week $149-469;) This colony of cottages whispers good taste, all sage green linens and British colonial–style dark wood furniture. All units have kitchenettes and flat panel TVs; even the smallest have private patios. None are more than a few minutes' walk from the small private beach. The central lobby has a kind of tropical ski lodge feel, with a fireplace and charmingly dim pub. The formal dining room is one of the island's best restaurants (dinners $22 to $35), serving Caribbean-tinged dishes such as grilled lobster tail or guava-glazed rack of lamb.

New Plymouth Inn HOTEL $$
(242-365-4161; newplymouthinn.com; Parliament St, New Plymouth; s/d $100/130;) There's something slightly spooky about this imposing pink colonial, built in 1830. Maybe it's the creaky, great-aunt's-house vibe of the nine guest rooms, each with period touches like quilts and pedestal sinks. Maybe it's the old-fashioned walled garden, like something out of a 19th-century romance novel. Or maybe it's the ghost of the home's original owner, Captain Billy

Green Turtle Cay

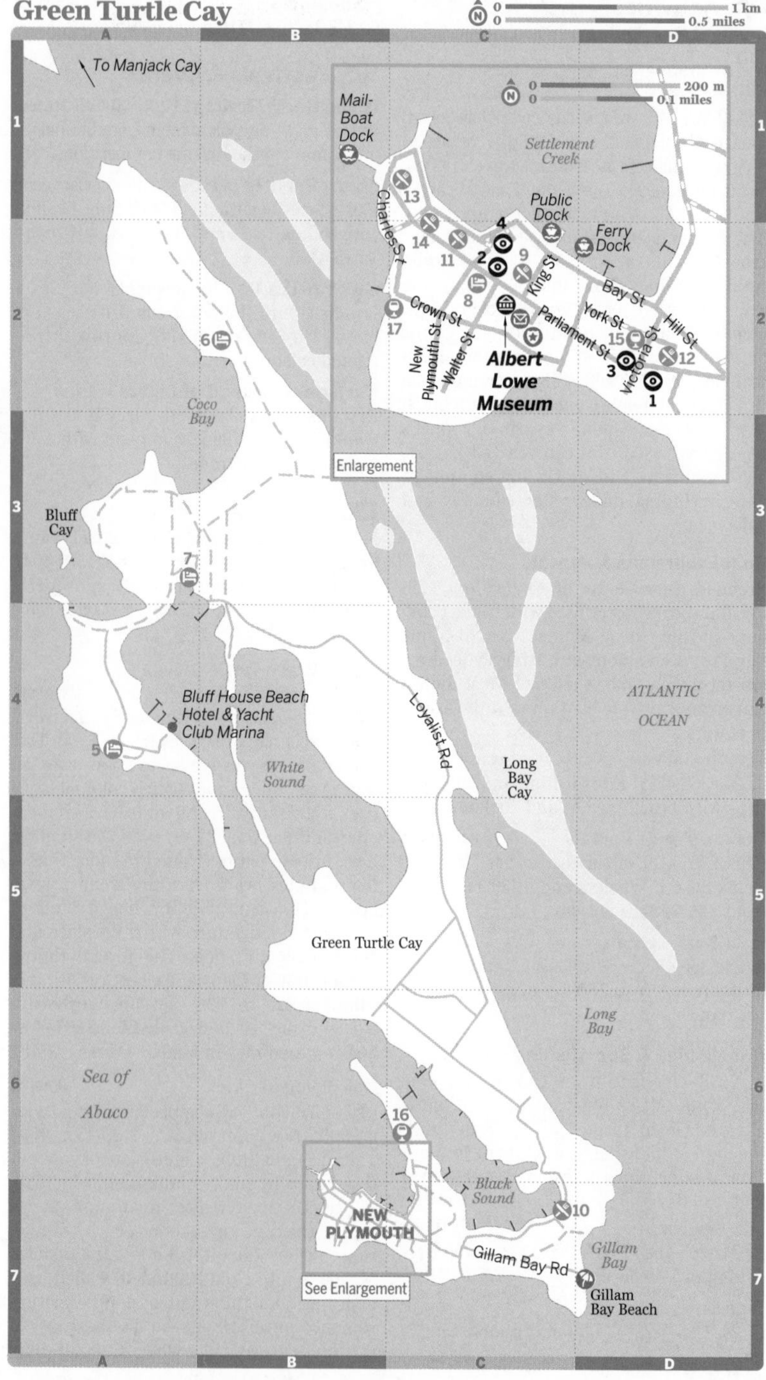

Green Turtle Cay

Top Sights

Albert Lowe Museum C2

Sights

1 Cemetery D2
2 Loyalist Memorial Sculpture Garden C2
3 Old Gaol D2
4 Vert's Model Ship Shoppe C2

Sleeping

5 Bluff House Club A4
6 Coco Bay Cottages B2
7 Green Turtle Club & Marina A3
8 New Plymouth Inn C2

Eating

Jolly Roger's Bar & Bistro .... (see 5)
9 Laura's Kitchen C2
10 Lizard Bar & Grill C7
11 Lowe's Food Store C2
12 McIntosh Restaurant & Bakery D2
13 Plymouth Rock Liquor Store C1
14 Sid's Grocery C2

Drinking

15 Miss Emily's Blue Bee Bar D2
16 Pineapples Bar & Grill C6
17 Sundowners Bar C2

Roberts, who's said to enjoy rocking on the porch rockers at night. Don't worry, he's friendly.

Bluff House Club COTTAGES **$$$**
(☎242-365-4247; www.bluffhouse.com; White Sound;units per 3 nights $417-1647, per week $973-3843;) On a bluff overlooking the ocean, this swanky club rents out 'barefoot homes' – privately owned cottages and villas situated on the club grounds. All are upscale, all have three-night minimum stays. Guests can use the club's pool and its wooden deck dotted with palm- frond huts. There's a casual restaurant, the Jolly Roger (dinner $18 to $32), and a by-reservation-only formal clubhouse dining room.

Coco Bay Cottages COTTAGES **$$$**
(☎242-365-5464; www.cocobaycottages.com; Coco Bay; 2- to 4-bedroom units $250-700;) Secluded and fabulous with miles of beach. Self-contained cottages are bright and breezy, with kitchenettes and homey floral prints. Great for families.

Eating & Drinking

In addition to the hotel restaurants mentioned in the Sleeping section, there are plenty of casual lunch and dinner spots scattered around New Plymouth. The aforementioned hotels are the best places for classy cocktails; for Kalik-fueled fun, there are a number of ultra-casual bars in town.

McIntosh Restaurant & Bakery BAHAMIAN, AMERICAN **$**
(Parliament St, New Plymouth; mains $5-15; breakfast, lunch & dinner) It could be 1955 inside this humble New Plymouth cafe, with plastic-covered tables, carpeted floors and gut-busting Bahamian and American dishes like cracked conch, cheesy omelets and key lime pie. The attached ice-cream shop is a welcome stop on a hot afternoon.

Lizard Bar & Grill INTERNATIONAL **$**
(Leeward Yacht Club, Black Sound; mains $6-15; lunch & dinner) In the swanky Leeward Yacht Club, this outdoor bar serves upscale international nibbles like shrimp kebabs and ahi tuna burgers. Diners get to use the pool.

Laura's Kitchen BAHAMIAN **$**
(King St, New Plymouth; mains $6-12; lunch & dinner) Simple-but-good Bahamian fare such as grilled fish sandwiches and BBQ ribs, served in a personality-free dockside cottage.

Sundowners Bar BAR
(New Plymouth; www.sundownersbar.com; 5pm-late) Daily Happy Hours with free appetizers, a pool table, and a monthly full-moon party draw mostly local crowds to this bright-painted waterfront shack, which also serves burgers, pizzas and conch.

Pineapples Bar & Grill BAR
(Black Sound; www.othershoreclub.com; 5pm-late) Down a dirt road, this funky dockside bar heats up on weekends with live goombay music and famous fried conch fritters.

You can buy groceries at **Lowe's Food Store** (Parliament St, New Plymouth) and **Sid's Grocery** (Parliament St; New Plymouth). The **Plymouth Rock Liquor Store & Cafe** (Parliament Street, New Plymouth) has booze and deli sandwiches.

Shopping

Look for photo-realistic paintings by Green Turtle's most famous artist, Alton Lowe, sold at the gallery next to the Albert Lowe

THE GOOMBAY SMASH: THE BIRTH OF A CLASSIC COCKTAIL

Miss Emily, a Christian teetotaler who passed away in March 1997, came up with the seductively lethal trademark drink of **Miss Emily's Blue Bee Bar** (242-365-4181; Victoria St, New Plymouth; noon-10pm) when she was 'fooling around' with mixes about 20 years ago. This mix of rums and fruit juices is now as famous across the Bahamas and the world as the Bahama Mama cocktail. However, only family members are entrusted with the original cocktail's recipe – a still closely guarded secret.

The bar is now run by Miss Emily's charming daughter, Violet, who still brews the secret recipe at home in plastic jugs. The simple wooden hut has only rustic seating, and decor is provided by a large portrait of the kindly-looking Miss Emily (who should be toasted with respect), business cards festooning the walls, T-shirts hanging from the ceiling, and all manner of scribbles from happy customers. Yacht pennants from around the world also indicate the fame that this modest blue bar (named after a tiny fish) has justifiably gained.

Museum. The Plymouth Rock Liquor Store & Cafe doubles up as an art gallery too, with works by more than 50 local artists.

Native Creations CRAFTS
(Parliament Rd, New Plymouth; 9am-5pm Mon-Sat) Sells local soaps, handmade Bahamian dolls, and lathe work by artist Roddie Pinder, among other crafts.

Information

For communications, phone booths are in several locales, including outside the library and by the ferry dock. The library, adjoining the post office, has a good array of novels and general reference titles. Books are borrowed on the honor system.

Government Medical Clinic (242-365-4028; New Plymouth St, New Plymouth)

Police (242-365-4450; New Plymouth) Adjacent to the post office.

Post office (Parliament St, New Plymouth)

Getting There & Away

Green Turtle Cay is a Port of Entry for the Bahamas; **Customs & Immigration** (242-365-4077; Parliament St) is in New Plymouth. **Green Turtle Ferry** (242-365-4166; Airport Ferry Dock; one way/round-trip $7/15) departs from Green Turtle Cay for Treasure Cay at 8am, 9am, 11am, 12:15pm, 1:30pm, 3pm and 4:30pm. The ferries return at 8:30am, 10:30am, 11:30am, 1:30pm, 2:30pm, 3:30pm, 4:30pm and 5pm.

The ferries will drop you at White Sound for an extra $2. The skipper will also drop you off at the dock nearest your hotel, or radio ahead so that your rental's caretaker will be waiting for you. Ferries also operate on demand, at extra cost, for people with flights; call ahead.

Mail boat *Captain Gurth Dean* calls in once a week from Nassau. See p266 for more details.

Leeward Yacht Club (242-365-4191; Black Sound) has a full-service marina, as do the Bluff House Club and the Green Turtle Club.

Getting Around

The preferred mode of transportation is the monster truck-wheel outfitted golf cart, appropriate for off-roading on sand or mud.

Kool Karts (242-365-4176; per day $50) is right in front of the ferry dock.

Brendal's Dive Centre rents out bicycles ($15) and kayaks ($15 per hour).

SOUTH OF MARSH HARBOUR

The Great Abaco Hwy runs from Marsh Harbour to Sandy Point, at the southwestern end of the island.

Little Harbour

Be prepared for some very rocky and roughly hewn roads to get down to the beach at Little Harbour. To reach the jewel in the crown, Pete's Pub, abandon your car at the beach and walk across the sands toward an icy-cold beer and gorgeous views of this lovely bay, popular with yachters and turtles.

The perfectly sheltered crescent bay is held in the cusp of crumbling limestone cliffs and a kerosene-lantern lighthouse looms over the holiday 'shacks' of wealthy American expats. You can climb to the top for a view of the waves running in toward the reef and the wreck of the *Anne Bonney*.

The turnoff from Great Abaco Hwy is 15 miles south of Marsh Harbour and leads to Cherokee Sound. Two miles before Cherokee Sound, a turnoff leads to Little Harbour via a very rough dirt road; you're warned!

Froggies Out Island Adventures (p123) offers excursions to Little Harbour.

TOP CHOICE **Pete's Pub & Gallery** BAHAMIAN, AMERICAN **$$**
(☎242-366-3503; www.petespub.com; mains $8-18; ⏲lunch & dinner) Yes, this is why so many people torture their cars down the miles of gnarled rooster trails that count for roads in these parts. Pete's Pub is legendary, and for good reason. The two-story driftwood bar is the kind of place where locals and visitors become fast friends in the space of a Kalik or three, and the fat, sloppy cheeseburgers win raves on several continents. Booze it up at the sand-floored bar, made from an old ship's prow, or watch the sun set across Little Harbour from the top deck. Whatever you do, don't miss the sporadic pig roasts, which draw Abaconians and yachties from miles around. The adjoining **foundry** has some remarkable bronze sculptures of sea turtles, mermaids and more, made from an old-fashioned 'lost wax' method of bronze casting. They're considered highly collectible worldwide – the Vatican museum even owns one of the pieces, *St Peter Fisher of Men*.

Cherokee Sound & Casuarina Point

Visiting isolated Cherokee Sound (population 100), 25 miles south of Marsh Harbour, is like stepping back into a 1950s fishing village. The residents, many with the same red hair and freckles, are said to be descended from the same small band of Loyalists. The fishing village of Casuarina Point, with a beautiful beach, lies on the west side of Cherokee Sound.

Sandy Point

South of **Crossing Rocks**, a forlorn fishing village 40 miles south of Marsh Harbour, the Great Abaco Hwy sweeps southwest through vast acres of pineland and ends at Sandy Point, a picturesque fishing community backed by a coconut-palm plantation.

Rickmon's Bonefish Club (☎242-366-4477; ❄) is a big stucco McMansion perched on the very tip of the island and owned by a well-known bonefishing guide. Packages start at about $1500 per person for a two-day, three-night stay including fishing. For hardcore anglers.

Pete & Gay's Guest House (☎242-366-4119; r $90; ❄) also draws bonefishers. Rooms are motel-style and the restaurant is rather musty.

Bahamas Ferries (☎242-323-2166; www.bahamasferries.com; Nassau) makes the trip from Nassau to Sandy Point twice weekly (round-trip $100, four hours).

The *Captain Gurth Dean* mail boat sails from Nassau to Sandy Point weekly (see p266).

Twenty miles northwest of Sandy Point, **Moore's Island** is the only inhabited island off the west coast of the Abaco mainland. The settlements of **Hard Bargain** and the **Bight** have a long fishing tradition and a wild, rustic spirit. Mail boats do stop here.

Abaco National Park

The 32-sq-mile park was established in 1994 to protect the major habitat of the endangered Bahamas parrot. About 1500 parrots now live here along with some wild pigs and stunning orchids.

There's also an extensive limestone cave system to explore (the local parrot population is unique – the birds nest in holes in the limestone rocks), plus hiking trails, lonesome beaches, and incredibly wild and spectacular scenery along the Atlantic shore. A turnoff for the park is signed 10 miles south of Crossing Rocks.

DISNEY'S PRIVATE ISLAND

On a clear day, if you stand by the shore in Sandy Point looking west, you may just see the outline of a massive ship on the horizon. This is Castaway Cay, AKA Gorda Cay, a former drug-runners haven turned private Disney port. The Walt Disney Company bought the island for exclusive use of the passengers on Disney Cruises, who play in Swiss Family Robinson-style waterslides, snorkel around sunken vessels used in movies like *Pirates of the Caribbean*, and bike on an old airplane runway. Unfortunately for independent travelers, the only way to visit the island is to book a **Disney Cruise** (www.disneycruise.disney.go.com).

The dramatic headland at the southern tip of the island is dominated by red-and-white-hooped **Hole-in-the-Wall Lighthouse**, reached by a horrendously potholed and tortuous road that adds to the sense of separation from civilization. The mosquitoes are very active here, so if you want to climb the lighthouse for the view, make sure you come prepared!

NORTHWEST OF MARSH HARBOUR

Treasure Cay

Treasure Cay, 17 miles north of Marsh Harbour, is not a true cay but a narrow peninsula that has secreted away one of the Bahamas most idyllic and captivating beaches, Treasure Cay Beach.

The cay has attracted a large community of retired American expats, and the resulting infrastructure (sidewalks, tennis courts, strip malls) give the area a vibe that's more South Florida than Bahamas.

Sights

Treasure Cay Beach BEACH

This 4-mile-long crescent of sugar-soft white sand appears to melt into a vast expanse of glittering waters that extend to the horizon. Docile rays glide through the turquoise shallows and sea birds echo their movements across the sky. Voted one of the world's top 10 beaches, this treasure is protected by a ring of palm trees, although some private houses and condos have crept alongside the perimeter.

The beach is Treasure Cay's main event, so bring plenty of sunscreen, a towel and a good book.

Activities

There's decent bonefishing in the shallow waters on the south side of the peninsula. Treasure Cay Hotel Resort & Marina can organize sportfishing trips (from $375/500 per half-/full-day charter).

Treasure Divers DIVING, SNORKELING

(☎242-365-8465; www.treasure-divers.com; Treasure Cay Hotel Resort & Marina) Offer two-tank dives ($120), night dives ($110) and blue-hole dives ($110). Snorkeling is $60. It also rents snorkel gear ($15 per day) and arranges fishing and scuba charters.

JIC Boat Rentals BOAT RENTAL

(☎242-365-8465; Treasure Cay Marina) Rents boats from a 21ft Dusky ($160 per day) to a 27ft Rambo ($200 per day), with cheaper long-term rates. It also rents out fishing rods ($15) and snorkels ($10), and can arrange guided tours of nearby islands.

Treasure Cay Golf Club GOLF

(☎242-365-8045; Treasure Cay Rd; green fees $90) This is a 6985yd, 18-hole golf course that has a reputation for its narrow fairways. Guests and non-guests can also book the tennis courts ($20).

Festivals & Events

In May the **Annual Bahamian Arts & Crafts Show** is held here as part of the long-running **Treasure Cay Billfish Tournament** (www.treasurecayfishing.com), which takes place in June. The Abaco-wide **Abaco Regatta** (www.regattatimeinabaco.com) has a stop in Treasure Cay.

Sleeping & Eating

Island Dreams Rentals (☎242-365-8507; www.islanddreamrentals.com) has a variety of well-appointed villas, townhouses and cottages for rent.

Bahama Beach Club RESORT $$

(☎242-365-8500; www.bahamabeachclub.com; Treasure Cay Rd; d $350;) Pink beachfront time-share condos are all fully furnished according to their owners' tastes. Nicer units have high ceilings and slick amenities like granite countertops. A full compliment of amenities – two huge pools, two hot tubs, outdoor bar and grill, gym etc – make this feel like a genuine resort.

Treasure Cay Hotel Resort & Marina HOTEL $$

(☎242-365-8578; www.treasurecay.com; Treasure Cay Rd; r from $94;) Pleasant, unremarkable rooms are furnished with floral prints and wicker furniture. Two-bedroom condos with kitchenettes are good for families. Management is not particularly friendly, but it's a convenient spot, especially with its **Spinnaker Restaurant & Lounge** (mains $15-30; ⊙lunch & dinner). This is one of Treasure Cay's few sit-down restaurants, and serves competent Bahamian and American seafood and meat dishes.

Golden Harvest Supermarket GROCERY STORE $

(shopping center; ⊙8am-6pm Mon-Sat, 9am-1pm Sun) The area's only supermarket is well-stocked with canned goods and imported produce.

Shopping

The gift shop at the marina sells Abaco gold jewelry and resort wear.

Abaco Ceramics CERAMICS
(Treasure Cay Rd; ⌚9am-4pm Mon-Fri) Handmade and hand-painted kitchenware and adornments are manufactured and sold here.

Information

Most facilities exist here. Public telephone booths can be found north of the shopping complex, where the post office is based.

Corbett Medical Centre (☎242-365-8288; Wilson Ronald M Dr)

Police (☎242-365-8048; VHF Channel 19)

Royal Bank of Canada (☎242-365-8119; ⌚9:30am-2pm Mon, Tue & Thu) Has an ATM.

Getting There & Around

Air

Treasure Cay International Airport (TCB) is located 15 miles north of town. A taxi to/from the airport to Treasure Cay for two people is $15. For information on international flights to Treasure Cay, see the table on p261. There are daily flights between Marsh Harbour and Treasure Cay.

Bicycle, Scooter & Car

Cars rent from $80 per day, and bicycles from $10 per day. Weekly rentals should be cheaper. Most rental companies close on Sundays.

Cornish Car Rentals (☎242-365-8623)

Triple J Car Rental (☎242-365-8761)

Wendals Bicycle Rentals (☎242-365-8687)

Boat

Green Turtle Ferry travels between Green Turtle Cay and Treasure Cay; see p132 for details.

Mail boat *Captain Gurth Dean* sails from Nassau to Treasure Cay weekly; see p266 for more information.

Treasure Cay Hotel Resort & Marina has 150 slips and provides dockage for transient/long-term stays. Cable TV and all facilities are available, including dining and accommodations.

Golf Carts

Cash's Carts (☎242-365-8771; shopping center; ⌚8am-5pm) is one of several operators in town renting golf carts for $42/258 per day/week.

Taxi

A taxi to/from the ferry dock from Treasure Cay is $15. Call **Hart's Taxi Service** (☎242-475-0572).

Spanish Cay

On your way to Spanish Cay you will pass **Cooper's Town**, a center for commercial citrus farms. Spanish Cay, a 3-mile-long sliver of land 3 miles off the northern tip of Great Abaco, was once owned by Queen Elizabeth II. Four beautiful beaches line the eastern shore. Most of its 185 acres are covered in palm groves and tropical forest, with a few homes of the international gentry hidden in their midst.

Spanish Cay Resort & Marina HOTEL **$$**
(☎242-365-0083; www.spanishcay.com; r $215-295, villas $375-875; ❄≋) Accessible only by boat or private plane, Spanish Cay is owned by a Texan yacht builder who has a home on the island's far side. Accommodations range from dingy duplexes to luxurious condos, though extreme isolation and lack of swimming beaches mean few traditional tourists. Most guests are passing yachties or local lobster fishermen. The marina offers 82 slips and full facilities, including a restaurant, bar and provision store.

Little Abaco

Great Abaco finishes 5 miles northwest of Cooper's Town at Angel Fish Point, where SC Bootle Hwy swings west over a bridge onto Little Abaco island.

The population lives in four small and relatively poor settlements: Cedar Harbour, Mount Hope, Fox Town and Crown Haven. There's a post office, small hotel and police station in Fox Town. There are a few modest beaches and the bonefishing on the south side of the island is said to be excellent. The only reason most visitors would come this way would be to catch the ferry from Crown Haven to Grand Bahama (p115).

Grand Cay

Near the top of the Abacos chain, Grand Cay is divided into the larger, box-shaped, virtually uninhabited isle of that name and, to its east, Little Grand Cay and Mermaid Cay, both with small settlements. There are several beaches; the most spectacular is Wells Bay, which runs the 2-mile west shore of Grand Cay. The bonefishing here is superb.

If you should find yourself here overnight, **Rosie's Place** (☎242-353-1223; 242-353-1355; www.rosiesplace.com) has no-frills cottages and a restaurant. You'll need a private boat to get here.

Walker's Cay

This tiny rocky cay sits right at the northern end of the Abacos chain. It is fringed by a barrier reef that offers spectacular diving, often in less than 30ft of water. Highlights include old wrecks, including a WWII relic; Jeanette's Reef, boasting a large population of eels; caverns full of silver minnows; and Travel Agent Reef, a beautiful coral garden ideal for snorkelers and novice divers. At the time of research, the island was for sale and closed to the public, but ask around to see if anything's changed.

Eleuthera

TELEPHONE CODE 242 / POPULATION 7800 / AREA 198 SQ MILES

Includes »

Best Places to Stay

- » Rock House (p143)
- » Pink Sands Resort (p143)
- » Runaway Hill (p143)
- » Edge of the World (p150)

Best Places to Eat

- » Arthur's Bakery & Café (p146)
- » Landing Restaurant (p146)
- » Ma Ruby's (p146)
- » Rainbow Inn & Restaurant (p151)
- » Tippy's Bar & Beach Restaurant (p152)

Why Go?

So what do you do in Eleuthera, a 100-mile-long wisp curving east like an archer's bow? According to literature, research and dependable local gossips, most people come here to do...absolutely nothing. That's right. The beach bum is the true royal here, their every do-nothing need met by mile upon mile of obliging shores. These are the supermodels of the beach world: pink sand, sunlight dancing on cerulean waters, sheltered coves, dramatic cliffs.

For those looking for more than a suntan, Eleuthera offers a number of high energy distractions. Wreck divers can explore the Devil's Backbone, fashionistas and foodies can salivate at the upscale boutiques and bistros of Harbour Island, and seasoned surfers can catch the waves of the eastern shore. While Harbour Island, a celebrity favorite, is developed and pricey (though fabulous), 'mainland' Eleuthera is ripe for off-the-beaten-path exploration.

When to Go

Eleuthera

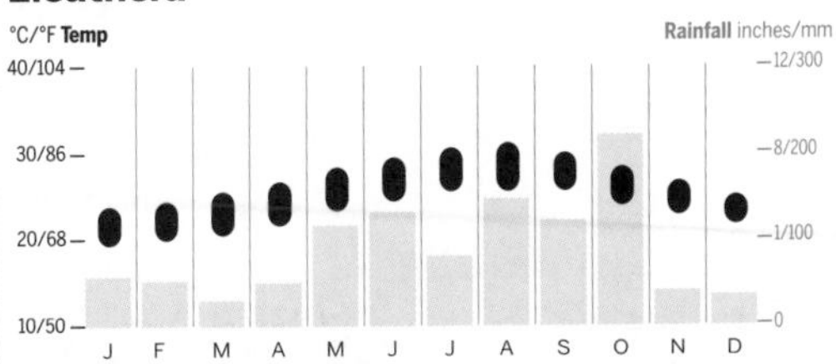

June Sleepy Gregory Town comes to life for the Pineapple Festival.

March–May Low season means you may actually be able to get a same-day dinner reservation on Harbour Island.

December–February High season brings pricier rates, bigger crowds and better celeb-spotting.

History

The name 'Eleuthera' comes from the Greek word *eleutheros*, meaning freedom (the Lucayans who originally settled the island called their home 'Cigatoo'). In 1648, English refugees fleeing religious persecution in Bermuda during the English Civil War era landed in Eleuthera after the Devil's Backbone reef ripped open their boats. They were later joined by Loyalists, who brought their slaves and founded new settlements.

Massive pineapple exports in the late 1800s and early 1900s were replaced with less intensive farming crops. Abandoned silos recall the thriving cattle and chicken industries that evolved in the 1950s. Alas, following independence the government bought out the farmers, and within a short period of time the farms were derelict.

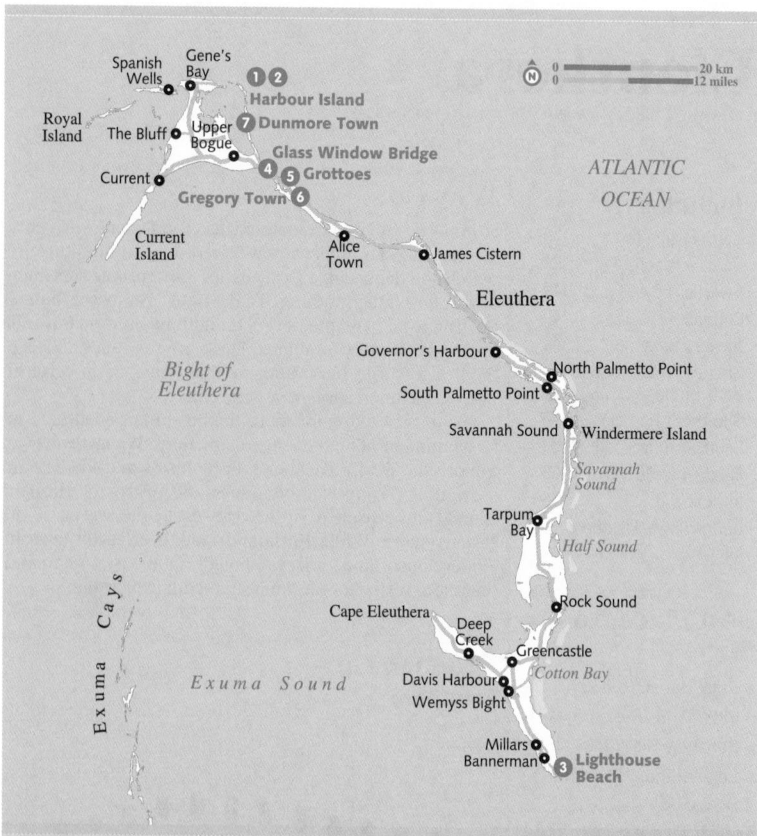

Eleuthera Highlights

1. Browsing the chichi boutiques of celeb-happy **Harbour Island** (opposite)
2. Strolling the ethereal **Pink Sands Beach** (p142 and p154)
3. Braving the rutted road to the secluded, jaw-droppingly beautiful **Lighthouse Beach** (p154)
4. Snapping a picture at the must-see-it-to-believe-it **Glass Window Bridge** (p149)
5. Splashing in the sun-warmed waters of the cliff-top **grottoes** (p151)
6. Rocking out with a who's who of island musicians at **Elvina's** (p150) in Gregory Town
7. Grooving the night away at the rumbustious **Vic Hum Club** (p147)

Since then, with the exception of Harbour Island, tourism on Eleuthera has also withered and many once-fashionable resort hotels are now closed. St Georges Island's Spanish Wells, however, has a thriving lobster industry.

Hurricane Andrew knocked the socks off much of North Eleuthera in 1992, and Hurricane Floyd hit the island with a right hook in 1999. The 2004 hurricanes also added to the general damage sustained by the infrastructure and many villages.

Getting There & Away

Most travelers to Eleuthera fly into Governor's Harbour Airport or North Eleuthera International Airport (if they are heading to Harbour Island). Others take the daily fast ferry from Nassau to Harbour Island. There are also two weekly fast ferries and one medium-speed ferry from Nassau to Governor's Harbour. A number of day trips to the cays from Nassau on super-zippy powerboats are also very popular. Cheaper but slow mail boats and expensive private boat charters round out the options.

Please refer to p263 for flight, ferry and mail-boat information to Eleuthera.

Getting Around

You'll need your own transportation if you want to explore Eleuthera outside of Governor's Harbour or Harbour Island. Fortunately, car-rental agencies can be found at the airport and through accommodations. If you fly in, you'll have to catch a ferry or water taxi to Harbour Island where bicycles or golf carts are the modus operandi; they're easily rented at the dock.

See individual destinations for specific details.

NORTH ELEUTHERA

Eleuthera is neatly divided by a tendril-thin strip of land called the Glass Window (p149), one-quarter of the way down the island. Immediately north, the isle broadens out in a rough triangle with Current Island to the west. To the east, Harbour Island and neighboring cays enclose a vast harbor. North Eleuthera includes Governor's Harbour.

Harbour Island

POP 1500

It is hard to live up to the accolade of being the prettiest island in the Caribbean, but 'Briland,' as it's known (try saying 'Harbour Island' three times fast), doesn't disappoint. The 3-mile speck is a winsome mix of rustic and chic – humble pastel cottages abut $800-a-night boutique hotels, wild chickens peck in the dust in front of sleek French bistros, local fishermen wave to millionaire businessmen as they speed past each other in identical golf carts.

Quaint **Dunmore Town**, on the harbor side, harks back 300 years. The town was laid out in 1791 by Lord Dunmore, governor of the Bahamas (1787–96), who had a summer residence here. Maybe the clip-clop of hooves has been replaced with the whir of golf carts, but the daily pace has not changed much. Once a noted shipyard and a sugar-refining center from which a rum-making tradition evolved, today most adults are employed at the hotels or in fishing.

On the opposite side of the island, the famed **Pink Sands Beach** is a miles-long stretch of powdery sand colored rosy by finely crushed coral. It's been called the world's most beautiful beach by a slew of international glossies, and we won't argue.

Briland's laid-back glamour has attracted an international mix of celebrities – if you spot Mick Jagger or Diane Von Furstenberg wandering around, just say 'good afternoon' and wander along.

Sights & Activities

One of the finest examples of loyalist architecture is the **Loyalist Cottage** (1797) on Bay St in Dunmore Town. The 1843 **Wesley Methodist Church** (cnr Dunmore & Chapel Sts, Dunmore Town), with beautiful hardwood pews and a huge model sailing ship that honors the seafaring tradition of the Brilanders, is close to the 1768 **St John's Anglican Church** (Dunmore St, Dunmore Town). St John's, near Church St, is claimed to be the oldest church in the Bahamas.

Also worth a visit are the ancient graves at the **cemetery** on Chapel St. Bahamians give it a wide berth at night, being fearful of spirits. The handsome 1913 **Commissioner's Residence** sits on Goal Lane at Colebrook St.

Eleuthera

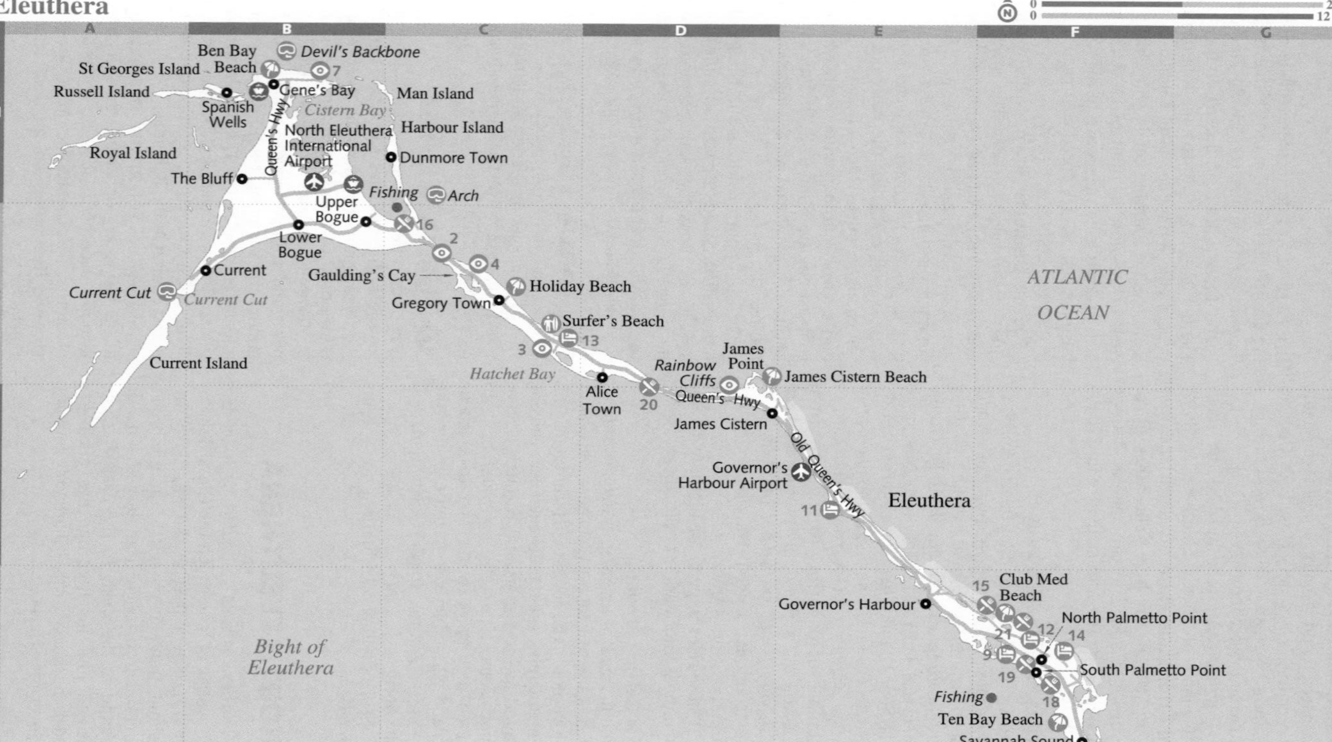
0
0
20 km
12 miles
ATLANTIC
OCEAN
Ben Bay Beach
Devil's Backbone
7
St Georges Island
Russell Island
Spanish Wells
Gene's Bay
Cistern Bay
Man Island
Queen's Hwy
North Eleuthera International Airport
Harbour Island
Royal Island
Dunmore Town
The Bluff
Fishing
Arch
Upper Bogue
16
Lower Bogue
2
4
Current
Gaulding's Cay
Holiday Beach
Current Cut
Current Cut
Gregory Town
Surfer's Beach
13
3
Current Island
Hatchet Bay
Alice Town
James Point
Rainbow Cliffs
James Cistern Beach
20
Queen's Hwy
James Cistern
Old Queen's Hwy
Governor's Harbour Airport
Eleuthera
11
Club Med Beach
15
Governor's Harbour
North Palmetto Point
12
14
21
9
19
South Palmetto Point
Bight of Eleuthera
Fishing
18
Ten Bay Beach
Savannah Sound
A
B
C
D
E
F
G
1
2
3
4

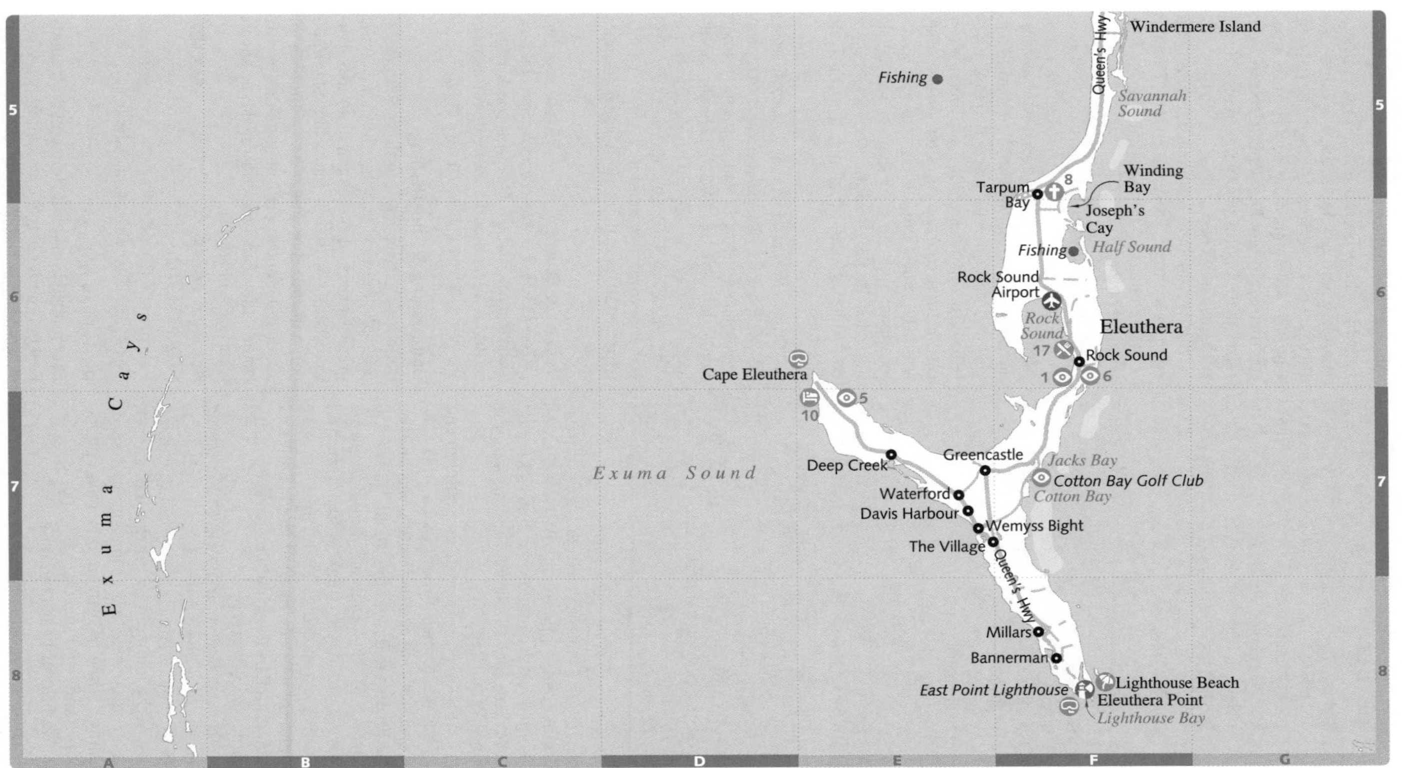

Windermere Island
Queen's Hwy
Fishing
Savannah Sound
Winding Bay
Tarpum Bay
Joseph's Cay
Fishing
Half Sound
Rock Sound Airport
Rock Sound
Eleuthera
Rock Sound
Cape Eleuthera
Exuma Cays
Exuma Sound
Deep Creek
Greencastle
Jacks Bay
Cotton Bay Golf Club
Cotton Bay
Waterford
Davis Harbour
Wemyss Bight
The Village
Queen's Hwy
Millars
Bannerman
East Point Lighthouse
Lighthouse Beach
Eleuthera Point
Lighthouse Bay

Eleuthera

Sights

Bahamas Out-Island Adventure (see 13)
1 Blow Hole F6
2 Glass Window Bridge C2
3 Hatchet Bay Cave C2
4 Hot Tubs C2
5 Island School E7
6 Ocean Hole F6
7 Preacher's Cave B1
8 St Columba's Church F5

Sleeping

9 Atlantic Suites Motel F4
10 Cape Eleuthera Resort & Marina E7
11 Cocodimama Charming Resort E3
12 Pineapple Fields F4
13 Surfer's Haven C2
14 Unique Village F4

Eating

15 Beach House F4
16 Bottom Harbour Beach Club C2
17 Four Points Marina Village & Restaurant F6
18 Island Farms F4
19 Mate & Jenny's F4
20 Rainbow Inn & Restaurant D2
21 Tippy's Bar & Beach Restaurant F4

There's a bizarre collection of **international license plates** and **driftwood signs** (painted with humorous limericks and aphorisms on Dunmore St, opposite the Royal Palm Hotel.

Cannons can be seen at the southern end of Bay St. Named **Roundheads**, this now overgrown 17th-century battery was built by the English to defend the island.

Next to the Harbour Island Club & Marina stand the ruins of the **Haunted House**, supposedly abandoned in the middle of the night by an ill-fated family and later gutted by fire. Now a mere skeleton, it's photogenically creepy.

No exaggeration, the wide and stunning length of **Pink Sands Beach** (p154) is really pink; a faint blush by day, turning a rosy red when fired by the dawn or sunset. The sea is great for swimming and snorkeling, while nearby hotels have public bars and restaurants. It's perfect for self-indulgent beach bumming.

Diving, Snorkeling & Water Sports

Fish have long been protected off Harbour Island, where groupers are so tame that they will nuzzle divers, hoping to be fed. The island is surrounded by superb dive sites, highlighted by the **Devil's Backbone**, with more than 3 miles of pristine reefs littered with ancient wrecks.

Dive prices here soar considerably with equipment rental costs included. The following companies rent snorkel gear for $20.

Some outfits:

TOP CHOICE **Valentine's Dive Center** DIVING, SNORKELING
(Map opposite; ☎242-333-2080; www.valentinesdive.com; Bay St, Dunmore Town) The island's biggest and best operator offers two-tank dives ($100), night dives ($105) and open-water certification courses. An afternoon snorkel trip ($60) takes in multiple reef and wreck locations. You can also sign on for kayaking trips in the shallow reef ($30/45 per half-/full day), and for all manner of private charters.

Lil' Shan's Watersports WATER SPORTS
(☎242-333-3532; www.lswatersports.com; next to Valentine's Resort & Marina, Dunmore Town) Rents jet skis ($120/350/475 per hour/half-/full day), kayaks ($10/35/50), Hobie Cats ($35/100/150) and more, and offers wakeboarding, waterskiing and tubing trips ($150 per hour) and snorkel tours ($50).

Ocean Fox Divers DIVING, SNORKELING
(☎242-333-2323; www.oceanfox.com; Harbour Island Marina) Just over 2 miles south of the center, is a small outfit that caters for up to six on its 34ft-long custom dive boat.

Bonefishing & Sportfishing

Bonefishing trips cost around $800/1200 per half-/full day, making this one of the priciest places in the Bahamas to fish. Bottom fishing trips run more like $300/500 per half-/full day. There are a number of bonefishing and sportfishing guides on the island (they can book up quickly). Ask at your hotel, or try:

Bonefish Stuart BONEFISHING
(☎242-333-2072)

Valentine's Dive Center SPORTFISHING
(☎242-333-2080; www.valentinesdive.com)

Horseback Riding

Easy guided horseback riding on Pink Sands Beach is around $20 per half-hour; wave down the gent strolling the sands with his untethered four-legged friends or call **Byron Bullard** (242-333-2317).

Festivals & Events

In October, yachties descend for the **North Eleuthera Sailing Regatta**, a three-day bacchanal of food, partying and... oh yeah, sailing.

Sleeping

Harbour Island is the priciest place to sleep in Eleuthera. If money's no object and rustic-chic luxury is your style, you'll be golden. Budget digs are trickier. Most wallet-conscious travelers stay on 'mainland' Eleuthera or band together with friends or family for group cottage rentals. For rentals, try either **Harbour Island Realty** (242-333-2278; www.harbourislandrealty.com) or **Red Apple Rentals** (242-333-2750; www.sugarapplebb.com).

TOP CHOICE **Pink Sands Resort** COTTAGE RESORT $$$
(242-333-2030; www.pinksandsresort.com; Chapel St, Dunmore Town; cottages $495-2600;) Rock stars, supermodels and other rich and famous types have long adored this 20-acre hideaway. Walking into the intimate open-air lobby, with its koi pond and carved Moroccan swing and ancient fig trees, feels like entering an Arabian Nights fairy tale. The 25 sleek cottages are their own private mini-kingdoms, with sitting areas and porches and minibars stocked with everything from champagne to Cracker Jacks. Some have million-dollar views of Pink Sands Beach, while others are tucked away beneath the trees. Stop in for a drink at the Blue Bar, an exquisitely minimalist beach lounge whose walls blend in with the sky.

TOP CHOICE **Rock House** BOUTIQUE HOTEL $$$
(242-333-2053; www.rockhousebahamas.com; Bay & Hill Sts, Dunmore Town; r incl breakfast $300-495, ste $575-950;) A seriously stylish crowd lounges on Moroccan-style swinging daybeds by the pool at this intimate hilltop retreat. Nine rooms are smallish but luxe, with crisp white decor broken up by designer touches like vintage birdcages and live orchids. Each comes with its own private cabana. The lobby area is like something out of a millionaire's Greek villa, all modern furniture and marble and floor-to-ceiling oil paintings. Even if you don't stay here, do dress up and drop by for evening cocktails at the outdoor tiki bar.

TOP CHOICE **Runaway Hill** BOUTIQUE HOTEL $$$
(242-333-2150; www.runawayhill.com; Colebrook St at Love Lane, Dunmore Town; r $325-475;) Built in the 1940s as the private estate of a wealthy American, this secluded hilltop hotel still has that WWII-era charm: black-and-white tiled lobby, dark wood library, flags flapping on the pole in the front yard. Rooms, both in the main house and several outbuildings, are done up in airy whites and vintage woods. There's a fabulous pool deck overlooking the slope down to the crashing sea. The friendly Canadian owners welcome children and are can arrange for all manner of boat charters.

Landing BOUTIQUE HOTEL $$$
(242-333-2707; www.harbourislandlanding.com; Bay St, Dunmore Town, r from $200;) It's 1926. You're the guest at the backwater island home of a British Empire functionary and his artistic-minded wife. You sleep beneath a white canopy in a simple gray-lavender room with creaking floors. There's little decor besides a few Picasso-esque sketches on the wall and a cut palm frond in a glass of water on top of the old mahogany vanity, but the way the sunlight plays across the walls is just exquisite. To amuse yourself, you swim in the small pool surrounded by rustic stone walls, or stand on the sloping veranda watching the villagers walk to and fro. Lovely.

Ocean View Club BOUTIQUE HOTEL $$$
(242-333-2276; www.oceanviewclub.org; east end of Court Rd, on the right, Dunmore Town; r $325-425;) Staying at this funky old beach house feels like crashing at the weekend home of an arty friend. Each room is painted a different jewel tone and filled with mix-matched antiques, folk art paintings, and charming random touches – a vintage tuba on the wall, a statue of Chairman Mao. The small lobby has a self-serve bar and shelves full of dog-eared photography books – grab one and relax on the Spanish tiled patio overlooking the ocean.

Tingum Village HOTEL $$
(242-333-2161; www.tingumvillage.com; Queen's Hwy, Dunmore Town; r $95-150, ste $160-250;) One of Briland's few mid-price accommodations, friendly Tingum Village has a range of spick-and-span rooms and suites surrounding a hillside garden. The cheaper rooms are simple, tiled and dim, while the fancier suites have stylish

Harbour Island

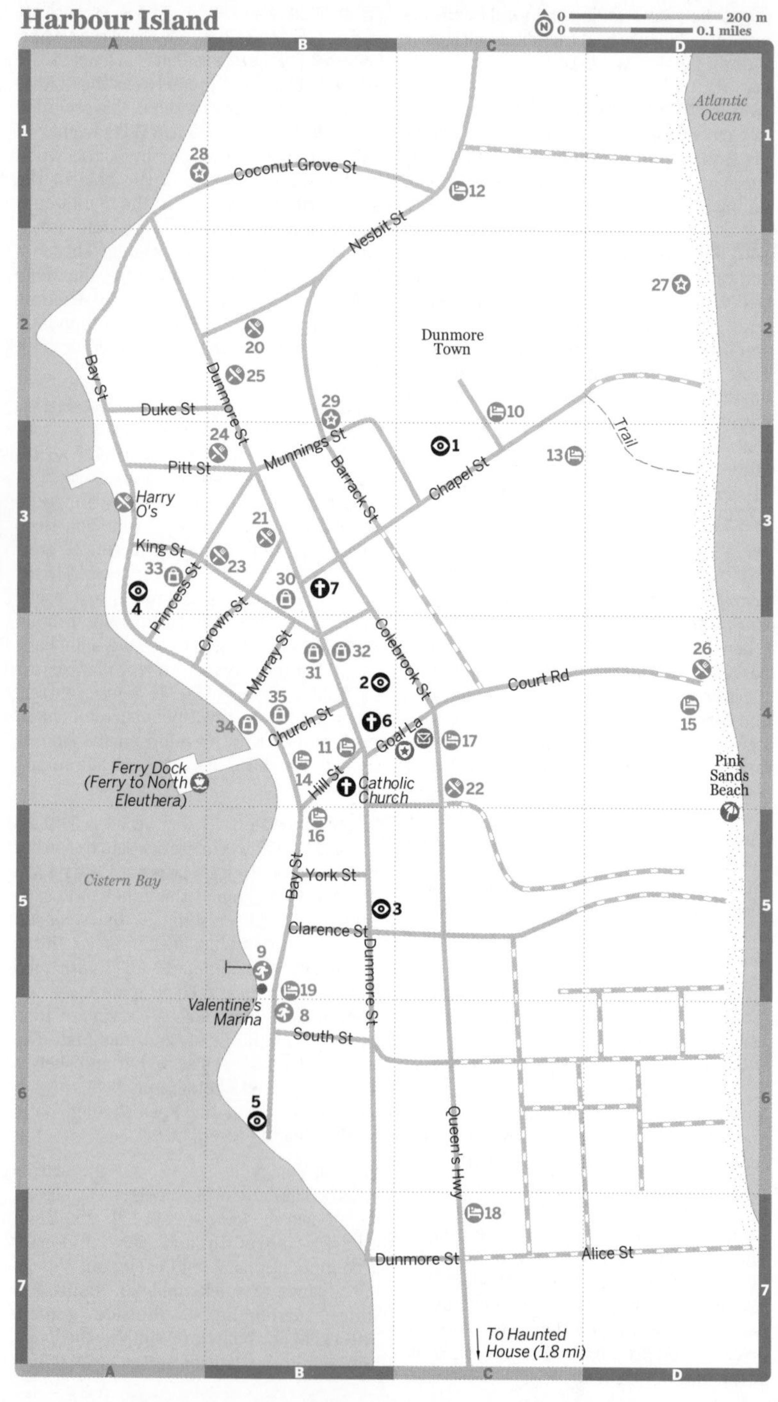

Harbour Island

Sights
1 Cemetery C3
2 Commissioner's Residence B4
3 Driftwood Signs B5
4 Loyalist Cottage A3
5 Roundheads B6
6 St John's Anglican Church B4
7 Wesley Methodist Church B3

Activities, Courses & Tours
8 Lil Shan's Watersports B6
9 Valentine's Dive Center B5

Sleeping
10 Pink Sands Resort C2
11 Bahama House Inn B4
12 Baretta's Seashell Inn C1
13 Coral Sands Hotel C3
14 Landing B4
15 Ocean View Club D4
16 Rock House B5
17 Runaway Hill C4
18 Tingum Village C7
19 Valentine's Resort B5

Eating
20 Angela's Starfish Restaurant B2
21 Arthur's Bakery B3
22 Avery's C4
23 Dunmore Deli B3
Landing Restaurant (see 14)
Ma Ruby's (see 18)
24 Patricia's Fruits & Vegetables Food Store B3
Rock House Restaurant (see 16)
25 Sawyer's Food Store B2
26 Sip Sip D4

Entertainment
27 Blue Bar D2
28 Gusty's A1
29 Vic Hum Club B2

Shopping
30 Blue Rooster B3
31 Dilly Dally B4
32 Miss Mae's Fine Things B4
33 Princess St Gallery A3
34 Straw Market B4
35 Sugar Mill Trading Company B4

touches like stone accent walls and in-room tubs. Bonus: the on-site restaurant, Ma Ruby's, serves one of the world's truly great cheeseburgers. Town and the beach are both short walks away.

Coral Sands Hotel RESORT **$$$**
(242-333-2350; www.coralsands.com; Chapel St, Dunmore Town; r $425-500, cottages $750-950;) The island's biggest resort, sprawling across 14 manicured seaside acres, has recently undergone a luxury facelift. Rooms, which are spread across several buildings, have a crisp British colonial chic: mahogany, simple white linens, ethnic print accent pillows. The nicest have straight-shot ocean views directly from the beds. The fully equipped cottages have sweet stone and tile bathrooms that are bigger than many NYC apartments.

Bahama House Inn B&B **$$**
(242-333-2201; www.bahamahouseinn.com; Dunmore St, Dunmore Town; r $165-210;) On a hilly side street, this cotton candy pink colonial has a pleasingly ramshackle charm. Its seven rooms are clean and simple, with tile floors and chenille bedspreads. A small garden tiki bar and a homey sitting room with a TV and couches add cozy touches.

Valentine's Resort HOTEL **$$$**
(242-333-2142; www.valentinesresort.com; Bay St, Dunmore Town; r $295-875;) The suites and rental apartments at this marina-side mini-village have a featureless corporate feel that seems at odds with Briland's arty, laid-back vibe. But with kitchens, comfy contemporary furniture and slick modern amenities, they're nice for long-term stays.

Baretta's Seashell Inn MOTEL **$$**
(242-333-2361; www.barettasseashellinn.com; Nesbit St, Harbour Island; r $120-250;) Just east of Dunmore Town, this friendly family-run motel has tidy rooms done up in faux wood and peach tones overlooking an overgrown garden.

Eating & Drinking

Harbour Island alone probably has more fine dining options than all the Out Islands combined. Reservations are definitely needed at the nicer places. Some of the island's best meals are served at the shacks lining Bay St north of the harbor. There's always

HARBOUR ISLAND'S BEST UNDERWATER SPOTS

While the **Devil's Backbone** is Harbour Island's most famous dive spot, there are plenty of other worthies. Among them are the ***Cienfuegos*** cruise ship, and the ***Potato & Onion***, a massive 19th-century wreck just 15ft down. Dive operators also head for the **Arch**, where sharks, rays and schools of jacks swim through a coral archway which begins at 75ft, and **Current Cut**, where you're whipped along at speeds of up to 10 knots, in depths down to 65ft. Here coral walls encourage voluminous sea life.

Snorkelers also have a lot of choice: **Bird Cay** has large populations of conch and fish; **Blue Hole's cavern** features a low-lying reef; **Gaulding's Cay** is where soft coral, sea anemone and bonefish abound across a large area; **Oleander Reef**, which is close to shore, has a tremendous variety of tropical fish; and **Paradise Beach's** barrier-reef system has heaps of coral and fish species. Moreover, **Pineapple Rock's** shipwreck, now claimed by myriad tropical fish, is great, as is **Seafan Gardens**, where gorgonians await, along with Baron, the friendly barracuda.

a line for Bahamian fare at **Harry O's** and people risk missing the ferry for a fresh, tart bowl of conch salad at **Queen Conch**.

TOP CHOICE **Arthur's Bakery & Café** BAKERY $
(Dunmore St, Dunmore Town; mains $6-13; 8am-2pm Mon-Sat;) One of the friendliest spots in town, this cornerside nook is the place to catch up on gossip, gather travel advice and relax over coffee, banana pancakes and croissants. Lunch means salads, sandwiches and lazy people-watching. Owner Robert Arthur is a one-time screenwriter and well-known man-about-town; co-owner wife Anna makes a mean key lime tart.

TOP CHOICE **Landing Restaurant** INTERNATIONAL $$$
(242-333-2707; www.harbourislandlanding.com; Bay St, Dunmore Town; mains $39-46; breakfast & dinner Thu-Tue) The Landing's Australian chef earns raves for his light touch with local and international ingredients. Modern international dishes range from New Zealand lamb over tahini sweet potatoes to grilled Bahamian grouper with pesto. If dinner is above your price range, drop in for a breakfast of ricotta hotcakes and Italian coffee in the airy 19th-century dining room.

TOP CHOICE **Ma Ruby's** BAHAMIAN, AMERICAN $$
(www.tingumvillage.com; Tingum Village, Queens Hwy, Dunmore Town; mains $10-20; lunch & dinner;) The 'cheeseburger in paradise' at this family-run patio restaurant is worth a trip to Harbour Island in and of itself. Cooked to order and served smothered with gooey cheese on thick slices of toasted brioche, it's earned legions of fans from across the globe – check out the collection of baseball caps above the bar, left by happy customers.

Sip Sip FUSION $$
(242-333-3316; Court Rd, Dunmore Town; mains $15-25; lunch Wed-Mon) Treat yourself to a little taste of fabulous at this pop art-y lime box, which sits preening at the far east end of Court Rd. Gourmet fusion lunches – lobster quesadillas, conch chili – are best nibbled on the crisp white deck. Here you can enjoy pink sand views while indulging in a little 'sip sip' – the local term for gossip.

Rock House Restaurant INTERNATIONAL $$$
(242-333-2053; www.rockhousebahamas.com; Bay & Hill Sts, Dunmore Town; mains $34-48; dinner) One of Briland's glammest dinner spots, the Rock House hotel's menu has the same international chic as its clientele: curried Colorado lamb with toasted couscous, local yellowfin with wasabi cream. Finish up with a poolside martini.

Angela's Starfish Restaurant BAHAMIAN $
(Nesbit St, Dunmore Town; mains $6-13; lunch & dinner) Grandmotherly Angela will cook you a heaping plate of conch with peas and rice at this cozy locals' joint, decorated in beachy kitsch like old street signs and tiki dancer dolls. Never refuse a slice of her homemade pineapple cake.

Aqua Pazza ITALIAN $$$
(242-333-3240; Harbour Island Marina, Dunmore Town; mains $30-35; lunch & dinner) On a grassy estate overlooking the harbor, this bright yellow open-air restaurant is the place to go for aperitifs (try the Veneziano – Aperol, Prosecco, club soda) and fancy pasta dishes.

Avery's BAHAMIAN $
(Colebrook St, Dunmore Town; mains $6-15; ⏲breakfast, lunch & dinner Thu-Tue) Sit at a plastic table on a porch strung with Christmas lights and tuck into plates of authentic Bahamian cuisine like pig feet souse, boil fish and grilled grouper with peppers.

For groceries, try **Dunmore Deli** (King St, Dunmore Town) for fancy imported cheeses, organic greens from Nassau's Goodfellow Farms and deli sandwiches, **Patricia's Fruits & Vegetables Food Store** (Pitt St, Dunmore Town) for homemade jams and candies, and **Sawyer's Food Store** (Dunmore St, Dunmore Town) for basics.

Entertainment

Top spots for elegant cocktails include the poolside bar at the **Rock House** and the seaside **Blue Bar** at Pink Sands.

TOP CHOICE **Vic Hum Club** NIGHTCLUB
(cnr Barrack & Munnings Sts, Dunmore Town; ⏲11am-late) This funky and sometimes fiery locale has a fine collection of rums, a checkerboard court that doubles as a dance floor, busy pool table and live reggae music by performers like Maxi Priest or the bar's own Paddy 'Big Bird' Lewis. Most importantly the world's largest coconut sits behind the bar. The place can get rowdy, fights often break out. Here's a promise, you won't suffer from ennui here. Pronunciation is key: vickum.

Gusty's BAR
(Coconut Grove St, Dunmore Town) Things get funky around 11pm at this ramshackle cottage crouched over the surf on the island's north end, with live music, dancing and pool. It claims to be Jimmy Buffett's original Margaritaville, but let's take that with a grain of salt (and a squeeze of lime).

Shopping

Harbour Island's not kidding around when it comes to boutiques, even earning kudos from *Travel + Leisure* as the best Caribbean island for shopping. Be sure not to miss the waterfront **straw market** facing Sugar Mill Trading Company. Most stores are closed Sundays.

Sugar Mill Trading Company BOUTIQUE, GIFTS
(Bay St, Dunmore Town) Owned by socialite designer and cousin to Prince Charles India Hicks, this upscale boutique has an impeccably edited selection of men's and women's clothes and island-inspired gifts.

Blue Rooster BOUTIQUE
(cnr King & Dunmore Sts, Dunmore Town) Try this blue-shuttered boutique for stylish sun dresses, wraps and accessories.

Dilly Dally BOUTIQUE
(Dunmore St, Dunmore Town) Boldly bright, unfussy, unabashedly jam-packed with flip-flops, bikinis, Briland tees and Bahamian books.

Princess St Gallery ART GALLERY
(Princess St, Dunmore Town) Local artists are represented here, along with Bahamian star-dauber Eddie Minnis. Works include original oils, acrylics and prints, hand-colored maps, antique prints and driftwood paintings.

Miss Mae's Fine Things BOUTIQUE
(Dunmore St, Dunmore Town) You wouldn't guess from the name or the flowered sign, but this store sells sophisticated designer resort wear; lots of cream linen and light cotton clothes.

Information

Public telephone booths sit along Bay St.

Bahamas Ministry of Tourism (☎242-333-2621; Dunmore St, Dunmore Town; ⏲9am-5:30pm Mon-Fri)

BaTelCo (☎242-333-2375; Colebrook St, Dunmore Town)

Harbour Island Medical Clinic (☎242-333-2227; Church St, Dunmore Town; ⏲9am-5pm Mon-Fri, to noon Sat)

Harbourside Pharmacy (☎242-363-2514; Bay St, Dunmore Town)

SPANISH WELLS

A mile offshore from Jean's Bay, the insular island community of **Spanish Wells** hasn't changed much since the days of the Eleutheran Adventurers. The deeply religious, largely white population keeps to itself – so don't expect a super-warm welcome as an outsider. There's not much to see here, other than a tidy little village of 200-year-old houses and a pretty beach on the north shore. Still, it's neat to experience the lost-in-time feel of such a closed community.

To visit as a day trip, hop the government ferry from the dock at Gene's Bay ($5 per person if sharing or $10 for a ride as a sole passenger for the five-minute journey).

Police (☎242-332-2111; Gaol St, Dunmore Town)

Post office (☎242-332-2215; Gaol St, Dunmore Town)

Royal Bank of Canada (☎242-333-2250; Murray St, Dunmore Town; ⏱9am-1pm Mon-Fri) The only bank here.

Tourist office (☎242-333-2621; Bay St, Dunmore Town)

Getting There & Away

Air

Most flights arrive at **North Eleuthera International Airport** (ELH; ☎242-335-1242), located in North Eleuthera, at the top end of the mainland, or at **Governor's Harbour Airport** (☎242-332-2321), halfway down the island. Some also fly to **Rock Sound Airport** (☎242-334-2177) down south.

For international flights to the Bahamas and Eleuthera please refer to p260.

These airlines fly between the Bahamian islands and Eleuthera:

Abaco Air (☎242-367-2266; www.abacoaviationcentre.com) Flies Marsh Harbour-North Eleuthera on Fridays and Sundays.

Bahamasair (UP; ☎242-377-5505; www.bahamasair.com) Hubs Nassau and Freeport.

Pineapple Air (☎242-377-0140; www.pineappleair.com) Flies three times daily from Nassau to North Eleuthera, Governor's Harbour and Rock Sound.

Southern Air (Nassau ☎242-377-2014; www.southernaircharter.com) Flies three times daily from Nassau to North Eleuthera, Governor's Harbour and Rock Sound.

Quoted fares are one way:

ROUTE	COST	FREQUENCY
Governor's Harbour-Freeport (Grand Bahama)	$135	2 weekly
Governor's Harbour-Nassau	$70	3 daily
Governor's Harbour-North Eleuthera	$30	3 daily
North Eleuthera-Freeport (Grand Bahama)	$135	2 weekly
North Eleuthera-Marsh Harbour (Abaco)	$90	2 weekly
North Eleuthera-Nassau	$70	3 daily
Rock Sound-Nassau	$70	3 daily

Boat

Also see p53 for daily boat excursions to Eleuthera and Harbour Island from Nassau.

FERRY **Bahamas Ferries** (☎242-323-2166, 242-322-8185; www.bahamasferries.com; Potters Cay, Nassau) offers a daily fast luxury passenger catamaran, the *Bo Hengy*, from Nassau to Harbour Island, North Eleuthera and Spanish Wells (one way/return $65/125), leaving at 8am. Another ferry goes to Spanish Wells on Wednesday, Friday and Sunday, taking two hours. Daily excursions from Nassau to Harbour Island are also offered, which include tours and a grand picnic lunch at Pink Sands Beach.

MAIL BOAT These leave from Potter's Cay dock in Nassau (one way from $30); please call the **Dockmaster's Office** (☎242-393-1064) for further details on these schedules.

Eleuthera Express Departs Nassau for Governor's Harbour and Spanish Wells on Monday and Thursday.

MV *Bahamas Daybreak III* Departs Nassau for Rock Sound, South Eleuthera, on Monday, and the Bluff and Harbour Island on Thursday.

MV *Current Pride* Departs Nassau for Current, Lower Bogue, Upper Bogue and Hatchet Bay every Thursday.

MARINAS Yachties have two docking options:

Valentine's Resort & Marina (☎242-333-2142; VHF Channel 16; www.valentinesresort.com; Bay St, Dunmore Town) Offers transient/long-term dockage and has all facilities.

Harbour Island Marina (☎242-333-2427; VHF Channel 16; www.harbourislandmarina.com; Queen's Hwy, Dunmore Town) Has 50 slips and offers transient/long-term dockage.

Getting Around

This information is solely for Harbour Island.

Flights arrive at **North Eleuthera International Airport** (☎242-335-1242), at the top end of the mainland. Taxis from the airport to the dock are $4 per person one way.

WORTH A TRIP

BOTTOM HARBOUR BEACH CLUB

A bit of a local's secret, the **Bottom Harbour Beach Club** (Map p140) is a funky orange beach shack at the far end of a verrrrry long and pitted dirt road. Head here on Sundays for its legendary all-day barbecue, with icy cold Kaliks, heaping plates of pork, and calypso bands jamming on the front porch. To get here from the south, turn right on the dirt road after the Glass Window Bridge. You can also hire a water taxi from Harbour Island.

GLASS WINDOW BRIDGE

The quintessential Eleuthera photo op, the single-lane **Glass Window Bridge** (Map p140) spans the island's narrowest stretch. On one side, the blue-black Atlantic pounds against the rocks. On the other, the calm green shoals of the Bight of Eleuthera sparkle in the sunlight. If you park your car on the side of the road and climb the rocky bluff overlooking the bridge, you get equal views of both sides. It's a sight that once inspired famed American painter Winslow Homer, who painted the Glass Window in 1895. A hurricane destroyed the natural arch that once connected north and south Eleuthera, so this cement substitute is the only thing that keeps the island from being two pieces. It's north of Gregory Town.

The dock for ferries to Harbour Island is 2 miles east of North Eleuthera International Airport.

Water taxis also operate from North Eleuthera to the ferry dock, Harbour Island ($5 one way).

Michael's Cycles (☎242-333-2384; Colebrook St, Dunmore Town) rents bikes ($12) and scooters ($40) per day.

Briland is a mini-LA – no one walks if they can help it. You can rent carts from taxi drivers and rental agencies who are based at the dock for $40 to $50 per day. Try **Johnson's Rentals** (☎242-332-2376; Bay St, Dunmore Town) or **Michael's Cycles** (☎242-333-2384; Colebrook St, Dunmore Town).

On Harbour Island taxis are slightly pricier than elsewhere in Eleuthera; try **Reggie Major** (☎242-333-2116).

Preacher's Cave

This large cave, about 2 miles east of Jean's Bay, is said to be where the Eleutheran Adventurers found shelter after foundering in 1648. They made an altar here and surely prayed to be rescued. Some remnants of their belongings remain, and regular prayer meetings held in the cavern keep their memories alive. The cave is fronted by a glorious beach, one of several beaches along the north coast. Finding the cave is tricky – follow the signs down a rutted dirt road and turn left towards the ocean. The adjacent **Tay Bay Beach** (p154) is secluded and utterly fabulous.

Current

Current may be the 'Oldest Settlement on the Island,' and some of the townsfolk claim to be descendants of Native Americans exiled here after a massacre at Cape Cod. While fishing is their industry, some are known for their basketware. Though not particularly scenic, Current is a good example of old-fashioned Bahamian life, with lots of children, chickens and old men hanging out on stoops. Follow the western road for 5 miles at Lower Bogue's junction, and don't miss the lovely beach on the west side of town.

The half-mile-long channel, Current Cut, separates North Eleuthera from Current Island. It is popular with very experienced swimmers who 'ride' the strong current.

A taxi from North Eleuthera International Airport will cost $28 one way.

Gregory Town

Gregory Town, once famous for its thriving pineapple industry, sits above a steep cove on a sharp bend in the Queen's Hwy some 25 miles north of Governor's Harbour. The second-largest settlement in mainland Eleuthera, it's a low-key collection of cottages clinging to the cliffs overlooking the glassy shoals. The pineapple industry is now so atrophied that local farmers have difficulty mustering a respectable supply of their usually large and succulent fruits to display at the annual Pineapple Festival. The town's young men have turned to lobstering, where the big bucks reside. A handful of older, surfer-type expats add an arty element to town life. And though quiet most nights, it gets funky every Tuesday and Friday at the legendary Elvina's.

Gaulding's Cay (p146), 3½ miles north of Gregory Town, is a splendid stretch of pure-white sand, while offshore the cay's waters are home to large communities of multihued sea anemones. The Cove Eleuthera (p150) offers a daily complimentary shuttle to Gauldings Cay for its guests.

At **Rebecca's Beach Shop** (☎242-335-5436, just off Queen's Hwy at bottom of hill), groovy American expat Ponytail Pete gives surf lessons ($70) and waxes at length about his wife's damn good Pirate's Revenge hot sauce. A few houses north, the **Island Made Gift Shop** (Queen's Hwy) is worth a stop to peruse the shell work, driftwood sculptures and jars of sweet, tangy local pineapple jam.

Sleeping & Eating

TOP CHOICE Edge of the World CABINS $

(☎242-335-5077; villas $50; 📶) Kim and Terry, a welcoming American-Bahamian couple, rent out three dollhouse-tiny cabins, all cleverly appointed with mini-kitchenettes and sleeping lofts. The sloping hillside property is lush with coconut palms and purple lilies; a meditation garden is in the works. A steep path goes down to the harbor, where you can launch a borrowed kayak for an afternoon paddle.

Cove Eleuthera HOTEL $$$

(☎242-335-5142; www.thecoveeleuthera.com; Queen'sHwy; r $245-294, ste $410-465; ❄🏊📶) Jaw-dropping views over the secluded green cove make up for slightly dated facilities that don't quite live up to their luxury billing. The cream-and-rattan restaurant is a friendly place for lunch with a view.

Drinking

Elvina's BAR

(☎242-335-5032; Queen's Hwy) Tuesday and Friday jam nights are legendary at Elvina's, an old-school party shack just around the bend from town. By 9:30pm the place is rumblin' to the rafters with half-hour sets by locals and visiting musicians. You might just see local landowner Lenny Kravitz strolling through the upbeat crowd of low-key locals, over-served yachties, sun-dried surfers and befuddled tourists who can't figure out where all these people came from.

Information

For emergencies call the **police** (☎242-332-2111).

Getting There & Around

Gregory Town is midway between the North Eleuthera and Governor's Harbour airports.

Cecil Cooper's Taxi Service (☎242-332-1575) and **Clement Cooper** (☎242-332-1726) taxi service will pick you up.

Gregory Town to Governor's Harbour

In the 25 miles between Gregory Town and Governor's Harbour there are only three towns of any size, from north to south: **Hatchet Bay**, **Alice Town**, and **James Cistern**. Hatchet Bay is a sleepy hamlet on a delicious stretch of oceanfront, Alice Town is the now-desolate former home of a cattle operation, and James Cistern is a picturesque waterfront hamlet, 3 miles north of the Governor's Harbour Airport.

The **Hatchet Bay Fest** in Alice Town each August features dinghy races and partying.

Sights & Activities

Surfer's Beach BEACH

Calling all surfers! This beach, 2 miles south of Gregory Town, has some killer breaks rolling in from the Atlantic. It's reachable only by an apocalyptically rutted and pot-holed 'road,' one of the worst we've seen, which keeps the casual day-trippers away.

JUICY & SWEET: ELEUTHERA'S PINEAPPLE FESTIVAL

Throughout the 18th century, pineapple production blossomed in Eleuthera, and a local variety – the Eleutheran sugar loaf – earned recognition for Eleuthera and Gregory Town as an especially succulent fruit. In 1900 production peaked, and 7 million pineapples were exported, many heading for London's Convent Garden Market. Alas, they were eventually supplanted by fruit from Cuba, Jamaica and Hawaii. Eleuthera's pineapple farmers are now a dying breed. Some pineapples are still grown here, but raising pineapples is labor-intensive, requiring backbreaking work that has little appeal for young people.

In early June the town hosts the three-day **Annual Eleuthera Pineapple Festival**, highlighted by the Miss Teen Pineapple Princess Pageant and the Pineathelon, which is a swim-bike-run competition. There's also the Pineapple-on-a-Rope Eating Contest in which participants with hands tied behind their backs attempt to nibble a dangling pineapple; a basketball shootout; a kayak race; and the Saturday-night Junkanoo Rush, a street party offering music, dancing and some easy fun. Look out for nonalcoholic pineapple smoothies, locally made pineapple rum and fragrant, juicy pineapple tarts. If you're not in town for the festival, pick up a jar of tangy pineapple jam at the Island Made Gift Shop in Gregory Town.

NATURAL HOT TUBS

North of Gregory Town down a sandy, rutted road, the violent Atlantic surf has pounded the cliffs into a psychedelic lunar landscape of tidal pools and grottoes. Locals call these pools the **hot tubs** (Map p140), as the sun tends to warm the standing water to near body temperature in summer. It's a fun place to explore, but don't get too close to the edge. To get here, head north on the Queen's Hwy 5 miles out of Gregory Town, then turn right at the faded round National Heritage sign. Leave your car and hike, lest you get stuck in the sand.

Bahamas Out-Island Adventures DIVING, SNORKELING
(Map p140; ☎242-335-0349; www.bahamasadventures.com; surf lessons from $60) Tom of Surfer's Haven (right) also runs this low-key tour company, with kayaking, surfing and snorkeling excursions, and is happy to customize. The vigorous drift snorkel trip at Current Cut is one-of-a-kind.

Hatchet Bay Cave CAVE
Turn south onto the dirt road near the three old silos to find the mouth to this half-mile-long **cave system** (Map p140). Descending into a vertical hole, you'll find several chambers bearing charcoal signatures dating back to the mid-19th century. Some harmless leaf-nosed bats reside within, as do stalactites and stalagmites – no touching! If you're going to explore the cave system beyond the first few chambers, bring a flashlight, long pants and a local guide.

Rainbow Cliffs GEOLOGIC FORMATION
North of Governor's Harbour, just past James Cistern, follow the National Heritage sign down an overgrown path and park your car where the road becomes impassible. Hike across the sandpits to the cliffs, where the pounding Atlantic surf has created an eerie moonscape of pitted rock and shallow tidepools.

James Cistern Beach BEACH
A bone-jarring dirt road leads north from James Cistern to this little-visited beach, where waves sometimes reach 10ft with a brisk south wind. There's a shipwreck offshore, which is a good spot for snorkeling when the water is calm.

Sleeping & Eating

Cocodimama Charming Resort HOTEL $$$
(Map p140; ☎242-332-3150; www.cocodimama.com; Queen's Hwy; r $210; ❄) A little slice of the Riviera in the Bahamas, Cocodimama's main house feels like an Italian beach villa owned by an arty Milanese jet-setter – think whitewashed walls, mosaic floors, avant-garde driftwood chandeliers. Guestrooms, in a series of pastel villas, are sunny and chicly minimalist. The resort's heavenly strip of private beach is lined with cute palm-thatch umbrellas. The fabulous nouvelle Mediterranean restaurant (mains $15 to $28) is all about Caprese salads and yellowfin tuna tartare, with a well-edited wine list.

Surfer's Haven GUESTHOUSE $
(Map p140; ☎242-333-3282; www.surfershavenbahamas.com; d/upstairs apt $55/75, camping sites $30; wifi) Run by Tom, a Nassau-born surfer boy with a friendly 'hey bro' attitude, this is one of the Bahamas' precious few backpacker-style guesthouses. Four homey rooms and a communal area cluttered with books and games and old *National Geographic* magazines give the place a sort of hippie frat-house vibe. Bring your own tent and camp beneath the lemon trees in the yard, with sloping views over the treetops to the beach. Tom's calculated the exact time it takes to carry your board from the house to the waves: seven minutes. You'll want a 4WD to get here, as the road leading to the guesthouse can only be described as hellish.

TOP CHOICE **Rainbow Inn & Restaurant** ITALIAN, INTERNATIONAL $$
(Map p140; ☎242-335-0294; www.rainbowinn.com; Queen's Hwy; mains $18-39; ⏲lunch & dinner) Wherever you happen to be staying on the island, the Rainbow's impressive steak dinners are worth a drive. Meat is flown in fresh from the Chicago stockyards, while organic veggies for the wood-fired pizzas and salads are grown on-site by the young Canadian owner. On a hillside overlooking the sea, the restaurant's dining room has a beach bar vibe, with lots of burnished wood, funky local art and a table made from the prow of an old shipwreck. On Saturday night, the Queen's Highway Band gets groovy. The Rainbow also rents several simple, sunny cottages ($100 to $250).

Governor's Harbour

This sleepy and amiable capital, wrapped around a broad, glassy harbor, is a good central location for exploring the island. People live quietly here, until the Friday and Saturday Fish Fry kicks off and the *goombay* beats (island music derived from the days of slavery) drift across the harbor. The smell of frying chicken entices the populace along for a beer and a bite, and the stars shine overhead in the clear sky.

There are many faded remnants of past glory days here. During the 19th century the harbor was filled with schooners shipping pineapples and citrus fruits to New York and New England, or unloading fineries for the wealthy merchants and their wives. The merchants' well-preserved old white clapboard houses nestle on the hillside east of Queen's Hwy, where royal poincianas blaze vermilion in spring.

Four miles south of Governor's Harbour, sleepy Palmetto Point is a spread-out village of fisherman's cottages mixed with expat-owned second homes. It's home to some of the area's better restaurants and hotels.

Sights & Activities

A stroll along the harborfront passes **St Patrick's Anglican Church** and cemetery; the historic, pink **Commissioner's Office**; and the lovely old **Haynes Library** (1897).

There are some beautiful little beaches over the hill on the Atlantic shore, where the azure seas lazily drift onto pink sands and where you can easily while away a day or three. **Club Med Beach** (p154), named after the long-gone resort, regularly pops up on 'World's Best Beaches' lists.

Clearwater Dive Shop (242-332-2146) in the town center offers dive and snorkel trips.

Sleeping

TOP CHOICE **Duck Inn** B&B $$
(242-332-2608; www.theduckinn.com; Queen's Hwy; cottages $150-300) In central Governor's Harbour, this 200-year-old colonial complex is clustered around the owner's carefully tended orchid garden. Three homey cottages are decked out in pink and lavender, with an eclectic mix of vintage furniture and shelves of dog-eared paperbacks. Cupid's Cottage has waterfront views and a full kitchen, Hunnypot is a tidy little studio, and Flora's Cottage is a charmingly creaky house. The liquor store's right around the corner – grab a bottle for cocktails by the mini waterfall on the patio.

Pineapple Fields CONDO HOTEL $$$
(Map p140; 242-332-2221; www.pineapplefields.com; Banks Rd, North Palmetto Point; 1-bedroom condos $160-270, 2-bedroom condos $250-370) On mainland Eleuthera, even the most charming accommodations tend to have a worn-in feel. Not so at Pineapple Fields, where 32 spankin' new yellow villas are set amid a meticulously kept garden of palms, hibiscus and aloe. Spotless one- and two-bedroom condos have kitchens, flat-panel TVs and private balconies. Guests, many of them families with children, lounge by the enormous pool or wander across the quiet road to the truly spectacular beach.

Unique Village HOTEL $
(Map p140; 242-332-1830; www.uniquevillage.com; North Palmetto Point; r $90-110) The white stucco buildings of this small resort complex have a Spanish Colonial feel, while the generic tiled guestrooms could belong to any chain motel in the universe. There's a casual restaurant, a nice pool and the beach just a few feet away.

Atlantic Suites Motel MOTEL $
(Map p140; 242-332-1882; North Palmetto Point; r $85) Right across from Unique Village, this spick-and-span little motel has rooms with kitchenettes and floral bedspreads. One of Eleuthera's few bargain digs.

Eating

On Friday evenings, the harbor-side town **Fish Fry** is the place to be, with oil drum cookers turning out fried turbot and conch fritters late into the night as locals dance.

TOP CHOICE **Tippy's Bar & Beach Restaurant** INTERNATIONAL $$
(Map p140; 242-332-3331; Banks Rd, North Palmetto Point Beach; mains $18-30; lunch & dinner) Almost too cool for its own good, this upscale beach shack is the current darling of visiting celebs, the *New York Times* and a host of fawning travel mags. Tippy's specializes in globally influenced seafood dishes – think lobster wraps, shrimp pizzas and hog fish with Thai curry. Jam-packed even in low season, it gets totally wild on busy weekend nights when the piano music starts up and those investment banker types at the next table start downing tequila shots.

Beach House TAPAS $$
(Map p140; ☎242-332-3387; Banks Rd, just south of Governor's Harbour; tapas $8-14; mains $20-28; ⊙lunch & dinner) The well-heeled expat clientele at this intimate tapas lounge all seem to know each other, but you'll be welcomed, too. Nosh on international tapas – spicy shrimp, Spanish chorizo, Indian-style chickpeas – on the patio. Or sit inside the warmly lit dining room, in a converted private home with yellow walls and poured concrete floors. The outdoor bar, with its incongruous hanging disco ball, is a fine spot for a glass of red.

Mate & Jenny's PIZZA $
(Map p140; South Palmetto Point; pizzas $10-28; ⊙lunch & dinner) Conch pizza and Goombay Smashes are the order of the day at this popular pizzeria, which also offers fried fish and a handful of sandwiches. Sports bar ambiance with multiple TVs and decked with American football memorabilia.

Some other selections:

New Sunset Inn BAHAMIAN $
(Queen's Hwy; mains $10-18; ⊙lunch & dinner) The ample patio of this friendly seaside bar and grill is the place to crack a cold Kalik at sunset while nibbling cracked conch and Christine's famous coconut pie.

Buccaneer Club BAHAMIAN $
(New Bourne St; mains $8-14; ⊙breakfast, lunch & dinner) This blue clapboard house is your best bet for traditional Bahamian breakfasts like boil fish and johnnycake, or for plates of fried fish with peas and rice.

Island Farms MARKET $
(Map p140; Queens Hwy, half-mile south of Palmetto Point; ⊙9am-4pm Mon-Sat) Stock up on local organic veggies and homemade jams at this sweet little farm stand. Fresh bread available on Tuesdays and Fridays.

Eleuthera Supplies Limited SUPERMARKET $
(downtown Governor's Harbour; ⊙6:30am-7pm Mon-Sat, to 2:30pm Sun) The local supermarket is the best-stocked on the island, but that ain't making any grand claim.

Drinking & Entertainment

Tippy's and the Beach House both have lively bar scenes in the early evening.

Ronnie's Island Hi-D-Way BAR
(Cupid's Cay) A lively bar with a pool table and wide-screen TV, plus dancing on Friday and Saturday; don't even think of arriving before 10pm.

Globe Princess Theatre CINEMA
(Queen's Hwy; admission adult/child $5.50/3) This town-center cinema shows movies at 8:15pm nightly, except Thursday.

Information

BaTelCo (Haynes Ave) Atop the hill. There's a phone booth here and another on Queen's Hwy.

First Caribbean International Bank (Queen's Hwy; ⊙9:30am-3pm Mon-Thu, to 4pm Fri) Has an ATM.

Government Medical Clinic (☎242-332-2774; Haynes Ave; ⊙9am-5pm Mon-Fri)

Police station (☎242-332-2111; Queen's Hwy)

Post office (Haynes Ave; ⊙9am-4pm Mon-Fri)

Tourist office (☎242-332-2142; Queen's Hwy)

Getting There & Around

Please refer to p263 for flight, ferry and mailboat information to Eleuthera and Governor's Harbour.

Governor's Harbour is served by the **Governor's Harbour Airport** (☎242-332-2321), about 10 miles north of town. Taxis from the airport to town are $25 one way for two people.

Many enterprising individuals act both as taxi drivers and car-rental agencies. This means that it is often easier to book a car rental from the airport with a taxi ride to the airport when you depart. Car hire costs from around $70 per day.

To hire a taxi or rent a car, call **Cecil Cooper's Taxi Service** (☎242-332-1576) or **Clement Cooper** (☎242-332-1726).

SOUTH ELEUTHERA

Heading along the Queen's Hwy, the accumulated effects of a series of hurricanes and a downturn in tourism on this part of the island are sadly all too apparent. But press on to find one of the world's most superb beaches (seriously), a flashy resort, and a one-of-a-kind marine biology school, among other things.

Windermere Island

Secluded, broom-thin Windermere Island boasts a pristine blush-hued beach running the 4-mile Atlantic shore. It is speckled with snazzy homes reflecting its long-standing status as one of the most exclusive hideaways for the rich and famous. The chic Windermere Island Club, once the Bahamas' most fashionable resort, was a favorite of Lord Mountbatten and,

BEACHES OF ELEUTHERA

The island's secluded shores are some of the best in the Bahamas for lounging, loafing, lollygagging and maybe, just maybe, a little beachcombing. Beach hunters should snag a copy of *The Elusive Beaches of Eleuthera* by self-proclaimed 'beachologists' Geoff and Vicky Wells ($24.95), which is sold at several gift shops around the island or online (www.elusivebeaches.com). The Tarbox map (US$10) sold at the Rainbow Inn & Restaurant is also good. Here are a few of the best starting from the north:

» **Pink Sands Beach** (p142) The sand at this iconic Harbour Island beach really does glow a light shade of pink, a result of finely pulverized coral. Follow Dunmore Town's Chapel St or Court Rd to public access paths to the Atlantic side shores. Hey, was that Mick Jagger strolling by? Probably.

» **Tay Bay Beach** (p149) Beyond Preacher's Cave, this utterly secluded strip has pinkish sands and calm waters.

» **Ben Bay Beach** About 10 miles from the North Eleuthera International Airport, this protected horseshoe-shaped beach has calm waters and good snorkeling not far offshore. The downside? It's impossible to find. We're not even going to try to give you directions here – ask a local or buy the detailed Tarbox map. It's worth the adventure.

» **Gaulding's Cay** (p149) This semisecluded central beach has shallow, gin-clear water and great snorkeling around a small rocky island. To get here, head 3½ miles north of Gregory Town and turn left opposite the two white apartment buildings on your right.

» **Surfer's Beach** (p150.) Windswept bluffs are a primo perch for watching surfers catching waves below. Follow the trail down to the protected beach. Two miles south of the Island Made Gift Shop in Gregory Town, take the rutted dirt road at the Surfer's Haven sign on the Atlantic side and follow the occasional marker to the bluffs and a small parking area.

» **Club Med Beach** (p152) Majestic pines sway beside a softly curving shore at this beautiful beach, one of the prettiest in the Bahamas. Known for years as Club Med Beach, for the resort that once stood here, it's occasionally called French Leave Beach as well. To get here, drive toward the Atlantic on Haynes Ave, passing the Quality Inn Cigatoo on your left. Turn right at the T-intersection, drive about 220yd to a dirt pull-off.

» **Ten Bay Beach** (below) South of Palmetto Point, this quiet, palm-shaded alcove borders Savannah Sound on the Caribbean side. Great for beachcombing, its shallows hold starfish and tiny conch shells. Heading south on Queen's Hwy, drive 3.5 miles past the Palmetto Point junction then turn right at the telephone pole with red reflectors.

» **Winding Bay** (opposite) This Atlantic-side charmer is a protected from the ocean's roughness by its C-shaped cove. The sand is wide, the water is sapphire blue and a mangrove inlet on the south side attracts all manner of interesting sea creatures. Heading south from Tarpum Bay, turn left at the signed road.

» **Lighthouse Beach** (opposite.) The harrowing drive down the impossibly rutted 3-mile road will feel so worth it when you emerge onto the dazzling crescent of sand that is Lighthouse Bay. Park here, then scramble up the hill to explore the stubby old lighthouse on Lighthouse Point. Down the other side of the hill is Lighthouse Beach, a pristine stretch of coral-pink sand backed by chalky white cliffs and thick forest. Calmer and shallower than other Atlantic-side beaches, it can have a strong undertow, so use caution. Bring a picnic and plenty of water.

later, Prince Charles and Princess Diana. The club is long closed and the beach is private, but if you ask nicely or enlist the help of a local, the gate guard may let you wander around.

On the opposite side of the Queen's Hwy, the near-destitute hamlet of **Savannah Sound**, which dates from the 18th century, enjoys roaming goats and chickens among its tumbledown shacks and collapsed colonial-era buildings. The sound is good for bonefishing and nearby is **Ten Bay Beach** (above), another beauty that calls out to you to abandon your life and live here for ever, padding along the soft sand and breathing in that clean sea air...

Rock Sound

The road south from Savannah Sound passes **Tarpum Bay**, a former pineapple-trading port, now a desolate place with some quaint old stone buildings, including **St Columba's Church**, and beaten-up clapboard houses. Bonefishing is good in **Half Sound**, south of the charming **Winding Bay** (opposite).

Rock Sound is a small, charming village from where the original townsfolk set out on their prime occupation – wrecking. Hence the settlement's early name, Wreck Sound.

There are several buildings of note, plus the **Ocean Hole** (below) and, on the shore south of town, the **Blow Hole** (Map p140), which erupts like a geyser during strong swells. Be sure to secure your car and belongings while you're looking at these natural wonders.

Rock Sound famously comes alive each summer during the **All-Eleuthera Regatta**, a vibrant let-your-hair-down affair, and the setting for all-out dinghy races. The area has a few nice beaches as well.

Junkanoo traditionally begins at 5am on Boxing Day (December 26), when various groups come together at Rock Sound.

In Rock Sound, everyone packs in to a little bungalow called **Sammy's Place** (just off Queen's Hwy behind the Catholic Church; mains $5-13; ⏲breakfast, lunch & dinner) for big plates of scrambled eggs, burgers and cracked conch. It also has got four rooms for rent ($100).

Just north down the road, **4 Points Marina Village & Restaurant** (Rock Sound; mains $7-20; ⏲breakfast & dinner Mon-Sat) is a big airy beach bar surrounded by palm trees. It's popular with both locals and visitors for broiled conch, lobster and rum cocktails.

For information on travel to Eleuthera and Rock Sound, see p263.

OCEAN HOLE

This crater-like curiosity, along Fish Rd on the south edge of Rock Sound, is said to be bottomless. No one knows, but it is a 100yd-wide tidal blue hole populated by saltwater fish that move to and fro through subterranean sea tunnels. If you're lucky, you'll spot one of the sea turtles transplanted here from the ocean as a visitor attraction. Brave swimmers can descend the metal ladder into the hole's black depths.

Rock Sound Airport is 3 miles north of town. A taxi from the airport to Rock Sound settlement costs $14.

Cotton Bay to Eleuthera Point

Mile-long Cotton Bay, 6 miles south of Rock Sound, is favored by wealthy expats who own fancy villas above the shore. Here, the Cotton Bay Golf Club, built by Pan Am founder Juan Trippe for his in-crowd of hobnobbing socialites, lies in utter ruin, its once-famed golf courses overgrown. There are rumors of a renovation and reopening sometime down the line – stay tuned.

South of Cotton Bay, the island flares out in a lopsided, inverted 'T.' At Wemyss Bight, Queen's Hwy splits. One branch heads towards **Bannerman**, where an unbelievably rocky 'road' leads to the extraordinary **Lighthouse Beach** (opposite).

The other branch leads north 10 miles to **Cape Eleuthera** via Davis Harbour and the mangrove swamp-fringed settlement of Deep Creek.

As you approach the tip of Cape Eleuthera, you'll notice an odd sight: several Space Age–looking domed buildings edged by solar panels. This is the amazing **Island School** (www.islandschool.org; 👪), a nonprofit eco-learning retreat. International student groups ranging from elementary schoolers to adults come here for a few days to two months to learn about marine biology and sustainability through hands-on projects – tagging bonefish, making biofuel from used cruise ship oil, farming tilapia. The fascinating campus, with an organic farm, boardwalks made from old tires, and dorms built from salvaged materials, is open for free tours Monday to Saturday at 11am and 1pm.

At the cape's furthest point, the shiny new **Cape Eleuthera Resort & Marina** (☎242-334-8500; www.capeeleuthera.com; villas from $199; ❄🏊📶) sits alone between two empty beaches. Though the facilities are snazzy – modern condos have granite countertops, crisp white linens, flat-panel TVs – the resort feels fairly desolate, and the lack of restaurants and food markets makes it a tough place to vacation. Well-provisioned yachties will be plenty happy, though. Day-trippers should consider coming down here to snorkel (rent gear at the reception area) and picnic on the small but lovely beach.

The Exumas

TELEPHONE CODE: 242 / POPULATION: 3540 / AREA: 121 SQ MILES

Includes »

Best Beaches

» Tropic of Cancer Beach (p165.)

» Cocoplum Beach (p163.)

» Pretty Molly Beach (p165.)

» Hooper's Bay Beach (p163.)

Best Places to Eat

» Café Alesha (p164.)

» Big D's Conch Spot (p164.)

» Santana's Grill (p166.)

» Club Thunderball (p168.)

Why Go?

The Exumas are an extraordinarily beautiful string of some 365 islands and cays, of which just a few are inhabited. Some of the cays are mere dots on the map, some are barren, and others luscious and fertile, but they all have glittering white sands and small harbors of turquoise water.

The main island, Great Exuma, is well set up for tourism, and is especially popular with yachties, many of whom stock up on supplies in tiny George Town before disappearing to explore the pristine beaches of the Exuma Cays. The island itself is well worth getting to know, however, boasting miles of great beaches and extremely friendly locals.

Elsewhere in the Exumas elegant Stocking Island has fine beaches, tranquil lagoons and is a hiker's paradise, while the Exuma Cays Land & Sea Park, which protects birds, marine life and the endemic iguanas, teems with life for birders, divers and nature lovers.

When to Go

George Town

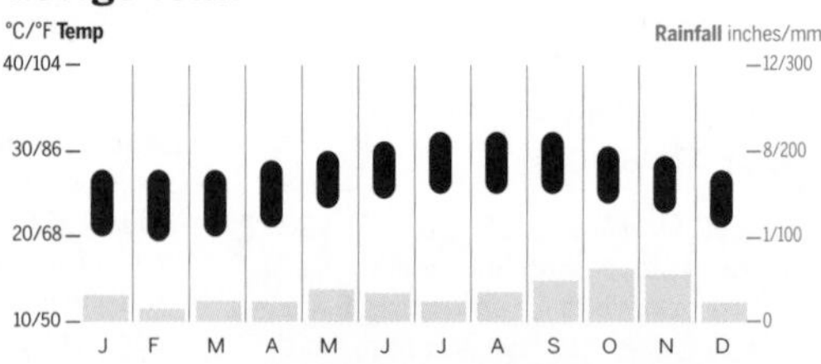

April Join the crowds at the annual four-day Family Island Regatta, the island's biggest festival.

October The annual Bahamas Bonefish Bonanza, held in George Town, attracts fisherfolk from around the world.

December Junkanoo begins on Exuma at 3am on Boxing Day – a noisy, colorful carnival you won't want to miss.

History

During the 17th century, many residents of New Providence settled Great Exuma to escape ruthless buccaneers, and made a living as salt rakers. Following the American Revolution, Loyalists under Lord Denys Rolle arrived with 140 slaves aboard a ship named the *Peace & Plenty*. Granted 7000 acres on which to plant cotton, Rolle's plantations blossomed until the chenille bug chewed through the cotton crop. The salt industry also (rather ironically) evaporated, done in by more profitable operations on neighboring islands. In 1834, the year of emancipation, most white people uprooted and left, while the newly freed slaves stayed and took over Rolle's land.

It was common back then for slaves to adopt the name of their master. Today every second person in Exuma is a Rolle, and since the 1890s every Rolle has been permitted to build and farm on common land. Rolleville and Rolle Town, the two most important historic settlements on Great Exuma, are certainly worth a look. Although now claimed by bush, there are decrepit forts and ruined plantations lying scattered around in between the farming and fishing villages.

The island plunged headlong into the modern world with the arrival of mass tourism in the shape of the Four Seasons Resort (now the Sandals at Emerald Bay), which opened in the 1980s and suddenly saw plane-loads of tourists touching down each week, changing the island's once quiet face forever.

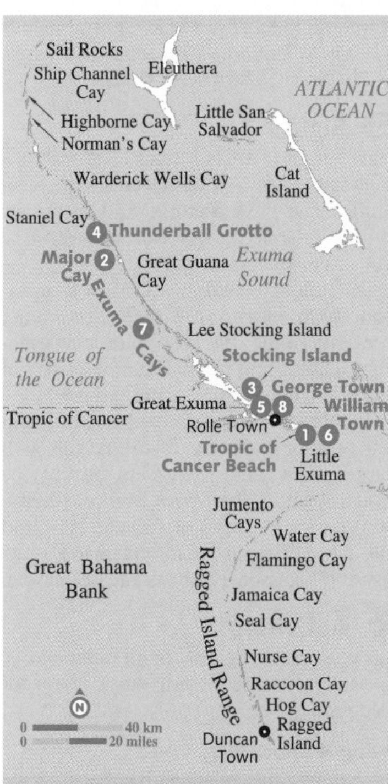

The Exumas Highlights

1. Lazing the day away on **Tropic of Cancer Beach** (p165)
2. Seeing the friendly swimming pigs of **Major Cay** (p168)
3. Discovering the hiking paths of beautiful **Stocking Island** (p163)
4. Snorkeling or diving in the exquisite **Thunderball Grotto** (p167)
5. Joining the crowds for the fabulous **Family Island Regatta** (p162)
6. Hearing tall stories about the making of *Pirates of the Caribbean* at **Santana's Grill** (p166)
7. Finding your own virgin beach cruising the incredible **Exuma Cays** (p166)
8. Chilling out and catching up on the local gossip in the bars and restaurants of **George Town** (p158)

Getting There & Away

AIR

Most travelers to Exuma fly into the small Exuma International Airport, 6 miles north of George Town. There are several flights (one way $85) per day on Bahamas Air, Western Air and Sky Bahamas, as well as international connections to Miami (American Eagle), Fort Lauderdale (Continental), Atlanta (Delta) and Toronto (Air Canada).

BOAT

If traveling in your own boat, George Town is the official port of entry to the Exumas. You'll need to call ahead to arrange clearance with **Customs** (☎242-345-0071) and **Immigration** (☎242-345-2569), both in the Government Administration Building on Queen's Hwy. You will also require a special sailing license for traveling around the islands.

FERRY An overnight ferry on **Bahamas Ferries** (www.bahamasferries.com) leaves Nassau (one way $60) at 8:30pm on Monday and Wednesday and arrives in George Town at 6:30am the following day.

MAIL BOAT If you fancy taking it slow, two mail boats connect the Exumas to Nassau.

Grand Master Departs Nassau for George Town (one way $40, 12 hours) at 2pm Tuesday and returns to Nassau at 7am on Friday.

Lady Eddina Departs Nassau for Exuma Cays, Barraterre, Staniel Cay, Black Point, Farmer's Cay and Highbourn's Cay (one way $40, 12 hours) at 1pm on Tuesday. It then carries on to San Salvador. The return journey begins at 9am Saturday in San Salvador. Contact the **Dockmaster's office** (242-393-1064) at Potter's Cay in Nassau for further details.

Getting Around

You will need your own transportation if you want to explore the island outside George Town's immediate vicinity.

Airport Car Rental (242-345-0090; taro@coralwave.com; Exuma International Airport) Has cars to rent from around $70 per day.

Don's Rent A Car (242-345-0112; donsrentacar@hotmail.com; Exuma International Airport) Rents vehicles from $70 per day.

Exuma Transport (242-336-2101; rjgray@yahoo.com; Queen's Hwy, George Town) Rents cars starting at $65 per day.

Bicycles can be rented from Pet's Place (p161) or Starfish (opposite) for around $25 per day.

GREAT EXUMA

The main island in the chain, Great Exuma is the starting point for most people exploring the islands, and where boaters and yachties will call in for their supplies.

George Town

POP 1050

Despite its interesting location, scattered around the sides of Lake Victoria (actually an inlet of the lagoon and a great natural harbor), George Town is a place most people visit to pick up supplies or run errands. While it has plenty of easy-going charm, there's nothing much to keep you here and most visitors move on quickly to Stocking Island, up or down the coast or to the cays.

Government Wharf is the focal point of most action, where townsfolk gather when the mail boat calls, fisherfolk return with their catch and a myriad of visitors' boats are always on the move.

The event of the year is April's **Family Island Regatta** (p162), considered one of the Bahamas' best. Hundreds of islanders still make the annual pilgrimage to George Town's Elizabeth Harbour for this event, for which boat builders proudly ship in their handmade dinghies from other islands aboard the mail boats. During the regatta, the town is transformed into an outdoor party venue. Another big event that draws an international crowd of keen fishermen is the annual **Bahamas Bonefish Bonanza**, held in George Town every October.

Sights

A few buildings are of interest. **St Andrew's Anglican Church** (1802) gleams whitely on a hill above Lake Victoria, and opens for Sunday services (it's well worth the stroll to peek at the gravestones out back).

The pink and white neoclassical **Government Administration Building** accommodates everything: the post office, police station, customs and immigration, Ministry of Education, magistrates' court and jail.

Regatta Park is a pleasant piece of land in the center of George Town that fills with market stalls and partygoers during the annual regatta. The **Straw Market** (9am-5pm) sits on the edge of Regatta Park and sells a small range of locally made straw bags and hats, some T-shirts and beachwear.

Activities

This is an excellent area for all water sports, especially boating of any kind, even for amateurs.

Diving & Snorkeling

The Exumas are replete with some fantastic snorkel and dive sites, including spectacular blue holes and caves, many of which have safety lines.

For great snorkel sites head for the schools of small and vibrant fish around **Bird Cay**; the odd-shaped **Duck Cay North**; **Duck Cay South**, a tiered reef that looks like an underwater wedding cake; and the shallow reefs of the **Three Sisters Rock**.

Harbour Buoy Portside is a very active reef with lots of marine life, as is **Jolly Hall**, a favored hatchery for grunts and yellowtail snapper. **Loaded Barrel Reef** has plenty of fish species inhabiting its wide sea beds, as well as staghorn coral. **Harbour Buoy Starboard** is home to large brain corals, as are the shallow reefs of **Liz Lee Shoals**.

There are some fabulous dive sites, and one of the easiest is **Stingray Reef**, where shallow waters are full of snapper, angelfish, grunts and stingrays.

Experienced daredevils may wish to try the **Angelfish Blue Hole**, a vertical shaft which starts at 30ft below the surface and falls to 90ft before leveling into a network of caves full of soft sponges and schooling angelfish. Another deep orifice, **Crab Cay Blue Hole** is a 40ft-wide crevasse up to 90ft deep, with archways inhabited by lobsters, snappers and stingrays.

South of Stocking Island, access to Mystery Cave (p163) begins at 15ft below the surface and drops to 100ft, and is another one for the experienced.

Some outfits:

Dive Exuma DIVING, SNORKELING
(☎242-336-2893; www.dive-exuma.com; February Point, Queen's Hwy) Highly recommended, this operator offers packages of six dives for $480 including all equipment, though there's a 10% reduction for a booking made four days in advance.

Turtle Divers DIVING, SNORKELING
(☎242-551-8807, 242-524-3305; Minn's Dock) Also offers diving ($70 per dive) and snorkeling excursions ($55 per trip). It operates out of Club Peace & Plenty in George Town.

Elvis Ferguson SNORKELING
(☎242-464-1558) A cheaper option for snorkeling trips. Offers trips to remote sites around Stocking Island.

Kayaking

Rolle's Sea Kayaking KAYAKING
(☎242-524-3172; www.rolleseakayaking.com) A family operation through and through and one that's all about kayaking – the owners are true enthusiasts. They cater to any level of experience and are very child-friendly.

Starfish KAYAKING
(☎242-336-3033; www.starfishexuma.com; Queen's Hwy) Starfish presents a variety of activities, including kayak rental by the day/week $50/225, and guided trips to Moriah Cay and around Elizabeth Harbour and the nearby beaches.

Bonefishing & Sportfishing

Exuma is one of the top spots for bonefishing in the Bahamas. A full list of guides can be obtained from the Bahamas Ministry of Tourism. Rates average around $300 per half-day or $400 to $500 per day.

Bandits Bonefishing Lodge & Pirate's Den
(☎242-358-7011; www.banditsbonefishin
Offers angling ($400 per day) and
packages, including accommodations and three nights/two days of fishing for $1450.

Marvin Bethel FISHING
(☎242-554-2873) Another recommended local guide, based in George Town.

Kitesurfing

Exuma Kitesurfing KITESURFING
(☎242-524-0523; www.exumakitesurfing.com) Offers a dizzying array of packages for kitesurfing including a learn-to-kiteboard three-day package ($985) and a five-hour Kiteventure package from $295.

Birdwatching

It is not only the marine parks that are fabulous for living creatures. Bird fanciers will jump for joy (quietly!) on the following islands that contain national bird reserves: Big Galliot, Channel and Flat Cays, Big and Little Darby Islands, and Guana, Goat, Betty, Pigeon, Cistern, Leaf, Harvey and Rocks Cays.

All these islands can only be reached by private boat and so you'll need your own vessel or book a day trip with a travel agency. Contact the tourist office in George Town for further information and more detailed maps.

Tours

There are a large number of tour operators operating tours of Great Exuma and the Exuma Cays. These typically involve a day on a boat, picnicking on pristine beaches, snorkeling, visiting caves and grottoes, seeing the famous swimming pigs of Major Cay, peeking at the 'sets' to *Pirates of the Caribbean*, and trying your hand at fishing or shark feeding. Shop around for the best deal and be clear about what you want: most tours are flexible. Prices average around $150 to $300 per person per half-day, depending on what's included.

Off Island Adventures (☎242-524-0524; www.offislandadventures.com)

Robert's Island Adventures (☎242-357-0224; www.robertsislandadventures.com)

Exuma Cays Adventures (☎242-357-0390; www.exumacaysadventures.com)

Four C's (☎242-464-1720, 345-2352)

Great & Little Exumas

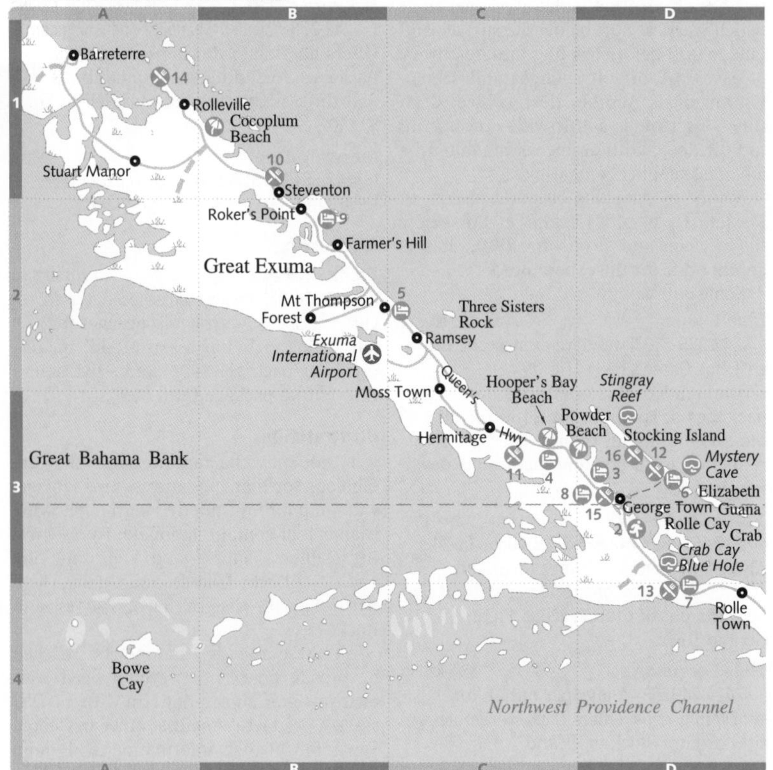

For an introduction to the history and culture of Great Exuma, join the excellent **East Exuma Native Bus Tour** (☎242-336-2857, $20), which departs the Sandals at Emerald Bay resort (p164) in Emerald Bay at 9:30am every day except Sunday, picking up in George Town at 10:15am, too. The tour takes in nearly all of the island's historic sights and includes time for a dip at Tropic of Cancer Beach and for some shopping in George Town.

Sleeping

There's a good variety of accommodations on Exuma, though bargains are fairly thin on the ground. The Bahamas Ministry of Tourism can supply a full list of guesthouses around the Exumas. Reserve lodgings well in advance at regatta time, as chances for last-minute accommodations are nil.

Regatta Point GUESTHOUSE **$$**
(☎242-336-2206; www.regattapointbahamas.com; Regatta Point; d $148; ❄) At the end of a promontory with great 360-degree sea views, this secluded spot is nevertheless just a couple of minutes' walk from the amenities of George Town. All six rooms enjoy full kitchens, outdoor spaces and pointedly have no TV or wireless. Rooms are fan-cooled, hot water is solar powered and the welcome is warm.

Club Peace & Plenty HOTEL **$$$**
(☎242-336-2551; www.peaceandplenty.com; Elizabeth Harbour; r from $219; ❄📶🏊) Built on the location of a slave market, this plucky hotel in the middle of George Town has 32 bright, Caribbean-style rooms set around a small pool, bar area and dock. The staff is very friendly and most rooms have great views towards Stocking Island. Snorkel gear and sailboards can be rented from Peace & Plenty Beach Club on Stocking Island,

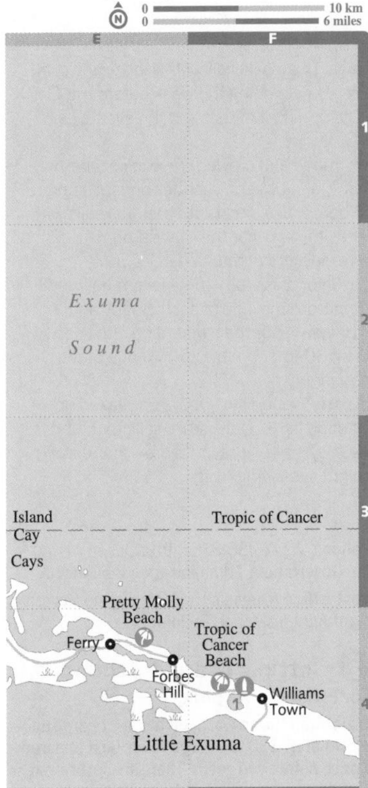

Great & Little Exumas

Sights

1 Doric Pillar F4

Activities, Courses & Tours

2 Dive Exuma D3

Sleeping

3 Sandals at Emerald Bay D3
4 Augusta Bay C3
5 Coral Gardens C2
6 Exuma Palms Hotel D3
7 Higgins Landing D4
8 Master Harbour Villas D3
9 Minns Cottages B2

Eating

10 Peace & Plenty Beach Club B1
11 Big D's Conch Spot C3
12 Café Alesha D3
13 Chat n Chill Bar & Grill D4
14 Cheater's Restaurant & Bar A1
15 Exuma Point Restaurant D3
16 Fish & Fry D3

which guests can reach by using the complimentary twice daily ferry.

Minns Cottages COTTAGES $$
(242-336-2033/2645; Queen's Hwy; 1-/2-bedrooms per week $875/1295;) Book ahead for these pristine, fully equipped and tasteful units just north of George Town, though be aware that it's not possible to rent them for less than a week at a time. The spacious cottages include an enclosed patio facing the sea (albeit from across the main road) and the kitchens have coffeemaker, microwave, oven and fridge.

Two Turtles Inn INN $
(242-336-2545; www.twoturtlesinnbahamas.com; George Town; r from $89;) This stone-and-timber lodge in the heart of George Town has nine rooms that were undergoing a total refit at the time of writing. A Chinese restaurant was due to open shortly, and two on-site bars make the whole complex something of a local watering spot for the entire town.

Eating & Drinking

A choice of groceries (and household goods) can be found at **Exuma Markets** (8am-6pm, to 11am Sun) in the town center. The Fish & Fry area (see p164), just north of George Town, has heaps of little eateries and is also worth a visit.

Eddy's Edgewater Club CAFE $
(Queen's Hwy; mains $7-12; 7am-10pm, to midnight Fri & Sat, closed Sun) This very reliable, friendly and informal restaurant serves up three tasty Bahamian meals a day, including changing daily specials. There's a pleasant terrace to sit out on with views over Lake Victoria, a more formal dining room at the back and a large bar that's always packed on Monday for the island's most popular rake 'n' scrape music evening.

Pet's Place DELI $
(242-336-3010; Queen's Hwy; mains $6-16; 7am-11pm Mon-Sat, to 10pm Sun;) It might not be giving New York a run for its money, but this new addition to George Town's limited eating scene opposite the Shell station is very welcome. Drop in for a freshly baked muffin and coffee in the

FAMILY ISLAND REGATTA

The wildly festive, four-day **Family Island Regatta** (www.nationalfamilyislandregatta.com) has been held every April since 1954. The party really gets going the week before the regatta, when breweries and rum companies sponsor a host of daft and fun events as a build-up to the main event.

Around 50 Bahamian sailing vessels (all locally made and crewed) race in Elizabeth Harbour, George Town, and everyone within miles – landlubbers, yachties and far-flung Bahamians – arrives to cheer on the sloops. The boats race along with their tall sails billowing, spilling the odd drunken crew member as they go. For the islands' boat builders, it is a chance to see their lovingly-built vessels prove their master's craft.

Races are divided into five classes, including a junior class for youngsters. A hallmark of the races is the 'pry,' a long wooden plank jutting from the side of each dinghy and sloop. The crew – often as many as six or seven people – put their weight on it to keep the boat balanced as it zips along, typically in a stiff 30-knot breeze. Knowledge of the winds, currents and boat-handling is essential to winning.

The celebrated regatta is also an excuse for a party; sound systems are tweaked up and accompanied by a colorful and raucous Junkanoo band, while stalls sell cracked conch and fried chicken. Everyone chatters while they sip their favorite brew in the sunshine. The dancing starts as dusk falls, and the night's festivities begin...

morning, or a filling soup and sandwich combination at lunch time. It also delivers.

Towne Café & Bakery CAFE **$$**
(Queen's Hwy; mains $12; ⏲7.30am-3pm Mon-Sat) This rather sterile-looking place in fact serves up a good Bahamian breakfast of boil fish (a type of stew) with onions and hot peppers, tuna-fish salad, or chicken souse with grits or mildly spiced johnnycake. Daily lunch specials include a great fried snapper.

City Wick Pizza PIZZA **$$**
(☎242-524-3247; pizza $10-30; Queen's Hwy; ⏲8am-9pm, to 10pm Thu-Sat) For those crying for some relief from fried fish and chicken dishes, obtain a take-out pizza here! It doesn't deliver, but will take orders by phone for you to pick up.

ℹ Information

Bahamas Ministry of Tourism (☎242-336-2430; www.bahamas.com; Queen's Hwy) In the same building as the Royal Bank of Canada and can offer lots of brochures, eating and lodging lists and free maps of the island.

Exuma Web Cafe (Queen's Hwy; per 30min $6; ⏲8am-8pm) It's between Eddy's Edgewater Club and BaTelCo.

Government Medical Clinic (☎242-336-2088) Based at the big pink and white Government Administration Building in George Town.

Pet's Place (Queen's Hwy; ⏲7am-11pm Mon-Sat, to 10pm Sun;) There's also access from a terminal and free wi-fi here.

Police (☎242-336-2666, 919; Queen's Hwy) In the Government Administration Building.

Post office (Queen's Hwy) Also in the Government Administration Building.

ℹ Getting There & Around

To/From the Airport

Taxis await the arrival of flights and charge approximately $30 to George Town; best to agree a price before you get in. There are several car rental agencies based at the airport.

Boat

To explore around the cays and Exuma Cays Land & Sea Park (p167), you will need a boat of some kind. Some lodgings provide boats for hire, but the rates offered by **Minns Water Sports** (☎242-336-3483; www.mwsboats.com; George Town) are especially good. It rents out boats from $45/90 per half-/full day, but the rates are reduced for bookings over three days. The boats vary in size from 15ft to 22ft, and a $200 cash deposit is required.

FERRY There are two separate ferries to different parts of Stocking Island departing from George Town. The main ferry is the water taxi from government wharf run by **Elvis Ferguson** (☎242-464-1558, $12 return), who offers a roughly hourly service to the Chat n Chill Bar & Grill and the St Francis Resort from 10am until 5pm daily.

A second service departs the dock at **Club Peace & Plenty** (☎242-336-2551; Elizabeth Harbour; round-trip $12, free for guests) for Stocking Island's Hamburger Beach at 10am and 1pm, returning at 1:10pm and 4pm.

Bus

Buses depart from and return to George Town daily via Emerald Bay ($3 one way) and Rolleville ($5). Ask at the Bahamas Ministry of Tourism for a bus schedule. While we don't recommend hitchhiking, it can be a more reliable way of getting around, and it's very common for locals to pick people up on the roadside.

Taxi

Exuma Transit Services (☎242-345-0232) and **Leslie Dames** (☎242-357-0015) both run taxi services around the island.

Stocking Island & Rolle Cay

Stocking Island, population 7, is a 600-acre, pencil-thin island lined with gorgeous beaches, about a mile offshore from Great Exuma. It's pleasingly remote and makes for a great day trip from George Town. You can go snorkeling, hike through some excellently maintained trails and enjoy a meal at the boisterous Chat n Chill Bar & Grill. The best snorkel spots are located at the cuts between Stocking Island and Elizabeth Island and between Elizabeth Island and Guana Cay.

Mystery Cave is a 400ft-deep blue hole on the Atlantic side and is said to be one of the few living intertidal stromatolite reefs in the world (the other major one is near Perth, Australia); a living fossil – dating back 3½ million years. Highborne Cay stromatolites (living fossils) are now being researched (see p166).

Peace & Plenty Beach Club (see right) will rent snorkel gear ($15 per day) and sailboards ($15/30 per half-/full day) to day-trippers, as well as small sailboats and paddleboats ($25 per half-day).

There are no roads on the island and access is by boat. For information about ferries to Stocking Island, see opposite.

Sleeping & Eating

Higgins' Landing BOUTIQUE HOTEL **$$$**
(☎242-357-0008, www.higginslanding.com; r incl dinner $495; ❄📶) This exquisite refuge from the world can almost justify its eye-wateringly high prices with its easy charm and genteel comfort. There are just four very private cottages (one of which accommodates two couples in separate rooms) and each boasts antique wooden furniture, white timber walls and private decks for sunbathing. The feel is much more of a private club than a resort here, with most things, from snorkeling equipment to use of the kayaks and the small gym, being free. Dinner is an elaborate affair, and the restaurant is considered to be one of the Exumas' best. The entire place is powered by solar energy and only rainwater is used in the bathrooms.

St Francis Resort RESORT **$$$**
(☎242-557-9629; www.stfrancisresort.com; r incl breakfast $260; ❄📶) This small getaway favorite is the second hotel on Stocking Island, and very lovely it is too. With 5 miles of sandy beach right on the doorstep and wonderful isolation to recommend it, it's easy to see why St Francis gets rave reviews. The rooms are not exciting, but they are spacious and comfortable, all with private decks overlooking the sea.

Chat n Chill Bar & Grill GRILL **$$**
(☎242-336-2800; mains $15; ⏰11am-7pm) This spirited and affable outdoor bar is a favorite with the yachtie crowd who descend on it each lunchtime for the simple menu of barbequed ribs, burgers and fresh fish and to share beers over tall stories of their morning's adventures. The Sunday pig roast ($15) is one of Exuma's social highlights; book in advance and enjoy a perfect Sunday afternoon on the beach here.

Peace & Plenty Beach Club GRILL **$$**
(☎242-336-2551; mains $8-15; ⏰lunch) This great beach club serves up delicious burgers that keep both locals and traveling yachties returning again and again. It enjoys a fantastic position on the suitably named Hamburger Beach.

North of George Town

Queen's Hwy runs north of George Town through a string of small settlements made up of traditional homes painted in Caribbean pastels and shaded by palms. Beautiful beaches line the shore, the very best of which are **Hooper's Bay Beach** and **Coco-plum Beach**. Access can be tricky as there are lots of private houses blocking beach access from the main road. Ask locals, or look for the sporadic 'Beach Access' signs.

A mile offshore opposite Mt Thompson sits **Three Sisters Rock**, a trio of craggy boulders rising from the sea. They're supposedly named for three sisters who each drowned herself here for the shame of bearing a child out of wedlock.

The historic settlement of **Rolleville**, 28 miles north of George Town, sits atop a hill at the northern end of Great Exuma. It's a poor village with many meager shacks and former slave homes, most in tumbledown condition, but it's brightened in late spring and early summer by African flame trees. The hamlet is the site of the **Rolleville Regatta**, held the first Monday in August. Several locals still make boats.

Sleeping

TOP CHOICE Coral Gardens B&B $
(www.coralgardensbahamas.com; Hooper's Bay; r from $99;) Run by retired Brits Peter and Betty, this charming house is located a few hundred meters inland from lovely Hooper's Bay and is one of the best deals on the island. The three bedrooms all have private bathrooms and two small apartments make this a great and good-value option. Peter, who can help with arranging all activities as well as car rental, is a mine of local information after a decade on Exuma. The owners also let out a range of beach-front **apartments** (www.bahamasbeachapartments.com) and a superb **beach house** (www.coralsandsbahamas.com) on Hooper's Bay.

Augusta Bay HOTEL $$$
(242-336-2551; www.augustabaybahamas.com; Hooper's Bay; r $315;) Brightly painted with an African theme, this is a solid choice for anyone looking for an upmarket hotel without the formality. An attractive pool area overlooks a small beach and the vibe is extremely welcoming. Bargains can often be had by calling the hotel directly.

Exuma Palms Hotel HOTEL $$$
(242-358-4040; www.exumapalms.com; Mt Thompson; r $230;) This motel-style accommodations has seen better days and has a rather lonely position overlooking an admittedly very beautiful beach. It has 12 large, air-con beachfront rooms and two cottages, all modestly but nicely furnished, with patio or balcony and satellite TV.

Sandals at Emerald Bay RESORT $$$
(242-336-6989; www.sandals.com; Queen's Hwy, Roker's Point; r $400-550;) This exclusive resort is rather isolated from everything else on the island, but is totally self-contained and so many visitors leave only to go to the airport. Centered on a golf course designed by Greg Norman, the resort complex features vacation townhouse rentals and beachfront villas, all in plantation-style architecture, plus gourmet restaurants, a health and fitness club, kids' clubs and a full-service marina.

Eating & Drinking

There are a few bars up this way that serve food.

TOP CHOICE Café Alesha MODERN BAHAMIAN $$
(242-336-2203; Queen's Hwy, Old Hooper's Bay; mains $14-25; lunch & dinner Mon-Fri, dinner Sat & Sun) This highly regarded newcomer has quickly sealed its local reputation with innovative takes on Bahamian cooking. Run by two sisters who are clearly ambitious to raise the bar of local cuisine, the restaurant is a spacious and relatively formal affair. The small menu includes novelspins on old favorites, such as mushroom-glazed pork chops with sweet potato or more standard grilled lobster tail and conch fritters.

Big D's Conch Spot SEAFOOD $$
(Queen's Hwy, Steventon; mains $10-26; lunch & dinner Tue-Sat) While it's tagline 'world-famous' might be pushing it a little bit, this brightly painted beachside restaurant exudes charm and retains fans across the island. The conch salad here is fantastic, though burgers, cracked lobster and whole snapper also feature on the menu. There's a great little beach here, too, so you can even take a cooling dip while waiting for your food.

Exuma Point Restaurant BAHAMIAN $$
(242-345-6244; Exuma Point, Rolleville; mains $12-15; lunch Sat & Sun, dinners by request) Well signposted out of Rolleville, this superbly located open-air restaurant right on a beautiful stretch of beach makes for a great weekend lunch spot. Enjoy the excellent Sunday buffer ($17) or a plate of ribs or cracked conch while taking in the sublime view.

Fish & Fry FAST FOOD $
(Queen's Hwy, btwn George Town & Hooper's Bay; mains $8-12; dinner) Definitely a local experience, this slice of island life may be a bit raucous for some, but it's one of the best opportunities you'll find on the island to mix with locals. Informal beach huts serve the day's catch to a beered up and almost exclusively male crowd, but the food is cheap and the atmosphere largely friendly.

South of George Town

South of George Town there's the wealthy, gated community of **February Point**, a selection of excellent and largely deserted beaches and several sights of local historical note. However, beyond that there's almost no tourist infrastructure and the ramshackle villages scattered along the Queen's Hwy get poorer and poorer the further south you go.

Many of the decrepit sun-bleached pastel buildings and clapboard shacks date back over a century and have withstood storms and hurricanes. Goats graze freely and chickens roam with their broods in neat little fluffy lines alongside the road.

Try not to miss visiting a very evocative piece of local history at the **Rolle Town Tombs**. Here lie a few solitary 18th-century tombstones, one of which is shaped like a double bed with headboard and footboard and dated 1792. The plaque notes that the 26-year-old wife of a Scottish overseer, Captain Alexander McKay, slumbers there with her infant child. The poor man died the following year, said to be from a broken heart.

Sleeping & Eating

Master Harbour Villas VILLAS $$
(242-345-5076; www.exumabahamas.com/masterharbour.html; Queen's Hwy; 1-/2-/4-bedroom villas $150/200/350;) These very clean and well-maintained villas are right on the beach and have their own dock, so they are popular with boaties. The owner Jerry can organize most activities, from diving to bonefishing, and car rentals.

Cheaters Restaurant & Bar BAHAMIAN $$
(242-336-2535; Queen's Hwy, South George Town; mains $12-25; 8am-10pm Tue-Sat) Local fare served at this simple eatery draws a friendly Bahamian crowd. The air-con room is shady and refreshing, although the decor is a little sparse. Typically Bahamian dishes include garlic shrimp and broiled grouper.

LITTLE EXUMA

Little Exuma lies only around 10 miles south of the Exuma International Airport, and is separated from the main isle by a 200yd-wide bight; a bridge fills the gap.

A number of ongoing developments for private beachside dwellings have yet to encroach completely over some lovely beaches. A nice day can be spent here relaxing on the white sands and paddling around in the perfectly clear water.

Pretty Molly Beach is one of the loveliest beaches on the island, despite the sorrowful origin of its name – a slave killed herself one day by simply walking into the waves off this beach. The stark beauty of these shores is a fitting monument to her spirit, which is said to still walk alongside these waters.

Ferry to Williams Town

Ferry is a small hillside settlement that lies immediately across the bridge from Great Exuma. Look out for **St Christopher's Anglican Church**, a whitewashed chapel (supposedly the smallest church in the Bahamas) festooned with a bougainvillea bower.

Forbes Hill, 12 miles southeast of George Town, has a 100yd-wide scimitar of pure white sand with turquoise shallows cusped by tiny headlands. Two miles south of Forbes Hill a side road leads east to **Tropic of Cancer Beach**, another true stunner that runs south, unblemished, for several miles – it's unusual to see anyone else here, so you don't have to worry about finding a spot, though there are no facilities or shops nearby.

The southernmost settlement is **Williams Town** (population 300), populated predominantly by Kelsalls, descended from or named for the foremost Loyalist family that founded the settlement. The Kelsalls established a cotton plantation and sold salt drawn from nearby salt ponds. The brush-entangled ruins of the plantation home – **Hermitage Estate** – still stand amid pinkish brine ponds.

You can see locals dressing their fresh catch of fish and conch at the rickety wharf behind and just south of St Mary Magdalene's Church in William's Town. North of town, on the bluff to the side of the road, you'll pass a tall **Doric pillar** transporting you (metaphorically) to ancient Greece. This column and a rusty cannon stand high above the rocky shore. The hulk of a ship lies dramatically on a white-sand beach fronting the village, within calling distance of the column meant to guide mariners.

Eating

Mom's Bakery (in Williams Town) is the place to stock up on tasty rum cake, banana bread, coconut tarts and bread. Two restaurants worth mentioning are the following:

WORTH A TRIP

RAGGED ISLAND RANGE

Few visitors ever reach this crescent of a dozen or so isles and a score of small cays that lie about 25 miles south of Little Exuma. The chain begins with the Jumento Cays, arcs west and south for about 100 miles and ends with the largest isle, Ragged Island. During the 19th century the chains' flats were used for salt-crystal farming. Today they are virtually uninhabited and the only settlement, Duncan Town (population 70) on Ragged Island itself is a small fishing village. The only way to make it here is to charter your own boat.

TOP CHOICE **Santana's Grill** BAHAMIAN $$
(242-345-4102; Queen's Hwy, Williams Town; mains $10-22; lunch Tue-Sat, dinner by arrangement) Pull up a bar stool at one of Exuma's most relaxed and enjoyable eateries. Run by the formidable Denise Rolle, this friendly grill offers the best-value fresh lobster on Exuma and its many regulars often entertain diners with increasingly tall stories from the *Pirates of the Caribbean* shoot, part of which happened at nearby Sandy Point (ask to see their photo albums). There's also a great beach just a matter of feet from the bar.

La Shanté BAHAMIAN $$
(242-345-4190; Queen's Hwy, Forbes Hill; mains $10-15; lunch & dinner Mon-Sat) On a small side road signposted off the Queen's Hwy, this place is known island-wide for its good lobster salad and the potent cocktails served up by its friendly owner, Dwight. There's a beautiful mini crescent beach right in front of the restaurant, which all-comers are welcome to use.

EXUMA CAYS

The Exuma Cays are a world unto themselves and the stuff of Caribbean fantasy. Tantalizingly inaccessible (you'll need to have your own boat or pay someone with one to make it to most places here), the cays begin at the barren Sail Rocks, 40 miles southeast of New Providence and continue in a long line of some 360 islets to Great Exuma. Though they may seem alike, each has its own quirky character and many are privately owned.

If you're in your own boat, a cruise around discovering new beaches, seeing wonderful Thunderball Grotto (opposite) or dropping anchor to snorkel around pristine reefs makes for an unbeatable Bahamas experience.

These waters are acclaimed as the 'finest cruising grounds in the Western Hemisphere.' *The Exuma Guide: A Cruising Guide to the Exuma Cays* by Stephen Pavlidis is a must-read for sailors.

Along with day trips to several of the cays from Nassau (see p53), or kayak and snorkel trips from George Town (see p158), you can always hire your own boat (see p162).

For details of the mail boat that visits some of the cays in this area from Nassau, see p157.

Getting There & Away

The following trips depart from Nassau, and are very popular:

Island World Adventures (242-363-3333; www.islandworldadventures.com; Nassau; adult/child $200/150) Provides day-long excursions on a high-powered speedboat from Paradise Island to Saddleback Cay's wonderful snorkeling and seven private beaches. Trips include lunch, an open bar and snorkeling gear.

Powerboat Adventures (242-363-2265; www.powerboatadventures.com; Nassau; adult/child $190/140) Offers a thrilling ride from Nassau as a powerboat zips you to Allan's Cays for snorkeling, then on to Ship Channel Cay for a nature hike and barbecue lunch on the beach.

Highborne Cay

This private cay, 2 miles south of Leaf Cay, is favored by yachties, who are permitted ashore if they are using the marina's facilities. The beach on the eastern side of the cay is one of the most beautiful in the Bahamas.

The **Highborne Cay Research Station** has recently been set up to research a year in the life of Bahamian stromatolites to see how they adapt to changing weather environments. For more information on stromatolites and Highborne Cay contact www.stromatolites.info.

The **Highborne Cay Marina** (242-355-1008; VHF channel 16; Nassau, New Providence) has a grocery store, pay phone and berths for yachts up to 130ft.

Norman's Cay

One look at the stunning beaches and you'll understand why 4-mile-long Norman's Cay was once an idyllic hideaway for the wintering wealthy, and then a less salubrious crowd. In the 1970s, most of the island was bought by Colombian drug lord Caelos Lehder Rivas. After his arrest and extradition to the US in 1987, his land was confiscated by the Bahamian government and sold to private investors. The bonefishing here is said to be superb.

Norman's Cay Beach Club at MacDuff's (242-357-8846; www.ncbcmacduffs.com; r $250;) has four one-bedroom villas that will sleep 16 people in all. The villas are pleasantly decorated and come with an equipped kitchen. Water sports are offered, and food can be stocked by arrangement. The restaurant and bar here is a popular lunch spot for yachties.

Exuma Cays Land & Sea Park

This park is an unspoilt underwater idyll teeming with all sorts of fish and marine life that scarcely notice your presence as they dart through a labyrinth of vast caverns, through blue holes and along miles of reef. It's the first marine 'replenishment nursery' in the world. The park consists of 175 sq miles of protected islands and surrounding seas, and was created in 1958. All fishing and collecting is banned. No marine or plant life, whether dead or alive, may be taken from here, including shells. Fish spawned in the park have now been proven to be breeding further afield and replenishing overfished areas, to everyone's delight.

The park runs 22 miles south from Wax Cay Cut (immediately south of Norman's Cay) to Conch Cut and Fowl Cay. It is 8 miles wide, extending 3½ miles east and west on each side of the islands. It has outstanding anchorages and even more outstanding dive sites.

On land, you may glimpse the Bahamian mockingbird, Bahamian banana quit, or the rare red-legged thrush. Sea birds abound, including terns, waders, and the elegant, long-tailed tropicbird, which nests in high bluffs. Land animals include curly-tailed and blue-tailed lizards, plump iguanas and endangered hutias, which look like oversized guinea pigs.

With no commercial development, the main cays in the park's vicinity are perfect for camping. There are no facilities, however, and you will need to take all food and water with you. The **Bahamas National Trust** (BNT; 242-225-1783; www.bnt.bs; Warderick Wells Cay; 9am-noon & 3-5pm Mon-Fri, 9am-1pm Sat) has posted information leaflets on several cays; park access is free.

Apart from day tours to the park from Staniel Cay or Nassau or kayaking tours from George Town, your best bet is to hire a boat and camping gear from George Town and enjoy exploring this wonderful region in your own time. Boaters must anchor at Hog Cay at the south end of Warderick Wells Cay. Moorings cost from $15 per day, depending on your vessel's length. Call 'Exuma Park' on VHF 16 at least 24 hours in advance to check availability.

Staniel Cay

This tiny cay (population 76) is the most sophisticated and visited settlement in the Exuma Cays and it is the main base from which to visit the Exuma Cays Land & Sea Park. The small, attractive village has all the necessities – grocery stores, post office, church and library (1776) – and the cay is lined with some lovely tranquil beaches on which to relax. The bonefishing is also excellent here.

The **New Year's Day Regatta**, always fun, is when locally built dinghies compete for prizes, and the town beach is where celebrations are held for the return of many local people and yachties for the festivities. The **Annual Staniel Cay Bonefish Tournament** in August is another big event that brings home the locals.

THUNDERBALL GROTTO

This crystalline grotto, just northwest of the cay, is another Bahamian jewel. The exquisite cavern – lit by shafts of light pouring in from holes in the ceiling that sear through the water highlighting a myriad of darting fish – was named for the James Bond movie *Thunderball,* scenes from which were filmed here. So, too, were scenes from *Splash* and another 007 movie, *Never Say Never Again*. Although you swim in at low tide, the current is pretty strong – inexperienced swimmers may

DON'T MISS

HAVE YOU SEEN THE LITTLE PIGGIES?

Only a short boat trip away from Staniel Cay, tiny Major Cay is a great place for a day of snorkeling and sunning. Don't forget a picnic for yourself and the friendly porcine population to enjoy! Yes, that's right, Major Cay has some famous swimming pigs that like nothing better than a 'plash, pat and a peanut-butter sandwich.

prefer to snorkel and swim elsewhere. Divers also love this spot.

Sleeping & Eating

The cay has two waterfront hotels that play to the boating crowd.

Staniel Cay Yacht Club & Resort RESORT **$$**
(242-355-2024; www.stanielcay.com; r from $165, mains $15-28;) This is truly a place for lovers of perfect seafront views. Spacious verandas overlook the sea and create a feeling of total relaxation. There are cool and comfortable cottages (with kitchenette) or suites (with kitchen) and great weekly rates. Use one of the resort's free *Boston Whalers* or *Sunfish* sailboats, take along the free scuba gear and go and visit gorgeous Major Cay. The restaurant here attracts a big crowd of yachties and can be packed in season – book ahead.

Club Thunderball BAHAMIAN **$$**
(242-355-2012; mains $10-25; lunch & dinner, closed Mon) This lively place is atop the bluff overlooking the Thunderball Grotto. It serves Bahamian food and has beach barbecues on Friday night (book a rib!), plus occasional pig roasts and a Super Bowl party in January. The club also features a pool table, satellite TV and dancing on weekends.

Great Guana Cay

The largest of the Exuma Cays, 12-mile-long Great Guana Cay, also has the cays' largest settlement, **Black Point** (population 253), and has a reputation for not being the friendliest place (it's generally not used to receiving visitors). Facilities include an airstrip, post office and a medical clinic. An **Emancipation Day Regatta** is held here each August.

De Shamons (242-355-3009; Black Point; r $100;) has four rooms with fridge, over its restaurant. The restaurant specializes in freshly caught fish served in traditional Bahamian style. Ask about the meals when making reservations.

Lorraine's Café (242-355-2201; Black Point; mains $8-15) is recommended for inexpensive Bahamian fare and freshly baked bread and cookies, though it's best to call in advance to ensure it will be prepared.

Adderley's Convenience Store (7:30am-6pm) sells a limited range of groceries.

Little Farmer's Cay

This cay is simply a stone's throw away from the southwest tip of Great Guana. It consists of a fairly small fishing village and bay. It hosts the annual **Farmer's Cay Festival & Regatta** in the first weekend of February as well as the spirited **Full Moon Beer Festival** in July.

Farmer's Cay Yacht Club & Marina (242-355-4017; r $100;) has four smallish rooms with TV. In the same building, a cosy **restaurant** (mains $10-25; lunch & dinner) serves everything from fish snacks to full lobsters and has a pleasant position overlooking the sea. Advanced notice is needed for dinner.

Ocean Cabin Restaurant (242-355-4006; www.oceancbn.com; mains $9-30; breakfast, lunch & dinner), a small, friendly bar in the hamlet, serves meals and beers, and has regular barbecues during the winter season. The owners also run two cozy rental cottages on Dabba Hill ($100 per night) as well as a private island to rent with a three-bedroom house ($1200 per week).

Cat & San Salvador Islands

TELEPHONE CODE: 242 / POPULATION: 2580 / AREA: 119 SQ MILES

Includes »

Best Beaches

» Port Royal Beach (p176)
» Greenwood Beach (p174)
» Pigeon Cay Beach (p175)
» Snow Bay Beach (p180)

Best Places to Stay

» Shannas Cove Resort (p176)
» Fernandez Bay Village (p173)
» Pigeon Cay Beach Club (p175)
» Riding Rock Resort & Marina (p179)

Why Go?

The childhood home of Bahamian screen legend Sydney Poitier, rural and undeveloped Cat Island is one of the country's most scenic places; blessed with the Bahamas' highest point (an incredible 206ft!), miles of virgin beach, superb diving and extremely friendly locals. Tiny 'San Sal' is one of the best wall-dive destinations in the world. There are more than 40 dive sites within 30 minutes of shore, and even more near Rum Cay and Conception Island. The island's waters are known for visibility up to 200ft; on special days it can exceed a miraculous 250ft!

Life on both islands continues much as it has for centuries, and the modern world couldn't really feel further away. However, don't expect island idylls; both Cat and San Sal are significantly poorer than the rest of the country.

When to Go

San Salvador

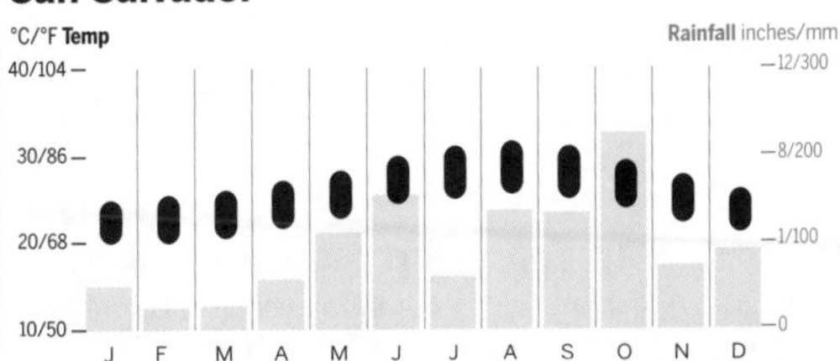

June The Annual Rake 'n' Scrape Music Festival is a fantastic chance to immerse yourself in Bahamian culture.

August Scores of Cat Islanders return from afar for the Cat Island Regatta.

October San Sal celebrates Discovery Day on October 12 with a party and regatta at Graham's Harbour.

CAT ISLAND

Cat Island is a fascinating place to visit and one where the heart of traditional African-Bahamian culture continues to beat, though you'll have to dig deep to discover: there is no tourism infrastructure handing you the island's culture on a plate; non-Bahamian visitors are rare, and those who come here go to several diving resorts on the south coast.

A single road, inventively named the Queen's Hwy, runs down the west shore, lined by plantation ruins and ramshackle settlements where unemployment and poverty are rife. Despite this, Cat Island is blessed with rolling hills and is crowned by Como Hill (206ft) and its atmospheric hermitage, while the Atlantic or 'north' shore is crowned with miles of blush-colored beaches and dramatic cliffs.

The wall-diving accessed from the southwest coast is exceptional and there is some great hiking along old logging and plantation trails.

History

Following the American Revolution, Loyalists arrived with many African slaves and established around 40 cotton and cattle estates. Many homes still retain traditional African ovens for baking bread and teacakes, while the African culture of bush medicine and obeah are still powerful influences. Some of the islanders are said to be skilled witches, always happy to prescribe a home-made cure.

Since emancipation, things in a material sense haven't changed much for most of the population. Many depend upon selling their few tomatoes, onions, and pineapples (planted in limestone pot holes, where nutritious soils are aided by guano or bat excrement, gathered from caves for fertilizer) and on small stipends from the National Insurance Board.

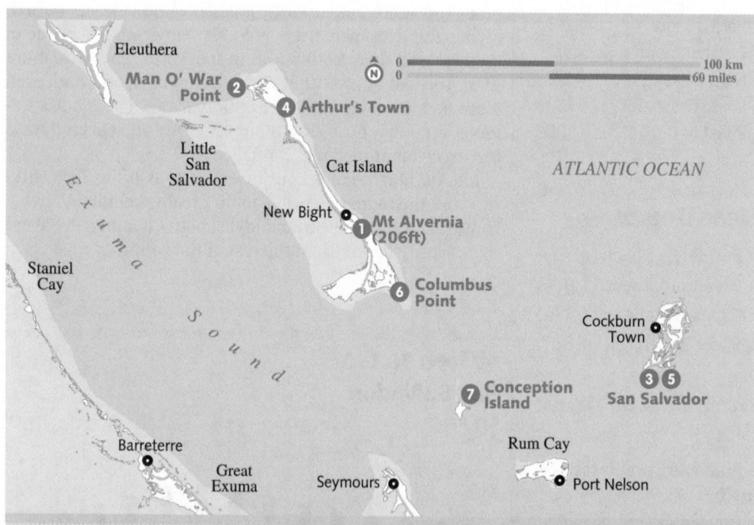

Cat & San Salvador Islands Highlights

1 Experience a Cat Island sunrise from Father Jerome's hilltop **Mt Alvernia Hermitage** (opposite)

2 Hike through dense scrub forest from Shanna's Cove to the beautiful beaches at **Man O' War Point** (p176)

3 Dive the pristine waters and numerous wall-dive sites of **San Salvador** (p177)

4 Chat with islanders in Arthur's Town about Bahamian history and **obeah** (p176)

5 Take a **guided walk** (p179) to learn about San Salvador's old plantations and bush medicine

6 Wander down Greenwood Beach along miles of virgin sand to spectacular **Columbus Point** (p174)

7 Dive with hammer head sharks, green turtles and huge eagle rays in the waters off **Conception Island** (p180)

Activities

There are several superb dive and snorkel sites down south at Morgan's Bay and Hawk's Nest Creek (p175). Dry Head, in shallow water close to the bay's shore here, also has prolific marine life.

Favored bonefishing spots include the flats of Joe's Sound Creek, a 20-minute boat ride south of Fernandez Bay A couple of recommendations:

Top Cat's Fishing Service FISHING
(☎242-342-7003; Devil's Point) Will tailor trips, priced accordingly.

Fernandez Bay Village FISHING
(☎242-342-3043; www.fernandezbayvillage.com; Fernandez Bay) Will arrange bonefishing with guide Mark Keasler ($200/290 per half-/full day), bottom fishing ($250/400) and a short-day fishing trip for children ($150).

Getting There & Away

AIR Cat Island is served by two airports, the northerly **Arthur's Town Airport** (ATC; ☎242-354-2046) and **New Bight Airport** (TBI; ☎242-342-2016), in the south. Cat Island Air flies between Nassau and both airports twice a day ($80 one way), as does Sky Bahamas ($79 one way).

BOAT For updated mail boat information call the **Dockmaster's Office** (☎242-394-1237; Nassau) or check the **Bahamas Ministry of Tourism** (☎242-302-2034; www.bahamas.com).

MV *Lady Eddina* This mail boat (one way $40, 14 hours) departs Nassau for Bennett's Harbour, Arthur's Town and Orange Creek on Thursday at 6pm, leaving Cat Island on Saturday at 2pm.

MV *The Sea Hauler* Mail boat (one way $40, 12 hours) services depart Nassau for Smith Bay, Old Bight and New Bight on Tuesday at 3pm, leaving Cat Island for Nassau on Monday at 7am.

MARINAS Many yachties hoist up in Fernandez Bay for food and water stores. Private boaters should check in with **Customs** (☎242-342-2016) in New Bight.

Hawk's Nest Resort & Marina (p175) has full service facilities, 28 slips, air-conditioned fish-cleaning sheds, accommodations and a private airstrip.

Getting Around

You'll need to rent a car to make the most of the island. Lack of visitor numbers makes this quite expensive however – expect to pay about $80 per day. All car hire companies can meet you at the airport with your car. Alternatively call for a **taxi pick-up** (☎242-342-3134, 242-464-6388). The following local car hire companies are recommended:

Gilbert's Inn & Car Rental (☎242-342-3011; New Bight)

New Bight Service Station & Car Rental (☎242-342-3014; New Bight)

Newbold's Car Rental (☎242-342-5041; New Bight)

Scratcher Car Rental (☎242-354-6070; Bennett's Harbour)

South Cat Island

NEW BIGHT AREA

New Bight originated as a free-slave settlement named Freetown. Much of the surrounding land has belonged to the local Armbrister family since 1780. It extends north to the tiny settlement of Smith Bay, where there's a **bat cave** amid the bush. A goat track leads from Smith Bay to **Pine Bay**, a good surf beach. Adventurous spirits can hike to **Turtle Cove**, a splendid spot on the Atlantic shore where marine turtles sometimes hang out. There are several beautiful casuarina-lined beaches, including **Fernandez Bay**.

Father Jerome's **Mt Alvernia Hermitage** is a tiny blanched-stone church with a Gothic-style bell tower, small chapel, tiny cloister, and guest cell on Como Hill. Reached by

BEASTS IN THE BLUE HOLES

Many of Cat Island's saltwater blue holes are thought to be the home of awesome beasts, including an island equivalent of Scotland's Loch Ness Monster.

The monster of **Big Blue Hole**, just off Dickies Rd near Orange Creek, is said to have an appetite for horses. Hence some horses that die on Cat Island are tipped into the lake! (Objects are sucked out of blue holes by strong tidal flows through subterranean passages that link the holes to the sea). And though freshwater lakes are less feared, at least one – **Mermaid Hole** (p174) – is said to be the home of a mermaid; another has a no less seductive merman.

Although Cat Island fisherfolk will readily travel many miles offshore, it's suggested that many of these same people cannot be induced to travel even 50ft on these lakes.

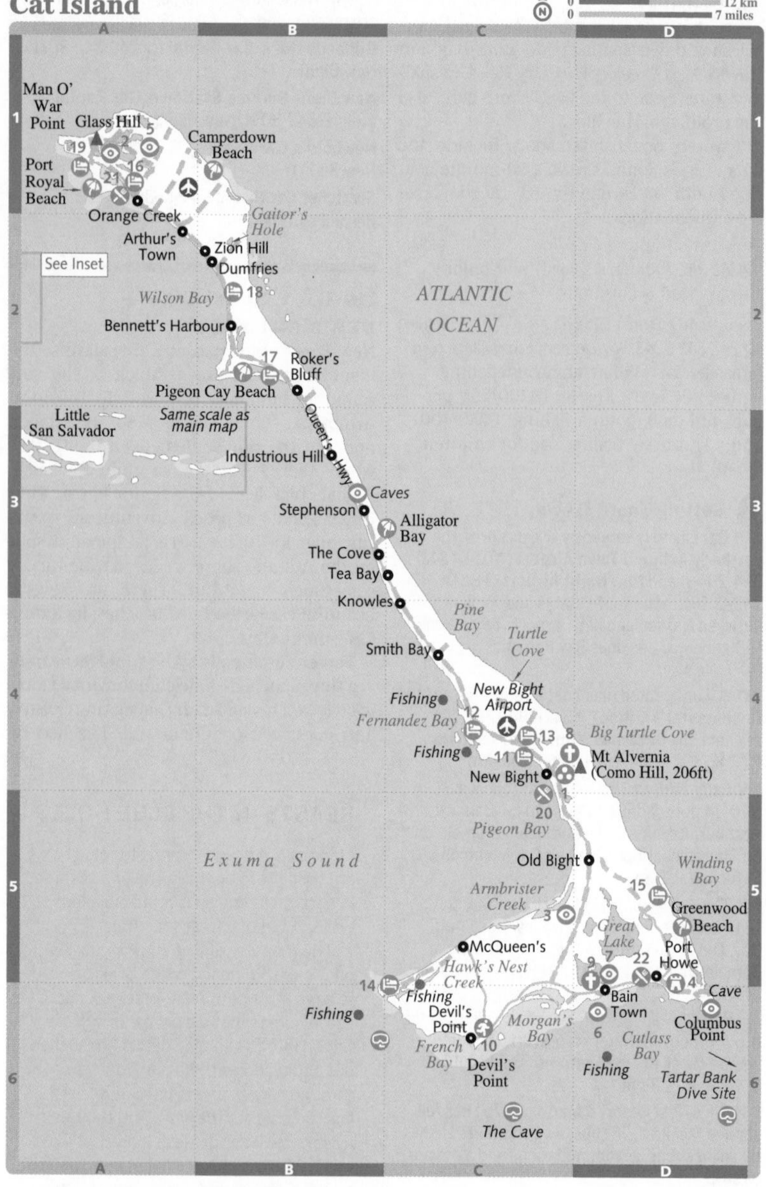

a rock staircase on the hillside, the views from here are wonderful. A rough track to the hermitage begins immediately south of the Government Administrative Complex on Queen's Hwy, north of the ruins of the old Armbrister Plantation – it's clearly signed off the road.

The biggest event of the year is the **Cat Island Regatta**, in August. Cat Islanders from far and wide head back to the island for the homemade-sailboat races, domino

Cat Island

Sights

1	Armbrister Plantation	C4
2	Big Blue Hole	A1
3	Boiling Hole	C5
4	Deveaux House	D5
5	Griffin Bat Cave	A1
6	House Rebecca	D6
7	Mermaid Hole	D5
8	Mt Alvernia Hermitage	C4
9	St John the Baptist Catholic Church	D5

Activities, Courses & Tours

	Fernandez Bay Village	(see 12)
10	Top Cat's Fishing Service	C6

Sleeping

11	Bridge Inn	C4
12	Fernandez Bay Village	C4
13	Gilbert's Inn & Car Rentals	C4
14	Hawk's Nest Resort & Marina	C5
15	Hotel Greenwood Beach Resort	D5
16	Orange Creek Inn	A1
17	Pigeon Cay Beach Club	B2
18	Sammy T's Beach Resort	B2
19	Shannas Cove Resort	A1

Eating

20	Blue Bird Restaurant & Bar	C5
	Hotel Greenwood Beach Resort	(see 15)
21	Perewinkle Bar & Restauran	A1
22	Sweet Tamarind	D5

tournaments and land-based fun of Emancipation Day (the first Monday in August). Bands congregate for the four-day **Annual Rake 'n' Scrape Music Festival**, held over the Labor Day weekend in June, which is organized by Sidney Poitier's daughter, Pamela.

Sleeping & Eating

Gilbert's Inn & Car Rentals INN $

(☎242-342-3011; New Bight; r $93; ❄) This budget two-story motel opposite the New Bight Food Market is very popular, so book ahead. Each room has a bed with a mirrored headboard, good bathroom, fridge and cable TV. Car rentals are also possible and the store across the road is well equipped.

Bridge Inn INN $$

(☎242-342-3013; www.bridgeinncatisland.com; New Bight; r $120; ❄📶) This attractive complex has native-stone walls and lofty wooden ceilings to keep the 12 rooms cool, though they are quite dark and worn. A restaurant and bar serves Bahamian food and has a rocking jukebox, and there are some good beaches within walking distance. The venue sometimes hosts a local rake 'n' scrape band.

Fernandez Bay Village RESORT $$$

(☎242-342-3043, 242-342-2088; www.fernandezbayvillage.com; Fernandez Bay; cottage $280-315 villa $370-425; 📶) Set on an absolutely superb crescent moon white-sand beach, this quiet and attractive resort has fabulous beachside stone and timber rooms, with private open-air bathrooms. The open-air bar and restaurant have a wonderful ocean backdrop and the offshore reefs are perfect for easy snorkeling. It offers free use of kayaks, canoes and bikes. There are also decent restaurants here.

Blue Bird Restaurant & Bar BAHAMIAN $$

(☎242-342-3095; New Bight; mains $10-15; ⏰lunch & dinner Mon-Sat) Right on the beach, this friendly place is run by a team of three sisters who serve up very tasty but simple Bahamian meals that you can eat on the small outdoor terrace. Sunsets are particularly good here. You should call before 3pm and let them know if you plan to come for dinner.

OLD BIGHT

Sitting on top of a little ridge beside the road is **St Francis Assisi Catholic Church**, a Father Jerome legacy. It has a Gothic facade topped by a cross and an engraving of St Francis with a flock of birds. Its interior has frescoes and sculptures. Mrs Burrows, across the road, has the key.

Worth a visit, too, is **St Mary's Church**, fronted by an African flame tree. The church was a gift of the family of Blaney Balfour, the British governor who read the emancipation proclamation.

Armbrister Creek leads to a crystal-clear lake called **Boiling Hole** that bubbles and churns under certain tidal conditions, fueling local fears that it is haunted by a monster. Baby sharks and rays can be seen cruising the sandy bottom. Birdlife also abounds in the mangrove estuary.

FATHER JEROME

John Hawes – hermit and humanitarian – was born in England in 1876 to an upper-middle-class family. He was a visionary, prize-winning architect before entering theological college in 1901, preparing to becoming an Anglican minister.

Once ordained, he vowed to emulate the life of St Francis of Assisi and lived briefly as a tramp. In 1908 he came to the Bahamas and traveled around the islands to rebuild churches that had been destroyed by a hurricane, utilizing thick stone and Roman arches. Hawes offended local sensibilities, however, while preaching on Harbour Island. He asked the congregation why the whites were sitting at the front and the blacks at the back, when all men are created equal. 'The congregation nearly fainted with shock and I was rushed out of the church as quickly as possible,' Hawes recorded.

Between bouts of preaching, the eccentric Englishman worked as a mule driver in Canada, a fox terrier breeder, a cattle wrangler, and a sailor. In 1911 he converted to Catholicism and studied for the priesthood in Rome before moving to Australia to serve as a bush priest during the gold rush.

In 1939 Hawes came to Cat Island to live as a hermit and began work on his hermitage atop Como Hill, renamed Mt Alvernia after the site in Tuscany where St Francis received the wounds of the cross. Meanwhile, he lived in a cave amid snakes, tarantulas and crabs, and took unto himself the name Father Jerome.

He built four churches on Cat Island, as well as a medical clinic, convent, monastery, technical school, and other projects throughout the Bahamas, all featuring his trademark medievalist architectural motif, made of quarried rock.

Undoubtedly, locals regarded him as a saintly figure. Many climbed the monastery steps to ask for money 'in a state verging on destitution,' and none was denied. Locals of all denominations attended his sermons, although apparently he converted only five people to Catholicism.

He died in 1956 and was buried, as per his request, barefoot and without a casket in the cave that had once been his home.

BAIN TOWN

The town lies along the shore south of the main road. There's a gas station east of town, halfway to Port Howe.

Look for **St John the Baptist Catholic Church**, another inspired Father Jerome creation, and **House Rebecca** built of local limestone and conch shells; owners Mr and Mrs Bain may invite you in to peek at the sitting room ceiling, made of 966 shells.

Legend has it that the 65ft-wide **Mermaid Hole** is inhabited by a mermaid (see p171). The lake is 10ft deep, but four holes in its bed lead into vast underwater chambers and passageways.

PORT HOWE AREA

The southeasternmost point of Cat Island, **Columbus Point**, lies 2 miles southeast of Port Howe at the south end of Churney Bay, but you will have to hike there from Port Howe. Cat Islanders cling to the belief – effectively debunked by recent evidence – that Columbus anchored here on October 12, 1492.

Around 1670 a small group of English settlers arrived from Bermuda and established themselves here, earning a living as wreckers. Then, in 1783, 60 English Loyalists arrived here and established large nearby plantations.

The decrepit **Deveaux House** mansion was presented to Colonel Andrew Deveaux, who saved Nassau from Spanish occupation in 1783. Note the old slave quarters.

Running for eight glorious, uninterrupted miles, down the southwestern coast of Cat Island along Winding Bay to the top of the island at Columbus Point, **Greenwood Beach** is a wonderful expanse of pink-white sand and one of the best on the island.

The diving off the south shore is superb; visit the **wall** which begins at 50ft and drops to 6000ft and **Tartar Bank**, covered by coral, sponges and sea fans. **Winding Bay** offers fabulous gorgonians and black coral.

Hotel Greenwood Beach Resort offers one-/two-tank dives ($60/80), night dives ($65) and snorkeling (half-day $25), and hires out snorkel gear for $5.

Sleeping & Eating

Hotel Greenwood Beach Resort RESORT $$
(242-342-3053; www.greenwoodbeachresort.com; Port Howe; r $110-30;) The area's only resort looks rather tired, but its location on an unbeatable 8-mile stretch of pink-sand beach more than compensates. It's run by a charming German couple, and many of the guests here are from Germany. The 15 rooms are nothing special, but are spacious and have tropical decor. Kayaks, snorkeling equipment and bicycles are complimentary for guests.

Sweet Tamarind BAHAMIAN $$
(242-342-5011; Port Howe; mains $15-20; breakfast, lunch, dinner) One of the very few good eating options is this little roadside hut that doubles as a souvenir stop, selling the owner's handicrafts and homemade jams. Call ahead for full meals, or just drop by for snacks, such as pigs' feet soup or chicken wings.

MORGAN'S BAY TO HAWK'S NEST CREEK

A badly potholed road leads west from the Deep South Roundabout, heading to Devil's Point, near McQueen's (founded in the 18th century by a Scottish loyalist, Alexander McQueen) and Hawk's Nest, a 15-mile drive from Deep South Roundabout.

There are several superb dive and snorkel sites locally including **Morgan's Bay**. Close to shore, **Dry Head** has one of the healthiest and most-populated shallow reefs in the Bahamas. **Devil's Point** has large formations of elkhorn and staghorn, tube sponges, and brain coral, while the flats and inland tidal creeks at Hawk's Nest are crowded with bonefish.

Hawk's Nest Resort & Marina (242-342-7050, 800-688-4752; www.hawks-nest.com; r $195;) is a friendly diving and fishing resort and marina offering cheerful and comfortable rooms with ocean views and patios. An honor bar, a good à la carte restaurant and a small beach right on the doorstep all add to the appeal. A private 1380yd hard-surface airstrip with tie-downs, deep-water marina with full services and some good packages make this a great option.

Contact the resort for tailor-made boating, fishing and diving trips; a top-notch small diving operation offers one-/two-tank dives ($65/85) and hires snorkel ($10) and diving ($35) gear.

North Cat Island

The northern Cat Island area is slowly developing, with a new diving resort having opened at the island's most northern tip.

ROKER'S BLUFF

Also known as 'Zanicle,' Roker's Bluff was founded by Scottish settlers and many locals have Scottish surnames. A dirt road leads a mile northwest to beautiful **Pigeon Cay Beach**, a stunning 3-mile-long stretch of white sand opening up into a beautiful bay of turquoise water.

Overlooking a simply fabulous beach, the charming self-contained cabanas of the **Pigeon Cay Beach Club** (242-354-5084; www.pigeoncaybahamas.com; r $140;) have comfortable, colorful furnishings and pleasant outdoor areas. An adjacent beach bar and barbecue is perfect for sunset dining. Activities on offer include fishing trips, snorkeling, kayaking and boat and bike rentals.

BENNETT'S HARBOUR

Bennett's Harbour sprawls beneath blazing-colored flame trees that continue down to a picturesque sheltered **cove**, once favored by pirates and salt traders.

The classy, intimate **Sammy T's Beach Resort** (242-354-6009; www.catislandbeachresort.com; r from $175;) has charming small cabanas with upmarket Caribbean furnishings and Bahamian artworks. Enjoy walk-off-the beach snorkeling, a beachside bar and seafood dishes. There are complimentary bicycles, kayaks and shuffle-boards.

ARTHUR'S TOWN

The island's second-largest settlement nevertheless feels like a village. Centered on Symonette Sq and the **St Andrews Anglican Church** (1870s), this neat little town was the childhood home of Sir Sidney Poitier, though there's no monument or museum to the Bahamas' most famous son.

For lunch and dinner try **Da Smokepot** (242-354-2077), which does hearty local cooking in a friendly venue and **Hard Rock Oasis** (242-342-7050), which does Bahamian standards but is also a popular local wateringhole in the evening.

ORANGE CREEK

There's good bonefishing in the mouth of Orange Creek, where it spills onto a beach. Call **Willard Cleare** (242-354-4143), local bonefishing guide. The turquoise waters offshore are superb snorkeling sites, with exquisite fan-coral formations.

From the head of Orange Creek, a trail leads west half a mile to the popular **Port Royal Beach**. Another leads north past **Oyster Lake** (good for spotting ducks and cormorants) and west to the beach at **Man O' War Point**, also perfect for snorkeling.

A third track leads northwest from the head of Orange Creek to **Glass Hill** (162ft), where there are beautiful views.

Dickie's Rd runs east to **Griffin Bat Cave** – once home to slaves who built walls and windows into the entrance and to a series of blue holes.

Sleeping & Eating

TOP CHOICE **Shannas Cove Resort** RESORT $$
(242-354-4249; www.shannas-cove.com; r from $170;) With quite simply one of the best positions of any resort in the Bahamas, this new and very friendly German-run miniresort is popular with divers and anyone enjoying seclusion. The wonderfully wide beach is just a short stroll down the steps from the five rooms, which are all spaciously simple with private terraces with great sea views. Diving is what brings most people here, and the owners organize bespoke diving trips, though nondivers will also love the beach and nearby hiking trails that lead to beautiful Man O' War Point.

Orange Creek Inn B&B $
(242-354-4110; www.orangecreekbahamas.com; r $82.50;) Sitting near the creek and above a good grocery store, a little to the north of Orange Creek, this very pleasant place has spacious and well-maintained rooms with TV. They are modestly furnished and a bit stuffy, but as many have kitchenettes, you can self-cater.

Shannas Cove Restaurant INTERNATIONAL $$
(242-354-4249; mains $13-17; lunch & dinner;) The restaurant at the Shannas Cove Resort is well worth a mention, as it makes for a pleasant change from the standard local fare – you won't find deep-fried anything on the menu. Instead tasty home made pizzas, fresh salmon and pineapple chicken are served up at this pleasant spot. Call ahead if you'd like to come for dinner.

Periwinkle Bar & Restaurant BAHAMIAN $$
(242-354-4151; Orange Creek; mains $12; lunch & dinner) This cheery little establishment is a popular watering hole and does a selection of local dishes ranging from peas and rice to conch and chicken dishes. There's a pleasant terrace overlooking the sea, though the view is sadly rather obscured by the fencing.

SAN SALVADOR

Known for its astonishingly clear waters that often give divers visibility over an amazing 200ft, tiny San Sal is the nation's

OBEAH

Obeah is the practice of interacting with the spirit world. Part folklore, superstition and magic ritual, it is deeply imbedded in the national psyche. Obeah (the word is Ashanti, from West Africa) was prohibited and severely suppressed by the Caribbean's colonial authorities.

The practice of obeah has diminished (legally banned, mostly due to pressure from the Baptist church) but still coexists alongside Christianity. Some faithful operate as 'balmists' who enact revenge or ensure successful romances. Firm believers sometimes heal, fall sick, or have been known to even die due to their faith in the power of obeah.

'Fixing' meanwhile is the deployment of a spell to protect property; it also means casting a spell or preventing a casting on or by other people. Many fixers ascribe their powers to God and place their 'fix' through directions 'derived' from the Bible.

Those trees with bottles dangling from them are not bearing strange tropical fruit – the bottles are spells to protect against thieves. Also stay clear of graveyards, which are littered with bottles for the spirits of the dead, who otherwise would bother the living for rum, according to local beliefs. Many houses, especially those north of New Bight, are also topped by spindles (like lightning rods) to ward off evil spirits.

On Cat Island the center of obeah is the Bight; on New Providence, it's the working-class area of Fox Hill.

outermost island. This 12-mile speck is ringed by superb reefs, and over 40 dive sites lie within easy reach of the shore, with even more near Rum Cay and Conception Island. Nondivers will also appreciate the 30 miles of gorgeous beach on the island, which are wonderful for walks and playing in the shallows.

The island's unique geography is a mixed blessing: acres of mangroves and saltwater lakes make much of interior inaccessible, making it home to very diverse wildlife, but also swarms of mosquitoes. Industrial strength bug spray is in order at dusk and dawn, and a warning: beaches are infested with no see 'ums, the vicious sand flies so tiny that you never see them, but with appetites that would embarrass a fast-food chain. Try the mariners' solution; Avon Skin So Soft.

Also be careful if you explore the brush areas. There are quick sands as well as poisonwood and manchineel trees.

On the plus side, San Sal offers excellent birdwatching. Ospreys (or 'chicken hawks') are everywhere. The cays off the north shore are favored by boobies and other sea birds. Egrets and herons pick for food in the brine pools. Besides diving and birdwatching, activities are quite limited, and the lack of tourist revenue and other industry of significant size has contributed to the island's sometimes visible poverty.

History

San Salvador, meaning 'holy savior,' was the moniker bestowed by Christopher Columbus on the first land he sighted in 1492. But, there is little evidence to support the entrenched claim that Columbus first landed here, a fact accepted locally as adamantly as the belief that the earth was flat.

Recent discoveries of Spanish artifacts are said to support the landfall claim – a claim effectively debunked by *National Geographic* in 1986 when it convincingly concluded that Columbus first landed at Samana Cay. However, in 1989 yachtsman Robin Knox-Johnson retraced Columbus' route using 15th-century instruments and ended up at...San Salvador. Take your pick!

Getting There & Around

AIR San Salvador is served by **Cockburn Town Airport** (ZSA; ☎242-331-2919/20), adjacent to town. There are daily flights (one way $100) between San Sal and Nassau on both Bahamasair and Cat Island Air.

BOAT Call the **Dockmaster's Office** (☎242-394-1237, Nassau) and check the **Bahamas Ministry of Tourism** (☎242-302-2034; www.bahamas.com) for the latest boat schedules and costs. The MV *Lady Francis* ($40, 18 hours) mail boat departs Nassau for San Salvador and Rum Cay on Tuesday at 1pm, departing for Nassau on Saturday at 9am.

CAR & BICYCLE Cars can be rented for about $80 per day, and the rental agencies are based in Cockburn Town. Riding Rock Resort & Marina (p179) rents bicycles/cars for $10/90 per day. For cars, also try **C&S Car Rental** (☎242-331-2714). For taxi services, try **Livingstone Williams Taxis** (☎242-331-2025).

MARINAS Boaters and pilots arriving from abroad must clear **Immigration** (☎242-331-2100) in Cockburn Town. Riding Rock Resort & Marina has 11 busy slips and facilities – it's always a important to book ahead.

Cockburn Town

San Sal's major settlement and administrative center, midway down the west coast, is a motley affair comprising two parallel roads crisscrossed by five narrow lanes. Tumble-down stone cottages and clapboard shacks in faded pastels mingle with new, often stylish houses squatting in unkempt yards picked at by goats and cockerels.

A 12ft plastic iguana guards the entrance to town where locals gather under the 'Lazy Tree,' a gnarled almond tree whose shade is preferred for taking it easy.

Sights & Activities

The small **San Salvador Museum**, housed in the old jail, has displays of Lucayan Indian remains and Columbus' conquest of the New World. Note the ceramic mural of Columbus. Ask for a key from the BaTelCo office.

The pretty pink **Holy Saviour Roman Catholic Church** (1992) was established by the Catholic Archdiocese of Nassau.

For divers, the following dive sites are recommended: ***Frascate***, a 261ft-long ship sunk in 1902 lies just 20ft down. Also **Rum Cay Wall**, which drops from 40ft to eternity. Nearby are remains of the **HMS *Conqueror***, a 19th-century British steam-powered battleship. **Telephone Pole** (a natural wall), begins at 45ft. At 100ft a wall decorated with large purple sponges and plate coral is also attractive to large pelagics.

Snorkel sites include **Flower Gardens**, where scattered coral heads feature caves

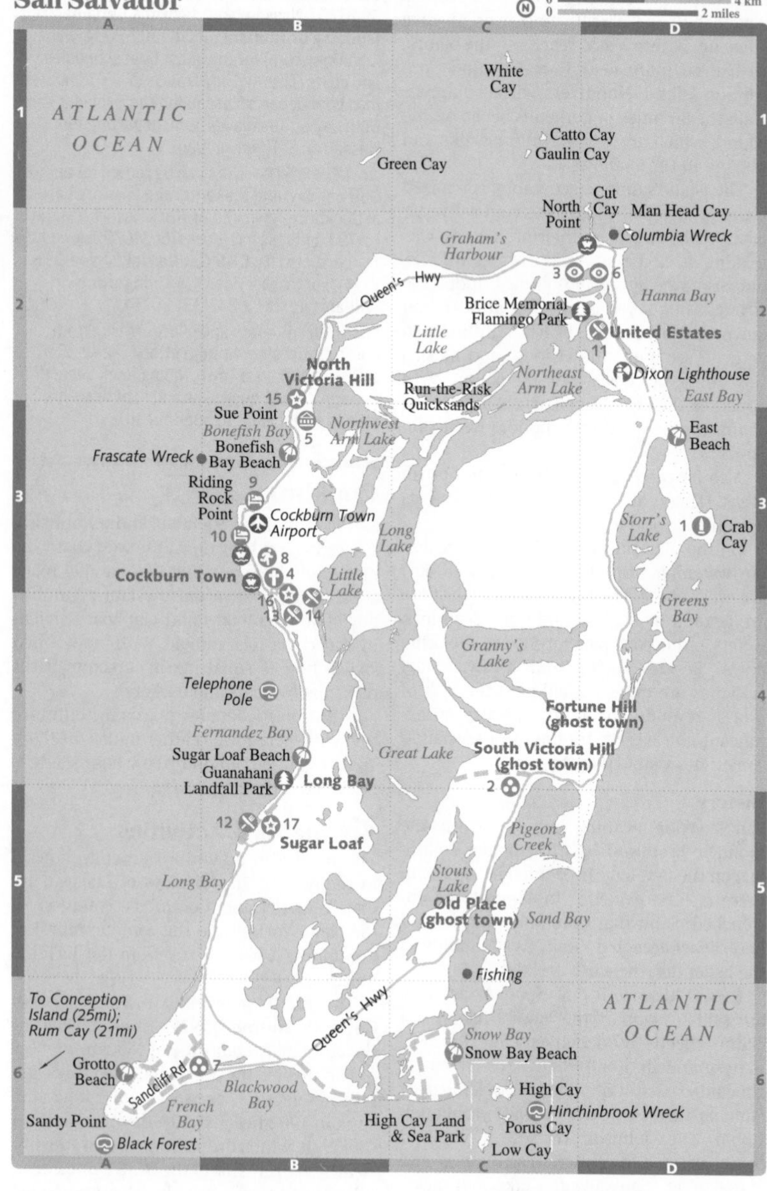

for exploring, and **Natural Bridges**, where a reef formation has natural arches. There's also **Sandy Point**, one of the best sites, and **Staghorn Reef**, where you'll find star and staghorn corals aplenty, as well as heaps of other marine life.

Riding Rock Resort & Marina (opposite) offers one-/two-tank dives ($70/90), and a 10-dive package ($355).

Island Venture Fishing Charters (☎242-331-2306) runs deep-sea fishing trips (half-/full-day $550/850) for a maximum of four people.

San Salvador

Lagoon Tours (242-452-0102; www.lagoon-tours-bahamas.com) runs guided walks and combined hiking and kayaking tours with informed and enthusiastic guides. Try the fascinating trip that takes in bush-medicine plants, an old plantation and lake-kayaking ($70), a birdwatching leisure hike through Watling's Castle to spot thrush, warblers, osprey and herons (prices vary), and lagoon tours ($90) with a peaceful boat ride along beaches to beautiful lagoons and a visit to the iguanas of Low Cay.

Riding Rock Resort & Marina (below) offers excursions to the Exumas and the Low and High Cays to see iguanas and osprey.

Sleeping & Eating

TOP CHOICE **Riding Rock Resort & Marina** RESORT $$
(242-331-2631, 800-272-1492; www.ridingrock.com; Cockburn Town; r standard/ocean-view $150/180;) This friendly and modern resort is loved by divers, and is very popular, so book ahead! Sparkling white rooms with tiled floors all have either beach or poolside views. There's a great nearby beach, tennis court, relaxed beachside bar and a good restaurant serving Bahamian dishes. The overall feeling is superbly relaxed.

Club Med Columbus Isle RESORT $$$
(242-331-2000; www.clubmed.com; r per week $1500;) This huge beachside resort is definitely geared toward French guests who want to party. The low-slung resort displays exotic antique art and units have custom-fashioned furniture and mod-cons. Tennis courts, a fitness center, water sports and other recreational activities including diving trips are on offer, and there's much lively nocturnal entertainment. This resort also charges for wireless access, something unheard of in most of the Bahamas. Expect to pay $5 per hour for the privilege, or a flat rate of $50 per week.

Three Ships Restaurant BAHAMIAN $
(242-331-2787; mains $6-20; breakfast, lunch & dinner, closed Sun) This friendly local mainstay serves boil fish and grits for breakfast, along with meat and fish dishes for lunch and dinner. Be sure to call ahead if you plan to eat here in the evening.

Other eating options on the island include **3JJ's Takeaway** (242-331-2787; United Estates), on the north coast, 6 miles from Cockburn Town, where you can get simple fast food dishes such as conch fritters and chicken wings to go. The main waterhole on the island is the **Sunrise Lounge** (Cockburn Town), which also serves burgers and fried chicken.

Entertainment

For nightlife, head to the **Driftwood Bar & Lounge** (located at Riding Rock Resort & Marina), exhibiting driftwood autographed by visitors from the '50s. Another local favorite is the **Harlem Square Club** (242-331-2777), which serves traditional food, has rap and dance nights on weekends, and lots of clattering dominoes during the day.

North Coast

The **Gerace Research Center** (242-331-2520; www.geraceresearchcentre.com; Graham's Harbour) primarily hosts scientific conferences and field courses for student groups. Scientists also run a coral reef monitoring project. Visitors are welcome.

Earthwatch (www.earthwatch.org) houses volunteers (including volunteer divers) for its program to preserve San Sal's reef at the Gerace Research Center. Volunteers snorkel four or five hours daily and make observations about coral health. It has two trips annually (from $2395).

Check out superb **Bonefish Bay Beach**, via North Victoria Hill, and the tiny **New World Museum**, displaying Lucayan Indian artifacts.

Graham's Harbour is good for swimming. A **Columbus Day Homecoming** and party is traditionally held here on Discovery Day (October 12) along with the annual **Columbus Bay Regatta**. The *Columbia*, wrecked in 1980, lies off North Point.

Club Arawak, next to the New World Museum, serves the usual fried chicken and fish dishes and does double duty as the local nightspot.

The northeast shore of the island is lined with lonesome beaches, including the rosy-pink 5-mile-long **East Beach.**

In United Estates (locally called 'U-E'), look for the blue house, **Solomon's Hill,** decorated with dozens of plastic buoys. U-E is pinned by the magnificent old **Dixon Hill Lighthouse** (⏲9am-noon & 2-5pm). From the balcony, there is a fabulous panoramic view of the entire island.

The weather-worn **Chicago Herald Monument** to Columbus stands at the south end of East Bay.

South Coast

This area was once the center of cotton and citrus plantations. The most notable ruins are **Farquharson Plantation** (1820s).

Pigeon Creek is an 8-mile-long ecological treasure (baby sharks swim here) that opens to the ocean at **Snow Bay**. There's an unmarked **Lucayan Indian archaeological site** at the northern end of Pigeon Creek.

Don't miss breathtakingly beautiful **Snow Bay Beach** where you can be alone with the gentle lapping of the waves and the cry of sea birds. The road runs inland from the shore for most of the way, passing a series of smelly salt lakes.

High Cay Land & Sea Park protects High Cay, Porus Cay and Low Cay, which are important nesting sites for ospreys, boobies and other sea birds. Endangered iguanas also cling to Low Cay. The reefs have claimed several ships, notably the ***HMS Hinchinbrook*** (sunk in 1913), a wreck that is much favored by scuba divers.

WORTH A TRIP

CONCEPTION ISLAND

This 3-mile-long, uninhabited, speck on the map is rimmed with reefs. It is approximately 25 miles southeast of Cat Island and it's protected as the **Conception Island National Park** by the Bahamas National Trust.

The island is an important nesting site for endangered green turtles as well as migratory sea birds, particularly boobies, which give their name to **Booby Cay**, east of the island.

Divers who enjoy deep dives will enjoy ferreting around the Black Forest Wreck spotting turtles, hammerhead sharks and eagle rays.

On the southwest coast, Fernandez Bay and Long Bay are lined by beautiful **Sugar Loaf Beach** while the peninsula's leeward shore is fringed by beautiful **Grotto Beach** and several caves.

Founded by a Loyalist settler, and named for the pirate, **Watling's Castle** ruins sit atop a hill with good sea views.

There's a **grocery store** and in Sugar Loaf, half a mile south of Guanahani Landfall Park the **Stansheka Bar** (Queen's Hwy).

Rum Cay

This 10-mile-long isle is lined by stunning beaches and the entire isle is fringed with coral. The **HMS *Conqueror*** (1861), a 101-gun British man o' war, sank in 30ft of water off Signal Point.

The only settlement is **Port Nelson.** The rest of the isle is a virtual wilderness of rolling hills browsed by feral cattle and donkeys, but it's popular with yachties and true adventurers.

The 18-slip **Sumner Point Marina** (☎242-331-2823; www.rumcaymarina.com) also has attractive one-bedroom **cottages** (r $125; ❄📶) for rent right on the beach from where you can watch the dreamy sunsets. The marina also has a charming restaurant, **Out of the Blue** (☎242-331-2823, mains $10-18) where you can enjoy simple lunches or bigger meals (reserve by 3pm). Diving and surfing can also be arranged.

See p177 for details of mail-boat stops at the cay.

Southern Bahamas

TELEPHONE CODE: 242 / POPULATION: 4957 / AREA: 1179 SQ MILES

Includes »

Best Beaches

- True Blue Beach (p191)
- Farquharson Beach (p194)
- Shell Beach (p190)
- Cape Santa Maria Beach (p185)

Best Places to Stay

- Chez Pierre Bahamas (p186)
- Cape Santa Maria Beach Resort (p185)
- Long Island Breeze Resort (p187)
- Beach Bungalow (p186)

Why Go?

Tear up what you think you know about the Bahamas when you come to the remote islands of the south. Yes, the sand is just as white, the water the same extraordinary blend of blues and the welcome just as friendly (if not more so) – but the simple difference here is that of development. No megaresorts or fast food restaurants blight the coastline, seeing another person on a beach is a crowd, and traffic is virtually nil.

The largest island in the Southern Bahamas is aptly named Long Island, though it's hard to imagine anywhere less like its New York namesake. While it is lined with great beaches and enjoying some beautiful scenery, there are just a handful of small resorts on the island and finding total seclusion is never a problem.

The other islands in the south are Crooked and Acklin Islands, both near-wildernesses with some of the country's best bonefishing, and the truly remote Inaguas, famed for salt production and flamingos. Look no further if you're seeking the off-the-beaten-path Bahamas.

When to Go

Mayaguana

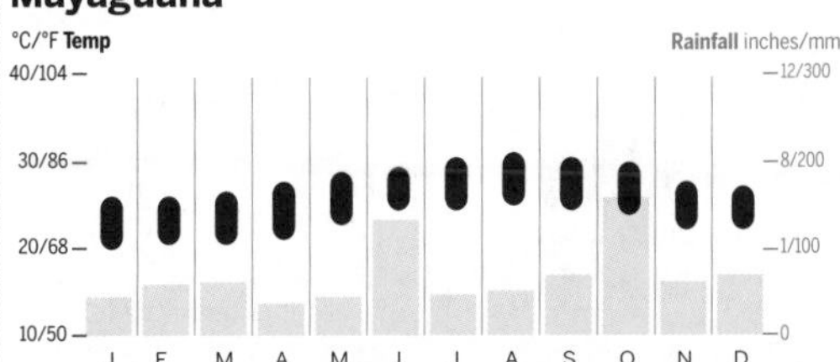

May Watch sloops from all over the country take part in Salt Pond's Long Island Regatta.

February & March This is the best time to see the flamingos at the Bahamas National Trust Park.

December Great Inagua's annual Junkanoo parade has lively dancing, music and great costumes.

LONG ISLAND

POP 2978

At over 80 miles from top to bottom and just a few miles across at its widest point, Long Island certainly lives up to its name. It's one of the most attractive islands in the Bahamas, boasting plantation ruins, stunning white and sky-blue Gothic churches, lush greenery, attractive villages and miles of virgin scrub forest.

You'll also come to a myriad of magnificent bays, blue holes, and miles and miles of beach. The island's inhabitants live in about 35 settlements, growing bananas

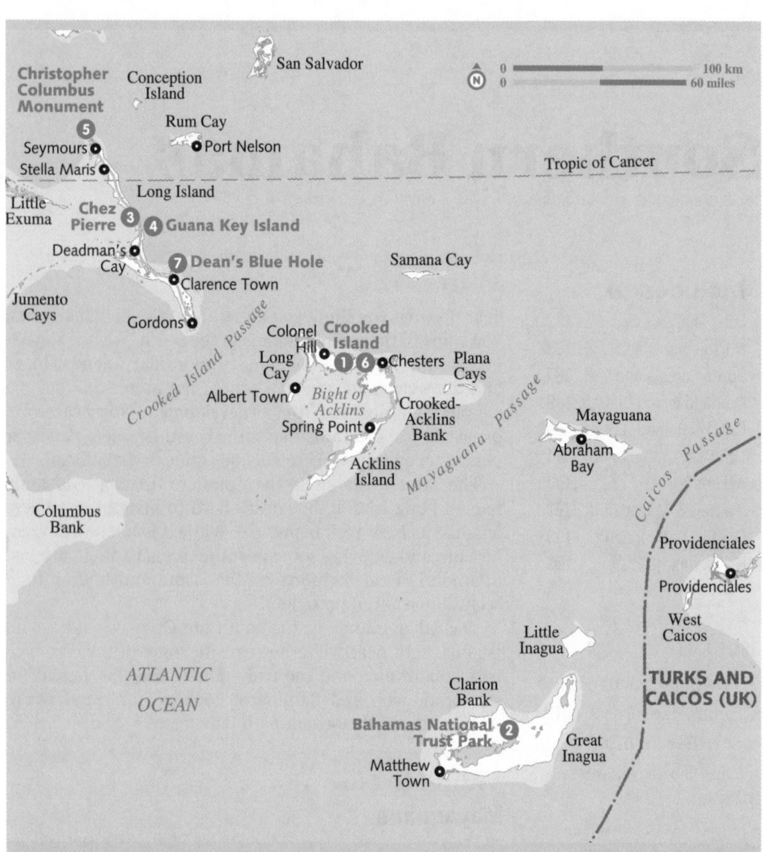

Southern Bahamas Highlights

1 Dive Crooked Island's wreck, the ***Million Dollar Mistake*** (p191), where maybe the odd quarter still lies

2 Birdwatch and flamingo count in the haunting landscapes of the **Bahamas National Trust Park** (p194)

3 Eat and sleep like a very comfortable Robinson Crusoe in a beach hut at **Chez Pierre Bahamas** (p186)

4 Head for Long Island's gorgeous **Guana Key Island** to see the snoozing resident iguanas (p187)

5 Hike up to the **Christopher Columbus Monument** (opposite) honoring the explorer's arrival in the new world

6 Charter a boat and enjoy a picnic on Shell Beach and a visit to **Long Cay** (p191), Crooked Island

7 Swim at incredible **Dean's Blue Hole** (p188), the 660ft-deep entrance to one of the world's largest underwater caverns

and rows of corn, along with vegetables and pineapples. On the east shore, Atlantic rollers crash against dramatic cliffs and offshore reefs, while the west coast consists of a string of shallow bays. In late spring hundreds of yellow butterflies appear.

This pristine diving paradise has untapped treasures, such as the newly discovered Neuritis Wall that drops off the Bahamas Banks, and the fast-paced action of Shark Reef is justifiably acclaimed. For those who prefer to eat fish rather than commune with them, the island also has top fishing year-round.

History

Long Island is notable for its rich history compared to many of the other islands in the country. The Lucayan Indian caves have yielded *duhos* (wooden seats) that archaeologists believe suggest chieftainship and ceremony, and *zemi* figurines bearing religious connotations. To the south, the island – Columbus' 'Fernandina' – ends at Cape Verde, where Columbus supposedly anchored on October 24, 1492.

A large percentage of Bahamians on the island are descendants of the 18th-century Loyalists. The colonists established a plantation system as viable as any in the archipelago.

Getting There & Away

AIR Long Island has two airports; Stella Maris Airport serves north Long Island and Deadman's Cay Airport is best for the middle and southern Long Island. Most flights to and from Long Island stop at both airports.

Pineapple Air and Bahamasair have one or two daily codeshare flights from Nassau to Stella Maris and Deadman's Cay (both one way $105). Southern Air also has one or two daily flights on the same route (one way $110).

BOAT The MV *Mia Dean* (one way $40, 12 hours) sails from Nassau to Clarence Town on Tuesday at noon and leaves Clarence Town for Nassau each Thursday at 8pm.

The MV *Sherice M* (one way $45, 15 hours) leaves Nassau each Monday at 5pm to call at Salt Pond, Deadman's Cay and Seymours. It leaves Long Island each Tuesday at 11am.

MARINAS The Stella Maris Resort Club & Marina (p185) is an official port of entry, and has a full-service marina with boat yard and slips for boats up to 70ft.

There is also the Flying Fish Marina (p189) in Clarence Town, which has a 15-slip marina, though isn't a port of entry.

Getting Around

You'll need your own transportation if you want to explore the island, and nearly all hotels can organize a rental car for you. Rentals are usually between $70 and $90 per day. Some recommended local agencies include the following.

Flying Fish Marina & Car Rental (☎242-337-3430; Clarence Town)

Mr T Car Rentals (☎242-337-1054; Deadman's Cay)

Williams Car Rentals (☎242-338-5002; Glintons)

Williams Car Rentals (☎242-338-5002; Glintons)

North Long Island

The north of the island is certainly worth exploring, from the Columbus Memorial to the vivid jade-colored seas that boast great snorkeling and diving. Take insect spray – mosquitoes and sand flies up this end of the island get pretty hungry at dawn and dusk.

STELLA MARIS

The upscale residential community of Stella Maris stretches for about a mile along the coast amid palms and scrub. Dominating the area is the Stella Maris Resort Club & Marina (p185).

Sights & Activities

The remote **Columbus Memorial**, a 15ft-tall stone obelisk, sits at the northern tip of Long Island, bearing a plaque dedicated to 'the peaceful aboriginal people of Long Island and to the arrival of Christopher Columbus.' The views and snorkeling around the headlands are stunning. Be careful on the mile-long very rough and rocky path that leads to the monument from Seymours.

The 3-mile-long **Galliot Cay** peninsula is linked to Long Island by a narrow spit with mangrove creeks, a gorgeous beach and turquoise shallows. Snorkeling is especially good at the reef gardens at the southern end.

The area's best beaches are the four pink-sand **Love Beaches** (the first has a shallow 'pool' perfect for small children). Head for Ocean View Dr.

The ruins of **Adderley Plantation** are smothered in vegetation, as are the graves in the slaves' cemetery.

At the shores of **Columbus Harbour**, a shallow bay lined with mangroves, you can cross the narrow tidal creek on a (semi-collapsed, but still passable) footbridge to reach **Newton Cay**, a small island with a

Long Island

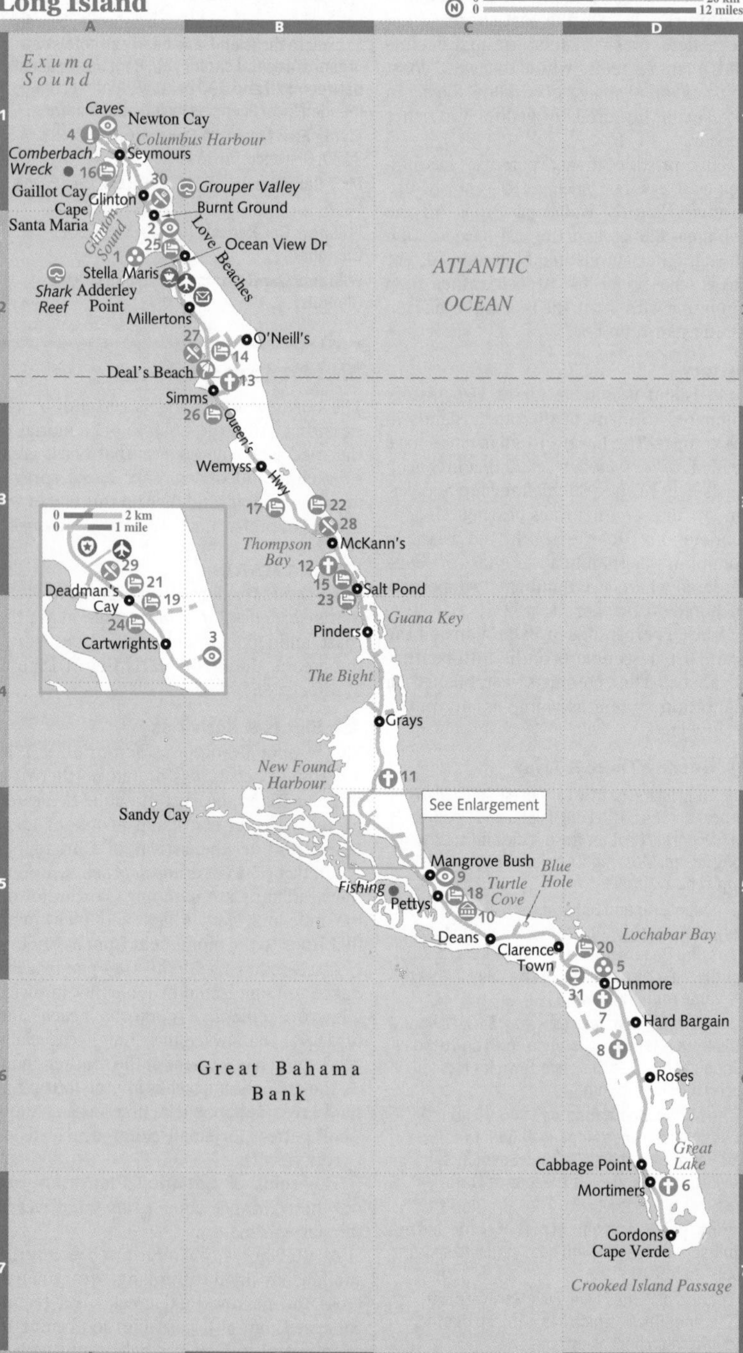
0 20 km
0 12 miles
Exuma Sound
Caves
Newton Cay
Columbus Harbour
Comberbach Wreck
Seymours
Gaillot Cay
Glinton
Grouper Valley
Burnt Ground
Cape Santa Maria
Glinton Sound
Love Beaches
Ocean View Dr
Stella Maris
Shark Reef
Adderley Point
Millertons
ATLANTIC OCEAN
O'Neill's
Deal's Beach
Simms
Queen's Hwy
Wemyss
0 2 km
0 1 mile
Deadman's Cay
Cartwrights
Thompson Bay
McKann's
Salt Pond
Guana Key
Pinders
The Bight
Grays
New Found Harbour
Sandy Cay
See Enlargement
Mangrove Bush
Blue Hole
Turtle Cove
Fishing
Pettys
Deans
Clarence Town
Lochabar Bay
Dunmore
Hard Bargain
Great Bahama Bank
Roses
Great Lake
Cabbage Point
Mortimers
Gordons
Cape Verde
Crooked Island Passage

Long Island

Sights

1 Adderley Plantation A2
2 Bonafide Bonefishing A2
3 Cartwrights Caves B4
4 Columbus Memorial A1
5 Dunmore Plantation (Ruins) D5
6 Father Jerome Church D7
7 Father Jerome Church D6
8 Father Jerome Church D6
9 Hamilton's Cave C5
Jail ..... (see 13)
10 Long Island Library & Museum C5
11 St Athanatius Church C4
12 St Joseph's Anglican Church B3
13 St Peter's Anglican Church B2

Sleeping

14 Beach Bungalows & Bonefishing Lodge B2
15 C-Shells B3
16 Cape Santa Maria Beach Resort A1
17 Chez Pierre Bahamas B3
18 Constantakis Bay View Appartments C5
19 Ellen's Inn A4
20 Gems at Private Paradise Beach Resort D5
21 Keva's Villas A3
22 King's Bay Resort B3
23 Long Island Breeze Resort B4
24 Smith & Well's Bonefish Lodge A4
25 Stella Maris Resort Club & Marina A2
26 Sunset Beach Villa B3

Eating

27 Beach Bungalow B2
Chez Pierre Bahamas ..... (see 17)
28 Club Washington B3
Long Island Breeze Restaurant ... (see 23)
29 Max's Conch Bar & Grill A3
30 Pratt's Restaurant & Bar A1

Drinking

31 Forest D5

beach on the Atlantic shore. There are caves around the headland to the north.

Stella Maris Resort Club & Marina (right) offers two-tank dives (without/with gear, $90/120) and resort courses (from $130). The resort also offers waterskiing for $50 and rents boats ($350 for a 27-footer).

Cape Santa Maria Beach Resort (below) offers diving (two-tank dives $90) and snorkeling ($45), and rents water sport, scuba and snorkeling equipment. They also offer bonefishing (half-/full-day $450/500), reef fishing (half-/full-day $500/600), as well as deep-sea fishing (full-day $600) for up to four people.

Guided bonefishing is offered by **Bonafide Bonefishing** (242-338-2035, 242-357-1417; www.bonafidebonefishing.com; Queen's Hwy, Burnt Ground) and its owner 'Docky' Smith is one of the best local guides on the island. Bonefishing (half-/full-day $300/350) and reef-fishing (full-day $550) are both offered.

Sleeping & Eating

Cape Santa Maria Beach Resort RESORT $$$
(242-338-5273; www.capesantamaria.com; Cape Santa Maria; r $325, villa $795) This luxurious resort on one of the Bahamas' best beaches manages to retain an intimate and relaxed feel despite its relatively large size. With 20 plush bungalows right on the beach and a long row of even smarter luxury villas further down, Long Island's largest resort attracts couples and families looking for an up-market getaway. A wooden walkway leads to an airy and handsome two-tier restaurant and bar in gingerbread plantation style and offering vast views. Activities available include catamarans, sailboats, sailboards, volleyball, diving, and snorkeling.

Stella Maris Resort Club & Marina RESORT $$
(242-338-2051, 800-426-0466; www.stellamaris resort.com; Stella Maris; s/d $160/190, cottage $235-675) The ocean views are stunning from this comfortable and well-equipped old plantation, now a resort, dotted with modern and breezy hillside rooms, suites and cottages all of which enjoy views of the ocean. The cottages, which run from one bedroom to four with a private pool, are better than the rooms, which are fine but a little worn and a little standard. With no TVs or phones in the rooms, this is a place for escape. Other features include a fantastic saltwater pool, a great walk way along the beach from where there are frequent humpback whale sightings and free snorkeling trips from the Stella Maris Marina.

Pratt's Restaurant & Bar SEAFOOD $$
(242-338-7051; Burnt Ground; mains $10-20; lunch & dinner) Run by a local fisherman who cooks up his own catch each day, this friendly spot won't win any design awards, but it's one of the best options in northern Long Island. We recommend the seafood platter ($25). Call ahead to let them know you're coming.

STELLA MARIS TO SALT POND

Between Stella Maris and Salt Pond, the coastal Queen's Hwy passes **Deal's Beach**, which has fabulous snorkeling over a sea-fan garden. You can follow a road east from here to **O'Neill's**, a tiny hamlet with two beaches that also offer good snorkeling.

Simms, a quaint seaside hamlet about 10 miles south of Stella Maris, dates back to the plantation era. It is dominated by well-kept **St Peter's Anglican Church**. The most endearing structure is a prim little **post office** and, nudging up behind it, an equally diminutive **jail** still bearing the sign 'Her Majesty's Prison.'

South of Simms, the road moves inland until it touches the shore again at **Thompson Bay**, about 5 miles further south. The bay is scenic, but far more spectacular is the one at **McKann's**, about half a mile east; turn east at the sign for King's Bay Resort.

Sleeping

TOP CHOICE Chez Pierre Bahamas RUSTIC LODGE $$
(242-338-8809; www.chezpierrebahamas.com; Miller's; s/d half board $125/175;) This is one of our favorite places in the Bahamas and a superb choice for a sublime rustic escape. A bumpy gravel road leads you to this perfect crescent beach, which is totally undeveloped save Pierre's six beach huts, which are just simple, tree-hut like structures with a double bed and full bathroom. If you stay five nights or more, there's a $20 per night discount on the room price. This is not a place for those looking to be pampered – air-con and swimming pools are unknown – but for those who appreciate simple luxury, look no further.

Sunset Beach Villa VILLA $$
(www.sunsetbeachvillabahamas.com; Wemyss; villa from $165;) This large and cleverly designed villa right on the beach is perfect for a big family holiday, sleeping as it does up to nine people when booked in its entirity. It can also be split into two properties, making it perfect for smaller groups. There are kayaks to use, a fully equipped kitchen for self catering and a superb terrace with fantastic sunset views.

Beach Bungalows & Bonefishing Lodge BUNGALOWS & FISHING LODGE $$
(242-338-8444, 242-472-1122; www.beachbungalowsbahamas.com; Deal's; bungalow $150;) A brand new addition to Long Island's accommodations options is this very attractive two-floor plantation-style house. All white timbers and green trim, it contains four spacious apartments, each sleeping up to four people. Deal's Beach is just on the other side of the main road, where you'll also find the Beach Bungalow Restaurant.

King's Bay Resort RESORT $
(242-338-8945; r $85; lunch & dinner) This rather worn place enjoys a fabulous and breezy location atop the dunes on the Atlantic shore north of McKann's. There's a huge beach and snorkeling equipment is free for guests. There's a restaurant and bar serving Bahamian food.

Eating

TOP CHOICE Chez Pierre Bahamas INTERNATIONAL $$
(242-338-8809; Miller's; mains $18-25; breakfast, lunch & dinner) The restaurant here is one of the best on the island, though unless you're a guest at the hotel you should definitely call ahead, as the eponymous Pierre can be a little cantankerous when people simply drop by unannounced. The interesting menu is French and Italian with a heavy emphasis on pasta and seafood, accompanied by a good wine list and all served up in the stylishly simple dining room.

Beach Bungalow INTERNATIONAL $
(Deal's; mains $8-16;) This new beach restaurant is a great spot to kick back with a cold beer at the end of the day on the terrace overlooking lovely Deal's Beach. It's also a great spot for a meal, with very tasty pizza, burgers, a killer steak sandwich and a range of Bahamian dishes.

Club Washington BAHAMIAN $$
(242-338-0021; McKann's; mains $10-15) This two-story blue building on the Queen's Hwy serves up local dishes and is a popular local spot for a beer at any time of the day.

SALT POND

Salt Pond, in the middle of the island, is the main centre of business, despite its small size. There's a fish-processing plant, several well-stocked stores and a gas station that's open on Sunday. With the arrival of the Long Island Breeze Resort here, this is a place that's set to become even more prominent in the future.

Just north of Salt Pond is **St Joseph's Anglican Church**, enjoying a sublime setting on a ridge above the beach and boneflats. Break out your camera!

Immediately north of HSC supply store there is a road that leads east to the Atlantic shore and a headland with blush-pink beaches and a craggy, untouched shoreline. You can hike trails that lead south for several miles.

At Pinders, about 2 miles south of Salt Pond, another road (this one is in appalling condition) leads to **Guana Key**, a beautiful, well-protected, shallow bay; Guana Key Island is a short swim offshore. In good weather you are able to snorkel over the wreck of an old freighter in 15ft of water.

The highlight of the island's annual calendar is the **Long Island Regatta**, a four-day event that's held at Salt Pond in mid-May.

Activities

The snorkeling and diving here are simply superb. Divers should head for **Cape Santa Maria Ship's Graveyard** or **Grouper Valley** where thousands of these friendly (and possibly endangered) fish gather to spawn every November. There is also **Grouper Village**, where resident groupers and Brutus, a mammoth jewfish, expect to be fed. **Ocean Blue Hole**, a dramatic, ever-widening funnel, is worth seeing. Some like the adrenalin of feeding sharks at **Shark Reef** although this practice is now widely frowned upon.

Snorkelers should head for **Coral Gardens** – Hawksbill turtles favor these awesome caves, overhangs, and valleys – and **Eagle Ray Reef** where rays flutter around guarded by a friendly grouper. **Flamingo Tongue Reef** and **Watermelon Beach** are both favored by countless species of corals and fish. Some very experienced divers have set up shop at Salt Pond, but they cover all the dive sites.

Sleeping & Eating

Long Island Breeze Resort RESORT **$$**
(☎242-333-0170; www.longislandbreezeresort.com; Salt Pond; s/d from $80/105; ❄≋📶) This very smart new resort has just eight plush rooms, but planning permission for a further 40 makes this potentially the biggest resort on the island. So far we like what we see: the quality wooden floors, tasteful furnishings and grand style of the bigger suites that include a state-of-the-art kitchen. Snorkeling and kayaking is free, there's a coin-operated laundry and a small pool and smart terrace area right on the water. This is definitely one to watch.

C-Shells STUDIOS **$**
(☎242-338-0103; www.cshellsguestquarters.com; Salt Pond; r $95-110; ❄👪) These five gleaming white units just a short wander from the beach all come equipped with a kitchen, DVD player and a front and back terrace. This is a very friendly place and a great bargain option.

Long Island Breeze Restaurant INTERNATIONAL **$$**
(☎242-333-0170; Salt Pond; mains $10-25; ⏲lunch Tue-Sun, dinner Thu-Sat; 📶) The attractive restaurant at this resort is open to the public and makes a great spot for lunch out on the terrace by the sea. The menu runs from steaks and sandwiches to lobster dishes, catch of the day and pork chops. They ask non-guests to reserve for dinner.

There are two large and well-stocked supermarkets in Salt Pond, both on the Queen's Hwy near to the Long Island Breeze Resort.

South Long Island

There is a lot to see and enjoy down this end of the island, with caves, some gorgeous beaches, and supposedly the world's deepest blue hole (663ft) leading to a vast underwater cavern and magnificent cove. The soaring church spires of Clarence Town is another attraction, as is nearby Lochabar Bay with yet another vast blue hole and a superb white-sand beach.

DEADMAN'S CAY AREA

Deadman's Cay is the site of Long Island's second airport. There is no discernible center to the town, but Max's Conch Bar & Grill is the next best thing if you want friendly gossip and information.

Sights & Activities

History buffs might enjoy the overgrown ruins of **Grays Plantation**, 2 miles north of Lower Deadman's Cay near Grays.

Lower Deadman's Cay is dominated by **St Athanatius Church**, which dates from 1929.

Cartwrights Caves, near the settlement of Cartwrights, immediately south of Deadman's Cay, were once used by Lucayan Indians. Harmless bats now live in the 150ft-long caves. They are half a mile east of the main road – look for the sign. **Hamilton's Cave**, at the hamlet of Pettys, 4 miles southeast of Deadman's Cay, is 1500ft long and is one of the largest caves in the Bahamas. It, too, contains bats, as well as stalactites, stalagmites, and a stone walkway with salt water on one side and fresh water on the other.

Reached from Queen's Hwy by a side road beginning at the Hillside Tavern, 1 mile south of Cartwrights, the fishing hamlet of **Mangrove Bush** is a center for traditional boatbuilding. Today the wooden vessels are built exclusively for racing regattas.

The **Long Island Library & Museum** (242-337-0500; adult/child $3/0.50c; 8am-4pm Mon-Fri, 9am-1pm Sat) in Dead Man's Cay has a collection of photographs and artifacts that chronicle the island's history and culture.

Sleeping & Eating

Ellen's Inn B&B $

(242-337-1086/0888; Queen's Hwy, Buckleys; s/d $75/90;) This little white bungalow is an immaculate and homely guesthouse. A guest lounge is comfortably furnished and even pastries and sweets are put out for guests. The guest kitchen makes this an affordable and good-value option. Rates are inclusive of taxes and Ellen also rents out cars for $65 per day.

Constantakis Bay View Apartments APARTMENTS $

(242-337-0644; Pettys; one/two bedroom apts $85/100;) These attractive green lodgings are again in a perfect location for a fisherman in need for bed, balcony and a beer. However, the comfortable kitchen, cable TV and two bedrooms also make this ideal for a family looking for a quiet spot that overlooks the sea, although there is not really a beach here.

Keva's Villas STUDIOS $

(242-337-1054; Queen's Hwy, Deadman's Cay; r $80;) Within walking distance of Max's Conch Bar & Grill, these very plain but clean units are also good value, comfortable enough and owned by Mr T, who also runs a car rental agency.

Smith & Wells Bonefish Lodge FISHING LODGE $$$

(242-337-0246; www.deadmansbones.com; Queen's Hwy; $1970 all inclusive per person per week;) Sitting on the quiet edge of town, and adjacent to the water, this is the place for fishing fans who want nothing more than a simple but clean place to sleep and a screened veranda for a beer in the evening. It sleeps up to six people in three two-bedroom units and the all inclusive fee includes a fishing guide, making this a good deal.

Max's Conch Bar & Grill BAR & GRILL $

(Deadman's Cay; mains $8-15; lunch & dinner) THE hot spot in town. Everything you need to know and want to share, you can do whilst sitting around this circular outdoor bar. A lively and convivial host is well-matched by his customers and family. Unsurprisingly, conch in all its glorious forms is the house specialty.

CLARENCE TOWN AREA

The peaceful harbor settlement of **Clarence Town** and its surrounds are perfect for those seeking some solitude, or a few quiet days living on a beach and pottering around. Long Island's administrative headquarters is very quiet, and has a lovely hillside setting that falls gently to the clear and sparkling waters of the town's small harbor.

Sights & Activities

Even the spiritually unattached will be inspired by the simple beauty of the two churches that rise over the town; **St Paul's Anglican Church** and the sparkling white and blue **St Peter's Catholic Church**. Both were designed by Father Jerome, the enigmatic architect-hermit-cleric of Cat Island (see p174). The first was designed prior to, and the second after, his conversion to Catholicism. You can climb the ladders within one of its two medieval spires for a marvelous bird's-eye view.

Immediately east of town is **Lochabar Bay**, a stunning half-mile-wide, flask-shaped cove that funnels east to a vast **blue hole**. It is rimmed by a splendid and lonesome white-sand beach, surrounded on three sides by dense thickets of thatch palm and scrub. Coral reefs lie just offshore, with staghorn coral at 30ft.

The 2-mile wide **Turtle Cove** near Deans, has a fabulous beach and turquoise shallows. Its real treasure, however, lies to the southeast beyond a headland, where perhaps the world's deepest **Dean's Blue Hole**

(663ft) leads to the world's eighth-largest underwater cavern. The neck of the aquamarine hole opens to a beautiful cove rimmed by gorgeous white sands. It's an incredibly beautiful spot, and you'll usually have it all to yourself. Bring a picnic.

The **Flying Fish Marina** (☎242-337-3430; www.flyingfish-marina.com; Clarence Town) has an excellent 15-slip marina, provisions store, laundry, bathrooms and showers and a bar with good food.

Sleeping

Winter Haven HOTEL $$
(☎242-337-3062; www.winterhavenbahamas.com; Clarence Town; r $150;) With eight spacious rooms in two colorfully painted blocks on a bluff overlooking the ocean, Winter Haven is a great spot to relax. Rooms are comfortable and modern, with wicker furniture and private terraces. There is no minimum-stay requirements and the adjacent Rowdy Boy's Bar & Grill is one of the best on the island.

Gems at Paradise Private Beach Resort RESORT $$
(☎242-337-3016; www.gemsatparadise.com; Clarence Town; r $160;) A mile away from town at Lochabar Bay, Gems has a wonderfully secluded location and its own great beach. Spacious studio apartments and little villas have sponge-painted wooden walls, tile floors, a kitchenette and wide French doors that open to a patio facing the bay, all with the beautiful white-sand beach just a step or two away.

Eating & Drinking

TOP CHOICE **Rowdy Boy's Bar & Grill** BAHAMIAN $$
(☎242-337-3062; Clarence Town; mains $8-18; ⏲1-10pm) Housed in an imposing pink building overlooking the sea, this airy and gleaming restaurant is one of the best on the island, with a far more interesting menu (pan roasted mahi-mahi, seared tuna steaks) than most you'll find here.

Outer Edge Grill & Bar GRILL $$
(Flying Fish Marina, Clarence Town; mains $14-17; ⏲11:30am-8pm daily) This tiny outdoor harborside bar and restaurant serves up cheap sandwiches ($4 to $7) as well as steaks, seafood and fish dishes. It's a great sundowner spot too and popular with the marina crowd.

The Forest BAR $
(☎242-337-3287; Queen's Hwy; mains $8-15) This is a lurid-pink bar and restaurant that also doubles as the area's hotspot with live music and dancing at weekends.

DUNMORE TO CAPE VERDE

The final 15-miles of the Queen's Hwy will take you past three exquisite **Father Jerome churches**, whitewashed and painted in trademark blue, in **Dunmore**, the wonderfully named **Hard Bargain**, and **Mortimers**.

Also just north of the church at Dunmore are the gates to some overgrown **plantation ruins**, named for a former governor of the Bahamas who had an estate producing sisal, cotton, and pineapples. You can follow a dirt track half a mile to the ruined hilltop mansion.

The road then passes turnoffs for shell-covered **Cabbage Point Beach**, some abandoned salt ponds and desolate villages until it reaches **Gordons**. From here you can hike the mile to **Cape Verde**, the island's southernmost point.

CROOKED ISLAND DISTRICT

POP 342

Crooked Island District consists of Crooked Island, Acklins Island, Long Cay, and outlying Samana and Plana Cays. These southerly islands are not developed for tourism, which is definitely part of their allure, but they are also not wealthy. Electricity still hasn't reached many areas and the island's descendants still fish, tend the land, and draw an income from stripping cascarilla bark and selling it to the manufacturers of Campari liquor (it is also used in medicines).

Crooked Island

One of the most beautiful Out Islands, Crooked is covered with lakes, bisected by tidal inlets and surrounded by wonderful beaches. Rich in nature, strictly Seventh Day Adventist and almost totally undeveloped, look no further for the 'real Caribbean'. The island is poor by Bahamian standards, with many villages having become ghost towns as the last remaining inhabitants have died or moved to Nassau to look for work. But that said, the island has plenty of natural charm and is a great spot to kick back and relax.

COLUMBUS STOOD HERE

No one disputes that Columbus' first landfall in the New World in 1492 was in the Bahamas. But the question of which island he landed on has aroused considerable controversy. Nine first landfalls have been proposed, although, incredibly, no one had taken into account 'dead reckoning' – the cumulative effect of current and leeway (wind-caused slippage) on a vessel's course – in tracing the route of the round-bottomed fleet.

In November 1986, following five years of extensive study by Joseph Judge and a team of scholarly interests under the aegis of the National Geographic Society, *National Geographic* magazine announced that it had solved the 'grandest of all geographic mysteries.' Judge ordered a new translation of the Columbus diaries, drew the first-ever track of the log, then input all the variables into a computer to adjust for leeway, current and magnetic variation, and traveled to the islands to find actual evidence. Judge's team also was the first to track Columbus' course using the Spanish league (2.82 nautical miles), not the English league (2.5 nautical miles) previously used. Presto! The exact landing spot turns out to be the island of Samana Cay, 23 miles off Crooked Island.

One main road runs along the north shore and leads to Landrail Point and Colonel Hill, the island's main villages, which run on farming and fishing, a number of generators and a lot of faith. As around 60% of the islanders are Seventh-Day Adventists, be prepared for the island to come to a total standstill from Friday sundown until Saturday sundown.

Getting There & Away

The main airfield is just east of Colonel Hill, and Pittstown Point Landing has its own 2000ft airstrip.

Bahamasair connects Colonel Hill Airport with Nassau every Wednesday and Saturday (one way $100), while Pineapple Air flies the route on Monday and Friday ($135). Flights also stop on Acklins Island.

MV *United Star* (one way $70, 14 hours) sails from Nassau weekly, stopping at Landrail Point. Contact the **Potter's Cay Dockmaster's Office** (242-393-1064) in Nassau for mail-boat departure times.

Getting Around

Contact **C&C Car Rentals** (242-344-2359, 466-9770) for car rental. They will meet you at the airport or dock with your hire vehicle ($60 per day).

A small, free passenger ferry runs between Cove Point, Crooked Island, and Lovely Bay, Acklins Island at 9am and 5pm daily except Sunday.

Ask at the **Land Rail Marina** (242-344-2676; Landrail Point) to see if any boats will take you to Long Cay or on sightseeing trips.

LANDRAIL POINT AREA

Landrail Point is the main settlement of Crooked Island and has most of the amenities and sights nearby, most impressive of which is a small, coral-encrusted cay a mile offshore from Pittstown Point. It is pinned by a stately 115ft-tall **Bird Rock Lighthouse** (1876), erected to guide ships through the treacherous Crooked Island Passage. The cay is a prime nesting colony for snowy white terns and tropical birds, and is a five-minute boat ride from Pittstown Point.

Bat Caves lie 100yd inland from the shore, near Gordon's Bluff near Gordon's Beach. They're easily explored, the walking is level and there are stalactites in the depths.

Brine Pool is a lagoon, stretching from Landrail Point north to Pittstown Point, along whose shore several expats have built modest homes, and sea birds, ospreys and sometimes flamingos flock.

Marine Farms, a salt farm on an island in the midst of the pond, began life as a cotton plantation and a Spanish or British fort that is said to have managed a firefight with US warships in the War of 1812. Cannons still can be seen lying amid the ruins and salt pans. **Great Hope House**, about a mile south of Landrail Point, was once the centerpiece of a 19th-century plantation.

The lovely **Shell Beach** and **Bathing Beach** stretch south from Landrail Point for 7 miles to **French Wells**. Snorkeling is divine, with fabulous coral heads just below the water.

Sleeping & Eating

Crooked Island Lodge RESORT $$
(242-344-2507; www.pittstownpoint.com; Landrail Point; r $150-225;) The island's

biggest resort has just twelve tasteful and spacious rooms, though the bathrooms are looking a bit worn. The small beach is just meters away, snorkeling is free and kayaks can be hired. For $65 per day you can take the full meal plan served in the attractive little beach hut restaurant

Casuarina Villas VILLAS **$$**
(☎242-344-2197, 242-457-7005; Landrail Point; s/d/apt $125/145/220;) With five units set in a great location just by the beach, these villas come with full kitchen facilities and a deck, and are located a short walk from Landrail Point. The friendly owners can organize diving expeditions and car rental for guests.

Gibson's Restaurant BAHAMIAN **$$**
(☎242-344-2020; Landrail Point; mains $15-20; lunch & dinner Sun-Fri, Sat by arrangement) This veritable institution and social hub is the place to head to catch up with locals and swap stories with other island visitors. Friendly owner Willie Gibson serves up tasty meals of chicken and fish in generous servings and her homemade lemonade is superb. Call ahead to let them know you'll be coming for dinner.

Landrail Point is also home to **Green Valley** (7am-7pm Sun-Fri), the best-stocked supermarket and general store on the island.

COLONEL HILL AREA

The settlement of **Colonel Hill** (population 240) may have the island's airport, but in other senses it's a bit of a backwater. The village comprises a few dozen ramshackle clapboard huts, emancipation-era houses, and pastel-painted modern concrete homes. The only building of note is **St John's Baptist Church**, atop the hill.

The road leads northwest 1½ miles to the lime-green **All Saints Church**, surrounded by African flame trees in Cabbage Hill, and the small **Baptist church**, fronted by a tiny bell tower in Cripple Hill.

Two recommended lodging options can be found in nearby Major's Cay. **Tranquility on the Bay Resort** (☎242-344-2563; www.tranquillitybayresort.com; r $190;) is notable for the hugeness of its pristine rooms and the accuracy of its name, sitting as it does on a lovely and peaceful bay. The enthusiastic owners are trying very hard to build up a tourism industry here and are extremely helpful. They also operate the **Conch Shell Restaurant** (☎242-344-2563, mains $10-15), one of the very few on the island. Next door you'll find **Sonsette Beach Resort** (☎242-344-2041, r $150;), three attractive beach-front studios with lovely terraces.

COLONEL HILL TO COVE POINT

Follow the north shore to **Major's Cay**, a hamlet facing turquoise-jade waters rimmed by the narrow but beautiful **True Blue Beach**. Further east, the road becomes a narrow track leading to **Cove Point**, 12 miles east of Major's Cay. There's nothing here but a tiny concrete wharf where the ferry departs for Acklins Island.

Long Cay

This small island is separated by a mile-wide channel from Crooked Island. Columbus, it seems, landed here on October 19, 1492. The explorer named the island Isabela after the Spanish queen who funded his jaunts to the New World.

The island was later known as Fortune Island and once boasted thriving sponging and salt industries. Flamingos wade in the bight on the south side of the island and an endemic subspecies of iguana inhabits two tiny cays – Fish Cay and Guana Cay – that lie 7 and 10 miles southeast of Long Cay.

In the 19th century **Albert Town**, also called Windsor and the island's only settlement, was the main base in the archipelago for transatlantic mail and freight ships hiring and dropping off stevedores, or 'coast crew.' Wild goats have taken over the ruins, though the largest **Anglican church** south of Nassau still stands.

A MILLION DOLLAR MISTAKE

This famous **plane wreck** is in 12ft of water about 50yd offshore Long Cay. The plane was on a drug run when it crashed at sea. Locals found a suitcase containing about $1,000,000. It was handed to an official from Nassau who, it seems, pocketed the money and went on to live the life of Riley. Nowadays divers hoping for any crumbs of this hoard will find no money but a wealth of fish and marine-life instead.

ACKLINS ISLAND

POP 435

Separated from Crooked Island by a shallow passage called 'The Going Through,' 45-mile-long Acklins Island is another totally undeveloped semi-wilderness of an island with some excellent bonefishing lodges, miles of scrub forest and very little else.

The main settlement is **Spring Point**, midway down the west coast. Public electricity arrived in 1998, although plenty of homes still use a small generator. To bathe, most locals scoop water from barrels, while their earnings come from fishing and beating the Cascarilla bark, a vital ingredient for Campari.

Sights & Activities

A partially excavated **Lucayan Indian site** along the shore of Pompey Bay, immediately south of Spring Point, may have been the largest Lucayan settlement in the Bahamas. The only other site of interest is the remote **Castle Island Lighthouse** (1867) at the southern tip of the island. A dirt road runs all the way to the poor Salinas Point Settlement, after which there's just a hiking trail to the end of the island.

The bonefishing is as good as it gets, as the Bight of Acklins has more than 1000 sq miles of knee-deep water. All hotels can arrange fishing trips.

Sleeping & Eating

TOP CHOICE **Acklins Island Lodge** FISHING LODGE $$

(242-344-199; www.acklinsislandlodge.com; Mason's Bay; $865 per person all inclusive for two nights;) Wonderfully situated at the top of a hill with views to both sides of the island, this charming complex of six fully equipped studios and the excellent Spice Kitchen restaurant is a great choice.

Gray's Point Bonefish Inn FISHING LODGE $$

(242-344-3210; www.greyspointbonefishinn.com; Pinefield; r $1500 per person all inclusive for two nights;) This six-room lodge has clean and spacious rooms in a beautiful position with easy access to the water and is aimed squarely at bonefishers.

Nai's Guesthouse MOTEL $$

(242-344-3543; 422-3310; r $130;) Nai's has six rooms in a low-slung white building opposite Acklins' only gas station. This is a good budget option, as guests can use the small kitchen.

Club Rolex GRILL $$

(242-344-3156; Mason's Bay; mains $10-12; 8am-9pm;) This is the island's most reliable eating spot, serving up unexciting but passable Bahamian snacks and full meals for which its best to call in advance.

There are several other bonefish lodges on the island including **Chester's Highway Inn** (242-557-3597; www.chestershighwayinn.com; Chesters; r per night/week from $285/1995) and **Top Choice** (242-344-3530; Mason's Bay; r from $250), both of which offer simple accommodations.

Getting There & Around

Spring Point Acklins airport is a mile south of Spring Point and has services to Nassau twice a week on Bahamas Air and once a week on Pineapple Air.

A free passenger ferry runs from Cove Point (Crooked Island) to Lovely Bay, 3 miles west of Chesters, twice daily except Sunday, leaving Acklins at 8:30am and 4:30pm, returning 30 minutes later.

Cars can be rented for $80 per day from Big Brother Car Rental at Chester's Bonefish Lodge.

INAGUAS & MAYAGUANA

Great Inagua is also the southernmost Bahamian island and is known for its vast flamingo sanctuary, local salt industry and proximity to both Cuba and Haiti. Neighboring Little Inagua is an uninhabited isle to the northeast of Great Inagua, while Mayaguana can rightfully be called one of the most lonesome of all Bahamian islands, lying just 50 miles northwest of Providenciales (Turks and Caicos).

Half of Great Inagua lies within Bahamas National Trust Park and therefore much of the island is only accessible with some arduous trekking through brush, with vast acres of exceedingly briny lakes where wild pigs, goats, horses and donkeys roam (the latter two outnumber humans by five-to-one). The birdlife is however the real draw card here, including five species of egret, the rare Bahamian Green Parrot and the hemisphere's largest flock of West Indian flamingos.

The islands' climate is hot and tourist infrastructure cannot even be said to be in its infancy. However the islands are blissfully free of other tourists and you'll be a curiosity to locals wherever you go.

History

Great Inagua's human settlement was financed and supported by salt. 'Crystal farming' was began in the late 18th century. The island became a major salt exporter (as told in *Great Inagua* by Margery O Erickson).

Great Inagua's southernmost position also makes it a prime piece of real estate for drug-runners heading in from Colombia and other drug-producing nations. So many islanders profited from the drug trade in the 1980s that when a policeman became overzealous, locals burned down the police station and took him hostage. The Drug Enforcement Administration now have a permanent presence on the islands.

Getting There & Around

Most visitors fly into Great Inagua or Mayaguana. Others catch the weekly mail boat from Nassau.

You'll need your own transportation if you want to explore the islands or visit Little Inagua. A couple of people rent cars in Matthew Town, though as much of the island is a restricted national park, you aren't able to drive freely around it.

Great & Little Inagua

POP 951

With salt traders and birds the most recognizable visitors, Great Inagua remains totally off the beaten path for travelers. The main attraction of the island is the birdwatching in the national park, where thousands of flamingos nest between February and June.

Matthew Town is the only settlement on the island and is a center for the Morton Salt Company, who produces nearly a million pounds of salt here annually. Sport fishing and scuba-diving fans will enjoy these pristine waters but will need their own gear.

MATTHEW TOWN

POP 452

The white gold of former years is still a regular income for most of the town's folk, while others get by on fishing and farming. The faded bungalows and old two-story whitewashed houses with green shuttered windows make up the town center along with a few shops and bars.

Sights & Activities

The small **Moreton Museum** (☎242-339-1863; Gregory St) contains profiles on salt production and native fauna, including flamingos. Ask the librarian to open it for you if it's closed, or call ahead to arrange a visit.

The **Great Inagua Lighthouse** (☎242-339-1370; Southwest Point) is one of four kerosene lighthouses in the country that must be wound by hand every 1½ hours throughout the night.

Sleeping & Eating

Morton Salt Company Main House GUESTHOUSE $
(☎242-339-1267; Gregory St; d $60-90; ❄📶) You'll feel like a traveling salesperson in a 1930s American novel if you stay at this endearing and well-maintained two-story guesthouse. Rooms are well equipped and staff are friendly when they're around, although unfortunately it's right opposite the very noisy town power plant, which may bother light sleepers. It's right in the center of town.

Enrica's Inn GUESTHOUSE $
(☎242-339-2127, 3339-1271; cnr Victoria & Taylor Sts; $75-110; ❄📶) The three new and beautifully maintained wooden houses look very swish by local standards and are the most comfortable option in town. Each house contains five rooms, and there's a communal kitchen for guests to use.

Gaga's Nest GUESTHOUSE $
(☎242-339-2140/1666; r $80; ❄📶) This pleasant place offers three decent rooms each with a fridge, TV and microwave in a colonial style house some way from the center of town.

Cozy's BAHAMIAN $$
(☎242-339-1440; William St; snacks $4-9, mains $10-12; ⊙lunch & dinner Mon-Sat) This place doesn't really live up to its name, but by local standards it's like the Ritz, with tablecloths and a relatively wide choice of food. Lunch is the best time to eat here, where full meals are served, while in the evenings you're limited to a range of smaller snacks such as burgers and hot wings. Look for the violent lime-green building.

A couple of other eating options include **Inagua Island Restaurant** (☎242-339-1414; mains $10-16), a very friendly family-run place where you'll find free wi-fi and a relatively wide selection of dishes. **S & L Restaurant & Bar** (☎242-339-1677; Kortwright St; mains $10-15) is another place to eat as well as being a popular local bar with a pool table.

FLAMING FLAMINGOS

The West Indian (or roseate) flamingo is restricted to Great Inagua, the Turks and Caicos, Bonaire, portions of the Yucatán Peninsula, and Cuba. Around 10,000 of these leggy birds inhabit 12-mile-long Lake Rosa in the Bahamas National Trust Park. In season (November through June) the birds can be seen in great flocks in the park, most magnificently, taking off en masse in a pink blizzard. The birds mate in December and January and nest from February to April. Each spring a **bird count** is undertaken. You're welcome to volunteer, simply contact the Bahamas National Trust (www.bnt.bs) head office in Nassau.

Inagua General Store (Gregory St; ⌚8am-6pm Mon-Fri, until 1pm Sat, closed Sun) is the pricey but surprisingly well-stocked island supermarket located in the same building as the Moreton Salt Company Main House.

Information

There is a Bank of the Bahamas branch (but no ATM), a post office and police station on Gregory St. There's a Government medical clinic on Victoria St.

Getting There & Around

Matthew Town Airport (☎242-339-1680) is 2 miles north of town. There are rarely taxis at the airport, but it's easy enough to get a lift into town on arrival, as the thrice-weekly flights from Nassau are big events here and the airport is always crowded.

Bahamasair flies from Nassau to Matthew Town, normally stopping at Mayaguana on the way there or back (one way $110, Monday, Wednesday and Friday).

The *United Star* (one way $70, 24 hours) sails from Nassau weekly to Inagua and Mayanagua. Call the **Dockmaster's office** (☎242-393-1064) on Potter's Cay in Nassau for exact schedules.

Matthew Town Harbour (☎242-339-1427) has slips and fuel, and you can enter the country at **Immigration** (☎242-339-1234; Gregory St). There is also a US Coast Guard looking out for Cuban and Haitian refugees.

For car rentals call **Laverne Ingraham** (☎242-339-1677/1515).

NORTH OF MATTHEW TOWN

About 4 miles past Matthew Town, the dirt road passes between the southernmost part of the Morton Salt Works' salt pans. The road finishes at **Farquharson Beach**, a protected bay and a prime snorkeling and bonefishing spot.

The **Morton Salt Works** are the second-largest solar saline plant in the hemisphere; comprising 34,000 acres of reservoirs and salt pans surrounding a cleaning, storage, and bulk-freight loading facility.

BAHAMAS NATIONAL TRUST PARK

The extraordinary salt-scorched landscape of this 287-sq-mile national park is truly haunting, and a visit here is *the* reason to come to Great Inagua. Home to the world's largest breeding colony of West Indian flamingos as well as roseate spoonbills, five types of egret, ospreys, pelicans, avocets, cormorants, tricolored Louisiana herons, burrowing owls, Bahamian pintails, endemic Bahamian woodstar hummingbirds, American kestrels and endangered Bahama parrots; the park has the most diverse birdlife in the Bahamas.

You can only enter the park with the warden **Henry Nixon** (☎242-225-0878, 242-464-7618; VHF Channel 16) on a tour ($50 for up to four adults, including vehicle and tip). It's best to call several days in advance to arrange the visit as Mr Nixon is often busy.

Hawksbill turtles also come ashore to nest and freshwater turtles inhabit ponds on these isles. **Union Creek Reserve** lies at the park's northwest corner and encompasses tidal creeks and beach where sea turtles feed and come ashore to nest. The sanctuary is the only natural feeding ground in the Caribbean region and mid-Americas where sea turtles are not hunted or exploited in any way.

The plain **Camp Arthur Vernay** (☎242-225-0878, 242-464-7618; dm per person $30) bunkhouse sleeps nine and has two shared showers with cold and lukewarm water and an outdoor kitchen. Take your own food, but the BNT warden Henry Nixon may cook for you on request; be prepared to tip extra.

LITTLE INAGUA

This 30-sq-mile island, 5 miles northeast of Great Inagua, is uninhabited, despite its relatively rich soils, which support a dense stand of Cuban royal palm and sizeable populations of wild burros and goats. Several bird species and marine turtles also nest here. You can visit from Great Inagua by chartering a boat in Matthew Town.

Mayaguana

POP 251

The silent beaches, rugged and rocky shores, and unspoilt reefs entice occasional boaters to this 25-mile-long isle that is barely 6 miles wide, and is located 65 miles from Great Inagua. Some fantastic snorkeling can be enjoyed here and **Booby Cay**, offshore, is an important nesting site for sea birds.

Abraham Bay, on the south coast, is the largest of three small settlements on the island. Roads northwest lead to the other settlements: **Pirate's Well** and **Betsy Bay**. Electricity and a full telephone service arrived here only in 1997.

The charming **Baycaner Beach Resort** (242-339-3726; Pirate's Well; r $143;), offers 16 simple rooms in its little single-story yellow building. You're just a stone's throw from a fantastic beach, and the restaurant and bar here serve up reliable local fare and cold beers all day long.

Most visitors fly here, but it's possible to catch the weekly mail boat from Nassau. The airfield is 2 miles west of Abraham Bay.

Turks & Caicos

CHRISTOPHER BAKER/LONELY PLANET IMAGES ©

Turks & Caicos

Includes »

Why Go?

The Turks and where? That's the reaction most people have when you mention these tropical isles. Like all great Shangri-Las, this one is hidden just under the radar. Be glad that it is, as this tropical dream is the deserted Caribbean destination you've been looking for. And the best part – it's only 90 minutes by plane from Miami.

So why would you want to go there? How about white-sand beaches, clear blue water and a climate that defines divine. Secluded bays and islands where you'll see more wild donkeys than other travelers. Historic towns and villages where life creeps along at a sedate pace.

Divers and beach aficionados will rejoice: clear warm waters teem with marine life, yet are devoid of crashing waves. Islands like Grand Turk – set in a time long since past, with its dilapidated buildings, salt ponds and narrow lanes – contrast with the ever expanding Providenciales. While development is on the rise, all one has to do is catch a boat to the next island over and the solace of solitude returns.

Best Beaches

- » Grace Bay Beach (p202)
- » Mudjin Harbor (p211)
- » Bambarra Beach (p211)
- » Governor's Beach (p214)

Best Places to Eat

- » Grace's Cottage (p207)
- » Terrace (p209)
- » Coyaba (p207)
- » Osprey (p215)

When to Go

Turks Island

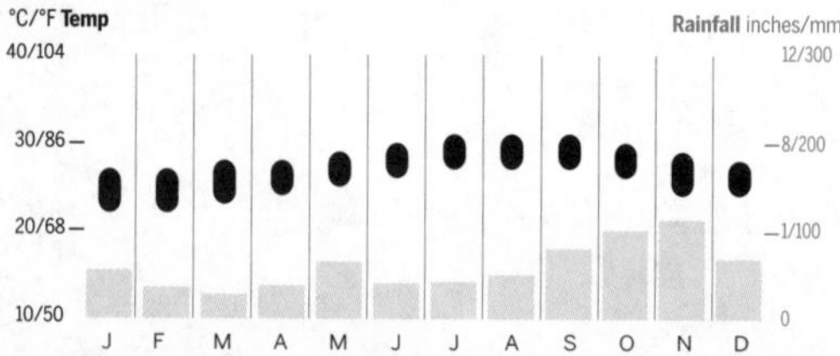

January–April The islands' high season is rightly popular – the weather is normally dry and warm.

July The country's biggest fishing competition, the Grand Turk Game Fishing Tournament, arrives.

November Blow a conch shell or just head for the tasting tent at the Turks & Caicos Conch Festival.

Itineraries

THREE DAYS

Spend the day admiring Grace Bay on Providenciales then wake up the next day to go for a snorkeling trip to French Cay to frolic with some stingrays. On the last day rent a bike and explore the island under your own steam.

ONE WEEK

Add on a trip to the islands of North Caicos and Middle Caicos and discover what solitude is really all about. Complete the trip by heading to Grand Turk to explore the town, do some great diving and spend a day or two on Salt Cay – the best-kept secret in the country.

GETTING TO NEIGHBORING ISLANDS

There are no scheduled ferry services to neighboring islands from the Turks and Caicos. Flying is the way to get around and there are regular flights to Nassau (Bahamas), Puerto Plata and Santiago (Dominican Republic), Cap-Haïtien and Port-au-Prince (Haiti) and to Kingston (Jamaica).

Essential Food & Drink

» **Conch** This grilled gastropod remains the dish of choice across the islands, and rigorous controls on the fishing industry mean that its numbers are not declining here.

» **Lobster** Don't miss tasting the fresh lobster during your stay – traditionally served in a butter sauce with lime, it's the culinary highlight of the country.

» **Turk's Head** The local brew is a great way to cool down in the height of the Caribbean afternoon.

AT A GLANCE

Currency US$

Language English

Money ATMs abundant on Providenciales, less common elsewhere

Visas Not required for citizens of the US, Canada or Western Europe

Fast Facts

» **Area** 430 sq miles

» **Capital** Cockburn Town

» **Telephone code** ☎+649

» **Emergency** ☎911

Exchange Rates

Australia	A$1	$1
Canada	C$1	$1
Eurozone	€1	$1.40
Japan	¥100	$1.22
New Zealand	NZ$1	$0.74
UK	£1	$1.62
US	$1	$1

For current exchange rates see www.xe.com

Set Your Budget

» **Budget hotel room** $80

» **Two-course evening meal** $50

» **Museum entrance** $5

» **Beer** $3

Resources

» **Official tourism website** (www.turksandcaicostourism.com)

» **Government website** (www.tcgov.tc)

» **Time of the Island** (www.timespub.tc)

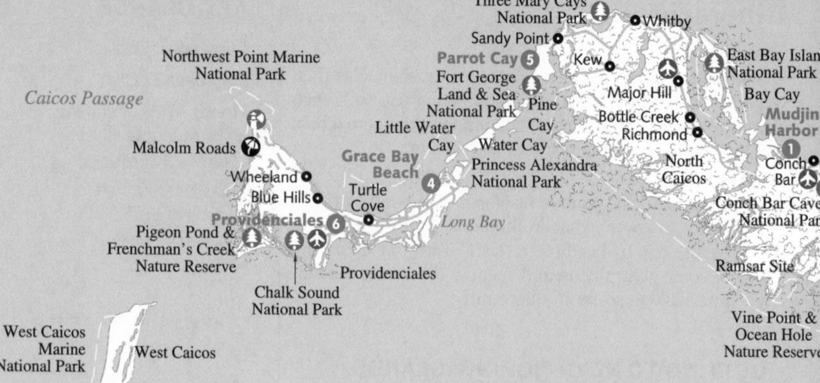

Turks & Caicos Highlights

1. Seeking out stunning **Mudjin Harbor** (p211) – one of the best beach entrances anywhere in the Caribbean

2. Joining a **whale-watching trip** (p216) in Salt Cay and see huge humpback whales breaching the ocean, an unforgettable experience

3. Diving into the water at **Grand Turk** (p214), where the fish are plentiful and the reef pristine

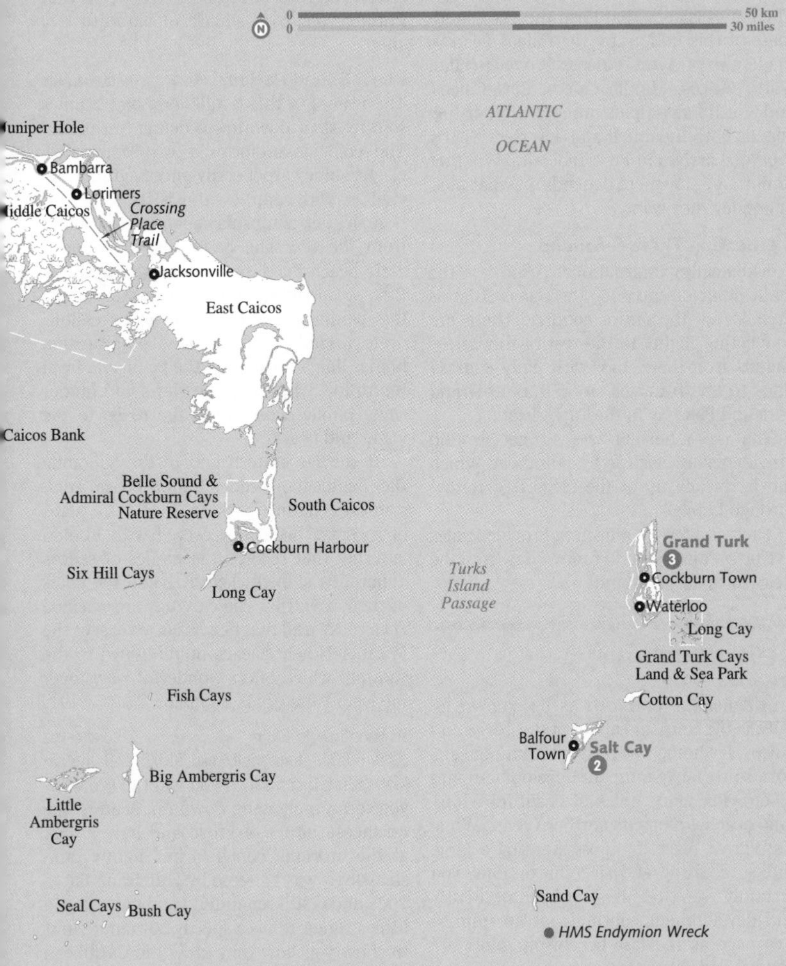

0 50 km
0 30 miles

ATLANTIC

OCEAN

Juniper Hole
Bambarra
Lorimers
Middle Caicos
Crossing Place Trail
Jacksonville
East Caicos
Caicos Bank
Belle Sound & Admiral Cockburn Cays Nature Reserve
South Caicos
Cockburn Harbour
Six Hill Cays
Long Cay
Turks Island Passage
Grand Turk
3
Cockburn Town
Waterloo
Long Cay
Grand Turk Cays Land & Sea Park
Cotton Cay
Fish Cays
Balfour Town
Salt Cay
2
Big Ambergris Cay
Little Ambergris Cay
Sand Cay
HMS Endymion Wreck
Seal Cays
Bush Cay

4 Finding your own slice of heaven on miles of white powder sand at **Grace Bay Beach** (p202)

5 Pampering yourself by booking a room at the sumptuous **Parrot Cay** (p209), for the ultimate in Caribbean elegance and luxury

6 Enjoying cosmopolitan pursuits in **Providenciales** (p202) – shopping in its many malls, eat in its great restaurants and enjoy cocktails on the beach

CAICOS ISLANDS

The fan of islands that form the main landmass of this nation are the Caicos Islands, made up of West Caicos, Providenciales, North Caicos, Middle Caicos, East Caicos, and South Caicos, plus numerous other tiny islands both inhabited and deserted. Nearly everyone arrives in Providenciales. Whether or not they stay there depends on what kind of holiday they want.

Getting There & Around

Providenciales International Airport is the main point of entry for the Caicos Islands as it is for the entire country. There are connecting flights to the rest of the Caicos Islands from here, too, with daily connections to South Caicos, as well as to Grand Turk and Salt Cay in the Turks Islands.

The most normal way to get around Providenciales itself is by rental car, which can be picked up at the airport or rented through hotels.

There is a ferry connecting Providenciales to North Caicos several times a day from the western tip of the island.

Providenciales

POP 8900

Providenciales, or Provo as it's known locally, is the tourism capital of the Turks and Caicos. It's home to a busy international airport, some fairly rampant development and its crowing glory, miles of beautiful white-sand beaches along its northern coast. While it's a great place for those wanting a large choice of eating and sleeping options, you certainly won't be alone in heading here – and development continues at an impressive pace as the last beachfront plots are divided and sold.

But there are still pockets of the island that haven't succumbed to the developers' attentions, and thankfully much of the island's western side is protected land, including the Pigeon Pond & Frenchman's Creek Nature Reserve and the Chalk Sound National Park.

Sights

Grace Bay Beach BEACH

The biggest attraction on the island is this world-famous stretch of sand, notably long and beautiful even by Caribbean standards. This stunning stretch of snow-white sand is perfect for relaxing, swimming and evening up your sunburn. Though it's dotted with hotels and resorts, its sheer size means that finding your own square of paradise is a snap.

Chalk Sound National Park NATIONAL PARK

The waters of this 3-mile-long bay, 2 miles southwest of downtown, define 'turquoise.' The color is uniform: a vast, unrippled, electric-blue carpet eerily and magnificently studded with countless tiny islets.

A slender peninsula separates the sound from the sea. The peninsula is scalloped with beach-lined bays, notably **Sapodilla Bay**. A horribly potholed road runs along the peninsula; although it is accessible, drive carefully. Unfortunately, large vacation homes line both sides of the peninsula from top to toe, which clip the views and hinder some public access from the roads to the water and beaches.

At the far eastern end of the Sapodilla Bay peninsula, a rocky hilltop boasts **rock carvings** dating back to 1844. The slabs of rock are intricately carved with Roman lettering that records the names of sailors apparently shipwrecked here and the dates of their sojourns. The carvings are reached via a rocky trail that begins 200yd east of the Mariner Hotel; it leads uphill 200yd to the summit, which offers wonderful views over the island and Chalk Sound.

Provo Conch Farm CONCH FARM

(☎946-5643; tour adult/child $10/5; ⏰9am-4pm Mon-Fri, until noon Sat) If you want to see what you've been chowing down on, head to the northeast corner of Provo and have a look at this working conch farm. Slightly ramshackle (it was battered by Hurricane Ike in 2008 and is still rebuilding) and more than a little strange, it has a speedy 20-minute tour to show you how they grow the Caribbean Queens. There are also green turtle feeding sessions each day at 9.30am and 3.30pm and at 10am Saturday.

Other Sights

If you feel inclined to tear yourself away from the beach and see some other sights, there are a few worth taking in. Though the options are limited, there are some historic points that should perk scholarly interest. Check out the ruins of **Cheshire Hall** (Leeward Hwy), a plantation house constructed in the 1790s by British Loyalists.

If you've got a rental car that can handle a bit of dirt road, be sure to check out the lighthouse at **Northwest Point**, 8 miles from Providenciales. Caution is the word as the road has been known to swallow cars whole.

Once you get all that history out of your system go for an anti-intellectual cleanse and seek out the sparkling beach at **Malcolm Roads**. From the settlement of Wheeland, northwest of downtown, a rough dirt road leads to this top-notch sandy spot.

Protecting reefs off of Provo's west shore, Northwest Point Marine National Park also encompasses several saline lakes that attract breeding and migrant waterfowl. The largest is **Pigeon Pond**, inland. This part of the park is the Pigeon Pond & Frenchman's Creek Nature Reserve. Other ponds – notably **Northwest Point Pond** and **Frenchman's Creek** – encompass tidal flats and mangrove swamps along the west coast, attracting fish and fowl in large numbers. You'll have to hike here, and come equipped with food and water.

Activities

Diving & Snorkeling

All the dive operators offer a range of dive and snorkel options, from introductory 'resort courses' to PADI certification ($350 to $395).

Most offer free hotel pick-up and drop-offs. Dive sites include the other Caicos islands and cays.

Art Pickering's Provo Turtle Divers DIVING
(☎946-4232; www.provoturtledivers.com; Turtle Cove Marina) Has been going strong for 35 years now; it offers two-tank/night dives for $119/85. Visits all the major dive sites – the company is all about service.

Dive Provo DIVING
(☎946-5040; www.diveprovo.com; Ports of Call plaza, Grace Bay Rd) Has two-tank/night dives ($119/85) at sites around the island, plus photo and video services.

Ocean Vibes DIVING
(☎231-6636; www.oceanvibes.com; Leeward Marina) Is the only dive operation on the island run by Belongers. It specializes in small groups and an intimate feel to its aquatic adventures. Two-tank dives are $125 and there's a host of good deals on the website.

Fishing

Boat charters and trips can be arranged from Leeward and Turtle Cove Marinas (see right). Try the following:

Catch the Wave Charters FISHING
(☎941-3047; www.catchthewavecharters.mobi; Leeward Marina) Runs a variety of boat charters to suit your taste. Fishing costs $500 for half a day. Deep-sea/bottom fishing is $750 for a half-day rental of a boat that will fit four fishers.

Bite Me Sportfishing FISHING
(☎231-0366; biteme@tciway.tc) Is not just a great name, but a good group of folks to help you land the big one.

Grand Slam Charters FISHING
(☎231-4420; www.grandslam-fishing.com) Offers the biggest charter boat on the Turks and Caicos for some serious deep-sea fishing!

Boat Trips

Undersea Explorer Semi Submarine BOAT TRIP
(☎231-0006; www.caicostours.com; Turtle Cove Marina; adult/child $55/40; 👪) This is a moving underwater observatory that's a big hit with kids and those with a phobia of actually getting wet. It's a cool way to see three different sections of the reef – as long as you're not claustrophobic. There are tours leaving at 10am, noon and 2pm each day, and your ticket includes a free pick-up and drop-off at any hotel in the Grace Bay area.

Water Sports

Windsurfing Provo WINDSURFING
(☎241-1687; www.windsurfingprovo.tc; Ocean Club, Grace Bay) Has windsurfing ($40 per hour), sailing ($150 per day) and kayaking ($25 per hour) on offer.

Sleeping

Provo most definitely isn't lacking in places to spend the night. Hotels, condos and resorts dot the island with a frequency that may make you wonder if there really are possibly enough tourists to fill all these rooms. Most budgets are accommodated for, but there is a skew to the higher end so those with deeper pockets will be spoilt for choice. At present, supply outnumbers demand so there are some good deals to be found, especially in the low season.

DOWNTOWN & TURTLE COVE

Coral Gardens BEACH HOTEL $$$
(☎941-5497; www.coralgardensatgracebay.com; Turtle Cove; r from $249; ❄📶🏊) This modern and sleek resort right on the beach manages to feel both relaxed and classy. All rooms,

Providenciales

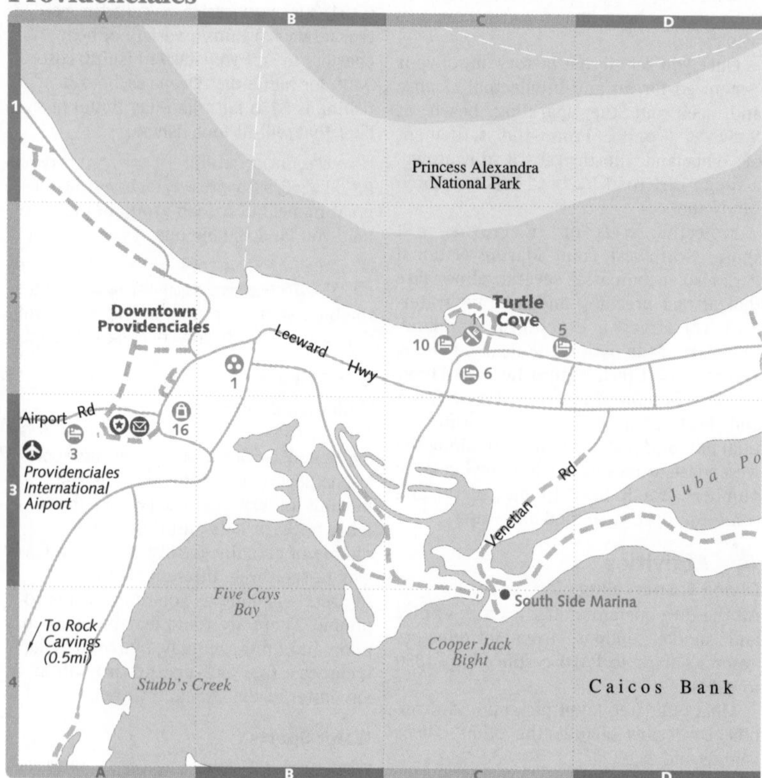

from the modest garden category to the three-bedroom ocean-front suites, are very plushly appointed and on top of that there's a fantastic and unusually social beach bar and restaurant.

Turtle Cove Inn INN $

(☎946-4203; www.turtlecoveinn.com; Turtle Cove Marina; r from $79; ❄☰☒) If you're here to dive and lounge by the pool, this older but friendly and well-run property in the heart of the Turtle Cove Marina is a good option. The rooms have fridge and a safe, but are otherwise frill-free, but staying here puts you in a great location. There are numerous restaurants a few steps away, and dive boats, fishing charters and rental cars all leaving from the doorstep.

Miramar Resort RESORT $

(☎946-4240; www.miramar.tc; Turtle Cove; r $89; ❄☰☒) Has bright, clean and spacious rooms with patio, fridge and good views of Turtle Cove from the hill above. It does lack a bit of character and there are some quirks to the place. It's also a fair trek from the beach. But it has a pool, tennis courts and a gym to keep you busy, and there is the excellent Magnolia Restaurant & Wine Bar in the adjacent building. Note also that there's a three-night minimum stay requirement.

Airport Inn HOTEL $$

(☎941-3514; www.airportinntci.com; Airport Plaza; s/d $130/140; ❄☰) Sporting unencumbered views of the runway, the Airport Inn isn't the sort of place to spend your holiday, but is worth considering if you have an early flight. It is also actually a great option if you're not here for the beach – the rooms are huge and very comfortable given the price. There are also plenty of eating options nearby, all with a local flavor.

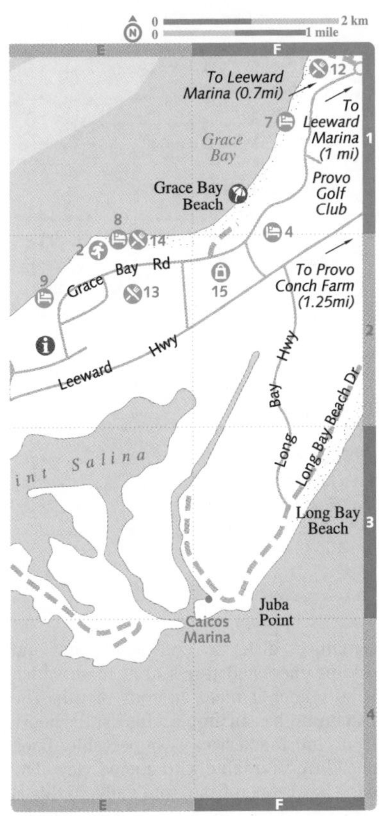

are right on Grace Beach, while the cheaper cottages are clustered around the pool in blocks of four, and still afford generous privacy and space. The entire place feels far removed from the bustle of the other resorts and this makes it a great place to escape to.

Comfort Suites SUITES $$
(☎946-8888; www.comfortsuitestci.com; Grace Bay; r from $105;) If you're searching for an affordable resort and are willing to accept that it isn't beachfront (though not far off!), this is a great option. Clean and spacious rooms stack in three stories above the pool and chilled poolside bar. Couches in the rooms and chilled-out staff are thrown in. There are even designated chairs on the beach for guests. Nothing too special, but if you're here to dive, lie on the beach or not liquidate your finances, this is the place to stay.

Ocean Club West RESORT $$$
(☎946-5880; www.oceanclubresorts.com; Grace Bay; r from $289;) With a great location in the heart of Grace Bay, the OC is a safe bet. The wonderful pool is complete with an arch-bridge-appointed 'river' and the requisite swim-up bar. Rooms are a bit cramped, but the kitchenettes and balconies more than make up for it. Guests here are also able to use the facilities at the nearby Ocean Club, effectively giving you access to two resorts for the price of one.

Sands RESORT $$$
(☎946-5199; www.thesandstc.com; Grace Bay; r from $285;) This mammoth place is a great family option with a kiddy pool, and kitchenettes in every room. The 118 suites cluster around the superb pool area or face onto the beach where there are tiki huts, for the sun worshippers and the excellent Hemingway's Bar and Grill on-site.

GRACE BAY & EAST PROVIDENCIALES

TOP CHOICE **Sibonné Beach Hotel** BEACH HOTEL $$
(☎946-5547; www.sibonne.com; Grace Bay; r incl breakfast $125-235, apt $350;) Deservedly popular and occupying a divine stretch of sand on Grace Bay, Sibonné is a real anti-resort and it gets our vote. With five room categories ranging from comfortable to luxurious and a friendly relaxed feel (no officious security guards here) this is a great place to enjoy the beach in a low-key surrounding.

Point Grace Luxury Resort & Spa RESORT $$$
(☎946-5096; www.pointgrace.com; Grace Bay; r $475, ste from $915;) The 28 rooms and cottages at this very up-market resort right on the beach are all very sophisticated and luxurious with freestanding bathtubs and vast four-poster beds. The very best suites

Eating & Drinking

Provo has by far the best eating options in the country: those on a budget have the choice of some fun pubs and family-style restaurants, while those looking for a truly memorable experience have several excellent options.

DOWNTOWN & TURTLE COVE

Baci Ristorante ITALIAN $$
(☎941-3044; Harbour Towne Plaza, Turtle Cove; mains $10-30; ⊙lunch & dinner) Maritime chic at its best with wrought-iron scrollwork

Providenciales

Sights
1 Cheshire Hall B2

Activities, Courses & Tours
Art Pickering's Provo Turtle Divers .... (see 10)
2 Caicos Cyclery E2
Dive Provo .... (see 15)
Undersea Explorer Semi Submarine .... (see 10)
Windsurfing Provo .... (see 7)

Sleeping
3 Airport Inn A3
4 Comfort Suites F1
5 Coral Gardens C2
6 Miramar Resort C2
7 Ocean Club West F1
Point Grace Luxury Resort & Spa (see 14)
8 Sands E2
9 Sibonné Beach Hotel E2
10 Turtle Cove Inn C2

Eating
11 Baci Ristorante C2
Calico Jack's .... (see 15)
Carambola Grill & Lounge .... (see 3)
12 Coyaba F1
13 Danny Buoy's Irish Pub & Restaurant E2
14 Grace's Cottage E2
Graceway Gourmet .... (see 4)
Green Bean .... (see 11)
Island Scoop Ice-Cream .... (see 13)
Magnolia Restaurant & Wine Bar.. (see 6)
O'Soleil .... (see 9)
Somewhere Café & Lounge .... (see 5)
Tiki Hut .... (see 10)

Shopping
Marilyn's Crafts .... (see 15)
15 Ports of Call Plaza F2
16 Town Centre Mall A3

lining the ceilings, all with an authentic Italian-infused flavor overlooking the marina. There's a cheap lunch menu offering paninis and pasta ($10 to $14), while the evening menu is more traditionally Italian (carpaccio, *scaloppini al limone*, steaks). Book ahead for the evening.

Magnolia Restaurant & Wine Bar MODERN CARIBBEAN **$$$**
(☎941-5108; Turtle Cove; mains from $22-35; ⏰dinner Tue-Sat) Sitting on the hill overlooking Turtle Cove, Magnolia is a great place for a romantic meal, with superb (if pricey) cooking and an equally lovely view over the lights of the cove. The fairy-light-rimmed balcony is the perfect setting for the signature dish, a cracked-pepper and sesame-encrusted rare-seared tuna, which is so tender it melts in your mouth. The restaurant has an ample wine list to choose from and the service is impeccable. Book ahead to get a table with a good view. The wine bar is open from 4pm daily, so this is also a great spot for a sundowner cocktail, even if you don't plan to eat.

Somewhere Café & Lounge MEXICAN **$$**
(Coral Gardens, Leeward Hwy, Turtle Cove; mains $12-25; ⏰breakfast, lunch & dinner) This charmingly laid back two-floor beach cabaña is a treat any time of the day. Good breakfasts, spicy Mexican dishes, delicious pastries and a lively bar make this one of the few

JOJO: A NATIONAL TREASURE

Since the mid '80s a 7ft bottle-nosed male dolphin called JoJo has cruised the waters off of Provo and North Caicos. When he first appeared, he was shy and limited his human contact to following or playing in the bow waves of boats. He soon turned gregarious and has become an active participant whenever people are in the water.

JoJo is now so popular that he has been named a national treasure by the Ministry of Natural Resources. This treasure is protected through the **JoJo Dolphins Project** (☎941-5617; www.deanandjojo.com; PO Box 153, Providenciales, Turks and Caicos). In addition to looking out for JoJo, it educates and raises awareness of issues affecting the ocean.

JoJo, as with any wild dolphin, interprets attempts to touch him as an aggressive act, and will react to defend himself, so please bear that in mind if you're lucky enough to experience his playfulness and companionship for a while.

places in Provo where you'll meet a young and fun crowd.

Tiki Hut INTERNATIONAL $$
(Turtle Cove Marina; mains from $16; ⏲11am-10pm Mon-Fri, 9am-10pm Sat & Sun) Set right on the wharf at Turtle Cove Marina, this popular spot is where you can sit with a cold beer and watch the boats returning to port. There are cheap sandwiches and burgers ($10 to $12) or more substantial dishes such as baby ribs, cracked conch or lobster pasta.

Carambola Grill & Lounge GRILL $$
(☎946-8122; Airport Hotel Plaza; mains $16-26; ⏲lunch & dinner) The huge menu at this popular downtown spot can be overwhelming, but it's safe to say you'll find something you want, from lobster thermidor to Cajun shrimp and chicken pasta. It offers a pick-up service from Grace Bay hotels, simply call ahead.

GRACE BAY & EAST PROVIDENCIALES

There is a wide choice of dining options in this neck of the woods. The Ports of Call shopping plaza has a stack of midrange options and nearly all hotels and resorts in this area have restaurants that are open to the public.

TOP CHOICE **Grace's Cottage** INTERNATIONAL $$$
(☎946-8147; Point Grace Luxury Resort & Spa, Grace Bay; mains $25-50; ⏲dinner) Tucked out of the way from the main road, this charming cottage has tables spread out among the trees and in romantic hidden enclaves. Crisp white-linen tablecloths adorn the surfaces and service is excellent. The menu encompasses inventive seafood dishes and pasta, and vegetarians are well catered for. There's also a superb wine list. Reservations are usually essential.

TOP CHOICE **Coyaba** CARIBBEAN $$$
(☎946-5186; www.coyabarestaurant.com; Paradise Inn; mains from $35; ⏲dinner Wed-Mon) Off Grace Bay Rd, Coyaba somehow treads the line of fine dining while retaining a relaxed atmosphere. The food is a clever fusion of Caribbean flavors and faithful classics. The legendary chef shows his skills with daily specials that outnumber the menu standards. This is a real food-lovers' paradise. Be sure to make a reservation – word's out about this one.

Green Bean CAFE $
(Leeward Hwy, Turtle Cove; mains $8-15; ⏲7am-6pm) This excellent initiative pairs up healthy eating and environmental awareness and is leading where hopefully others will follow, using organic produce, compostable packaging and, where possible, locally sourced ingredients. Try its excellent salads or make your own, get a fresh smoothie or panini to go, or just chill out with a range of tea and coffee.

O'Soleil SEAFOOD $$$
(☎946-5900; The Somerset, Princess Dr; mains $26-40; ⏲dinner) Fresh seafood is the specialty in this stylish eatery. The Mediterranean-influenced architecture provides the perfect backdrop for the culinary designs created in the kitchen. Be sure to try the Turks and Caicos chowder: it's loaded with fresh seafood and the secret ingredient that makes it nearly irresistible – Caribbean rum.

Calico Jack's BAR & GRILL $$
(Ports of Call plaza; mains from $12; ⏲dinner) Comes with a generous helping of nautical paraphernalia and is named after the English pirate who popularized the skull and crossbones flag. Nightly drink specials, Spanish armada–sized portions and a friendly atmosphere make it a locals' favorite. The conch is awesome, and be sure to swing by on a Thursday when the place really hops to the sounds of live music.

GO FLY A KITE

The steady winds that buff the coastline of the Turks and Caicos mixed with the reef-sheltered shoreline are the perfect combination for the snowboarding of the aquatic world – kitesurfing. The bastard child of stunt kite flying, wakeboarding and windsurfing, this sport is going off right now. Imagine flying the biggest kite you've ever seen, strapping yourself onto a wakeboard and holding on for dear life. Depending on how much sugar you like in your tea, it either sounds terrific or terrifying. The warm T&C waters are already on the radar of the sport's elite – but don't be put off, it's also a great place to learn. Chat to Mike at **Windsurfing Provo** (☎241-1687; www.windsurfingprovo.tc; Ocean Club, Grace Bay) to get hooked up with the how-to ($150 for a two-hour lesson). Who said all there is to do in the Caribbean is lie on the beach?

Danny Buoy's Irish Pub & Restaurant PUB $
(Grace Bay Rd; mains from $10; ⏲lunch & dinner) This dark but lively pub offers up traditional Irish fare mixed with Caribbean classics. The Guinness on tap is good, but you'll need a lot of them to believe you're in the old country!

Island Scoop Ice-Cream ICE CREAM $
(Grace Bay Plaza, Grace Bay Rd; ice cream $3; ⏲10am-9pm) When the sun is shining and it's all starting to get just a bit too hot, slide into Island Scoop for the therapy you need. Twenty-four flavors of goodness to choose from, piled into homemade waffle cones.

The best supermarket in Providenciales is **Graceway Gourmet**, just next to the Scotiabank and Comfort Suites in Grace Bay. It may be eye-wateringly expensive, but its selection of fresh fruit and vegetables can't be beaten anywhere else in the country.

Shopping

Providenciales has a large selection of shopping malls spread out along the Grace Bay Rd. These largely contain international brand shops and prices aren't particularly good, as everything has been imported. Locally produced items are generally of very little interest to travelers, there are few local arts and crafts, and most items on sale come far more under the heading of 'tourist tat' that genuine souvenirs.

A large selection of beachy items, casual clothing and batiks is offered at Tattooed Parrot, Marilyn's Crafts and the Night & Day Boutique, all in the Ports of Call plaza.

Information

Associated Medical Practices Clinic (☎946-4242; Leeward Hwy) Has several private doctors. The clinic has a recompression chamber.

Cable & Wireless (☎111; Leeward Hwy) Make calls here. It has telephone information and can sort you out with a cell phone. There are also public phone booths at several roadside locations. You dial ☎111 to place credit-card calls.

Fire (☎946-4444)

Police (☎946-4259; Old Airport Rd)

Post office (Old Airport Rd; ⏲8am-noon & 2-4pm Mon-Thu, 8am-12:30pm & 2-5:30pm Fri) Next to the police station.

Provo Discount Pharmacy (☎946-4844; Central Sq Plaza, Leeward Hwy; ⏲8am-10pm)

Tourist information booth (Arrivals Hall, Providenciales International Airport)

Turks & Caicos Tourism (☎946-4970; www.turksandcaicostourism.com; Stubbs Diamond Plaza, ⏲9am-5pm Mon-Fri)

Getting There & Around

Air

For flight information to and from the Caicos Islands, see p221.

There is no bus service from Providenciales International Airport. A taxi from the airport to Grace Bay costs $20 one way for two people; each extra person costs $5. Some resorts arrange their own minibus transfers.

Bicycle

Both **Scooter Bob's** (☎946-4684; scooter@provo.net; Turtle Cove Marina Plaza) and **Caicos Cyclery** (☎941-7544; www.caicoscyclery.com; Grace Bay Rd) rent out bikes for $25 per day.

Boat

A plethora of boat charters and trips can be arranged to the islands and cays from Turtle Cove and Leeward Marinas (see p222).

Car & Motorcycle

You'll find the following rental agencies on the island:

Budget (☎946-4079; www.budget.com; Providenciales International Airport)

Hertz (☎941-3910; www.hertztci.com; Providenciales International Airport)

Rent-a-buggy (☎946-4158; www.rentabuggy.tc) Specializes in 4WD rentals.

Scooter Bob's (☎946-4684; scooter@provo.net; Turtle Cove Marina Plaza) Rents out cars and 4WDs from $75 per day and scooters from $50 per day. It also rents out bicycles for $25 per day and snorkeling gear for $15 per day.

Taxi

Taxis are a popular way of getting around the island. Most are vans and although unmetered the pricing is consistent. It's best not to be in a hurry as they often take forever to come pick you up. Your hotel can arrange a taxi for you and they meet all flights at the airport. Here are a couple of good options:

Nell's Taxi Service (☎941-3228)

Provo Taxi & Bus Group (☎946-5481)

The Cays

The smaller islands around Providenciales are known simply as the Cays, and most of them boast superb beaches and total isolation, being accessible only by a private boat charter.

PARROT CAY

Look no further for true indulgence than **Parrot Cay** (☎941-7544; www.parrotcay.como.biz; r from $938; ❄@🛜🏊), which is definitely the best hotel in the Turks and Caicos, and one of the very best in the Caribbean. On its own eponymous private island, Parrot Cay is part resort with its infinity pool, water sports, diving school and superb restaurants, and part spa, with a firm emphasis on healthy treatments, yoga and 'wellness' provided by the international spa brand Como Shambala. The rooms, which run from simple but sublime one-room garden-view rooms to the incredible five-bedroom Residence, are done in beautifully understated teak furnishings and white timbered walls. The main restaurant, **Terrace**, is a sublime experience catering for all needs with cuisines ranging from macrobiotic to gourmet. Of course, if you need to ask about the price, you probably can't afford it, but if you're looking for a once-in-a-lifetime splurge or you happen to be a Wall Street banker, then this is the place for you.

Northeast of Provo and separated from it by the 400yd-wide channel, **Little Water Cay** is a nature reserve within Princess Alexandra National Park and is the home of about 2000 endangered rock iguanas. If you land here, do not feed or touch the iguanas, even though they are generally easy to approach. Also keep to the trails to avoid trampling their burrows and the ecologically sensitive plants. Next door **Pine Cay**'s primary residents are celebrities. The 2 miles of ocean separating it from the northeast edge of Provo is plenty of moat to keep the riffraff out.

Fort George Cay is home to the remnants of an 18th-century British-built fort built back in the day to protect the islands. Now the only invaders are divers and snorkelers there to inspect the gun emplacements slowly becoming one with the sea bottom. The site is protected within Fort George Land & Sea National Park, which is also home to a protected iguana population. **Dellis Cay** has some of the best shells around on its beautiful beaches, but being in the park precludes you from taking them home.

Parrot Cay is home to the Turks and Caicos' most luxurious and famous hotel (see above) and is very private indeed.

Some way south of Providenciales, the old pirate hideaway of **French Cay** is now more frequented by migrating birds than swashbuckling scoundrels. Uninhabited and a permanent wildlife sanctuary, this small island 15 miles south of Provo is home to a staggering number of bird species. Just offshore the waters are teeming with stingrays who use the calm waters as a nursery. Nurse sharks (entirely harmless creatures) gather here in summer where they feed, breed and scare swimmers. You can snorkel among the menagerie of sea life on a day trip from Provo.

North Caicos

POP 1500

There was a time a century ago when bountiful North Caicos, with its lush farmland and bustling towns, was the center of action in the island chain. But those times have long since passed. These days there are only stone ruins and a few small towns to show for these early expansions. But don't despair; there remains a pristine tropical isle that is a joy to visit.

There are a few tiny settlements, more groups of dwellings than towns – but that is where the charm lies. There is a distinctive lost-world feel to this island. As you wander along the empty roads, shell-strewn beaches and green interior you can't help but feel glad that Provo-style development doesn't yet threaten this beautiful spot.

Sights & Activities

The Kew area has several historic ruins, including the interesting **Wades Green Plantation**, granted to a British Loyalist by King George III. The owners struggled to grow sisal and Sea Island cotton until drought, hurricanes and bugs drove them out. The plantation lasted a mere 25 years; the owners abandoned their slaves and left. It's a sobering place to visit and worth the effort.

Beaches along the north coast of North Caicos include **Pumpkin Bluff**, **Horsestable** and most importantly, **Whitby Beach**. On any one, yours will be the only Robinson Crusoe footprints. Pumpkin Bluff beach

THE CLOCK IS TICKING

For as long as everyone can remember North Caicos has always been the ultra-quiet neighbor to Provo. But times are a changing – there is an unprecedented amount of development underway on the island. Granted, it's not going to look like Miami Beach any time soon, but there are quite a few new projects under way. The new ferry has increased numbers and there's a deep-water harbor under construction that will make bringing building materials to the island much easier. This translates into more people, and soon more options for places to stay, eat and drink. Sadly it does signal the end of a very quiet era on North Caicos; the days when you got the beaches all to yourself are numbered. So if you want to see NC the way it's supposed to be – quiet as a mouse – you better get here ASAP.

is especially beautiful and the snorkeling is good, with a foundered cargo ship adding to the allure.

Cottage Pond, a 150ft-deep blue hole on the northwest coast, attracts waterfowl such as West Indian whistling ducks, grebes and waders. Bellfield Landing Pond, Pumpkin Bluff Pond and Dick Hill Creek also attract flamingos, as does a large brine lake, **Flamingo Pond**, which floods the center of the island. Here the gangly birds strut around in hot pink. The ponds are protected as individual nature reserves.

A series of small cays off the northeast shore are protected within **East Bay Islands National Park**, and a trio of cays to the northwest form **Three Mary Cays National Park**, another flamingo sanctuary and an osprey nesting site. The **snorkeling** is good at Three Mary Cays and further west at Sandy Point Beach.

Sleeping

Generally accommodations on North Caicos are set up with self-catering in mind. All the options listed here come standard with kitchenettes, except for the Pelican Beach Hotel, which cooks for you.

Ocean Beach Hotel BEACH HOTEL **$$$**
(☎946-7113; www.turksandcaicos.tc/oceanbeach; r $225-275; ❄📶👪) Popular with families and often full of returning guests, Ocean Beach is a treat. Beautifully maintained with simple homely touches, it feels like you're staying at a friend's cottage – with the best view money can buy. There are rooms here accommodate every type of group; big or small it will sort you into the right spot, while the complimentary local cell phone will make organization that much easier. Ocean Beach has been a trendsetter in sustainability from its inception: the 'so simple it's clever' solar-heated rooftop water-collection system provides all the water for the hotel. It doesn't stop there: compact fluorescent lighting, room orientation to take advantage of the wind and avoid air-con use, and a commitment to reducing linen and towel washing. Big hotels around the world could learn a lot from this little inn on North Caicos.

Pelican Beach Hotel BEACH HOTEL **$$**
(☎946-7112; www.pelicanbeach.tc; r $145, s/d half board $160/225; ❄📶) For those looking for a relaxed, back-to-basics place to stay, this is an excellent option. Suzie and Clifford's place is getting a bit old and tired, but the old-school feel adds to the experience. There is nothing fancy here; plain TV-less rooms sit in a row only a few feet from the beach. It's well worth taking the half-board option as Suzie is a legend in the kitchen! There are also free bicycles for guests.

Hollywood Beach Suites BEACH HOTEL **$$$**
(☎231-1020; www.hollywoodbeachsuites.com; ste from $235; ❄📶) Housing just eight guests, finding space on the beach won't be an issue. The rooms are tidy, modern and well set up for a relaxing holiday, with couches, TV and DVD player for when the stress of sun worshipping just gets to be too much. There are complimentary kayaks and bikes for guests. Your dinner is cooked for you the first night of your stay too – go for the lobster!

Eating

You can buy produce and groceries at KH's Food Store in Whitby and at Al's Grocery in Bottle Creek.

Silver Palm CARIBBEAN **$$**
(☎946-7113; Ocean Beach Hotel; mains $10-18; ⏰breakfast, lunch & dinner) Lobster and conch are the specialties here – all of course sourced locally. Informal and friendly, small and intimate, this place epitomizes the North Caicos experience: simple and delicious.

Frank's Café GRILL **$$**
(☎243-5256; mains from $15; ⏰10am-10pm Mon-Sat) Some way down the coast away from

much of the development on the rest of the island, this friendly place serves up great seafood dishes as well as a mixture of international cuisine, from Italian dishes to burgers.

Information

There's a post office in Kew, and Bottle Creek has a small public library. The nearest hospital is in Provo (p208).

Government clinic Bottle Creek (☎946-7194); Kew (☎946-7397)

Police Bottle Creek (☎946-7116); Kew (☎946-7261)

Getting There & Around

For information on getting to/from the island by air or boat, see p222. A taxi from the airport to Whitby costs $10 or about $40 from the ferry landing, one way. **M&M Tours** (☎231-6285) will pick you up; be sure to prebook. Most hotels and condos offer complimentary bikes to their guests.

Car rental costs are around $80 per day. Try the following options:

Al's Rent A Car (☎946-7232)

Pelican Car Rentals (☎241-8275)

Middle Caicos

POP 300

If you're really looking to get away from it all, treat yourself by checking out Middle Caicos. With an area the size of North Caicos and with such a small population you'll be lucky to see *anyone*. The topography is much the same as North Caicos, with a green, lake-filled interior surrounded by white-sand beach and azure water. Recently a causeway has been completed connecting North and Middle, making the visiting process a whole lot easier. There are few places to stay on the island and even fewer places to eat, so those not intending on a self-catered, pre-arranged stay would do well to plan a day-trip. But for those who do decide to stay, your efforts will most certainly be rewarded – this is the way the Caribbean used to be.

Sights & Activities

There are a few tiny settlements dotted along the island; Conch Bar and Bambarra are the largest, but there still isn't much to them. **Bambarra Beach**, however, is possibly the Caribbean beach you've been dreaming about. Impossibly white sand, robin egg–blue water and not a soul around. On the quiet end of a blissfully uninhabited island, this beach sees little traffic of any sort.

The aim of the game on Middle is to relax – but if you're keen to get the blood flowing a bit there are a few options worth checking out. Five miles west of Bambarra Beach, directly in front of Blue Horizon Resort, is **Mudjin Harbor** – the rocky shore rears up to form a bit of rare elevation. Walking along the cliff top you'll be surprised to see a staircase appear out of nowhere, leading into the earth. Take it down through the cave and emerge on a secluded cliff-lined beach. Looking seaward you'll be entertained by the waves crashing into the offshore rocks in spectacular fashion.

A great way to get a feel for the island is to go for a walk on the **Crossing Place Trail**. Hugging the northern edge of Middle Caicos and crossing into North Caicos, this easy-to-follow and straightforward track supports good ocean views and birdwatching opportunities. It's easily picked up from Mudjin Harbor or from other points along the main road – keep an eye open for the signs.

Sleeping

At present there are only a couple of sleeping options on Middle Caicos. The emphasis is on longer-term stays where self-catering is a must.

TOP CHOICE **Dreamscape Villa** VILLA **$$$**
(☎946-7112; www.middlecaicos.com; Bambarra; per week $2000; ❄👪) OK so its interior design won't win any prizes, but this villa is magnificently located on a pristine section of Bambarra Beach, just a few yards from the sea. The house itself has three bedrooms and is set up to sleep four comfortably. It has all the modern conveniences and is perfectly arranged for a week of relaxation. There are bikes and sea kayaks to keep you busy, and great snorkeling, right out front, if the mood strikes. Nice touches such as an outdoor shower, hammocks and a barbecue add up to make this great for a family holiday.

Blue Horizon Resort RESORT **$$$**
(☎946-6141; www.bhresort.com; Mudjin Harbor; cabins from $230; ❄) This beautiful property at Mudjin Harbor boasts its own 2200ft stretch of private beach and a wonderful setting amid the foliage. The five cabins are spread out among the greenery, all with prime ocean views. The decor is nothing special, but the views and the seclusion more than make up for the slightly dated sense of style. The units all have kitchens

WORTH A TRIP

BEST OF THE REST

If you really want an adventure and want to escape from any sort of tourist infrastructure, then all you have to do is head to either South or East Caicos. These islands are a paradise for those with a phobia of development, tourism or other people.

East Caicos is the least inhabited island in the chain. There is a Haitian immigrant community on the island but little else. The beaches are renowned and odds are you will have them all to yourself. East Caicos is not linked by air or a ferry service to elsewhere in the country, however, so the only way to get here is by boat charter or your own yacht. As there is almost no infrastructure on the island, the latter is far preferable.

South Caicos is the place to go for unspoilt scuba diving. The waters are pristine and prized for the effort required to get there. The land itself is a windswept wasteland of sand and scrub. The towns are microscopic and you really will find more donkeys than people here. Each May things spark up a bit for the annual **Big South Regatta** – but don't worry, this is still way off the radar of most T&C visitors. South Caicos is connected by two daily flights from Providenciales (from $48 one way).

and you can provide a shopping list so the cupboards are full for you when you arrive.

Information

There are few services to speak of on the island, save the odd seemingly abandoned gas pump (which may or may not have gas) and a few phone booths that have seen better days. The proximity to North Caicos dictates that traveling over to the neighboring island is the way to go if you want to buy groceries or head out for a meal.

TURKS ISLANDS

The Turks group comprises Grand Turk and its smaller southern neighbor, Salt Cay, in addition to several tiny cays. The islands lie east of the Caicos Islands, separated from them by the 22-mile-wide Turks Island Passage.

Getting There & Away

For flight information, see p221.

Getting Around

TO/FROM THE AIRPORT

Taxis meet incoming flights; to Cockburn Town (1 mile north of the airport) costs about $10. There are no buses, but pre-booked rental cars will meet your plane.

BICYCLE

Most, if not all, hotels on Grand Turk provide bikes for their guests as they are the perfect way to get around the tiny island. On Salt Cay, **Trade Winds Guest Suites** (☎946-6906; www.tradewinds.tc; Victoria St, Salt Cay) will get you pedaling for $15 per day.

BOAT

A ferry runs biweekly from Grand Turk to Salt Cay (round trip $12). Contact **Salt Cay Charters** (☎231-6663; piratequeen3@hotmail.com). Arrangements can also be made with any of the Grand Turk dive companies to take you over to Salt Cay; costs vary depending on numbers.

CAR & SCOOTER

Car hire is very simple to arrange on both Grand Turk and Salt Cay. Expect to pay around $70 per day. All hotels can either arrange car rental or point you in the direction of local companies.

TAXI

Taxis are an inexpensive and reliable way to get around Grand Turk. A taxi from the airport to town will cost you about $10 though prices vary according to distance; the entire island can be reached from the airport for up to $25. Be sure to settle on a price before you head out as the cabs are unmetered. Your hotel can easily sort you a cab, or call **Carl's Taxi Service** (☎241-8793).

Grand Turk

Happily lacking the modern development that has enveloped Provo, Grand Turk is a step back in time. At just 6½ miles long, this dot amid the sea is a sparsely populated, brush-covered paradise. Cockburn Town, the main settlement, is still the capital of the country and is lined with buildings that date back to colonial times. Narrow streets are frequented by wild donkeys and the odd local cruising by. That of course can change in an instant if a large cruise ship docks off Grand Turk and several thousand day visitors crowd out this tiny Caribbean town.

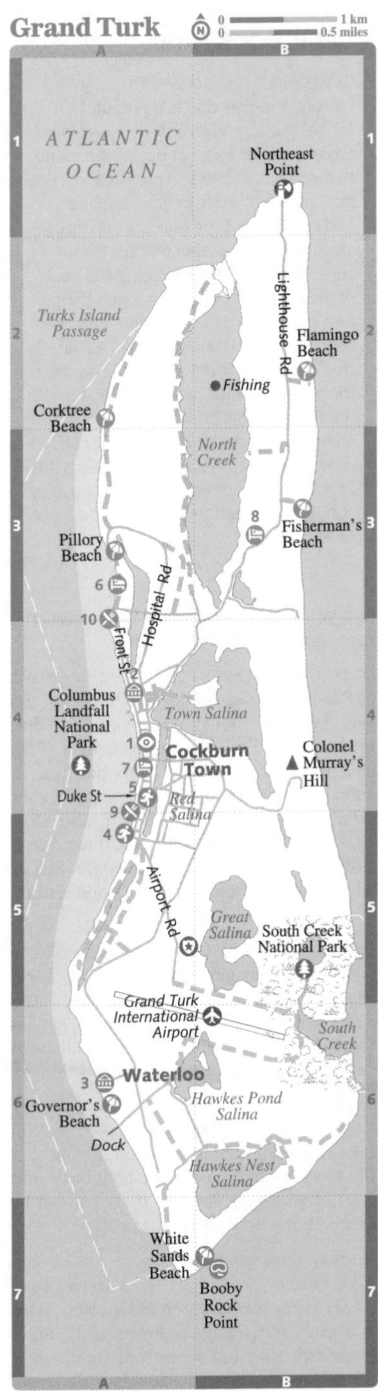

Where salt was once the main industry, tourism has taken over and you are blessed with a slew of charming guesthouses to choose from. Beaches rim the land and calm blue water invites you in for a refreshing swim. There is a quiet peace to the island and a feel among the locals, discovered long ago, that this is the place to be.

COCKBURN TOWN

POP 5500

Without knowing beforehand you'd be hard pressed to guess that sleepy Cockburn is the capital city of the Turks and Caicos. What it lacks in polish and sophistication it more than makes up for in rustic charm. The town itself comprises two parallel streets that are interconnected with narrow laneways. Colonial-era houses line the tiny streets and former salt-storage sheds hark back to a bygone era of dusty roads and donkey-filled lanes.

The heart of town is sandwiched between the ocean and the salt pond named Red Salina.

Sights

The Turks & Caicos Island Tourist Board, the museum and most hotels have free *Heritage Walk* pamphlets. **Front St**, which runs along the waterfront, has some magnificent buildings. The salt air and the rough treatment of time have not been kind to many of these structures and some have begun the slip into dilapidation. But there are still highlights here, and a walk among the architecture is recommended.

Grand Turk

Sights

1 General Post Office A4
2 Waterloo A4
3 Turks & Caicos National Museum A6

Activities, Courses & Tours

4 Grand Turk Diving Co A5
5 Oasis Divers A4

Sleeping

6 Island House A3
7 Bohio Dive Resort & Spa A4
8 Grand Turk Inn B3

Eating

Osprey .... (see 4)
9 Sand Bar A4
10 Taste of the Island A3

The **General Post Office** is a relic of a forgotten era, and still shines brightly. Nearby, four large cannons point to sea, guarding the site that Columbus supposedly set foot upon land – the reality of that claim is still up for grabs, but it does make for a nice photo. The fringing coral reef just offshore is protected within the confidently named **Columbus Landfall National Park**.

The little **Turks & Caicos National Museum** (www.tcmuseum.org; Front St; admission nonresidents $5; ⏲9am-4pm Mon, Tue, Thu & Fri, to 6pm Wed, to 1pm Sat) boxes above its weight with a great selection of displays. Everything from shipwrecks to messages in bottles and crash-landing spacecraft are covered – be sure to ask to see the cabinet of cannons.

South of the heart of downtown, Duke St narrows off to form a twisting lane of old buildings. Even the most jaded of futurists will be left enchanted by the colonial-era structures.

The long and pothole-covered road to Northeast Point is the way to get to the old cast-iron **lighthouse**. It's open when cruise ships are in port and offers a good vantage point of the crashing waves.

Waterloo (1815) is the official Governor's residence. The island's dock is here, and the old US missile-tracking station sits as a reminder of the Cold War. In 1962 Grand Turk was briefly put on the world stage when astronaut John Glenn splashed down in his Mercury spacecraft off the coast of the island. He made landfall at this dock and was debriefed at the missile-tracking post.

Beaches

A dirt road leads south to **White Sands Beach**, which is great for snorkelers, and on to lovely pine-shaded **Governor's Beach**, 1½ miles south of town, a popular place for a picnic and a dip in the sea.

Dirt roads lead east to three prime **bird-watching spots**: Hawkes Pond Salina, Hawkes Nest Salina and South Creek National Park, which protects the mangroves and wetlands along the island's southeast shore.

To the north of Cockburn Town are remote **Corktree** and **Pillory Beaches**. Both are good for bathing and out of the way enough that you'll have the sand to yourself.

Activities

Diving is the main reason to come to Grand Turk. The following diving operators will take you snorkeling if you're not a diver, and run courses if you want to learn.

CRUISE CONTROL?

Grand Turk's popularity with its many visitors is largely due to its reputation for being a forgotten oasis of quiet in the eastern Caribbean, not having succumb to the megaresorts and package tourists that are a fact of life in Providenciales and beyond. But the building of a cruise-ship harbor and an accompanying leisure and shopping complex in the south of the island has rather changed things. Like some sort of per-molded, pseudo-Caribben port, it sticks out like a palm tree on a plain. But it's certainly changed the economic face of Grand Turk, too – this is the port of call for most cruise ships coming to the Turks and Caicos Islands. On a busy day, two ships will be in port – off-loading nearly 7000 people, suddenly outnumbering the residents of Grand Turk.

Oasis Divers DIVING, SNORKELLING
(☎946-1128; www.oasisdivers.com; Duke St) Will take you down on a two-tank dive ($85), a single tank in the afternoon ($55) or a night dive ($60). It rents out gear at good rates and has a great reputation for service and professionalism. It also runs trips to Gibbs Cay, where you can hand-feed stingrays ($60 plus diving rates), as well as whale-watching and kayak trips and renting snorkeling equipment.

Grand Turk Diving Co DIVING, SNORKELLING
(☎946-1559; www.gtdiving.com; Duke St) Local legend Smitty runs this excellent outfit. There are two-tank dives for $75 and singles for $50 and night dives for $60. Full PADI courses are offered for $450.

Screaming Reels FISHING
(☎231-2087; www.screamingreelstours.com) Will take you out and help you land the big one. Charters are based on a per-boat basis and start at $500 per day, but that cost can be shared between up to eight people.

Chukka Caribbean Adventures ADVENTURE, SAFARI
(☎232-1339; www.chukkacaribbean.com) This is a great one for horse lovers as there's a horseback ride and swim tour (adult/child $74/52) as well as a kayak safari ($65) and

river tubing ($64/45) available, to name just a few.

Salt Cay Charters WHALE WATCHING
(☎231-6663; piratequeen3@hotmail.com) The leading whale-watching operator in the Turks and Caicos offers 2½-hour trips to see the migrating humpbacks every year between February and March. Trips cost $125 per person and include snacks and drinks. Boat charters and other tours are also available.

Sleeping

There are several accommodations options in both downtown Cockburn and elsewhere on the island. Everything is close enough that staying on one end of the island doesn't preclude you from enjoying the other.

TOP CHOICE **Island House** GUESTHOUSE $$
(☎946-1388; www.islandhouse.tc; d $190;) Walking through the doors at Island House you'll be met with Mediterranean-influenced architecture, whitewashed walls and arched doorways. Further in you'll discover the inviting pool and opulent courtyard. The rooms are airy and nicely put together. Guests, who mostly come here to dive and purchase packages when they book, have free use of a car while staying and there are bikes too, if you're feeling energetic.

Grand Turk Inn GUESTHOUSE $$$
(☎946-2827; www.grandturkinn.com; Front St; ste $300;) This beautifully restored Methodist manse is definitely Grand Turk's most atmospheric place to stay. The Balinese bamboo furniture sets the tone and the owners, two sisters, make you feel immediately at home. There are full kitchens in each of the five suites and its central location in Cockburn Town is hard to beat.

Bohio Dive Resort & Spa DIVING RESORT $$
(☎946-2135; www.bohioresort.com; Front St; r $190;) Boasts a prime location on a stunning stretch of sand, excellent value dive packages and a friendly atmosphere. The staff here is top notch and the rooms are pleasant and clean. There are kayaks, sailboats, snorkeling gear and even yoga classes available. The resort is just north of the town center.

Eating

Osprey INTERNATIONAL $$
(☎946-2666; Duke St; mains from $10-25; lunch & dinner) Make sure you drop by on Wednesday or Sunday night for the legendary barbecue: amazing seafood, poultry and beef grilled before your eyes, bombarded with salads and served up poolside. There are great ocean views and the band gets going after dinner so you can dance off that dessert.

Taste of the Island CARIBBEAN $
(West St; mains from $10; lunch & dinner) Come to this locals' beachside restaurant and bar to work on your Creole or enjoy a swim in the sea while you wait for your food. The offerings are simple, fresh and cheap and it can get loud and a little crazy, making it a real taste of the island. It's just north of the town center.

Sand Bar BAR & GRILL $
(☎946-1111; Duke St; mains $8-15; noon-1am) This small yet lively bar is a popular hot spot with locals, expats and tourists alike. It has yummy burgers if you've got the munchies, and the potential for spotting the green flash (a Caribbean phenomenon where you can see a green flash as the sun sets into the ocean) is great, especially if you've had a few Turk's Heads first.

Shopping

The best shopping to be found on the island is in the street stalls that open up on Duke Street when the cruise ships are in port. There is a good variety of locally made goods, Haitian artwork and hand-drawn maps. Conversely if you are seeking cheap T-shirts, snow globes and shot glasses, head to the cruise-ship center (opposite) where you will be inundated with an ocean of cheap rubbish.

Information

Businesses and government offices close at 3pm on Friday. Some businesses open from 9am to 1pm on Saturday. Public phones can be found at most central places.

General Post Office (☎946-1334; Front St)

Grand Turk Hospital (☎946-2333; Hospital Rd)

Turks & Caicos Islands Tourist Board (☎946-2321; www.turksandcaicostourism.com; Front St)

Getting There & Around

The town center is 1 mile north of the Grand Turk International Airport; a taxi ride from the airport into town costs about $10. Bikes are often provided to hotel guests and are a great way to get around. You're hardly likely to need a car in town, but do pay attention anyway to the one-way system along Duke and Front Sts. You can rent cars ($70 per day) from **Tony's Car Rental**

(☎946-1879; www.tonyscarrental.com; Airport Rd), located at the airport.

For details about getting around Grand Turk, see p212.

Salt Cay

If you can't quite envision what the Turks would have been like in the 19th century, take a trip to Salt Cay. Like stepping into a time machine, this picturesque island is the sort of hideaway that you search your whole life to discover. A few dusty roads interconnect the handful of structures, and donkeys wander aimlessly through the streets intermixed with friendly locals. While the land is quiet, the sea surrounding the island is awash with life. Turtles, eagle rays and the majestic humpback whale (see right) all frequent the waters. Hard to get to and even harder to leave, this place is a true haven for scuba divers and for those seeking an escape from the modern world.

Salt Cay Divers (☎241-1009; www.saltcaydivers.tc) is a one-stop dive shop. The owner is a long-term local who has her finger in most pies on the island. The staff can take you out for a dive ($45 per tank), and sort you out with accommodations and a hearty meal too. The annual humpback whale migration (February to March) is a big draw, and this operation takes pride in showing off the whales yet not disturbing them ($75 for divers, $95 for non-divers).

For details on getting to/from Salt Cay, see p212.

Sleeping

Pirate's Hideaway Guesthouse GUESTHOUSE $$$
(☎244-1407; www.pirateshideaway.com; Victoria St; r from $200; ❄📶🏊) The colorful owner Nick goes out of his way to make you feel at home here. Cool features include an 'infinity bed' in the crow's-nest room and a new freshwater pool to cool you off. You can see the whales from the upstairs rooms as they pass by, or just hang out with the parrots – it is a pirate's place after all.

Trade Winds Guest Suites RESORT $$
(☎241-1009; www.tradewinds.tc; Victoria St; r $190; ❄📶) Right on the beach, just a few steps from town. Trade Winds is a great spot to base yourself for an extended stay: there are weekly rates and the location is tops. There are complimentary bikes and dive packages available, too. The rooms are tidy, ocean-facing and good value.

Eating

Island Thyme Bistro BISTRO $$$
(☎242-0325; mains from $20; ⊙breakfast, lunch & dinner) This little restaurant and bar is set to be the big memory of your Salt Cay stay. The food is great and is prepared and presented with a sense of fun. There's also a popular guest-chef night, where you get to strut your stuff in the kitchen. Friday is pizza night and the restaurant prides itself on a flexible menu – try the Filipino roast sucking pig if you really want a treat.

Green Flash Cafe GRILL $$
(Main Dock; mains from $12; ⊙lunch & dinner) Right off the main dock and the perfect vantage point to watch out for its namesake. Nothing pretentious here, just simple food enjoyed on picnic tables in a beautiful setting. Great burgers, conch and cold beer – what more could you want?

UNDERSTAND TURKS & CAICOS

History

Recent discoveries of Taíno (the indigenous population) artifacts on Grand Turk have shown that the islands evolved much the same indigenous culture as did their northern neighbors. Locals even claim that the islands were Christopher Columbus' first landfall in 1492.

A WHALE OF A TALE

Salt Cay could very well be one of the best places on earth to see humpback whales – by the thousands. Every winter the gentle giants make their annual pilgrimage to the warm seas of the Caribbean to mate and give birth. From the sandy shores of Salt Cay you can watch the majestic beauties of the sea saunter past from February to March. They are plain to see from the beach but you can also get among it on a whale-watching trip or dive trip organized from either Grand Turk (p215) or Salt Cay.

The island group was a pawn in the power struggles between the French, Spanish and British, and remained virtually uninhabited until 1678, when some Bermudian salt rakers settled the Turks islands and used natural *salinas* (salt-drying pans) to produce sea salt. These still exist on several islands.

Fast forward to the mid-20th century: the US military built airstrips and a submarine base in the 1950s, and John Glenn splashed down just off Grand Turk in 1962, putting the islands very briefly in the international spotlight.

Administered through Jamaica and the Bahamas in the past, the Turks and Caicos became a separate Crown colony of Great Britain in 1962 then an Overseas Territory in 1981. In 1984 Club Med opened its doors on Providenciales (Provo), and the Turks and Caicos started to boom. In the blink of an eye, the islands, which had lacked electricity, acquired satellite TV.

The Turks and Caicos relied upon the exportation of salt, which remained the backbone of the British colony until 1964. Today finance, tourism and fishing generate most income, but the islands could not survive without British aid. The tax-free offshore finance industry is a mere minnow compared with that of the Bahamas, and many would be astonished to discover that Grand Turk, the much-hyped financial center, is just a dusty backwater in the sun.

Illegal drug trafficking, a major problem in the 1980s, has also been a source of significant revenue for a few islanders.

Relations between islanders and British-appointed governors have been strained since 1996, when the incumbent governor's comments suggesting that government and police corruption had turned the islands into a haven for drug trafficking appeared in the *Offshore Finance Annual,* and opponents accused him of harming investment. Growing opposition threatened to spill over into civil unrest.

Things were made far worse in 2009, when the Governor of the Turks and Caicos imposed direct rule on the country following a series of corruption scandals that rocked the islands in 2008. The scandals concerned huge alleged corruption on the part of the Turks and Caicos government, including the selling off of its property for personal profit, and the misuse of public funds.

The imposition of direct rule from London was attacked by members of the suspended Turks and Caicos government, who accused the UK of 'recolonizing' the country, but the general reaction across the country was a positive one, as faith in the local political system had been extremely low in the years leading up to the suspension.

The British government is looking to hold elections for a new Turks and Caicos government at some time in 2011. Despite the ongoing problems of corruption, it's likely to create a resurgence in calls for independence, or even a slightly wackier idea that has been kicking around the country for some time: a union with Canada.

The Turks & Caicos Way of Life

The culture of the Turks and Caicos is that of a ship that is steadied by a strong religious keel. There is a very strong religious core to these islands, and the populace is friendly, welcoming and a bit sedate. Native Turks and Caicos islanders, or 'Belongers' as they are locally known, are descended from the early Bermudian settlers, Loyalist settlers, slave settlers and salt rakers.

There are a few expats lurking about calling the Turks home; Americans because of the proximity, Canadians because of the weather and Brits because of the colonial heritage. Some have come to make their fortunes, some to bury their treasure like the pirates of old and others to escape the fast-paced life that permeates much of the developed world.

More recently hundreds of Haitians have fled their impoverished island and landed on the Turks and Caicos Islands; for some this is only a port of call on their way to America, while others are happy to stay. Some Belongers are wary of these new immigrant communities, while some locals are sympathetic or even indifferent.

Nightlife in the Turks and Caicos is of the mellow variety for the most part. There are a few night spots in Provo, and some beachside bars on the outer islands. Those seeking a roaring party of a holiday should look elsewhere – having said that, the local rake 'n' scrape music can really get the crowd going. For those not in the know, rake 'n' scrape or ripsaw (as it is locally known) is a band fronted by someone playing a carpenter's saw by rhythmically scraping its teeth with the shaft of a screwdriver; sometimes other household objects are used as percussion.

The art scene in the Turks and Caicos is slowly evolving. Traditional music, folklore and sisal weaving evolved during colonial days, have been maintained to this day. Paintings depicting the scenery are popular and the quality appears to be improving. The Haitian community has had a strong influence on the Turks and Caicos art scene.

There are a few shops in Provo that have a good selection of locally produced art; unfortunately, except for a few choice locations, most of the art that's available outside Provo is tourist paraphernalia, made in China and slapped with a T&C sticker.

The Landscape & Wildlife

Much of the Turks and Caicos can be described as flat, dry and barren. The salt industry of the last century saw fit to remove much of the vegetation from Salt Cay, Grand Turk and South Caicos. Low-lying vegetation now covers the uninhabited sections of these islands. The larger islands are in a much more pristine state, with vegetation and a higher degree of rainfall prominent on North, Middle and East Caicos. Small creeks, inland lakes – often home to flamingos – and wetlands make up the interior of these larger land masses.

On Providenciales the most common sight on land is not anything natural but the explosive degree of development. Everywhere you look, there seems to be another new property and resulting heap of construction garbage. The scrubby landscape is still visible among the fresh buildings – but for how long?

All the islands are rimmed with stunning beaches. Most are great and some are exceptional – truly world-class stretches of sand worthy of every accolade and hyperbolic description of sun, sand and gentle surf.

Walking down a dusty laneway and coming upon a donkey is a quintessential T&C experience. Their forebears once carried 25lb burlap bags of salt from the ponds to the warehouses and docks.

Iguanas once inhabited much of the Turks and Caicos until they lost their lives to introduced dogs and cats, and their habitats to development. Now Little Water Cay, Fort George Cay and the Ambergris Cays are all protected iguana reserves.

The waters are favored by four species of turtle: hawksbills (an internationally endangered species, although sadly not recognized in this region), green, loggerheads and, occasionally, leatherbacks.

Countless species of sea birds and waders have been sighted, both migratory and nonmigratory. Ospreys are numerous and easily spotted, as are barn owls and sparrow hawks. Flamingos – once numerous throughout the chain – are now limited to West, North and South Caicos, where you may also see Cuban herons.

A flourishing population of bottlenosed dolphins lives in these waters. Also, some 7000 North Atlantic humpback whales use the Turks Island Passage and the Mouchoir Banks, south of Grand Turk, as their winter breeding grounds between February and March. Manta rays are commonly seen during the spring plankton blooms off of Grand Turk and West Caicos.

SURVIVAL GUIDE

Directory A–Z

Accommodations

Accommodations in the Turks and Caicos are mostly in hotels, resorts and the odd smaller establishment. On Provo you'll mostly find larger resorts, but there are still a large number of smaller hotels and guesthouses, most of which are well established and reasonably priced. In high season budget rooms go for around $80 to $100 a night, though options are limited. Midrange hotels average $100 to $200 per night, while upscale resorts and hotels begin at $200 per night upwards. As you head out to the less populated islands the establishments get more intimate.

The **Turks & Caicos Hotel Association** (www.turksandcaicoshta.com) has a useful website with an exhaustive list of accommodations options, while the following agencies arrange villa rentals:

Coldwell Banker (www.coldwellbankertci.com)

Grace Bay Realty (www.gracebayrealty.com)

Prestigious Properties (www.prestigiousproperties.com)

Turks & Caicos Sotheby's (www.turksandcaicossothebys.com)

Activities

The most popular activities are diving and snorkeling, fishing and boating. Diving highlights include Salt Cay (p216) where you can dive with humpback whales during their annual migration. Grand Turk (p212) has pristine reefs and spectacular wall-diving. And then there is diving off Provo (p203), where you might just get the chance to share the sea with JoJo the dolphin.

In Caicos, a two-tank dive typically costs around $100 and a half-day snorkeling trip is around $65. Fishing can cost $400 to $800 per half-/full day, while windsurfing averages $30 to $40 per hour.

A two-tank dive in the Turks typically costs from $40 to $80 and snorkeling around $50 per half-day. Fishing is around $300 to $400 per half-/full day.

Books

» *Turks & Caicos Islands – Beautiful by Nature* (by Julia and Phil Davies) A beautiful coffee-table book.

» *Water and Light* (by Stephen Harrigan) A splendid memoir by a Texan who spent several months diving off of Grand Turk.

» *Turks & Caicos Islands: Land of Discovery* (by Amelia Smithers) Covers the history and idiosyncrasies of these charming islands.

» *Living in the Turks & Caicos Islands: From Conch to the Florida Lottery* (by Charles Palmer) A 'Belonger,' as those born on the islands describe themselves, depicts island living and the changes from the early 1950s to the current day.

Business Hours

We've only listed business hours where they differ from the following standards. Expect limited hours away from Provo or touristy areas.

Bars	to 1am or 2am
Businesses	9am to 5pm Monday to Saturday
Restaurants	breakfast from 8am, lunch from noon, dinner 6:30pm to 9pm

EATING PRICE BANDS

In restaurant reviews throughout this chapter, we've indicated the price band.

» $ means a budget place where a main dish is less then $10

» $$ means midrange; mains are $11 to $20

» $$$ means top end; mains are more than $20

Children

The Turks and Caicos is a fantastic kid-friendly destination, although you will struggle to find specific programs and activities aimed at younger travelers. Crime is low, traffic is sparse, waves are tiny and the locals are friendly. Some hotels are specifically non-kid-friendly so it's a good idea to check with your hotel beforehand. We have used the icon to denote places that are suitable for children in this chapter.

Dangers & Annoyances

There are few real worries on the islands. Crime is nearly unheard of, but normal precautions are advised, such as not leaving valuables on the beach unattended. Also, be aware that break-ins to hotel rooms on Grace Bay Beach in Provo are not entirely unheard of. Most hotels with beach frontage leave clear instructions to put valuables out of view when you leave your room. Break-ins remain very rare, but it's worth taking these simple precautions.

Electricity

Turks & Caicos uses the US and Canadian two- or three-pin style plugs.

Embassies & Consulates

There are no foreign embassies or consulates in the Turks and Caicos. Contact the relevant officials in Nassau (see p255) in the Bahamas.

Festivals & Events

Big South Regatta Held on South Caicos in late May, this regatta is a classic for the sea dogs.

Annual Music & Cultural Festival Held in July and August, this annual event is the islands' biggest party – good times and hangovers guaranteed.

Grand Turk Game Fishing Tournament Held end July/early August. I once caught a fish that was this big...

Marathon Run Held each December. Why relax when you can run 26.2 miles?

Christmas Tree Lighting Ceremony Grand Turk hosts this special event in mid-December for kids of all ages.

Gay & Lesbian Travelers

As in most Caribbean destinations, the attitude toward gay and lesbian travelers in the Turks and Caicos is far from progressive. While totally legal, gay sex remains a taboo subject here, particularly with reference to gay men. That said, as more gay and lesbian cruise ships enter port and mix with the locals, some degree of acceptance has been forthcoming. There is however, no openly gay scene or gay bars to speak of.

Holidays

Turks and Caicos national holidays:

New Year's Day January 1

Commonwealth Day March 13

Good Friday Friday before Easter

Easter Monday Monday after Easter

National Heroes' Day May 29

Her Majesty the Queen's Official Birthday June 14 (or nearest weekday)

Emancipation Day August 1

National Youth Day September 26

Columbus Day October 13

International Human Rights Day October 24

Christmas Day December 25

Boxing Day December 26

Internet Access

Internet access in the Turks is getting easier all the time. Wireless internet is offered free of charge in nearly all hotels and many restaurants and bars, while internet cafes and in-house terminals are getting rarer. It's a good idea to bring a smart phone or laptop with you to guarantee ease of access.

Maps

Tourist maps of Provo and Grand Turk are easily acquired from the tourist offices, the arrivals hall in the airport and at most hotels. The tourist offices have some substandard maps of the less populated islands, but finding one with any sort of detail is a challenge.

Medical Services

There are small hospitals on Provo and on Grand Turk. There are clinics on the smaller islands and a recompression chamber in Providenciales.

Money

The Turks and Caicos are unique as a British-dependent territory with the US dollar as its official currency. The treasury also issues Turks and Caicos crowns and quarters. There are no currency restrictions on the amount of money that visitors can bring in.

The country is pricey, with a hefty 30% duty slapped on all imports. When you consider how much is imported to this tiny and barren group of islands, the high price of food suddenly makes sense. Credit cards are readily accepted on Provo and Grand Turk, as are travelers checks. Elsewhere, you may need to operate on a cash-only basis. Foreign currency can be changed at banks in Provo and Grand Turk, which can also issue credit-card advances and have ATMs. Major credit cards are widely accepted in the Caicos and Grand Turk. However, credit cards are not widely accepted for small transactions in the more remote cays and islands. Travelers checks are accepted in the Caicos and Grand Turk, but you may be charged a transaction fee of 5%.

If you find yourself in need of an emergency cash injection, you can arrange a telegraphic or mail transfer from your account in your home country via **Western Union** (Grand Turk ☎946-2324; Dots Enterprises, Pond St; Providenciales ☎941-5484; Butterfield Sq, Leeward Hwy).

Post

Post offices can be found on Provo, Grand Turk and North Caicos. To send a postcard to the US it will cost $0.50; a letter is $0.60.

Telephone

The Turks and Caicos country code is ☎649. To call from North America, dial ☎1-649 + the local number. From elsewhere, dial your country's international access code + ☎649 + the local number. For interisland calls, dial the seven-digit local number. We've included only the seven-digit local number in Turks and Caicos listings in this chapter.

Phone calls can be made from **Cable & Wireless** (☎1800-804-2994), which operates a digital network from its offices in Grand Turk and Provo.

Public phone booths are located throughout the islands. Many booths require phone cards (see below).

Hotels charge $1 per local call. Frustratingly, some also charge for unanswered calls after the receiving phone has rung five times.

Some useful telephone numbers:

Directory Assistance (☎118)

International Operator Assistance (☎115)

Local operator (☎0)

CELL PHONES

Most cell phones will work in the Turks and Caicos; you can either set your phone up for global roaming prior to leaving home or purchase a SIM card for it once you get here. Global roaming is both easier and more expensive; be sure to check rates with your phone company prior to dialing. If you have a GSM phone that is unlocked you can purchase a new SIM card for it ($10 from Cable & Wireless outlets). This gives you a local number to call from and is much cheaper in the long run.

PHONE CARDS

Phone cards cost $5, $10 or $15, and can be bought from Cable & Wireless outlets, as well as from shops and delis. You can also bill calls to your Amex, Discover, MasterCard or Visa card by dialing ☎1-800-744-7777 on any touchtone phone and giving the operator your card details (there's a one-minute minimum).

Tourist Information

Turks & Caicos Tourism (www.turksandcaicostourism.com; ⏲9am-5pm Mon-Fri); Grand Turk (☎946-2321; Front St, Cockburn Town); Providenciales (☎946-4970; www.turksandcaicostourism.com; Stubbs Diamond Plaza)

Travelers with Disabilities

Some of the larger hotels have rooms that are wheelchair accessible, but it's best to enquire before arriving.

Visas

No visas are required for citizens of the US, Canada, UK and Commonwealth countries, Ireland and most Western European countries. Citizens from elsewhere require visas, which can be obtained from British representation abroad.

Women Travelers

The Turks and Caicos is a relatively safe place to travel and no special precautions are required for women travelers.

Work

Those wishing to work in the Turks and Caicos will need to get a work permit from the **immigration department** (www.immigrationboard.tc). See the website for details.

Getting There & Away

Entering Turks & Caicos

All visitors, including US citizens, need a valid passport to enter the country. Proof of onward transportation is required upon entry, so make sure you have your return flight confirmation to show immigration officers if they ask.

Air

AIRPORTS There are three airports handling international traffic to Grand Turk and Provo, but nearly all international flights arrive at Provo. The Provo airport has a tourist information booth in arrivals, car rental offices, a restaurant and not much else. Other islands just have airstrips with no amenities.

Grand Turk International Airport (GDT; ☎946-2233)

Providenciales International Airport (PLS; ☎941-5670)

South Caicos International Airport (XSC; ☎946-4255)

AIRLINES There are good air connections elsewhere within the Caribbean from Turks and Caicos, including to Jamaica, the Bahamas, Haiti and the Dominican Republic. To get to elsewhere in the region, you may have to hop to Miami. The following airlines fly into Turks and Caicos:

Air Canada (www.aircanada.com)

Air Turks & Caicos (www.airturksandcaicos.com)

American Airlines (www.aa.com)

Bahamas Air (www.bahamasair.com)

British Airways (www.ba.com)

Delta Airlines (www.delta.com)

US Airways (www.usairways.com)

West Jet (www.westjet.com)

Getting Around

Air

Following are airlines flying within the Turks and Caicos:

Air Turks & Caicos (946-4999; www.airturksandcaicos.com) Flies from Providenciales to Grand Turk six times daily, North Caicos (airport is just north of Major Hill) three times daily, Middle Caicos (near Conch Hill) four times per week, South Caicos twice daily and Salt Cay daily. It also flies from Grand Turk to Salt Cay daily.

Bicycle

Cycling is a cheap, convenient, healthy, environmentally sound and above all fun way to travel. Bicycles are complimentary to guests at many hotels or can be rented at concessions for around $20 per day.

Boat

TCI Ferry Service (946-5406) is a small passenger ferry operation taking people from the Leeward Marina on Providenciales to North Caicos (round trip $30), eliminating the need for the expensive and inconvenient flight. There are four departures each way daily, leaving Leeward Marina daily at 10.30am, 12.30pm, 3pm and 4.30pm. On Sunday there are just two services in each direction each day.

A ferry runs biweekly trips from Grand Turk to Salt Cay (round trip $12); contact **Salt Cay Charters** (231-6663; piratequeen3@hotmail.com) for details.

Car, Motorcycle & Scooter

Taxis get expensive in the long run so renting a car makes sense if you plan to explore Provo or Grand Turk. The local companies are very good, and may be cheaper than the internationals. Rentals average around $80 per day and the cars are generally in good nick; most rental companies offer free drop-off and pick-up. A government tax of $15 is levied on car rentals ($8 on scooter rentals). Mandatory insurance costs $15. A minimum age of 25 years may be required.

Driving is on the left-hand side. At roundabouts (traffic circles), remember to circle in a clockwise direction, entering to the left, and give way to traffic already on the roundabout.

Speed limits in the Turks and Caicos are 20mph (around 32km/h) in settlements and 40mph (around 65km/h) on main highways.

Please refer to island destinations for rental companies.

DRIVER'S LICENSE

To rent a car, citizens of the US, Canada, and the UK and Commonwealth countries are required to have a valid driving license for stays of up to three months. Everyone else requires an International Driving Permit. You must get this permit before you arrive on the Turks and Caicos Islands.

FUEL

Gas stations are plentiful and usually open from 8am to 7pm. Some close on Sunday. Gasoline costs about $5.50 per US gallon – luckily most destinations are pretty close. Credit cards are accepted in major settlements. Elsewhere, it's cash only, please!

Taxi

Taxis are available on all the inhabited islands. Most are minivans. They're a good bet for touring, and most taxi drivers double as guides. The cabs are unmetered (though pricing is consistent), so be sure to negotiate an agreeable price before setting out.

› Understand The Bahamas

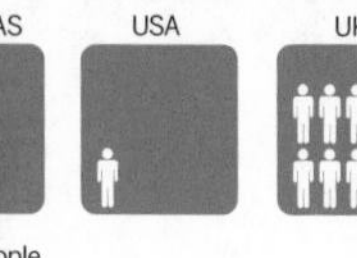

The Bahamas Today

Economic Ups & Downs

The Bahamas' tourism-based economy took a hard hit with the global recession of 2009. The slowdown continued in 2010, with hotels closing and construction projects halting. Grand Bahama, which had still been recovering from the hurricanes of 2004, was especially wounded. In Nassau, the crisis has not stopped the $2.6 billion Baha Mar project, however, which aims to turn Cable Beach into an Atlantis-style mega-resort. Despite controversies over the use of Chinese workers, Baha Mar was slated to break ground in early 2011.

The offshore banking industry, another economic mainstay, has slowed down too following government cleanups in the early 2000s.

» Population: 310,400 (2010)

» GDP: $8.9 billion

» GDP per capita $28,600

» Unemployment: 7.6%

The Prime Minister & the Blonde

In the 2007 election, Bahamians ousted the Progressive Liberal Party (PLP; a populist leftist party), who had ruled since their landslide victory in 2002. Why the change of heart? Shortly before the election, Prime Minister Perry Christie came under fire for allegedly fast-tracking the residency visa of the late Playboy bunny Anna Nicole Smith. Smith had been hiding out in the Bahamas to avoid paternity testing of her infant daughter. Immigration Minister Shane Gibson, who approved the permit, was forced to resign after pictures surfaced of him and Smith locked in a romantic embrace.

The new Prime Minister, Hubert Ingraham, of the Free National Movement party (FNM; which is moderately conservative), was also an old Prime Minister – he had previously governed from 1992 to 2002.

Etiquette

» Greet everyone you see – bus drivers, pedestrians, clerks – with 'hello' or 'good afternoon'

» Make eye contact; looking away is considered rude

» Keep swimwear on the beach; Bahamians are generally modest (unless going out dancing!)

» Use honorifics – Mr, Mrs, Professor – until a first name is explicitly offered

» Arrive on time when invited to dinner or a party, but don't be surprised if Bahamians keep 'Bahamian time'

Top Books

» *Wind from the Carolinas,* Robert Wilder; historical fiction

» *Bahamas: In a White Coming On,* Dennis Ryan; poetry

» *The Story of the Bahamas,* Paul Albury; history

» *Bush Medicine in the Bahamas,* Leslie Higgs

belief systems
(% of population)

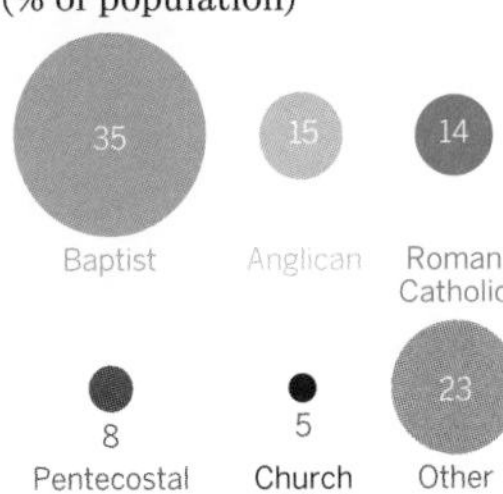

if The Bahamas were 100 people

85 would be black
12 would be white
3 would be Asian or Hispanic

Crime Conundrums

'Murder Rates at All-Time High' screamed newspaper headlines in 2010 and 2011. Though violent crime is still relatively rare in the Bahamas – and extremely rare for tourists – it's hard to ignore the regular gun deaths, most of which take place in Nassau's working-class Over-the-Hill neighborhood. Most of these murders are motivated by drugs and desperation, the latter a rising concern in an uncertain economy.

The continuing involvement of Bahamians in the cocaine trade between South America and the US also worries many. A 2009 report from the US Drug Enforcement Agency revealed that there are 12 to 15 drug-trafficking organizations currently operating in the Bahamas.

A Growing Environment Conscience

Though the Bahamas have never been on the cutting edge of the environmentalist movement, the country is increasingly savvy about saving its precious resources. Sea turtles, a traditional delicacy, were pulled from menus in 2009 following a nationwide ban on the hunting, selling and consumption of turtles or turtle parts. And due to concerns over overfishing, the Bahamas has regulated its conch industry in recent decades, with populations currently considered stable.

Another hot-button environmental issue has been the development of the Bimini Bay Resort & Marina (see p99), which threatens the island's rich mangrove swamps. Environmentalists have been locked in a battle with developers for years, and the situation continues to unfold.

There are few genuine ecolodges in the country, though resorts are beginning to respond to consumer demand. Consider letting hotel management know how important recycling and energy conservation are to you – the tourism dollar speaks!

» Miles of coastline: 2201

» Number of islands: 29

» Number of cays: 661

» Airports: 62

» National flower: yellow elder

Musicians

The Baha Men Modern Junkanoo music, most famous for 'Who Let the Dogs Out?'
Ronnie Butler Popular calypso and rake 'n' scrape artist
Andre Toussaint A founder of Bahamian calypso
Brettina Robinson LA-based Bahamian jazz singer

Bahamians

Sidney Poitier Movie star; from Cat Island
Kimbo Slice Huge mixed martial arts star; born in Nassau
Rick Fox LA Lakers and Boston Celtics basketballer; from Nassau
Roxie Roker TV actress and mother of Lenny Kravitz; born to Bahamian immigrants

Filmed Locally

Never Say Never Again Underwater scenes off New Providence
Thunderball Paradise Island's original Cafe Martinique
The Silence of the Lambs Final scene in North Bimini
Pirates of the Caribbean II and III Grand Bahama

History

The peaceful Lucayans knew a good spot when they found one. They paddled into the Bahamas' glistening seas as early as the 6th century and decided to stay. Smart, those guys.

Unfortunately for them, they weren't the only ones with eyes on the turf. The Spanish sailed through in the 1500s, searching for gold and carting off Lucayans to use as slaves. A century later, British settlers arrived, seeking religious freedom. Butting heads with the Spanish, they declared the territory ungovernable and let pirates run rampant in Nassau. Some of the most interesting moments in Bahamian history come from this time period, with notorious villains like Blackbeard, Calico Jack and Stede Bonnet turning Nassau into a nonstop pirate party.

But the party was over in 1718, when English pirate fighter Woodes Rogers became the first Royal Governor of the Bahamas and booted the bad guys. More Englishmen arrived later that century, Loyalists fleeing the newly formed United States after the Revolutionary War. The population tripled, with many new arrivals being African slaves brought down to work the Loyalist plantations.

The abolition of slavery in 1834 brought an end to the plantation system, and the Bahamas soon found another economic niche: a base for Confederate blockade running during the American Civil War. Sixty years later, it served a similarly shady role as a jumping-off point for rum-runners during Prohibition.

The 20th century brought two major developments: the decline of the British Empire and the rise of the tourism industry. Americans began flocking to the country in the 1960s, after the embargo against Cuba made Havana a no-go. In 1973, the Bahamas became fully independent from England, hence its current name: The Commonwealth of the Bahamas.

By the way, no one is sure of precisely where the name 'Bahamas' comes from. Some say it's derived from the words *baha mar*, Spanish

TIMELINE

500s

The Lucayans paddle into the Bahamas from Cuba or Hispaniola in their dugout *kanawas* (or, as we now know them, canoes). They settle and begin subsistence farming and fishing.

1492

Genoese explorer Christopher Columbus sets sight and foot onto the New World, mostly likely on the Bahamian island of San Salvador or Samana Cay.

Late 1400s

A number of Spanish ships wreck off the coast of Abaco and the horses in the cargo hold swim ashore; their descendents are now the legendary wild horses of Abaco.

for 'shallow seas,' while others think it's based on the Lucayan name for Grand Bahama island, ba-ha-ma.

Lucayan Living

Living primarily off the sea, the Lucayan people, a tribe of Arawaks, evolved skills as potters, carvers and boat-builders, and they spun and wove cotton into clothing and hammocks, which they traded with neighbors. Religion played a central role in Arawak life. They worshiped various gods who were thought to control the rain, sun, wind, and hurricanes. The little that remains of their culture is limited to pottery shards, petroglyphs, and English words such as 'canoe,' 'cannibal,' 'hammock,' 'hurricane,' and 'tobacco.'

Columbus & the Spanish

Christopher Columbus's first glimpse of the New World came on October 12, 1492, during the first of his four voyages to find a westward route to the East Indies.

The expedition had sailed west and after 33 days and more than 3000 miles, the shout of *'Tierra!'* (Land!) went up and an island gleamed in the moonlight. Columbus planted the Spanish flag on an island he named San Salvador (likely current-day San Salvador or Samana Cay).

Columbus and his fellow expeditionaries were underwritten by monarchs and merchants whose interest was economic. Gold, or at least the thought of it, filled the sails. The Spaniards did not linger in these barren coral islands. The Lucayans told Columbus that gold might be found in Cubanacan (middle Cuba), which he translated as 'Kublai Khan.'

As the search for gold dominated all adventurers' priorities it was no surprise that the Spanish returned in 1495, and started shipping out enslaved Lucayans from the Bahamas to work their gold seams in Hispaniola.

The Lucayans were worked to death. Those who resisted perished by the sword, the rest by European diseases or mass suicide. Within 25 years the entire Lucayan population of 50,000 was gone. The Spaniards then casually sailed away, leaving the island chain devoid of human life.

Eleutheran Adventurers

In 1648, a group of English Puritans sailed from Bermuda to found a brave new colony in the Bahamas. En route, their ship was wrecked on the Devil's Backbone reef at the north end of what's now Eleuthera. The Eleutheran Adventurers limped along for several years, farming the island's sandy soil, before branching off to settle New Providence and found the city of Charles Town (later renamed Nassau). They then settled

Top Historic Towns

- Nassau
- Hope Town, Elbow Cay, Abaco
- New Plymouth, Green Turtle Cay, Abaco
- Dunmore Town, Harbour Island, Eleuthera

Best History Museums

- Pirates of Nassau, Nassau
- Albert Lowe Museum, Green Turtle Cay, Abaco
- Bimini Museum, Bimini
- Wyannie Malone Museum, Hope Town, Elbow Cay, Abaco

1513

Spanish explorer Ponce de León arrives in the northern Bahamas on his journey to find the Fountain of Youth, and discovers that the Lucayan population has been decimated.

1600s

Pirates like Blackbeard, Calico Jack and Stede Bonnet turn Nassau into a 17th-century Sin City of brothels, pubs and lawless debauchery. Many are said to bury their plunder throughout the Bahamas.

1648

The Eleutheran Adventurers, a group of English puritans, set out from Barbados but shipwreck on Eleuthera's Devil's Backbone reef, where they're forced to spend a season living in a cave.

1695

Charles Town is rechristened as Nassau in honor of the Netherland's William III, a member of the Dutch House of Orange-Nassau.

in to live a life of subsistence farming and wrecking – scavenging the wrecks that washed up on the islands' dangerous shores.

The **National Archives of the Bahamas** (www.bahamasnationalarchives.bs/index.html) has all sorts of maps, pictures and documents dating back to the 17th century; it's an especially good source for genealogical research.

Golden Age of Piracy

The Spanish were none too pleased with the Eleutheran's little wrecking enterprise, especially when their own wrecked ships were often the subject of looting. In retaliation, they burned Charles Town and the Eleutheran settlements to the ground.

England, the colonist's mother country, was busy fighting the French back home. Since the Royal Navy couldn't effectively patrol the Caribbean, the crown sponsored privateers to capture enemy vessels and plunder foreign cities. A combination of absentee landlords and the growing number of ruffian residents meant that the city descended into the hands of pirates such as Henry Jennings and 'Blackbeard' (Edward Teach), who terrorized his victims by wearing flaming fuses in his matted beard and hair. Blackbeard took over New Providence, establishing a lawless city that by 1666 was lined with brothels and taverns.

Spain, of course, was outraged, especially since it still claimed title over the Bahamas, and on at least four occasions attacked and razed Charles Town. In 1718 Governor Woodes Rogers (himself a former privateer) was appointed by the British king to finally suppress piracy. Rogers arrived with three warships and issued the king's ultimatum to pirates: 'death or pardon'. He described his own tenure: *Expulsis Piratis – Restituta Commercia* (Pirates Expelled - Commerce Restored), words that still adorn the official seal of the Bahamas.

20,000 Leagues under the Sea by Universal/Williamson in 1916 was the first underwater motion picture ever made, and it was shot in the Bahamas.

Damned Yankees & Spanish Scourge

The Bahamas lay close to the North American colonies, and the outbreak of the American Revolution in 1775 put the Bahamas in the firing line. Not for the last time, the American Navy fell upon Nassau, intent on capturing arms and explosives (the first-ever foreign invasion by US forces). The Yankees occupied Nassau, carousing for two weeks before sailing away.

In 1782 a joint Spanish–French–US force again took advantage of England's weakened position to capture the city. Spain declared possession of the Bahamas and then made life intolerable for the city's inhabitants.

Andrew Deveaux, a Loyalist, recaptured the Bahamas for England a year later with 200 pro-British mercenaries. The Spaniards watched from afar as longboats ferried soldiers ashore. As the landing point was hidden from view, the soldiers stood up for the journey to shore and then the same men lay out of sight for the journey back to the

1706

The Spanish and the French team up for the infamous Raid on Nassau, where they trash the city and drive out the English privateers and settlers.

1718

English sea captain Woodes Rogers sails into Nassau and drives out the pirates. The Bahamian nation's motto 'Pirates Expelled-Commerce Restored' is coined; Rogers becomes the first Royal Governor.

1775

The American Revolution starts an exodus of Loyalists and their slaves to the region. Many set up shop on the islands off Abaco, now known as the Loyalist Cays and still populated with their descendants.

1782

The Spanish are back! Working with the Americans, they capture Nassau and declare possession of the Bahamas. A year later, British Loyalists retake the islands.

ship, repeatedly. Thus the Spaniards gained the impression that thousands of troops were landing. The Spaniards packed their belongings and set sail for Cuba. The Treaty of Versailles formally ceded the Bahamas to England from Spain.

Loyalists Land

Following the American Revolution, more than 8000 Loyalists and their slaves resettled in the Bahamian islands between 1783 and 1785, tripling the existing population. They introduced two things that would profoundly shape the islands' future: cotton and slaves, but the land was ill-suited to cotton. Then in 1807 the British banned slave trading, and brought their liberated 'cargoes' to the Bahamas. The abolition of slavery in 1834 and transition to a free society went smoothly, but a white elite minority of merchants and administrators now ruled over an ill-represented black majority, a state of affairs that would last for more than a century.

MALONE

The most famous Loyalist of them all was a South Carolina widow named Wyannie Malone, who arrived at Elbow Cay, Abaco, with her four children and settled the island almost single-handedly. Today it seems like half of all islanders bear the last name Malone.

Rhett Butler Slept Here: The Bahamas in the US Civil War

The US Civil War (1861–65) gave the Bahamas another economic boost, with the Bahamas becoming the major trading center for the blockaded South. Ships such as the *Ballymena* became infamous blockade-runners, running supplies to the South and returning with holds full of cotton. Author Margaret Mitchell, in *Gone with the Wind,* presents Rhett Butler as a well-known figure in Nassau, where he loaded his schooner with luxuries for the Confederacy.

But the end of hostilities burst Nassau's bubble again, and the ensuing decades witnessed an exodus of migrant labor to the US.

Rum, Gambling & GIs

The islands were again granted divine deliverance in the 1920s with Prohibition, which forbade the sale of alcohol in the US. The Nassau waterfront soon resembled a vast rum warehouse. Millions of gallons of alcohol were whisked across the water to Florida or New Jersey's Rum Row. Construction boomed and the islands' first casino opened, attracting gamblers and gangsters alongside a potpourri of the rich and famous. However the repeal of Prohibition again shattered Nassau's economic hopes, the Depression followed, and the Bahamas hit skid row.

During WWII the islands served as a base for Allied air and sea power. Exhausted GIs came to the islands to recuperate and were joined by wealthy Canadians and Americans wanting some winter sun.

» An abandoned slave home on Cat Island

1834

The British abolish slavery and the plantation system crumbles. Freed slaves establish villages, but indentured servitude exists for another four years and racial inequalities persist for well over a century.

1860s

The Bahamas become a base for Confederate blockade-runners sneaking supplies into Charleston during the American Civil War. The economy flourishes, though it will tank again post-war.

Independence 'Soon Come'

The decision to promote tourism coincided with the arrival of the jet age and the Cuban Revolution in 1959. During the 1950s, Havana was the mecca for American tourists. When Fidel Castro spun Cuba into Soviet orbit in 1961, the subsequent US embargo forced revelers to seek their pleasures elsewhere, and Nassau became the new hot spot.

The Bahamas was redefined as a corporate tax haven, aided by statutes modeled on Switzerland's secrecy laws. Tourism and finance bloomed.

The upturn in fortunes coincided with (and perhaps helped spark) the evolution of party politics and festering ethnic tensions, as the white elite and a growing black middle class reaped profits from the boom.

Only a small number of black representatives (mostly wealthy black businessmen) sat in the assembly, which remained dominated by the Bay Street Boys, descendants of the white Loyalists, and British appointees. Middle-class blacks' aspirations for representation coalesced with the pent-up frustrations of their brethren who remained impoverished.

In 1953 a local firebrand named Lynden Pindling formed the Progressive Liberal Party (PLP) to seek justice for the nation's black majority at the ballot box. In 1963 the tensions bubbled up into a violent national strike supported by the PLP. A new constitution, proposed by Britain,

Top Historical Sites

» Fort Fincastle, Nassau

» Mt Alvernia Hermitage, Cat Island

» Elbow Cay Lighthouse, Abaco

» Preacher's Cave, Eleuthera

A RIGHT ROYAL RENEGADE

In 1940 the Duke and Duchess of Windsor arrived as governor and governess. Formerly King Edward VIII of England, the duke abdicated the throne in 1936 to marry an American divorcee; Wallis Simpson, 'the woman I love.' The couple ensured that the rich and famous poured into Nassau in postwar years, and set the trend for the ruling Brits and their romances to hit the headlines.

Edward, who had suffered great humiliation in Britain, proved as controversial in the Bahamas as he had at home. Some claim that he made strides to right the colony's backward and racist politics. Others believe he endorsed the corrupt ways of the 'Bay Street Boys,' an oligarchy of white lawyers and merchants that dominated the islands' assembly for many years.

It is argued that the duke was sent to the Bahamas as a punishment. Other evidence suggests that on the eve of WWII, the Nazis were planning to kidnap the duke – who had settled in the south of France – and restore him to the throne as a puppet after Hitler's forces had conquered Great Britain. Edward had shown sympathies toward Nazism. Winston Churchill, the prime minister, urged King George VI to send his brother to the Bahamas to place him out of harm's way.

Nonetheless, the duke was beloved by many in the Bahamas and became the topic of several endearing songs and poems.

1920s

Prohibition in the United States turns the Bahamas into a rum-runners haven, particularly Bimini and the West End area of Grand Bahama, both just a hop, skip and jump from Florida.

1955

The Hawksbill Creek Agreement establishes the city of Freeport, and heretofore undeveloped Grand Bahama is soon dotted with mid-century modern hotels and casinos, a hit with Rat Pack-era jetsetters.

1958

Exuma Cays Land & Sea Park becomes the first marine fishery reserve in the world. Its pristine waters and beaches are still a haven for vacationers.

1959

Pan Am airlines founder Juan Tripp opens the swanky Cotton Bay Club on Eleuthera, turning the island into a jet-set destination.

was drawn up with the aim of creating a more representative legislature and providing for internal self-government. Voting, however, was restricted to male property owners, a provision overwhelmingly favoring whites. The United Bahamian Party (UBP), led by white Bahamian Roland Symonette, gained power in a national election by a slender majority, and Symonette became premier. The close race allowed for white dominance to be somewhat diluted, but black aspirations had barely been appeased.

Pindling and PLP followers refused to recognize the parliamentary speaker's authority. In 1967 the PLP finally boycotted parliament altogether, but not before winning an elimination of the property-ownership qualification. A new election was held, and Pindling's PLP came to power, a position it would maintain for the next 25 years.

On July 10, 1973, the Bahamian islands officially became a new nation, The Commonwealth of the Bahamas, ending 325 years of British rule.

Most Historic Hotels

- » Graycliff Hotel, Nassau (1740)
- » British Colonial Hilton, Nassau (1900)
- » New Plymouth Inn, Green Turtle Cay (1830)
- » The Landing, Harbour Island (1800)

Corruption & Drug Running

Pindling initially continued the progressive economic policies first adopted by his predecessors, based on tourism and finance. However, foreign-owned development interests enjoyed preferential treatment and when his government tried to redress these problems the economy stalled.

Kickbacks to government members had become a staple of political life by the early 1980s and the Bahamas' hundreds of islands, marinas, and airstrips had become the frontline staging post for narcotics en route to the US. Bahamians from all walks of life made hay on the trade, and the government seemed disinclined to crack down on it.

In 1984 it was suggested by an American TV program that Colombian drug barons had corrupted the government at its highest levels. Pindling and his ministers were accused of involvement in drug trafficking, and a Bahamian royal commission found against several ministers. Pindling was cleared, however the report noted that his expenditure was eight times his declared income.

The country's drug-heavy reputation tarnished its reputation abroad. Tourism and financial investment declined, so the government belatedly launched a crackdown led by the US Drug Enforcement Agency (US DEA).

The electorate had become frustrated, and voted in a conservative and business-orientated government, the Free National Movement (FNM) party, in 1992. Lynden Pindling died in August 2000.

The most famous example of a foreigner's view of the Bahamas is *Out Island Doctor* by Evans Cottman, a Yankee teacher who fell for the Crooked and Acklin Islands in the 1940s.

Hurricanes & Hope

In August 1999 Hurricane Dennis raked the Abacos and Grand Bahama. A month later, Hurricane Floyd – a 600-mile-wide whopper – pounded Cat, San Salvador, Abaco and Eleuthera with winds up to 155mph. In

1962
Women gain the right to vote. Half a century later, though, women still don't have the same legal protections as men – they can't confer citizenship on their children, and marital rape remains legal.

1965
Category 4 Hurricane Betsy slams into Abaco and New Providence, raging above the city of Nassau for three hours and doing so much damage it became known as 'Billion-Dollar Betsy.'

1967
The Bay Street Boys, a group of rich, white businessmen who've controlled the economic and political scene for decades, are toppled by the election of the Afro-Bahamian–led Progressive Liberal Party.

1973
The country achieves independence from Great Britain and becomes the Commonwealth of the Bahamas. Lynden Pindling, already Prime Minister, is considered the 'Father of the Nation.'

2004 two more hurricanes, Frances and Jeanne, hit these same islands in quick succession. Massive flooding and the destruction of many buildings again hit the villages and tourism industry of these already-struggling islands.

As tourism alone accounts for more than 60% of the Bahamas' GDP, the country scrambled to rebuild. Though the global recession of 2009 hit the islands hard, the country continues to forge ahead with large-scale tourism projects like New Providence's Baha Mar megaresort. In the first part of 2011, tourism was up, and Bahamians are crossing their fingers that the trend will hold.

1998

South African hotel magnate Sol Kerzner opens the first part of his Atlantis megaresort on Paradise Island. The massive hotel, casino, shopping and water park complex continues to expand.

2004

Hurricanes Frances and Jeanne lash the islands, doing the most damage in Grand Bahama and completely destroying corn crops on Cat Island and Long Island.

2009

The hunting, sale and consumption of sea turtle is banned nation-wide following years of environmentalist lobbying. Conservationists cheer, while many traditional Out Islanders grumble.

2010

Colton Harris-Moore, the teenage American airplane thief known as the 'barefoot bandit', is captured off Harbour Island by police, after a week-long manhunt.

Bahamian Life

Bahamians are a friendly bunch. Step on a public bus or ferry, and expect to be greeted with a 'good afternoon' by fellow passengers. Outside of Nassau, almost everyone seems to know each other; on some of the smaller islands, they're probably related. With a per-capita income of around $22,000, the Bahamas is one of the wealthiest countries in the region. Half of the archipelago's population is employed in the tourism industry; another 10% work in banking and finance. On the Out Islands, economies often function on the barter system and pockets of poverty are still visible. Life is much faster-paced in Nassau and Grand Bahama than on the Out Islands, where unemployment is high and midday loafing with a Kalik and a plate of cracked conch is not reserved for weekends.

Food & Drink

Africa meets England meets the US South meets the Caribbean on the Bahamian plate, reflecting the country's multicultural origins. Many of the country's best-loved dishes – johnnycake, peas 'n' rice – were born in African slave kitchens, while others, such as roasts and pies are distinctly British in flavor. American fast-food dishes like burgers (albeit with an island slant) are ubiquitous, while foods like fried chicken and benne (sesame seed) cakes are Southern US with roots in West Africa. Everything's flavored with local bounty – seafood, pineapple, guava, plantain.

Dining options range from humble beachfront conch shacks to flashy celebrity chef-run palaces of haute cuisine, though options are limited in the more rural regions. If you're staying on the Out Islands, we hope you like conch.

Must-Try Bahamian Dishes

- Cracked conch
- Boil fish
- Guava duff
- Peas 'n' rice
- Mac 'n' cheese
- Souse
- Johnnycake

Breakfast

Breakfast, even on the Out Islands, tends to come in two varieties: American-style (eggs, toast, cinnamon rolls etc) or Bahamian-style. The latter is heavy on grits (coarsely ground corn) – grits with eggs, grits with sardines, grits with corned beef – and seafood. Look for boil fish or stew fish, a clear soup of fish (usually grouper) cooked with potatoes, onions, salt pork and lime. It's often served with johnnycake, a type of flat cornbread. Souse, a thick brownish stew made with chicken, mutton, pork

EATING PRICE BANDS

In restaurant reviews throughout this book, we've indicated the price band.

- $ means a budget place where a main dish is less than $12
- $$ means midrange; mains are $12 to $25
- $$$ means top end; mains are more than $25

feet, sheep tongue or pretty much whatever meat bits the cook can get her hands on, is another breakfast favorite. It's a bit of an acquired taste.

If you're staying at a resort, you may be treated to a full English fry-up – eggs, bacon, toast, beans, fried tomato etc – a legacy of the island's colonial days.

Classic Dishes

When it comes to meat, chicken is king. Southern US–style fried chicken is ubiquitous at diners and fast-food joints, curried chicken is a classic takeout dish, and BBQ chicken is a favorite of family cook-outs. Pork is a close runner-up – look out for savory, black pepper-dusted pork chops and delectably greasy BBQ ribs. Mutton is common too, often served as a curried stew or souse.

Peas 'n' rice, a humble combination of rice and red beans, is the island's top starch, its name synonymous with home for lonely overseas Bahamians. Mac 'n' cheese – dense squares of baked noodles mixed with gooey cream cheese and topped with bubbling cheddar – vies for a close second. Other down-home favorites include potato salad, pea soup with dumplings (chunks of boiled pastry dough), coleslaw and plantains.

Meat patties, spiced ground beef or chicken served in a fried pastry shell, are a lunchtime treat, as is roti, a West Indian dish of flatbread and meat or vegetables.

Colonial cultural hangovers are often retained on menus in tourist spots as well as in residential suburbs. Regular dishes include steak and kidney pudding, bangers and mash, and shepherd's pie.

If you're overwhelmed by all this meat and starch, keep your eyes open for roadside stands selling local fruits like plantains, cassava, mangoes, finger chilis, papayas, pineapples and soursops.

CANDIES

In Nassau, Mortimer Candies has been serving up sweet treats like benne (sesame seed) bars, fudge, and mints in the colors of the Bahamian flag for more than 80 years. You can find their products in grocery stores nationwide.

Seafood

Many Bahamians still make their living pulling fish from the glittering turquoise seas, and seafood is unsurprisingly a staple of Bahamian cuisine. Look out for conch, crab, grouper, jack, shrimp, snapper, turbot, and tuna, often fried or served in sandwiches or stews. Caribbean spiny lobsters (crawfish) are a favorite. They're delicious cooked in butter with peppers and onions.

After conch, grouper is the hands-down favorite seafood. With mild, firm white flesh, it holds up well to frying – deep-fried 'grouper fingers' are a mainstay.

Dessert

The trademark Bahamian dessert is guava duff, a boiled jellyroll filled with sweetened guava paste and topped with guava butter or rum-infused cream sauce. Another yummy favorite is coconut tart, a thin baked pie with a sweetened shredded coconut filling. Banana bread, coconut bread, cassava cake and carrot cake are staples of local bakery cases. On Eleuthera, look out for sweet, tangy pineapple tarts and good-enough-to-eat-with-a-spoon pineapple jam. Rum cakes, often sold in decorative

DOS & DON'TS

- Do tip 15% with a smile at all restaurants and bars.
- Do take a small gift when dining at someone's home.
- Don't smoke indoors at restaurants.
- Don't assume drinking alcohol is the norm, many islanders are teetotalers.

THE UBIQUITOUS CONCH

Conch (pronounced 'conch') is the de facto national dish of the Bahamas, a staple of every home, restaurant and roadside takeout stall in the country. A type of sea snail with a large, lovely cone-shaped shell, it's fished from the shallows and brought live to market, then extracted through a hole in the shell. Its tough flesh, comparable to calamari, takes some TLC to tenderize. Chefs usually pound the meat, score it with sharp knives, or marinate it in lime – the mark of a top cook is the tenderness of her conch. The top conch dishes are cracked conch (battered and fried), conch salad (chopped and tossed with onions, tomatoes and lime juice; choose either skin-on on skin-off), conch chowder, roast conch, conch souse (stew) and conch fritters (deep-fried balls of minced conch and batter).

Conch stands – beachfront or roadside wooden shacks with primitive kitchens – are often the best place to sample conch in all its forms. Ask a local for their favorite; everyone has an opinion on who serves the best conch!

Conch shells also make wonderful souvenirs – buy a polished specimen from any local straw market or gift shop, or look for your own on an uncrowded beach. Jewelry made from the rosy coral interior of the shell is also popular, as are the rare pink conch pearls sometimes found inside.

tins, are a popular souvenir. Around Christmas, a liquor-soaked fruit cake called black cake is a holiday treat.

Drinks

The Bahamian beer Kalik (say 'Ka-LICK') is fantastic, with golden bubbles and a sharp flavor. Sands, a newer brew, is also wildly popular, comparable to light Mexican beers like Corona. The national Bahamian cocktail could be the Goombay Smash, a lethally easy-to-drink fruit juice and rum cocktail (see also p132), although the Bahama Mama is better known. At the fish fry, locals suck down Sky Juice, a high-octane blend of gin, coconut water and nutmeg.

The infamous rum that bottoms up local cocktails is simply called 151, as it is 151 proof. There is an excellent range of duty-free quality rums available in Nassau, including the Bacardi line. Rums flavored with coconut, mango or pineapple are also popular.

Wine is widely sold, but costly. Be aware that some bottles will have been exposed to the heat. Wine connoisseurs should head to the Graycliff Hotel in Nassau, with 250,000 bottles of the rarest and finest vintages in a jaw-dropping cellar.

Non-alcoholic potables include Goombay Punch, a teeth-judderingly sweet fruit punch–flavored soda; Goombay Junkanoo, a lemon-flavored version of the same; and Vitamalt, a malt-flavored soft drink. Canned coconut water is popular as well, and fresh pineapple and mango juices are common in higher-end hotels.

You may notice that a large number of downtown Nassau restaurants seem to be Greek-run. Greek-Bahamians, who immigrated to work in the sponging industry in the late 19th century, are a visible minority in New Providence, where many of them today work in the restaurant or hotel business.

Bahamas Best Bars

- Nipper's Beach Bar & Grill, Great Guana Cay, Abaco
- Blue Bar, Harbour Island, Eleuthera
- Margaritaville Sandbar, Grand Bahama
- Dune, Paradise Island

Where to Eat & Drink

Our rule of thumb: the uglier the conch shack, the better the conch. Don't be put off by the ramshackle appearance of some down-home cafes and takeouts – they often serve the tastiest, most authentic food at the best prices.

The bigger tourism areas have a huge variety of international cuisine, from avant-garde sushi joints to steakhouses to cozy French bistros. Since most food is imported, prices tend to be high. A fancy meal in the Bahamas can easily set you back 50% more than the same meal in New York.

Nassau and Grand Bahama have high-quality, if pricey, supermarkets. On the Out Islands, pickings are slimmer – the smallest islands may have only a tiny convenience store selling chocolate bars and dusty cans of peas.

Religion

A Christian Nation

Christianity is a dominant force in the Bahamas, where the overwhelming majority of islanders are devout believers who profess to live by the word of God. Virtually every taxi driver has a Bible at hand, as do many office workers. State functions and the school day begin with prayers. Church affairs make headline news, while major international events are relegated to the inside pages. Every political speech is peppered with biblical quotations and is considerate of the Church's position on social issues.

The Bahamian nation claims the greatest number of churches per capita in the world. The vast majority of the populace are mainstreamers; Baptists (35%), Anglican/Episcopalian (15%) and Catholic (14%). The official state religion is the Anglican Church, although some Christian priests hedge their bets and mix a little good-willed obeah (folk magic) into their practice.

Every island is a veritable jumble of chapels and churches, usually Baptist revival centers, referred to as 'jumper churches' by locals. Often you'll see as many as a dozen churches in settlements with barely 200 people. Most of these churches are maintained with much love and with money the congregation can ill-afford.

Sundays really are blessed days, when businesses outside main tourist centers are closed. Bahamians normally dress up to show respect even if they are working (as with Nassau's taxi drivers) and the churchgoers are resplendent in big hats and shiny new suits.

'Potcake' is the Bahamian term for the many skinny-ribbed stray dogs that wander the Out Islands. The canines got the nickname because housewives used to leave their cooking pots outside the house so the dogs could eat the caked-on rice – or 'pot cakes' – at the bottom.

POTCAKE

Spirit Beliefs

Despite the force of Christianity in society, many Bahamians still keep spirit beliefs held over from slave days, when African religions melded with Christianity. Rooted in the animist beliefs of West Africa (animism has nothing to do with animal spirits; the name is derived from the Latin word *anima,* meaning 'soul'), they are based on the tenet that the spiritual and temporal worlds are a unified whole.

A core belief is that spirits live independently of the human or animal body and can inhabit inanimate objects. They can communicate directly with humans and are usually morally neutral; it is the service to which humans call them that determines whether they will be a force of good or evil. Cantankerous, onerous people beget evil 'sperrids'; kind and thoughtful people beget good spirits. Spirits particularly like to live in silk cotton trees, of which many Bahamians are extremely wary.

BAHAMA MAMA

Here is the makings of a classic Bahamian cocktail.

- ½ fl oz (15ml) dark rum
- ½ fl oz (15ml) coconut liqueur
- ¼ fl oz (8ml) 151%-proof rum
- ¼ fl oz (8ml) coffee liqueur
- ½ lemon, juiced
- 4 fl oz (120ml) pineapple juice

Combine the ingredients and pour over ice. Garnish with a cherry.
Skol! Slàinte! Cheers!

FISH FRY

From Nassau to the tiniest Out Islands, local social life revolves around the Fish Fry. A Fish Fry is both a place and an event. As a place, it's usually a collection of brightly painted wooden shacks in a central location, either downtown or by the harbor. During the day, it's empty, but at night it lights up as an outdoor food market, each shack serving plates of fried seafood – conch, turbot, lobster – and hearty sides like peas 'n' rice. Everybody gathers at the Fish Fry to eat, drink, gossip and dance, fueled by homemade wine and rake 'n' scrape beats. It's one part church picnic, one part neighborhood party, one part food court, one part nightclub. On some islands, the Fish Fry only happens on Friday or Saturday night, while on others it's a nightly event. Nassau's Arawak Cay is the island's most famous Fish Fry, but Out Island versions are even more fun for mixing and mingling with locals.

All kinds of practices have evolved to guard against evil spirits. Even physicians are known to tie a black cord around a newborn baby's wrists to guard against evil spirits. A Bible is often placed at the head of a sleeping child for the same reason. And if this fails, a Bahamian may attempt to dispel a malicious spirit by marking Xs all around and repeating the all-powerful phrase, 'Ten, ten, the Bible ten.'

The term 'Conchy Joe' is used to refer to white Bahamians with longtime roots in the islands. Though many locals playfully apply the term to themselves, it can be considered derogatory.

The Arts

Relative to its neighbors, the Bahamas' intellectual tradition is comparatively weak and, for a capital city, Nassau has been surprisingly unsophisticated in the visual and performance arts. Things have been changing, however, especially in music and art – and with the opening of the National Gallery in Nassau, displays of really impressive works are gaining their rightful place in Bahamian society.

Literature

While the Bahamas has produced no writer of world renown, the nation does have its literati. Few, however, are known even within the Caribbean region.

Bahamian Anthology (published by the College of the Bahamas) is a selection of poetry, stories and plays by Bahamian writers. In a similar poetic vein, try *Bahamas: In a White Coming On* by Dennis Ryan.

The Bahamas has been the setting for work of more notable, non-Bahamian writers. Ernest Hemingway's *Islands in the Stream* is a fictitious but accurate look at the Biminis' history and his own brutish ways during WWII.

Robert Wilder's *Wind from the Carolinas* is a historical novel that tells of the settlement of the Bahamas in the form of a generational saga. And Barbara Whitnell's *The Salt Rakers* follows suit.

A more contemporary romp is Herman Wouk's *Don't Stop the Carnival*, the tale of a publicist who gives it all up to open a hotel on a fictitious Caribbean isle.

The Luis de Torres Synagogue in Freeport is the only Jewish temple in the Bahamas. It's named after a Spanish Jew who sailed with Christopher Columbus on his voyage to the New World.

WHOSE FAMILY?

The term 'Out Islands' or 'Family Islands' refers to all the Bahamian islands except New Providence and Grand Bahama. The 'family' in 'Family Islands' refers to the fact that nearly all Bahamians, most of whom live in Nassau or Freeport, have families back on the more remote, less developed islands, such as Abaco, Eleuthera or Andros.

A CONSERVATIVE CULTURE

Despite their laid-back attitudes and friendliness, Bahamians as a group are quite conservative.

The islands are traditionally hostile to homosexuality (see p66), though they do have a small, under-the-radar gay population, especially in Nassau and Grand Bahama. The moralistic-minded Bahamas Plays and Films Control Board decides which movies are 'decent' to be shown in the country. In 2006, it raised quite a stink by banning the gay cowboy blockbuster Brokeback Mountain, an action the *Nassau Guardian* decried as prejudiced and out-of-touch.

Feminism has made headway since women got the vote in 1962, though Bahamian women still can't pass their citizenship to their children born overseas (only men can do that), and a bill to outlaw marital rape failed to pass in 2009.

Though welcoming of tourists, the Bahamas is quite xenophobic when it comes to one group of foreigners: Haitians. Haitians, who have been immigrating to the Bahamas since the 1950s, are generally treated as a dirty underclass – headlines in 2010 decried the eviction of 1500 Haitian immigrants from an Abaco shantytown, and accusations of abuse of Haitians by Bahamian immigration officials are rampant.

Music

Whether it's hotel beach parties or the raw-sound-system dance clubs of Over-the-Hill, Nassau's poorer quarter, the Bahamas reverberates to the soul-riveting sounds of calypso, soca, reggae and its own distinctive music, which echoes African rhythms and synthesizes Caribbean calypso, soca and English folk songs into its *goombay* beat.

The Hermit of Cat Island, by Peter F Anson, tells the fascinating story of Father Jerome, the hermit architect who blessed Cat and Long Islands with splendid churches. These miniature Gothic buildings are everywhere.

Goombay

Taking its name from an African word for 'rhythm', *goombay* derives its melody from a guitar, piano or horn instrument accompanied by any combination of goatskin *goombay* drums, maracas, rhythm (or click) sticks, rattles, conch-shell horns, fifes and flutes, and cowbells to add a uniquely Bahamian *kalik-kalik-kalik* sound. It's typified by a fast-paced, sustained, infectious melody. *Goombay* is to the Bahamas what reggae is to Jamaica and is most on display during Christmas and midsummer Junkanoo celebrations.

Goombay draws on a heritage of folk music introduced by African slaves from North America, Jamaica and other neighboring islands. Particularly important are the 'talking drums,' once used to pass along information, and folk songs developed in the cane fields to ease the backbreaking labor. Over generations, European elements, such as the

FOLKTALES & CHILDREN'S STORIES

Several books trace the evolution and meaning of Bahamian folktales, including *Bahamian Lore: Folk Tales and Songs* by Robert Curry. Patricia Glinton-Meicholas is another name to look out for, this prolific writer has a real panache in bringing oral histories and folktales to life. Her collection *An Evenin' in Guanima: A Treasury of Folktales from The Bahamas* is a great introduction to the Bahamas.

Telcine Turner's *Once Below a Time: Bahamian Stories* is an illustrated collection of short stories for children. Likewise, youngsters might enjoy *Climbing Clouds: Stories & Poems from The Bahamas*, also edited by Turner, and *Who Let the Dog Out? (Dottie's Story)* by Carole Hughes, a story about a Dalmatian born into Green Turtle Cay who heads off to explore the world.

French quadrille introduced by planters, were absorbed as well, creating a unique style.

Other Bahamian Styles

The Bahamas' down-home, working-class music is rake 'n' scrape, usually featuring a guitar, an accordion, shakers made from the pods of poinciana trees and other makeshift instruments, such as a saw played with a screwdriver.

Rake 'n' scrape music can be heard at local bars throughout the islands, and is a highlight of many festivals such as Family Island regattas. Grand Turk has a fabulous annual festival when these musicians gather from across the Turks and Caicos region to display and enjoy their talents.

Dance hall, a kind of Caribbean rap and the in-vogue working-class music of the formerly British Caribbean islands, has evolved its own style in the Bahamas, where it is known as 'chatting.' It is performed entirely in local dialect by DJs with their own mobile discos.

The Bahamas has an adult literacy rate of almost 96%, putting it ahead of Singapore and Portugal, but behind the US and England.

Visual Arts

The so-called father of Bahamian art is Amos Ferguson, the nation's foremost folk artist. Ferguson is intensely spiritual. His naive, palette-bright canvases focus upon religion, history, nature and folklore, or 'ol' story.' Ferguson began making bird figurines, tumblers and jars for the

JUMPING AT JUNKANOO

You feel the music before you see the main event...a frenzied barrage of whistles and horns overriding the cowbells, the rumble of drums and the joyful blasts of conch shells. Then the costumed revelers stream into view, whirling and gyrating like a kaleidoscope in rhythm with the cacophony. This is Junkanoo, the national festival of the Bahamas – its equivalent of Carnaval or Mardi Gras – and it is a mass of energy, color and partying that starts in the twilight hours of Boxing Day.

The name, pronounced *junk-uh-NOO*, is thought to come from a West African term for 'deadly sorcerer.' Others say the festival is named for John Canoe, the tribal leader who demanded that his enslaved people be allowed to enjoy a festivity. With its origins in West African secret societies, the parade evolved on the plantations of the British Caribbean among slaves who were forbidden to observe their sacred rites. The all-male cast of masqueraders hid their identity, following West African mask-wearing traditions.

At first Junkanoos were suppressed by the Bahamian colonial government, which feared they might get out of hand and lead to slave uprisings. Later, planters encouraged them. Creole elements found their way into the ceremony, along with British Morris dancing, polkas and reels. On Jamaica and other islands, Junkanoo was suppressed to extinction, but in the Bahamas it became an integral part of the culture.

Junkanoo is fiercely competitive and many marchers belong to 'shacks,' groups who vie to produce the best performance, costume, dancing and music. The most elaborately costumed performers are one-person parade floats whose costume can weigh over 200lb and depict exotic scenes adorned with a myriad of glittering beads, foils and rhinestones. Many spend a year planning their costumes, keeping their designs a carefully guarded secret.

The energy of this carnival is that of a joyous and frenetic explosion. In Nassau the first 'rush,' as the parade is known, occurs on Boxing Day (December 26); the second happens on New Year's Day and the third in summer, when the shacks go over their game plans. Head for the Fish Frys if you won't be there for the festival, this is where the shacks rehearse their dances and the music for the big nights. Thursday nights are practice night in Grand Bahama. In the Family Islands the summer 'rushes' are on different days to Nassau. Parades start around 3am and finish by noon in time for a big lunch.

Bahamian Art 1492–1992 by Patricia Glinton-Meicholas, Charles Huggins and Basil Smith is a splendid book on Bahamian visual art.

tourist trade. You can see a permanent collection of his works in the Pompey Museum in Nassau.

Brent Malone, Max Taylor, Rolph Harris and Alton Roland Lowe – the Bahamas' artist laureate for more than three decades – are also all writ large in the Bahamian art world.

The islands' plastic arts (ceramics, sculpture, painting, woodcarving and textiles) have been late in flowering, and with the exception of straw-work, the crafts industry is relatively undeveloped. It has been influenced in recent years by the influx of Haitians, who have inspired intuitive hardwood carvings, often brightly painted and highlighted by pointillist dots.

Island Landscapes

From the vast pineyard forests of Andros to the chalky bluffs of Eleuthera to the endless mangrove swamps of Abaco to the humid subtropical palm groves of Cat Island, the Bahamas has a splendiferous variety of landscapes to explore. Birdwatch in national forests, dive in eerie water-filled caves, bonefish in sandy-bottomed shallows, sail from cay to cay – the islands beckon.

The Archipelago

Geology & Geography

The Bahamian islands are the surface projections of three massive limestone platforms rising sheer-sided from the deep seabed. These platforms, known as the Bahama Banks, are the result of nearly 150 million years of deposits; the islands as we know them today began to take their present form only about 500,000 years ago.

The mostly linear islands are strewn in a general northwest–southeast array. Several – Great Abaco, Eleuthera, Long Island, Andros – are as much as 100 miles long. Few, however, are more than a few miles wide. All are low lying, the terrain either pancake-flat or gently undulating. Cat Island's Mt Alvernia, the highest point in the Bahamas, is a less-than-dizzying 206ft above sea level.

These shores are lined virtually their entire lengths by white- or pinkish-sand beaches – about 2200 miles in all – shelving into turquoise shallows. Some islands – notably Bimini and Andros – sit on the edge of the banks, with dizzying drop-offs into deep ocean trenches less than a few miles from shore.

Most islands have barrier reefs along the length of their eastern shores, anywhere from 200yd to 2 miles out, that offer protection from Atlantic waves.

Blue Holes

The islands' porous limestone is pocketed with deep water-filled sinkholes called blue holes. These holes can occur inland, in which case they resemble dark ponds or water-filled cave mouths. Inland blue holes often have subterranean tunnels leading to the sea – divers have been shocked to find sharks swimming around in what they believed to be an old rock quarry! The holes can also occur beneath the sea, their deep blue color standing at contrast with the surrounding pale teal. Some are even walking distance from the shore.

Divers have long been enthralled with the blue holes' inky depths – the deepest, Long Islands' Dean's Blue Hole, plunges 663ft. Andros is especially well known for its blue-hole diving, though Abaco and Grand Bahama have their fair share as well.

Bonefishing is always catch-and-release, and sportfishing is highly regulated by Bahamian law – billfish, like marlin, are always catch-and-release, while others are subject to strict size limits/daily quotas.

Best Blue Holes

- Uncle Charlie's Blue Hole, Andros
- Stargate, Andros
- Ben's Blue Hole, Grand Bahama
- Dean's Blue Hole, Long Island

Unique creatures have evolved to exist solely within the gloom of the underwater caverns, including blind, pigmentless fish. Because of the lack of oxygen at the bottom, biological matter like skeletons can be preserved here for eons – divers have discovered Lucayan skeletons, prehistoric crocodile skulls and more.

Local lore attributes deadly mermaids, mermen and sea monsters to many of the holes. Even without mythological beasties, the blue holes can be extremely dangerous – outgoing tides can create a 'suck' that's hard to swim away from.

Tongue of the Ocean

If you look at a satellite image of the Bahamas, you'll see what honestly looks like a long blue tongue unfurling itself between Andros and New Providence. This is the Tongue of the Ocean (TOTO), a 6000ft-deep ocean trench that drops suddenly off the eastern shore of Andros.

The US government uses the TOTO abyss as a deep-water testing facility. The Atlantic Underwater Testing and Evaluation Center (AUTEC) is a top-secret Andros facility used to try out undersea weapons, acoustic instruments and submarines.

TOTO's proximity to Andros makes it an easy location for wall dives. Brave divers can take the plunge from the shallow sandy bottom into the dizzying drop-off.

ASTRONAUTS

Early American astronauts used to splash down in the waters off Grand Bahama, where a missile base tracked their missions across the skies.

Hurricanes

The Bahamas location, though felicitous in many ways, is a disadvantage in one major respect: it's smack in the middle of the Atlantic hurricane pathway. Hurricanes shape everything from the pattern of sands on the beaches to the growth rates of forests, not to mention their impact on human life. Hurricane season, which lasts from June to November but is usually busiest in August and September, is taken seriously here: islanders always have one ear cocked for the weather report.

Hurricanes that hit the Bahamas form off the coast of Africa and whip in a westerly direction across the Atlantic. The first stage of a hurricane's approach is called a tropical disturbance. The next stage is a tropical depression. When winds exceed 40mph, the system is upgraded to a tropical storm and is usually accompanied by heavy rains. The system is called a hurricane if wind speed exceeds 75mph and intensifies around a low-pressure center called the 'eye of the storm.'

The strength of a hurricane is rated from one to five. The strongest and rarest hurricanes, the Category-5 monsters, pack winds that exceed 155mph. Hurricanes travel at varying speeds, from as little as 6mph to more than 31mph.

If you are caught by an approaching hurricane, follow local warnings. Hotels are typically of concrete and steel construction capable of withstanding strong winds. If you have an oceanfront room, relocate inland.

In August, 1999, Hurricane Dennis raked the Abacos and Grand Bahama. A month later, Hurricane Floyd, a 600-mile-wide whopper, pounded Cat, San Salvador, Abaco and Eleuthera with winds up to 155mph. In late 2004 two more hurricanes, Frances and Jeanne, hit these same islands along with Grand Bahama in quick succession. Massive flooding and the destruction of many buildings again hit villages and the tourism industry. Luckily, few lives were lost.

For warnings, check the USA National Hurricane Center's **Tropical Prediction Center** (www.nhc.noaa.gov).

National Parks

The Bahamas has 26 national parks, reserves and protected areas which include large sections of the barrier reef. These parks protect more than 700,000 sq miles of territory.

The parks are used for both scientific research and for protecting endangered species, and are maintained by the **Bahamas National Trust** (BNT; ☎242-393-1317; www.bnt.bs; Retreat, Village Rd, Nassau). Notably, the 175-sq-mile Exuma Cays Land & Sea Park was created in 1958 as the first marine fishery reserve in the world. The park now teems with prehistoric life forms, coral reefs, turtles, fish and endangered rock iguanas and hutias.

The boxed text (p244) does not include all the Wild Bird Reserves, obtainable from the **Department of Agriculture** (☎242-325-7413; Levy Bldg, E Bay St, Nassau).

One of the worst storms to hit the Bahamas was 1965's Hurricane Betsy, which smashed through the Abacos then hunkered down over Nassau for a full three hours, before heading to the US. The damage was so expensive the storm was nicknamed 'Billion-Dollar Betsy.'

Flora & Fauna

Mammals & Reptiles

The archipelago has only 13 native land mammal species. Twelve of them are bats. All are endangered. The most common is the leaf-nosed bat, an ugly/cute little thing with a piglet-y pink nose and enormous ears. Bats consume large amounts of insects, especially mosquitoes, and act as important seed dispersers and pollinators for flora.

The only native terrestrial mammal is the endangered hutia, a cat-size brown rodent akin to a guinea pig. A small population lives on a small cay in the Exumas.

Wild boar roam the backcountry on larger islands, especially Andros, where they're often hunted for meat. Bahamian raccoons, once considered a distinct species, are now believed to have been introduced relatively recently from the US. They make quite a pest of themselves on Grand Bahama.

Many Bahamian islands have unique species of reptiles, such as the Cat Island Turtle. Great Inagua also has its own terrapin, while Bimini has a unique boa constrictor.

There are frogs, too, including the Cuban tree frog, whose mucus is poisonous.

Rock iguanas are shy and harmless vegetarians that have been virtually eradicated by humans, feral dogs and cats, and now inhabit some outlying isles. Look for them in the Exuma Cays.

For most visitors, the most obvious animals are the chickens, who run rampant in many of the Out Islands, even chichi Harbour Island. If you don't like being woken up at 5am by a rooster, invest in some earplugs. Horses and donkeys meander the rural island as well, and Exuma is home to a unique colony of swimming pigs.

Beware the poisonwood tree. Endemic across the Bahamas, it causes rashes similar to poison ivy in susceptible individuals. You'll recognize the tree by its scaly reddish bark and glossy green teardrop-shaped leaves.

Birds

Birdwatchers exalt in the Bahamas' 300 recorded species of feathered creatures. Only a few are endemic, including the Bahama swallow, endangered Bahama parrot and the Bahama woodstar hummingbird, which weighs less than a US nickel.

The West Indian (Caribbean) flamingo, which is the national bird, inhabits Crooked Island, Long Cay and Great Inagua, a sanctuary with over 50,000 birds.

From September through May, the forests swarm with visitors. Vireos, flycatchers, thrushes and plovers visit, migrating between summer and winter habitats. Birdwatchers also can spot Bahama whistling ducks, guinea fowl, quails, snipes, coots, herons and gallinules in the wetlands.

WILDLIFE RESERVES IN THE BAHAMAS

PARK	FEATURES
Abaco National Park	32 sq miles; endangered Bahama parrot
Black Sound Cay National Reserve	small mangrove island; wintering habitat for waterfowl & avifauna
Pelican Cays Land & Sea Park	2100 acres; extensive coral reefs, undersea caves, abundant terrestrial plant & animal life
Tilloo Cay National Reserve	20-acre area of pristine wilderness; vital nesting site for tropical birds
Conception Island National Park	temporary station for migrating birds & nesting green turtles
Exuma Cays Land & Sea Park	175 sq miles; world's first marine fishery reserve (1958); coral reefs, turtles, fish, endangered rock iguanas & hutias
Peterson Cay National Park	1½-acre cay & surrounding coral gardens
Lucayan National Park	world's longest known underwater cave & cavern system; mangrove wetland; birds
Rand Nature Centre	100-acre site & BNT HQ; captive flamingo flock, native boa constrictors & curly tailed lizards
Bahamas National Trust Park	287 sq miles; world's largest breeding colony of West Indian flamingos
Union Creek Reserve	7 sq miles; tidal creek & marine turtle research facility
Little Inagua	no fresh water on the island or human habitation, with undisturbed biodiversity
Harrold & Wilson Ponds	250 acres; 100 avian species including herons, egrets & cormorants
The Retreat	11 acres; very large collection of palms & tropical plants; hardwood forest supports diverse plant species & features; BNT HQ

The pinelands of the northern Bahamas support a wide variety of resident summer nesters, plus migratory songbirds in winter.

The red-tailed hawk is one of several birds of prey commonly seen soaring high overhead, as is the jet-black turkey vulture, unmistakable with its undertaker's plumage and bald red head. The beautiful and diminutive osprey and kestrel prefer to spy from atop telegraph poles.

Each summer, swarms of giant Androsian land crabs scuttle hither and thither in a mating frenzy. Many of them will wind up on a dinner plate, caught by quick-reflexed crabbers carrying flashlights and net bags.

The islands are also home to the burrowing owl and the barn owl. Both are protected species.

Marine Life

Different sources claim that the Bahamas has between 900 and 2700 sq miles of coral reef. What is certain is that there are thousands of species of marine life inhabiting these coasts, such as bonito, inflatable porcupine fish, three species of stingrays, moray eels, lobsters, parrotfish, sharks, kingfish, groupers, barracudas, jewelfish and deep-blue Creole wrasse.

Many dive outfitters offer trips to encounter wild stingrays. Up to 5ft across, stingrays are quite gentle and will take food from your hand.

ACTIVITIES	LOCATION	PAGE
hiking, birdwatching	Abaco	p133
walking, birdwatching	Abaco; adjacent to Green Turtle Cay	p115
yachting, snorkeling, diving, birdwatching	Abaco	p126
hiking, birdwatching	Abaco, between Marsh Harbour & Pelican Cays	p126
diving, birdwatching, yachting, snorkeling	between Long Island and San Salvador	p180
yachting, snorkeling, diving, hiking	Exuma Cays	p167
yachting, snorkeling, diving, hiking	Grand Bahama	p90
yachting, snorkeling, diving, hiking, birdwatching	Grand Bahama	p90
hiking, birdwatching	Grand Bahama	p75
birdwatching tours organized through Nassau's BNT office	Great Inagua	p194
tours organized through Nassau's BNT office	Great Inagua	p194
contact BNT for access	Little Inagua	p194
hiking, birdwatching	New Providence	p40
walking	New Providence	p47

Humpback whales pass through the waters windward of the Bahamas and blue whales are also frequently sighted. Atlantic bottlenose dolphins frequent these waters, as do the less-often-seen Atlantic spotted dolphins.

Three species of marine turtles – green, loggerhead and, more rarely, hawksbill – use the islands' beaches as nest sites. Turtles migrate thousands of miles to nest and lay their eggs here, as they have for at least 150 million years. Unfortunately, these gentle creatures are endangered, though a recent ban on turtle-hunting shows promise.

Perhaps the Bahamas' least welcome creature, the sand flea, AKA the no-see-um, comes out at dusk to nip the flesh of unsuspecting beachgoers. Though not painful or poisonous, its bite is highly irritating. Bring bug spray. Always.

Plants

The Bahamas' thin, rocky soil, underlain by limestone, is not conducive to lush vegetation. Nonetheless, the islands together boast more than 1370 species of plants, including 121 endemics, such as Bahamian mahogany and Bahamian pine.

Lignum vitae (also known as Ironwood), the national tree – which you may recognize by its clusters of dark-blue blooms – has the heaviest timber of all known woods and is much in demand among carvers (its bark, gum, fruit, leaves and blossoms also serve useful purposes, including medicines for gout and syphilis).

The waxy branches of the candlewood tree, another endemic species, were once lit as torches by Lucayans.

Environmental Issues

Outside of the national park system, inappropriate development, pollution and overexploitation threaten wildlife and marine resources. Although the Bahamas was the first Caribbean nation to outlaw long-line fishing as a threat to the marine ecology, the islands' stocks of Nassau grouper, spiny lobster and turtle all face the consequences of over-fishing.

Commercial poaching, mostly by Cuban-Americans from Florida in the west and by Dominicans in the east, has also been a significant problem. From the late 1970s the problem stirred several island communities to establish their own nongovernmental reserves.

Coral reefs have also experienced damage by anchors, careless divers and snorkelers as well as by Bahamian fishermen. The biggest culprit, however, is Mother Nature: hurricanes cause as much devastation as a minor war.

The destruction of mangrove swamps, a natural hurricane barrier and fertile spawning ground for many fish species, has been a hot topic of late, as environmentalists battle against development in the North Bimini wetlands.

The government – which knows which side its bread is buttered – has taken an increasing interest in sustainability, joining an international council on sustainable tourism and promoting alternative energy sources like wind power. It remains to be seen, however, whether this will have much impact on the ground.

Top Eco-Resorts

- » Small Hope Bay Lodge, Andros
- » Higgins Landing, Exuma
- » Tiamo, Andros
- » Club Peace & Plenty, Exuma

While queen conch is considered 'commercially threatened' (though not endangered) in some parts of the Caribbean, Bahamian populations are considered well-regulated and stable and are not subject to any international bans or censures.

Ecosystems of The Bahamas

Whiteland Coppice Shrubby, thin, salt-sprayed forest near the ocean, full of cacti and wind-bent trees; common trees include Cabbage palm, gumbo-limbo, poisonwood and sea grape.

Blackland Coppice A dense, primeval forest in the islands' interior. Full of mahogany, red cedar and pigeon plum, with a shady canopy and orchids and bromeliads growing in the understory. Much of the old-growth blackland coppice has long since been logged, but you can still find ancient trees on Little Inagua.

Rocky Coppice A transitional zone between mangrove swamps and pineyard forest, set atop limestone outcroppings and often flooded at high tide.

Pineyard Forest Endemic to four Bahamian islands, including Grand Bahama, this is a sparse forest full of tall, skinny Caribbean pines once used for lumber.

ARE DOLPHIN ENCOUNTERS GOOD FOR DOLPHINS?

Dolphin encounters are a popular attraction in the Bahamas and elsewhere, but they are not without controversy. Some experts, like celebrity zookeeper Jack Hanna, promote dolphin swims as a way for humans to learn about the importance of protecting marine life, while others, like the Humane Society, condemn the encounters are harmful to the animals' wild way of life.

Experts tend to agree that captive dolphins live shorter lives than wild dolphins, perhaps due to the stress of confinement. Most of the dolphin swims we recommend in this book involve either wild dolphins, or dolphins who live in ocean lagoons but are not kept captive. Bill and Nowdla Keefe's Bimini Wild Dolphin Adventures (p98) involves completely wild dolphins, who only show up when they want to. Grand Bahama's Underwater Explorers Society (UNEXSO) dolphin experience (p77) also earns high marks, with dolphins who are free to swim in the open ocean. Nassau's Blue Lagoon program (p53) has received accreditation from the Alliance of Marine Mammal Parks, an international organization that promotes quality control for the care of captive sea mammals.

Mangrove Swamp Where the ocean meets the land, these brackish wetlands are home to three types of thick, knobby mangrove trees – the black mangrove, the red mangrove and the white mangrove. Mangroves swamps are hugely important to the greater environment – the trees filter water through their roots, the shallows are an important hatching ground for many fish and sharks, and the forests themselves provide a buffer against hurricane damage.

Shoreline At the edge of the sand grows knee-high plants like sea purslane, bay marigold, bay geranium, sandfly bush and spider lily.

Coral Reef These underwater forests are built from the exoskeletons of tiny creatures called polyps. There's a stunning variety of coral shapes, from branched elkhorn, to swaying sea fans, to enormous brains. The reef is home to thousands of varieties of fish, and provides an important bulwark against the tides. Unfortunately it's also one of the most sensitive ecosystems, bleached by global warming and damaged by careless humans.

Island School

The Island School, a non-profit eco-learning retreat in Eleuthera, is teaching a new generation about the importance of sustainability, with an organic farm, solar power projects, sustainable fisheries initiatives and more.

Survival Guide

Directory A–Z

Accommodations

With a fantastic range of cheerful little cottages, welcoming inns, stylish condos, excellent hotels and all-inclusive resorts, the Bahamas caters for most tastes, if not for all budgets. You may come across some intimidating and often unjustified high rates when checking out accommodations, as many hotels of similar price vary dramatically in ambience and value.

Room taxes can be around 12% and, to add insult to injury, surcharges can hike up your bill by another 10% to 30%. These miscellaneous charges will be described as an energy surcharge, a 'resort levy,' or a per-diem fee for housekeeping service. The housekeeping service charge is legal, but the energy tab is left over from the oil crisis days of the mid-'70s and is definitely illegitimate. Check whether the service charges and taxes are per room or per person (even couples and children sharing rooms can sometimes be charged individually). Charges may also be added for credit-card payments.

Most hotels also have a price system tiered into peak- and low-season rates. Low or off season (summer) is usually mid-April to mid-December; high or peak season (winter) is the remainder of the year, when hotel prices increase by 25% to 50% or more.

Now for the good news: the off-season (or summer) encompasses many months of great weather, and during this time virtually all accommodation rates drop anywhere from 25% to 60%. During these times even the top-end hotels are usually looking to fill their rooms and may be affordable. So although this region is pricey, it is possible to find value-for-money lodgings and even some great bargains.

Even during peak times, many of the quieter accommodations offer some amazing specials. Your best bet is to contact the hotels directly by telephone and via their websites. These discounts and special website offers can save up to 30% on prices listed in this book and many need to be booked online.

BOOK YOUR STAY ONLINE

For more accommodations reviews by Lonely Planet authors, check out hotels.lonelyplanet.com/Bahamas. You'll find independent reviews, as well as recommendations on the best places to stay. Best of all, you can book online.

Rates

The listings in the sleeping sections of this guidebook come in three broad categories of 'budget', 'midrange' and 'top end'. We haven't included either taxes or hotel surcharges in our listings, unless they are included in the rates, which we have indicated. Rates for all budgets are generally for two people. In high season, decent budget rooms are around \$80 to \$100 a night, but choices in this price range are slim at best. Midrange hotels will usually cost \$100 to \$200 (with \$150 to \$180 being the average). Upscale resorts will cost from \$200 to \$800 per night as a standard, and above that, the stars are the limit.

Prices in the guidebook refer to room only; breakfast is not generally included unless mentioned.

Bed & Breakfasts

B&Bs haven't really taken off in the Bahamas, but there are a handful to be found. Often run by expats, they range from luxurious manor houses to humble suburban homes. They can be a great bargain, with rates starting around \$90, and are a lovely way to meet locals and get insider tips.

Bonefishing Lodges

Many people come to the Bahamas with the express purpose of hunting the gray ghost – the elusive bonefish.

A number of lodges are set up to accommodate anglers, mostly in bonefish-heavy areas like Andros, Abaco and Grand Bahama. Lodges range from ultra-barebones concrete bungalows to luxurious villas on private islands. Rates are all-inclusive, starting at $1000 per person per day for room, board and fishing. Cheaper rates for nonfishing spouses or partners can often be arranged.

Camping

The Bahamas does not encourage campers. Camping on the beaches is illegal and there are no official campsites, even in wilderness areas. However, many land and sea parks contain cays that are perfect for pitching a tent – ask a local first.

Guesthouses

While the Bahamas does not have any traditional hostels or backpacker-style accommodations, there are a number of casual guesthouses that are popular with international budget travelers. These range from barebones boarding houses in downtown Nassau to funky surfer-run cottages in Eleuthera.

Hotels & Resorts

Bahamian hotels run the gamut from humble motels with curly-tailed lizards scampering across the walls to opulent Colonial palaces with uniformed bellboys and acres of marble and mahogany. Boutique hotels have more intimate vibes, with unique decor and friendly staff. Resorts range from lavish luxury palaces packed with restaurants, bars and entertainments to modest beachfront complexes with a pool and snack bar. Many hotels and motels tack the word 'resort' onto their name without much justification; for us to classify an accommodation as a resort, it must have more to offer than simply beds. If an accommodation is categorized as a resort in this book, it generally has multiple pool areas, spacious grounds, activities such as scuba diving on offer, and at least one restaurant. Some resorts are just one building, while many consist of scattered cottages or villas.

All-Inclusive Resorts

All-inclusive resorts are popular with travelers looking for a no-stress getaway, especially honeymooners. You pay a set fee and (theoretically), don't have to touch your wallet again once you set foot inside. Take care with choosing an all-inclusive. Many properties have jumped onto the 'all-inclusive' bandwagon for marketing purposes. In reality you'll have to pay for booze and some extras, such as scuba diving. Check carefully for hidden charges for water sports, laundry, and other activities or services not included in the price. Rates begin at about $250 per day.

Rental Accommodations

For group or long-term stays, renting a cottage, villa or house is a good bet, and all the Bahamian islands have a wide variety of offerings. These properties range from modest units at $850 to lavish villas at $12,000 and more per week. Affordable, charming studios rent from $600 and three-bedroom houses from $2000 per week. Rates can fall as much as 30% in summer (May to November).

Many condos are attached to resort hotels to which you have access. These self-contained, fully-furnished apartments are normally timeshare properties with kitchens or kitchenettes, and daily housekeeping service.

WHAT YOU GET FOR YOUR MONEY

Budget (less than $100)

Anything from a barebones room with a sagging bed in a family-run guesthouse to a tidy, simple motel room to a rustic beach cabana. Almost all budget accommodations have cable TV, and an increasing number have wi-fi. Some have pools, others do not.

Midrange ($100 to $200)

Midrange hotels will generally have, at minimum, cable TV, wi-fi, a pool and a restaurant or bar. Many have minifridges or kitchenettes. At the low end of the range, rooms may be motel-style and lobbies basic and unwelcoming. At the high end, rooms may be spacious and chicly appointed, with palatial grounds and multiple restaurants, bars and outdoor areas.

Top End (more than $200)

A top-end hotel room should have a flat panel TV, wi-fi, deep soaking tub or spacious shower stall and fine linens. Boutique hotels may have a small but luxurious pool area and small fine-dining restaurant, while flashy resorts have multiple water park-like pools, many restaurants, onsite movie theaters and more. In terms of extra amenities – private butlers, massage, rose petals strewn on your bed – the sky (and your budget) is the limit.

The benefit of these types of accommodations is that you get to use the resort facilities such as pools, marinas etc. The downside is that privately-owned units are decorated by their owners – you never know what you're going to get!

Activities

Not the type to spend a full eight hours a day roasting on the sand? Lucky for you, the Bahamas has a wealth of laid-back and high-octane activities, from hiking to bonefishing to cave diving and beyond.

The island chapters have more-specific information, including details on sites of particular interest for each activity and contact information for local activity tour-operators.

Bicycling

Few people explore the islands by bicycle, but the relative flatness of the islands and the dearth of traffic on the Out Islands make cycling a lovely option. Many hotels and concessions rent bicycles ($12 to $20 per day). Some places have mountain bikes, but most have heavy single-gear beach cruisers, which are definitely not for touring. We'd avoid cycling in or around Nassau because of congestion, narrow roads and speeding minibuses.

Birdwatching

The Bahamas are heaven for birdwatchers (see p243). More than two dozen reserves in the Bahamas protect more than 230 bird species, including West Indian flamingos and Bahama parrots. Grand Bahama is a particularly popular birwatching spot. The Audubon Society's annual Christmas Bird Count is a well-attended event here, attracting birders from near and far.

The **Bahamas National Trust** (☎242-393-1317; Village Rd, Nassau; ⏰9am-5pm Mon-Fri) offers regular guided birdwatching walks and has information on the wonderful species that visit or live on these isles.

A list of all the Bahamian Wild Bird Reserves is available from the **Department of Agriculture** (☎242-325-7413; Levy Bldg, E Bay St, Nassau).

Boating & Sailing

With some 700 islands and cays scattered over 100,000 sq miles of ocean, the region is a boater's dream. Indispensable guidebooks include:

Yachtsman's Guide to The Bahamas and Turks & Caicos

Explorer Chartbook: Far Bahamas

Explorer Chartbook: Near Bahamas

Explorer Chartbook: Exumas

These all give details on cruising permits and customs regulations, plus a list of designated ports of entry.

Favored areas in the Bahamas are the protected waters of the Sea of Abaco (between Great Abaco and the Abaco Cays) and Exuma Sound and Exuma Cays Land & Sea Park. Both are good for beginning sailors, as the waters are shallow and sheltered, and land is always within sight.

BOAT CHARTERS

Experienced sailors and novices can charter sailboats, yachts and cruisers by the day or week. Most marinas offer boats with a skipper and crew, as well as 'bareboat' vessels on which you're your own skipper. You'll need to be a certified sailor to charter bareboat; usually you'll have to demonstrate proficiency before being able to sail away. All boats are stocked with linens and other supplies.

Charters can be arranged at most major hotels or by calling a local charter company. Many individuals offer sportfishing, but will happily take you exploring, diving and snorkeling. They charge anything from $350 to $800 per half-day, $600 to $1400 per day.

Bareboat charters are usually by the week; prices begin at $1200, depending on size. Crewed charters often cost about double that. Skippers can be hired for about $400 a day. See Activities sections in the island chapters for details on local charter companies.

Most resorts provide small sailboats called Sunfish, either as part of the hotel package rate or for an hourly rental fee. You also can rent motorboats, from small fry such as Boston Whalers to giant luxury cruisers, with price tags to match, from local marinas.

BOAT EXCURSIONS

Boat excursions for all sorts of activities abound, whether your thing is fishing, sailing,

RENTAL HOME WEBSITES

For some countrywide rental listings, check out these sites. For destination-specific rental information, look at the On the Road chapters.

Bahamas Home Rentals (www.bahamasweb.com)
Hideaways Aficionado (www.hideaways.com)
HG Christie (www.hgchristie.com)
Home Away (www.homeaway.com)
RentaVilla (www.rentavilla.com)
Vacation Rentals by Owner (www.vrbo.com)

PRACTICALITIES

Newspapers

» *Nassau Guardian* (www.thenassauguardian.com)

» *The Tribune* (www.tribune242.com)

» *Bahama Journal* (www.jonesbahamas.com)

» *Freeport News* (www.freeport.nassauguardian.net)

» *Bahamas Weekly* (www.thebahamasweekly.com)

» *Abaconian* (www.abaconian.com).

Radio & TV

» The government-owned Broadcasting Corporation of the Bahamas operates TV Channel 13 (ZNS) and several radio stations. Most hotels also offer American cable TV.

Smoking

» Banned in most hotels and restaurants.

Weights & Measures

» The British Imperial and metric systems are both in use. Liquids are generally measured in pints, quarts and gallons, and weight in grams, ounces and pounds. Miles are favored over kilometers.

kayaking, sightseeing or simply lazing on a boat sipping rum punch while someone else does all the hard work.

Ferry trips from Nassau are a cheap and fast way to get to a few of the Family Islands, and a great day out. Tickets start from $65 one way.

Day excursions are priced from about $85 to $200 depending upon your activities.

Caving

The islands are honeycombed with dozens of limestone caverns and water-filled blue holes, many only partially explored and mapped. In some, Lucayan Indian petroglyphs add to the allure. Many caves are also roosts for harmless bats. Use extreme caution if you're exploring without a guide.

Grand Bahama has the world's longest cave system in Lucayan National Park. Permits are required to dive these caves, while sightseeing adventure excursions are available.

Also see the Blue Holes boxed text on p26.

Diving & Snorkeling

These are the region's headline acts. The range of sites means that both novice and experienced divers and snorkelers can enjoy these waters and their exotic occupants. See the Activities sections in each island chapter, plus the Diving in the Bahamas chapter (p24), for details on key dive and snorkel sites and local operators.

It's possible to walk off a beach on the islands and be within yards of precious livingcoral teeming with fish. There is a range of operators that will take snorkelers out to a variety of sites. You may be reminded by the captains not to touch the coral. Don't take offence, as a mere tap with your fins is enough to kill whole sections of the reef, which then has the domino effect of wiping out the area's marine and fish life.

If you intend to do a lot of snorkeling or diving, it is worth bringing your own mask, snorkel and fins, otherwise it is about $15 per day to hire the equipment.

DIVING ORGANIZATIONS

The following organizations are good to know:

Divers Alert Network (DAN; US ☎919-684-2948; www.diversalertnetwork.org) Offers divers' health insurance, covering evacuation and emergency treatment.

National Association of Underwater Instructors (NAUI; in the USA ☎813-628-6284; www.naui.org) A worldwide diver-training organization; all dive shops should be either NAUI or PADI certified.

Professional Association of Diving Instructors (PADI; in the USA ☎949-858-7234; www.padi.com) A worldwide diver training organization; all dive shops should be either PADI or NAUI certified.

Dolphin Encounters

Several outfits across the Bahamas offer dolphin encounters, which range from hugging tame dolphins in shallow water to diving alongside wild pods in the open ocean; details are included in the islands' Activities sections. Bimini, Grand Bahama and New Providence have particularly good options. Some high-profile international organizations (the US Humane Society, for one) point out the detrimental effects that these encounters can have on the mammals and their lifespans, but Bahamian programs are generally well-run and humane.

Fishing

Very strict regulations are in place, and marine and sea parks are off-limits to all fishing fans, so check with the relevant authorities.

Bimini, Andros and Abaco are the big fishing hotspots.

These regions host major annual fishing tournaments (often held from April to June), from big-game contests for serious contenders to laidback, family-oriented contests.

BONEFISHING

The gin-clear waters of the sandbanks that shelve the perimeters of most islands are made for battles with the bonefish: pound for pound, one of the world's fighting champions. Related to the herring, it's named for its complex skeleton, and makes for bony eating. Many lodges are devoted to bonefishing and there are local bonefishing guides on all islands. Bait and tackle are sold and rods rented at many fishing lodges.

Andros, Grand Bahama and Abaco are all well-known for their bonefishing grounds, but all the islands offer bonefishing to some extent.

SPORTFISHING

As fans of Ernest Hemingway realize, the archipelago's ocean waters are a pelagic playpen for schools of marlin, dolphin fish, wahoo and tuna. And reef or bottom fishing for snapper or yellowtail is plentiful. Bimini, where Hemingway once spent his summers, is the country's top big-game fishing island due to its proximity to the Gulf Stream.

In the Bahamas, fishing is strictly regulated. Visiting boaters must have a permit for sportfishing. You can get a permit at your port of entry or in advance from the **Department of Fisheries** (☎242-393-1014; PO Box N-3028, E Bay St, Nassau), which can offer information on current fishing regulations. The capture, possession or molestation of coral, turtles and marine mammals is forbidden, as is long-line, spear and net fishing. Other restrictions exist.

CHARTER & GUIDE RATES

Dozens of commercial operators offer sportfishing charters, and will charge from $350 to $800 per half-day or $600 to $1400 per day with bait and tackle provided. You usually take your own food and drinks. Most charter boats require a 50% deposit (if you cancel, you should do so at least 24 hours before departure to avoid losing your deposit). Some operators keep half the catch. Discuss terms with the skipper before setting out.

Hiking

A few wildlife reserves have tracks, while several islands have tracks that were originally cut by lumber companies.

Always carry plenty of water and insect repellent, especially in summer, plus a small first-aid kit when hiking in remote places. Rarely will you be far from a settlement. The limestone terrain is too treacherous to permit you to walk off the track safely, as thick vegetation hides sinkholes and crevasses. Be especially wary of clifftops, which are often undercut and can give way easily.

A few tour operators offer a mix of kayaking, snorkeling and hiking tours in Grand Bahama's Lucayan National Park (p90). In the Abacos, several outfitters offer guided hiking in Abaco National Park,and Bahamas Outdoors (p54) has walking tours of the New Providence's central coppice forest. See those island chapters for more details.

There are hunters in Great Abaco's and Andros' backcountry seeking wild boar. Beware! Consider hiring a hunter as a guide.

Cat Island has some of the best hiking. The Fernandez Bay Village resort (p173) is a good starting point; the owners can provide maps and even a guide, if required.

On Great Inagua, trails lead into Bahamas National Trust Park (p194), a semi-arid, rugged landscape with fabulous birdwatching.

Kayaking

Miles and miles of creeks and flats provide wonderful entrances to the redolent world of the mangroves and wetlands of Grand Bahama and the Family Islands.

Many hotels and resorts rent kayaks or provide free use for guests. And several tour operators are now introducing kayaking as an organized activity.

Guided excursions are offered in the Caicos, Abacos and Grand Bahama. See the island chapters for contact information. The Exuma Cays Land & Sea Park (p167) is a particularly good destination for kayaking.

Water Sports, Surfing & Windsurfing

Most resort hotels either include water sports in their rates or offer them as extras. On offer are all kinds of beach and water sports, such as parasailing, waterskiing, and windsurfing. Typical rates are: sailboards $20 per hour; jet skiing $75 for 30 minutes; for a 15-minute banana boat ride $30 per person; parasailing $70 per hour; windsurfing $75 per hour; sailing $90 per half-day; and kayaks rent for $15 per hour.

For surfers seeking the ultimate wave, look elsewhere. There are a few spots on the Bahamas' east coasts, however, where surfers can find decent Atlantic waves, notably Surfer's Beach on Eleuthera and, most importantly, Garbanzo Reef off Elbow Cay, Abaco. Winter months are best.

Virtually the entire east side of the chain is fringed by an offshore barrier reef onto which the waves break, making surfing dangerous far out. The trade winds, however, continue to blow inside the barrier reef, so the placid stretches inside the reef are perfect for windsurfing (in the absence of other coral).

Resorts and concessionaires rent equipment on the main beaches of New Providence and Grand Bahama. Many hotels have free sailboard use for guests.

Business Hours

In Nassau and on Grand Bahama some banks close at 2pm and re-open from 3pm to 5pm on Friday, when they can be very busy. In the Family Islands, bank hours vary widely. Usually local banks are open only one or two days a week for two or three hours. A few local banks open 9am to noon on Saturday.

Few businesses and stores open on Sunday, outside of the tourist centers. In the Family Islands many stores and businesses will close for lunch during the week. Most restaurants and cafes in the tourist centers open seven days a week. The following hours should be regarded as a general guide.

Banks (9am-3pm Mon-Thu, 9am-5pm Fri)

Government offices (9am-5pm Mon-Fri)

Post offices (9am-5pm Mon-Fri, 9am-noon Sat)

Private businesses (9am-5pm Mon-Fri)

Restaurants (breakfast 7am-10am; lunch noon-2pm, dinner 6-9pm)

Shops (9am-5pm Mon-Fri, 10am-5pm Sat)

Tourist information (9am-5pm Mon-Fri)

Customs Regulations

All baggage is subject to a customs inspection, and Bahamian customs officials are serious about their business. All visitors are expected to complete a Baggage Declaration Form.

Individuals are allowed to import $10,000 cash, plus 50 cigars, 200 cigarettes or 1lb of tobacco, plus one quart (946mL) of spirits free of charge. Purchases of $100 are also allowed for all arriving passengers. You are allowed to bring in a reasonable amount of personal belongings free of charge. However, you may need to show proof that laptop computers and other expensive items are for personal use. You should declare these upon arrival.

Excess items deemed to be imported goods are subject to 35% duty (25% for clothing). The tariff is as much as 300% for certain items.

The following items are restricted: firearms, drugs (except prescription medicines), flowers and plants, honey, fruits, coffee, meats and vegetables (unless canned).

For more information, call the **Bahamas Customs Department** (242-325-6550).

Electricity

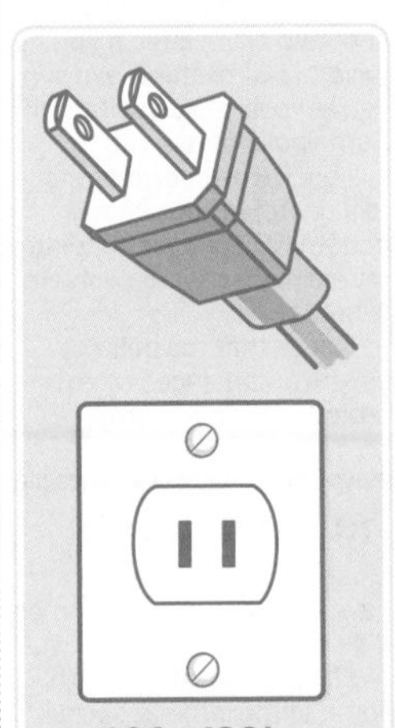

Embassies & Consulates

Most countries are represented by honorary consuls, individuals appointed to represent the respective country.

Australia (242-326-0083 Ext 107; 2 Nassau Ct, Nassau)

Canada (242-393-2123/4; Shirley St Plaza, Nassau)

Germany (242-394-61-61; Alliance House, E Bay St, Nassau)

Netherlands (242-3616-398; netherld@mail.bahamas.net.bs; Gladstone Rd, Nassau)

UK (242-325-7471; 242-323-3871; Bitco Bldg, E St, Nassau)

USA (242-322-1181/2/3; www.nassau.usembassy.gov; Mosmar Bldg, 42 Queen St, Nassau)

Gay & Lesbian Travelers

Immense prejudice against homosexuals still exists in the Bahamas; as a result most Bahamian gays and lesbians are still in the closet. Though homosexuality is not illegal, 'public' displays of homosexuality are punishable by law.

Refer to the boxed text on p66 as this information, both social and legal, basically applies across the whole region.

Health

From the medical standpoint, the Bahamas is usually safe. The most common travel-related diseases, such as dysentery and hepatitis, are acquired by consumption of contaminated food and water. Mosquito-borne illnesses are not a significant concern here, except during outbreaks of dengue fever.

No vaccinations are required to enter the Bahamas. However, a yellow fever vaccination certificate is required for travelers arriving within seven days of traveling in many central African and South American countries. See www.mdtravelhealth.com for a current list of infected areas. Vaccination protection lasts 10 years.

High-quality medical care is usually available, but expensive, in Nassau and Freeport. Medical care is limited elsewhere. Bahamian doctors and hospitals expect payment in cash, regardless of whether you have travel health insurance. If you develop a life-threatening medical problem, you'll probably want to be evacuated to a country with state-of-the-art medical care. Since this may cost tens of thousands of dollars, be sure you have insurance to cover this before you depart.

Many pharmacies are well supplied, but important medications may not be consistently available. Be sure to bring along enough supplies of all prescription drugs.

The scorching Caribbean sun is one of the biggest hazards for tourists in the Bahamas. To protect yourself from excessive sun exposure, you should stay out of the midday sun, wear sunglasses and a wide-brimmed sun hat, and apply sunscreen with SPF 15 or higher, with both UVA and UVB protection. Sunscreen should be generously applied to all exposed parts of the body approximately 30 minutes before sun exposure and should be reapplied after swimming or vigorous activity. Travelers should also drink plenty of fluids and avoid strenuous exercise when the temperature is high.

Insurance

A travel-insurance policy to cover theft, loss and medical problems is worth organizing for your trip. There is a wide variety of policies available, so check the small print.

Some policies specifically exclude 'dangerous activities' (eg motorcycling, rock climbing, canoeing, scuba diving and even hiking). If you're planning on doing any of those activities, be sure to hunt down the right policy to cover yourself.

You may prefer a policy that pays doctors or hospitals directly rather than requiring you to pay on the spot and claim later. If you have to claim later make sure you keep all documentation. Some policies ask you to call back (reverse charges) to a center in your home country where an immediate assessment of your problem is made.

Check that the policy covers ambulances or an emergency flight home.

Internet Access

Most Bahamian hotels now have wi-fi, though sometimes it's only in the lobby. It's usually free for guests, though some of the larger resorts like Atlantis like to squeeze an extra few bucks out of their guests by charging $10 to $15 a day. In Nassau and Grand Bahama, many high-density outdoor tourist areas such as Port Lucaya Marketplace are now free wi-fi hotspots. As wi-fi proliferates, internet cafes become increasingly obsolete. Most midrange and top-end hotels still have business centers with free computers for guests' use. Connections can be sketchy on the more remote Out Islands, but it's generally not too difficult to get online.

For a list of useful websites please refer to p258.

Legal Matters

Marijuana (ganja) and cocaine are prevalent in the Bahamas, which is used as a trans-shipment point for drug traffic into North America and Europe. At some stage, you may be approached by hustlers selling drugs.

Possession and use of drugs and the 'facilitation of drug trafficking' in these islands are strictly illegal and penalties are severe. The islands are swarming with US Drug Enforcement agents, and purchasing drugs is a risky business. Foreigners do not receive special consideration if caught and Bahamian prisons are notoriously nasty places.

Money

The Bahamian dollar is linked one-to-one with the US dollar, so you can use US currency everywhere. You'll often get change back in Bahamian coins. Major commercial banks maintain branches throughout the islands, although in the Family Islands they are scarce and may only be open once a week for a few hours. Most hotels and car-rental companies will take credit cards on the Family Islands, but do have some ready cash just in case.

ATMs

Automated teller machine (ATM) cards are a good way to obtain incidental cash. There are plenty of ATMs in the leading tourist centers, but they become rarer in the Out Islands. If you're headed away from Nassau or Grand Bahama, be sure to find out if there's an ATM in your destination, or bring plenty of cash. Most machines accept Visa, MasterCard and American Express via international networks such as Cirrus and Visa/PLUS.

Credit Cards

Major credit cards are accepted at most hotels and tourist-oriented restaurants in major centers such as Nassau and Freeport. On the Out Islands, some hotels and most restaurants accept cash only. You can use your credit card to get cash advances at most commercial banks. Companies that accept credit cards may add an additional charge of up to 5%.

Traveler's Checks

These are widely accepted throughout the Bahamas, except on more remote Family Islands, although some hotels, restaurants and exchange bureaus charge a hefty fee for cashing traveler's checks.

To report lost American Express traveler's checks in the Bahamas, contact **Destinations** (☎242-322-2931; 303 Shirley St, Nassau).

Post

Mail from the islands is slow. Airmail to North America usually takes about 10 days. Allow about four weeks for mail to Europe, Australia and New Zealand.

Postcards to the UK, US, or Canada cost $0.50. Airmail letters cost $0.65 per half-ounce to the US and Canada; $0.70 to the UK and Europe; and $0.80 to Africa, Asia, or Australasia.

Express mail services are listed in the *Yellow Pages*. Note that 24-hour service is not usually guaranteed from the Out Islands, as the express-mail services tend to rely on air-charter services.

You can have mail addressed to you 'Poste Restante' care of 'The General Post Office,' East Hill St, Nassau, The Bahamas. Mail should be marked 'To be collected from the General Delivery desk.' All correspondence is retained for three weeks.

Public Holidays

Bahamian national holidays that fall on Saturday or Sunday are usually observed on the following Monday.

New Year's Day January 1

Good Friday Friday before Easter

Easter Monday Monday after Easter

Whit Monday Seven weeks after Easter

Labour Day First Friday in June

Independence Day July 10

Emancipation Day First Monday in August

Discovery Day October 12

Christmas Day December 25

Boxing Day December 26

Telephone

Hotel telephone rates are expensive across the region and should be avoided when possible. Many hotels also charge for an unanswered call after the receiving phone has rung five times.

Most US toll-free numbers can't be accessed from the Bahamas. Usually you must dial ☎1-880, plus the last seven digits of the number.

The government-owned **Bahamas Telecommunications Corporation** (☎242-302-7000; John F Kennedy Dr, Nassau), or BaTelCo, has an office on most Bahamian islands. Even the smallest settlement usually has at least one public phone.

The Bahamian country code is ☎242. You need to dial this when making interisland calls. To call the Bahamas from the US and Canada, dial ☎1-242. From elsewhere, dial your country's international access code + ☎242 + the local number.

CELL PHONES

Unlocked European or Australian phones can be used with Bahamian SIM cards. Most US phones are locked, and can only be used when roaming. Service is poor on many of the Out Islands.

DOMESTIC CALLS

Local calls are free of charge, although hotels charge between $0.75 to $1 per call.

Current Time & Temperature ☎917

Directory Assistance ☎916

Interisland calls ☎1-242 followed by the seven-digit local number

International Operator Assistance ☎0

Weather by Phone ☎915

INTERNATIONAL CALLS

Many Bahamian phone booths and all BaTelCo offices permit direct dial to overseas numbers. It is far cheaper to call direct from a phone booth than to call from your hotel via operator-assisted calls. Assisted calls to the USA cost around $1.80 per three-minute minimum, then $0.90 per minute. Calls to Canada cost around $1.30, then $1.30 per minute, to Europe it costs $2.90, then $2.15 per minute while calls to Australia and New Zealand are just frightening.

Many national companies offer a service for their subscribers, issuing international charge cards and a code number. Costs for calling home are then billed directly to your home number. The following companies provide such cards.

AT&T USA Direct (1-800-225-5288)

British Telecom (0-800-345-144)

Canada Direct (1-800-389-0004)

MCI (1-800-888-8000)

Sprint (1-800-389-2111)

Telstra Australia (1-800-038-000)

PHONE CARDS

The majority of Bahamian public telephones accept only prepaid phone cards issued by **BaTelCo** (242-302-7827), available at stores and other accredited outlets near phone-card booths. The cards are sold in denominations of $5, $10, $20 and $50.

Safe Travel

In all likelihood, the most you will have to worry about on the islands are mosquitoes and 'no see ums' (sandflies).

Natural Hazards

Many of the reefs and beaches across the region have dangerous undertows and currents, so do take care. Blue holes and caves are especially dangerous – don't explore without an expert present.

Public warnings will be issued if a hurricane is due to come ashore. In the event of a hurricane, seek shelter in the sturdiest structure you can find. (For more on hurricane seasons see p242).

The manchineel tree, which grows along the Bahamian shoreline, produces small, applelike green fruits. Don't eat them – they're highly poisonous! The sap is also irritating. Take care not to sit beneath the tree, as even raindrops running off the leaves onto your skin can cause blisters. Poisonwood, a common tree, has a scaly reddish bark that can cause poison ivy-like itchy rashes when touched.

Human Hazards

Most Bahamians are extremely law-abiding citizens and their tolerance of thieves and criminals is extremely low.

Nassau is a distinct exception, where violent crime is dishearteningly common, though largely confined to young Bahamian men with connections to the drug trade. Most of the problems occur in the low-income area south of downtown called Over-the-Hill, an area avoided by most foreigners. Tourists are very rarely affected by violence, though robberies have been known to occur in downtown Nassau. Certain parts of Freeport on Grand Bahama are also affected by crime, most notably the Winn Dixie Plaza area after dark. The mellow Out Islands have little crime and many islanders still sleep with their doors open, though Marsh Harbour, Abaco has a few slum areas best avoided.

Most crime against travelers is petty opportunistic theft, so take sensible precautions with your valuables.

Tourist Information

Whatever the name, these places can be helpful with activity booking and hotel and restaurant recommendations, especially in major tourism centers like Nassau. On the Out Islands, offices may be understaffed, keep irregular hours, or generally show surprise to see tourists. But even on smaller islands, the visitor centers put out helpful brochures and maps that are often more useful than talking to an actual person.

The **Bahamas Ministry of Tourism** (800-422-4262; www.bahamas.com) has a central information office in the US that sends out literature. There are also regional offices across the USA and in other countries that can also help with information.

Also in the US is the **Bahama Out Islands Promotion Board** (US 954-475-8315; www.boipb.com; 1200 South Pine Island Rd, Suite 750, Plantation, FL 33324, USA).

Additional Bahamas websites include the following:

» www.bahamas-on-line.com

» www.cruisecritic.com

» www.geographia.com/bahamas

» www.thebahamasguide.com

» www.thenassauguardian.com

Travelers with Disabilities

Disabled travelers will need to plan their vacation carefully, as few allowances have been made for them in the Bahamas.

GOVERNMENT TRAVEL ADVICE

The following government websites offer travel advisories and information on current hot spots.

» **Australian Department of Foreign Affairs** (www.smarttraveller.gov.au)

» **British Foreign Office** (www.fco.gov.uk/countryadvice)

» **Canadian Department of Foreign Affairs** (www.dfait-maeci.gc.ca)

» **US State Department** (http://travel.state.gov)

New construction codes mandate ramps and parking spots for disabled people at shopping plazas and other select sites. Larger hotels are beginning to introduce features such as Braille instructions and chimes for elevators, bathrooms with grab bars, and ramps. However, only the most recent structures in Nassau and, to a lesser degree, Freeport have adopted these features.

The tourism boards can provide a list of hotels with wheelchair ramps, as can the **Bahamas Council for the Disabled** (☎242-353-7720; 11A Kipling Bldg, Freeport, Grand Bahama) and the **Bahamas Association for the Physically Disabled** (☎242-322-2393; Dolphin Dr, Nassau, PO Box N-4252, Nassau). The latter can also hire out a van and portable ramps for those with wheelchairs.

Visas

Residents of the US, Japan, Turkey, Europe, most of Latin American and almost all Commonwealth countries do not need a visa to enter the Bahamas for a 90-day tourist stay. See also Passport (p260).

Women Travelers

It is relatively unusual for women to travel alone in the Bahamas, and you will be asked on many occasions by curious men and women about your husband's whereabouts. This is a friendly enquiry, and it is often easier to reply that you are meeting up somewhere or that he is working, rather than get into the whole discussion about free choice.

There is no doubt that these amiable locals will be concerned about your welfare. Although single women have little to fear in the Bahamas, and cases of sexual assault are very, very rare, there is always the exception that proves the rule. Enjoy the warmth of their trepidation and take obvious precautions at night. Bahamian women rarely dress in shorts, belly-revealing shirts or bikini tops around town, especially on the smaller Out Islands, so take your cue from how the locals dress.

Bahamas Crisis Centre (☎242-328-0922; www.bahamascrisiscentre.org; Shirley St, Nassau) can assist in an emergency or if you need emotional support.

Transport

GETTING THERE & AWAY

With 29 islands and nearly 700 cays spread across 100,000 sq miles of ocean, the Bahamas isn't always an easy place for point-to-point travel. But isn't that part of its charm? Private boat-owners certainly believe so.

Nearly all the region's major international traffic flows through Nassau, New Providence. The main forms of transportation are scheduled flights and cruise liners. From Nassau, local carriers, a few ferries and the slower mail boats reach most inhabited islands and cays. Traveling between Out Islands is rarely simple; you'll usually have to fly back to Nassau to catch your next flight.

The skies are opening up, however, and it is now possible to take direct flights from the USA and Europe to a few of the other Bahamian islands.

Flights, tours and rail tickets can be booked online at lonelyplanet.com/bookings.

Entering the Bahamas

See also p255 for customs information.

Passport

Changes to the law in effect from 31 December 2005 mean US citizens and all visitors are now required to have a passport or 'other secure, accepted document' to enter or re-enter the United States from the Caribbean. Any American travel to and from the Bahamas by air needs a passport. Proof of onward travel is also required.

Visitors from most European and Commonwealth countries, most of Latin America, Turkey and Israel require passports but no visas for stays of up to three months. See the Visa section of the Directory for more information.

Citizens of the following countries require passports and visas for stays of any duration: the Dominican Republic, Haiti, India and all communist countries. Citizens of all other countries should check current entry requirements with the nearest Bahamian embassy. For information about extended stays or work (there are strict regulations for foreigners seeking work in the Bahamas), check with the **Ministry of Labor & Immigration Department** (☎242-322-7530; fax 242-326-0977; PO Box N-831, E Hill St, Nassau).

Air

Airports & Airlines

The Bahamas has six international airports, including two major hubs at Nassau and Freeport.

Exuma International Airport (GGT; ☎242-345-0095) Located in George Town, Exuma.

Freeport International Airport (FPO; ☎242-352-6020) Located in Freeport, Grand Bahama.

CLIMATE CHANGE & TRAVEL

Every form of transportation that relies on carbon-based fuel generates CO_2, the main cause of human-induced climate change. Modern travel is dependent on aeroplanes, which might use less fuel per kilometer per person than most cars but travel much greater distances. The altitude at which aircraft emit gases (including CO_2) and particles also contributes to their climate change impact. Many websites offer 'carbon calculators' that allow people to estimate the carbon emissions generated by their journey and, for those who wish to do so, to offset the impact of the greenhouse gases emitted with contributions to portfolios of climate-friendly initiatives throughout the world. Lonely Planet offsets the carbon footprint of all staff and author travel.

Marsh Harbour International Airport (MHH; ☎242-367-3039) Located in Marsh Harbour, Abacos.

Moss Town Exuma International Airport (MWX; ☎242-345-0030) Located in Moss Town, Exuma.

Lynden Pindling International Airport (NAS; ☎242-377-7281) Located in Nassau, New Providence.

North Eleuthera International Airport (ELH; ☎242-335-1242) Located in North Eleuthera.

AIRLINES FLYING TO/FROM THE BAHAMAS

The Bahamas is well served by flights from North America and Europe. Its proximity to Florida means regular, relatively inexpensive flights from Miami, Fort Lauderdale and Orlando, as well as other east-coast gateways. Nassau is less than three hours' flying time from the northeast USA and about 30 minutes by jet from Miami.

The national airline of the Bahamas, **Bahamasair** (☎242-377-5505, ☎Freeport 242-352-8341; www.bahamasair.com) has an unblemished safety record and the pilots have an excellent reputation (see www.airsafe.com for details). However, delays and lost luggage are regular occurrences. Bahamians say, 'If you have time to spare, fly Bahamasair.' You are warned.

The following major international airlines have offices at Nassau Airport.

Air Canada (AC; ☎1-888-247-2262, 242-377-8220; www.aircanada.ca; hubs Toronto & Montréal)

Air Jamaica (JM; ☎1-800-523-5585, 242-377-3301; www.airjamaica.com; hub Montego Bay)

American Airlines/American Eagle (AA; ☎1-800-433-7300, 242-377-2355; www.aa.com; hubs New York, Newark, Miami & Orlando)

Bahamasair (UP; ☎242-377-5505, ☎Freeport 242-352-8341; www.bahamasair.com; hubs Nassau, Freeport, Miami, Orlando & Fort Lauderdale)

British Airways (BA; ☎1-800-247-9297, 242-377-2338; www.british-airways.com; hubs Heathrow & Gatwick)

Continental/Gulfstream International (3M; ☎1-800-231-0856, 242-394-6019; www.continental.com, www.gulfstreamair.com; Star Plaza, Mackey St, Nassau; hubs Miami, Fort Lauderdale & West Palm Beach)

Delta Air Lines/Comair (DL; ☎1-800-241-4141, 242-377-7774, 800-354-9822; www.delta.com; hubs New York, Orlando, Cincinnati & Atlanta)

US Airways/US Air Express (US; ☎1-800-622-1015, 242-377-8886; www.usair.com; hubs New York & Miami)

CHARTER AIRLINES

Charter flights are available throughout the Bahamas via dozens of charter companies. Only fly with companies holding either a valid American FAA (Federal Aviation Administration) or a Bahamian AOC (Air Operator Certificate) certificate. Major charter companies flying in this region include the following:

Air Flight Charter (☎954-359-0320; www.airflightcharters.com; hub Fort Lauderdale Jet Center)

Cherokee Air (☎242-367-3450; www.cherokeeair.com; hub Marsh Harbour, Abaco)

Island Air Charters (☎954-359-9942; www.islandaircharters.com; hub Fort Lauderdale)

Twin Air Airways (☎954-359-8266; www.flytwinair.com; hub Fort Lauderdale Jet Center)

Yellow Air Taxi (☎888-935-5694; www.flyyellowairtaxi.com; hub Fort Lauderdale Jet Center)

Tickets

As an alternative to booking directly with airlines, there's a plethora of web-based companies selling flights to the Bahamas. The Connections to Nassau table includes average high-season prices for one-way tickets on popular routes. Many flights have layovers in Nassau, Miami or other cities.

Sea

Cruise Ship

Two and a half times more visitors arrive in the Bahamas by sea – usually by cruise ship – than by air. Those are impressive stats, even for the cruise-happy Caribbean. Nassau is the number one port of call, followed by Grand Bahama. While none of the Out Islands have their own cruise-ship ports, several cruise lines have bought isolated cays to use as private islands solely for their own passengers.

Cruise experiences vary vastly according to the cruise company and individual ship you choose. One person's sugar may be another's poison. For example, some passengers may wish to avoid the cruise liners now trotting out old rock bands such as REO Speedwagon or Foreigner for 'rock-nights,' while other travelers may whip out their snakeskin boots and shoulder pads, fix

FLIGHTS TO NASSAU

ROUTE	COST	DURATION	FREQUENCY
London-Nassau	$100	1hr	multiple daily
Miami-Nassau	$185	3hr	multiple daily
New York-Nassau	$240	9hr	multiple daily
Toronto-Nassau	$240	3hr	multiple daily

their combovers, and just get on down. *Caveat emptor!*

Cruise Line International Association (www.cruising.org) is a handy resource. Most cruises that visit the Bahamas depart from Florida and, less frequently, from New York.

Immigration and customs formalities are handled by the cruise companies upon arrival in port.

Some major cruise lines include the following:

Cape Canaveral Cruise Line (☎321-783-4052, 800-910-7447; www.cruisecanaveral.com)

Carnival Cruise Lines (☎305-599-2200, 800-327-9501; www.carnival.com)

Celebrity Cruises (☎305-358-7325, 800-437-3111; www.celebrity.com)

Costa Cruises (☎305-358-7325, 800-462-6782; www.costacruises.com)

Crystal Cruises (☎310-785-9300, 800-446-6620; www.crystalcruises.com)

Discovery Cruise Line (☎800-866-8687, 800-937-4477; www.discoverycruise.com)

Disney Cruise Line (☎407-566-3500, 800-511-8444; disneycruise.disney.go.com)

Holland America Line (☎206-281-3535, 800-426-0327; www.hollandamerica.com)

Norwegian Cruise Line (NCL; ☎305-436-4000, 800-327-7030; www.ncl.com)

Princess Cruises (☎310-553-1770, 800-421-0522; www.princess.com)

Royal Caribbean Cruise Lines (☎305-379-4731, 800-327-6700; www.royalcaribbean.com)

Ferry

Grand Bahama is close enough to Florida for day cruises. If you'd like to disembark and stay, these can be a valid alternative to flying.

Discovery Cruise Line (☎1800-937-4477; www.discoverycruise.com) Runs daily between Fort Lauderdale and Freeport, Grand Bahama ($129). It leaves Fort Lauderdale early in the morning, returning at 10pm. Rates include three main meals. There's a Las Vegas–style casino on board. If you want to disembark and stick around, you're free to do so. You can catch a ride home another day.

Bahamas Celebration (☎800-314-7735; www.bahamascelebration.com) Leaves Palm Beach in the afternoon, spends the night at sea, then docks in Grand Bahama the following morning for a day of island activities before returning that evening. More upscale and family-friendly than the party-hearty Discovery, it's got a spa and a kids' club onboard and cabins ranging from bare bones to luxe. You can stay overnight and cruise home later.

Mail Boat

The term 'mail boat' usually refers to the cargo freighters that travel between the Bahamian islands. Only one company offers passenger service to the United States aboard its cargo ships:

MailBoat Company (☎242-394-0847; www.mailboatbahamas.com) Runs slow, cargo-filled mail boats between Nassau, Freeport and Florida ($50 one-way).

Yacht

The sheltered waters of the 750-mile-long archipelago attract thousands of sailors each year. Winds and currents favor the passage south. Sailing conditions are at their best in summer, though you should keep fully abreast of weather reports, as summer is hurricane season. Use VHF channel 16 for emergencies and most other communications.

CUSTOMS

You must clear customs and immigration upon arrival in the Bahamas. For details of each port's marinas, see the destination chapters. Your crew and guests will each need either a passport or birth certificate (a driver's license is not proof of citizenship). You'll need to clear customs again upon arrival at *each* island. It's a hassle, but the Bahamas' drug problem is such that you should be sympathetic to this policy. Anticipate the possibility of being boarded and searched by the US or Bahamian coast guard.

Details of official requirements are given in the *Yachtsman's Guide to the Bahamas* (see opposite).

Specified marinas on each island are designated ports of entry (you may not enter at any other place):

Abacos Green Turtle Cay, Treasure Cay, Marsh Harbour, Spanish Cay, Walker's Cay.

Andros Congo Town, Fresh Creek, San Andros.

Berry Islands Chub Cay, Great Harbour Cay.

Biminis Alice Town, South Bimini, Cat Cay.

Cat Island Smith's Bay, New Bight, Bennett's Harbour.

Eleuthera Governor's Harbour, Harbour Island, North Eleuthera, Rock Sound, Spanish Wells.

Exumas George Town, Moss Town.

Grand Bahama Freeport Harbour, Port Lucaya Marina, Old Bahamas Bay Marina (West End).

Great Inagua Matthew Town.

Long Island Stella Maris.

Mayaguana Abraham's Bay.

New Providence Nassau (any yacht basin).

San Salvador Cockburn Town.

PERMITS

You'll require the regular documentation for foreign travel (see p260). There is a $150 charge for each foreign pleasure vessel under 30ft, and a $300 charge for vessels longer than 30ft with up to four passengers. Each additional person must pay $15. These charges cover customs and immigration services as well as fishing and cruising permits.

You must have a separate import permit for any pets on board. Contact the **Department of Agriculture** (242-325-7413; fax 242-325-3960; Levy Bldg, E Bay St, Nassau) for information.

MAPS, CHARTS & GUIDEBOOKS

You'll need accurate maps and charts for any voyage through the Bahamas' reef-infested waters. British Admiralty charts, US Defense Mapping Agency charts and Imray yachting charts are all accurate. You can order them in advance from **Bluewater Books & Charts** (US 1-954-763-6533, 1-800-942-2583; www.bluewaterweb.com).

No sailor should set out without the excellent *Yachtsman's Guide to the Bahamas* ($48). It provides detailed descriptions of just about every possible anchorage in the archipelago, and lists information on marinas throughout the islands as well as other invaluable information. Small sketch charts are *not* intended for use in navigation. It's available at bookstores and marinas in the Bahamas or online from (www.yachtsmansguide.com).

Likewise, refer to Mathew Wilson's splendid *Bahamas Cruising Guide* ($42), which is available at good bookstores, and Julius Wilensky's *Cruising Guide to the Abacos and the Northern Bahamas* ($20). These and many other regional boating guides can be ordered from **White Sound Press** (US 386-423-7880; www.wspress.com).

Waterproof Charts (800-423-9026; www.waterproofcharts.com) publishes a series of large-scale waterproof sectional charts of the Bahamas. The charts mostly show physical features and are of limited use as travel maps. Larger-scale (11in by 17in) versions of the charts can be ordered; they're highly detailed and durable. A complete set of six charts covers the major island groupings ($180).

US government charts of the region can be ordered through most marine stores, as can detailed charts from **National Oceanic & Atmospheric Administration** (NOAA; 301-436-6829; www.nws.noaa.gov).

CREWING

Crewing aboard a yacht destined for the Bahamas from North America or the Caribbean is a popular way of getting to the islands. Check the bulletin boards of marinas: often you'll find notes advertising for crew or you can leave one of your own.

GETTING AROUND

Perusing a map, you may be tempted to think that island-hopping down the chain is easy. But unless you have your own boat or plane, it isn't. Interisland air travel is centered on Nassau. Getting between the islands without constantly backtracking is a bit of a feat. Even the mail boats are Nassau-centric.

Air

Airlines in the Bahamas

Interisland flights offer the only quick and convenient way to travel within the Bahamas, and islanders ride airplanes like Londoners use buses. You don't save any money by booking interisland tickets for the Bahamas in advance. Inexplicably, some Bahamian airlines are cash-only, even major carriers.

The scene is dominated by **Bahamasair** (UP; 242-377-5505, Freeport 242-352-8341; www.bahamasair.com; hubs Nassau & Freeport). The airline runs on a hub-and-spoke system: Nassau is the main hub. If you island-hop a lot, you'll feel like a yo-yo and may need to stay in Nassau between flights. Budget accordingly.

There are several airlines operating in the Bahamas.

Abaco Air (242-367-2266; www.abacoaviationcentre.com; hub Marsh Harbour) Flies between Marsh Harbour, Abaco and Nassau, North Eleuthera and Moore's Island.

Cat Island Air (242-377-3318; www.flycatislandair.com; hub Nassau) Flies from Nassau to Cat Island, Rum Cay, San Salvador and the Berry Islands' Great Harbour Cay.

Flamingo Air (242-377-0354; www.flamingoairbah.com; hub Nassau, Freeport) Flies from Freeport to Moore's Island, Abaco and Great Harbour Cay, and from Nassau to Staniel Cay, Black Point, Harbour Cay, Exuma, and Mangrove Cay, Andros.

Pineapple Air (242-377-0140; www.pineappleair.com; hub Nassau) Flies from Nassau to Eleuthera (Governor's Harbour, Rock Sound, North Eleuthera) as well as Crooked Island, Acklins, Deadman's Cay and Stella Maris.

Regional Air (242-351-5614; www.goregionalair.com; hub Freeport) Based in Freeport, with services to Bimini, Abaco (Marsh Harbour, Treasure Cay, Walker's Cay), North Eleuthera and San Andros, Andros.

Sky Bahamas (242-377-8777; www.skybahamas.net; hub Nassau) A large carrier; flies between Nassau and Cat Island, Bimini, Freeport, Marsh Harbour and Exuma, as well as between Freeport and the Turks and Caicos.

Southern Air (242-377-2014; www.southernaircharter.com; hub Nassau) Flies from

Nassau to Governor's Harbour, Rock Sound and North Eleuthera, and to Stella Maris, Long Island.

Western Air (☎242-329-4000; www.westernairbahamas.com; hub Andros & Nassau) The country's largest private airline flies from Nassau to Freeport, Marsh Harbour, Andros (San Andros and Congo Town), Bimini, Exuma, and Kingston in Jamaica.

Tickets

Refer to the destination chapters for relevant inter-island flight information. The table below includes prices of one-way fares for connections to Nassau.

Charter Flights

See p261 for a list of the region's major charter airlines.

Bicycle

Cycling is cheap, convenient, healthy, environmentally sound and above all a fun way to travel. Major resort hotels rent bicycles for $20 a day. Unfortunately, the bikes are heavy, have only one gear and are virtually guaranteed to give you a sore bum. We don't recommend biking in smoggy, congested Nassau, nor on the dangerously narrow West Bay St.

Boat

Boat Excursions

There are a myriad boat excursions on offer, covering activities such as water sports, sightseeing, pleasure cruises, snorkeling and diving. Refer to the destination chapters for further information.

Ferry & Water Taxi

Water taxis zip back and forth between Nassau and Paradise Island. Several other offshore islands and their neighboring cays are served by private water taxis.

Government-run water taxis link islands that are a short distance apart, such as North Bimini and South Bimini; Mangrove Cay and South Andros; and Crooked and Acklins Islands.

In Abaco, the Green Turtle Ferry and Albury's Ferry serve the Loyalist Cays. See the Abaco chapter for schedules. In Grand Bahama, Pinder's Ferry travels between McLean's Town and Crown Haven, Abaco.

The only major inter-island ferry operator in the islands is **Bahamas Ferries** (☎242-323-2166/8; www.bahamasferries.com), which runs a high-speed ferry linking Nassau, Andros, Abacos, Eleuthera and the Exumas.

Mail Boat

Around 30 mail boats sail under government contract to most inhabited islands. They regularly depart Potter's Cay for Grand Bahama and all the Family Islands. Traditionally the boats sail overnight, and the journeys last between five and 24 hours. Always call the **Dockmaster's Office** (☎242-394-1237) and check with the **Bahamas Ministry of Tourism** (☎242-322-7500; www.bahamas.com) for the latest schedules and prices.

Car & Motorcycle

Bahamians are generally very cautious and civilized drivers. Main roads are normally in relatively good condition, but minor roads can be a riot of potholes and mud, barely passably except by four-wheel drive. Believe any Bahamian who warns you that a road is in bad condition.

Driver's License

To rent a car you must be 21 (some companies rent only to those 25 or older) and must have a current license for your home country or state. Visitors can drive using their home license for up to three months.

Fuel

Esso, Shell and Texaco maintain gas (petrol) stations on most islands. Gas stations are usually open from 8am to about 7pm. Some close on

FLIGHTS FROM NASSAU

ROUTE	COST	DURATION	FREQUENCY
Nassau-Abacos	$85	30min	3 daily
Nassau-Andros	$75	15min	2 daily
Nassau-Biminis	$85	20min	2 daily
Nassau-Cat Island	$75	1hr	2 daily
Nassau-Crooked	$105	2hr	2 weekly
Nassau-Eleuthera	$75	15min	2 daily
Nassau-Exumas	$80	1hr 20min	3 daily
Nassau-Grand Bahama	$85	45min	6 daily
Nassau-Inagua	$110	1½hr	3 weekly
Nassau-Long Island	$85	45min	1 daily
Nassau-San Salvador	$80	1¾hr	3 weekly

Sunday. In Nassau and Freeport you'll find stations open 24 hours a day. Gasoline is nearly $5 per gallon. Credit cards are accepted in major settlements; elsewhere, it's cash only.

Insurance

Damage-waiver insurance is $15 a day. On many Family Islands, however, no insurance is on offer at all.

Rental Agencies

Several major international car-rental companies have outlets in Nassau and Freeport, as do smaller local firms. In the Family Islands there are some very good local agencies. Ask your hotel for recommendations, or look for display boards at the airport. Local companies may not offer insurance.

You usually rent for 24-hour periods with rates starting at $70. Rates start from around $80 in Nassau, and from $60 on the smaller islands.

Golf carts can be rented on the smaller islands and cays for $40 per day.

Road Rules

Always drive on the left-hand side of the road. This can be tricky to remember, as most Bahamian cars are American imports, with steering wheels on the left! At traffic circles (roundabouts), remember to circle in a clockwise direction, entering to the left. You must give way to traffic already in the circle. You should also be aware that it is compulsory to wear a helmet when riding a motorcycle or scooter.

Hitchhiking

Hitchhiking is never entirely safe anywhere, and we don't recommend it. Travelers who do decide to hitch should understand that they are taking a small but potentially serious risk. Those who choose to hitch will be safer if they travel in pairs, and let someone know where they are planning to go. Hitchhiking by locals is fairly prevalent (and legal) in the Bahamas, especially in the Family Islands.

Local Transportation

Bus

Nassau and Freeport have dozens of jitney buses (private minibuses) licensed to operate on set routes.

There is very little public transportation on the Family Islands or at airports (the taxi drivers' union is too powerful). Few hotels are allowed to run a transfer service for guests.

FERRY SCHEDULES

February to April

FROM	TO	DAYS & TIME	COST	DURATION
Nassau	Harbour Island	8am daily	$65	2hr
Nassau	Governor's Harbour	7am Wed, 4:15 Fri & Sun	$50	2hr
Nassau	Current, Eleuthera	4pm Fri & Sun	$50	2hr
Nassau	Fresh Creek, Andros	8am Fri & Sun	$50	2½hr
Nassau	George Town, Exuma	8:30pm Mon & Wed	$60	10hr

April to December

FROM	TO	DAYS & TIME	COST	DURATION
Nassau	Harbour Island	8am daily	$65	2hr
Nassau	Governor's Harbour	7am Thu & Fri, 4:15pm Sun	$50	2hr
Nassau	Current, Eleuthera	4pm Fri & Sun	$50	2hr
Nassau	Morgan's Bluff, Andros	8am Sat	$50	2½hr
Nassau	Fresh Creek, Andros	8am Fri & Sun	$50	2½hr
Nassau	Sandy Point, Abaco	11am Fri & Sun	$60	3hr
Nassau	George Town, Exuma	8:30pm Mon & Wed	$60	10hr

MAIL BOAT SCHEDULE

DESTINATION	LEAVES NASSAU	RETURNS	BOAT	COST	DURATION
Abaco	6pm Tue	6pm Fri	*Gurth Dean*	$40	12hr
Andros (South)	11pm Mon	11am Wed	*Captain Moxey*	$30	7hr
Andros (Central)	noon Tue	1pm Sun	*Lady D*	$30	5hr
Andros (Mangrove Cay)	11am Tue	1pm Sun	*Lady Gloria*	$30	5hr
Berry Islands	6pm Fri	8am Sun	*Gurth Dean*	$45	7hr
Bimini	2am Thu	7pm Mon	*Bimini Mack*	$45	12hr
Cat Island (North)	6pm Tue	2pm Sun	*Lady Eddina*	$40	14hr
Cat Island (South)	3pm Tue	7am Mon	*Sea Hauler*	$40	12hr
Eleuthera (North)	7pm Thu	11am Tue	*Current Pride*	$30	5hr
Eleuthera (South)	6pm Wed	3pm Sun	*Bahamas Daybreak III*	$30	5hr
Eleuthera (Harbour Island)	5pm Mon	8pm Tue	*Bahamas Daybreak III*	$30	5hr
Eleuthera (Harbour Island)	7am Thu	1pm Sun	*Eleuthera Express*	$30	5hr
Exuma	2pm Tue	7am Fri	*Grand Master*	$40	12hr
Freeport	4pm Wed	8am Sun	*Marcella III*	$45	12hr
Long Island	noon Tue	8pm Thu	*Mia Dean*	$45	12hr
Mayaguana/Acklins Island/Crooked Island/Great Inagua	Call for schedule				
North Long Island	5pm Mon	11am Tue	*Sherice M*	$45	15
San Salvador	1pm Tue	9am Sat	*Lady Francis*	$40	12

Taxi

There's no shortage of licensed taxis in Nassau and Freeport, where they can be hailed on the streets. Taxis are also the main form of local transportation in the Family Islands, where they meet all incoming planes.

All taxi operators are licensed. Taxi fares are fixed by the government based on distance. Rates are usually for two people, with each additional person charged a flat-rate of $3. Fixed rates have been established from airports and cruise terminals to specific hotels and major destinations. These rates should be shown in the taxi. However, you should be aware of some crafty scams in Nassau and Freeport, where an unscrupulous driver may attempt to charge additional people the same rate as the first and second passengers.

behind the scenes

SEND US YOUR FEEDBACK

We love to hear from travelers – your comments keep us on our toes and help make our books better. Our well-traveled team reads every word on what you loved or loathed about this book. Although we cannot reply individually to postal submissions, we always guarantee that your feedback goes straight to the appropriate authors, in time for the next edition. Each person who sends us information is thanked in the next edition – and the most useful submissions are rewarded with a free book.

Visit **lonelyplanet.com/contact** to submit your updates and suggestions or to ask for help. Our award-winning website also features inspirational travel stories, news and discussions.

Note: We may edit, reproduce and incorporate your comments in Lonely Planet products such as guidebooks, websites and digital products, so let us know if you don't want your comments reproduced or your name acknowledged. For a copy of our privacy policy visit lonelyplanet.com/privacy.

OUR READERS

Many thanks to the travelers who used the last edition and wrote to us with helpful hints, useful advice and interesting anecdotes:

Jeff Baierlein, Jason Eldredge, Robert Leger, David Ma, Katy Mann, Daniel O'Rourke, Julie Porter, Stephanie Saur, Jerry Sterling, Peter Szasz

AUTHOR THANKS

Emily Matchar

Thanks to Robbin Whachell, Lyndah Wells, Lanelle Phillips and Harry Bahama for showing me around Grand Bahama and giving me such great Abaco and Nassau tips. Ditto to Erika and Ed Gates of Grand Bahama Nature Tours, and Katybel Taylor at the Seagrape. Thanks to Eugene at the Pineville Motel in Andros for sharing his vast local knowledge. Thanks to Katie and Grant at the Bimini Sands, for their great Bimini and Andros info. Thanks to Laurie Costanza, my Loyalist Cays partner in crime. And thanks as always to Jamin Asay for being my companion in travel and life.

Tom Masters

Huge thanks to a long list of Bahamian cast members who all went out of their way to help me during my trip. Particular gratitude goes to Peter and Betty Oxley in Exuma, to the very kind staff at the Moreton Main House in Inagua, to Bernard at Tranquility on the Bay and the friendly faces at Gibson's Restaurant on Crooked Island, to Margaret Cleare on Cat Island and the staff at Riding Rock on San Sal. A huge thanks too to the staff at the Orange Hill Beach Inn in Nassau, for making me feel at home during my numerous overnight stays in between poorly timed Bahamasair flights! In the Turks and Caicos, I'm very grateful to Sandra McLeod of the Turtle Creek Inn for all her local tips, and the staff at the Island House in Grand Turk. Thanks also to my co-author Emily Matchar, commissioning editor Heather Dickson and to Caroline Sieg.

ACKNOWLEDGMENTS

Climate map data adapted from Peel MC, Finlayson BL & McMahon TA (2007) 'Updated World Map of the Köppen-Geiger Climate Classification', *Hydrology and Earth System Sciences*, 11, 163344.

Cover photograph: Hammock swings below palm trees on a beach in the Bahamas/ Charles Register, Alamy. Many of the images in this guide are available for licensing from Lonely Planet Images: www.lonelyplanet images.com.

THIS BOOK

This 4th edition of Lonely Planet's *The Bahamas* guidebook was researched and written by Emily Matchar and Tom Masters. The previous edition was written by Jill Kirby; Jean-Bernard Carillet wrote the Diving in the Bahamas chapter for the last edition and he contributed to the text this edition. Christopher P Baker contributed the Beasts in the Blue Holes, Father Jerome and Obeah boxed texts in the Cat & San Salvador Islands chapter. This guidebook was commissioned in Lonely Planet's Oakland office, laid out by Cambridge Publishing Management, UK, and produced by the following:

Commissioning Editor Kathleen Munnelly
Coordinating Editors Catherine Burch, Kate Taylor, Gina Tsarouhas
Coordinating Cartographer Mark Griffiths
Coordinating Layout Designer Paul Queripel
Managing Editors Helen Christinis, Bruce Evans, Annelies Mertens
Managing Cartographer Alison Lyall
Managing Layout Designer Jane Hart
Assisting Editors Laura Crawford, Justin Flynn, Kristin Odijk, Fionnuala Twomey, Jeanette Wall, Simon Williamson
Assisting Cartographer Valeska Canas
Cover Research lonelyplanetimages.com
Internal Image Research Sabrina Dalbesio
Color Designers Tim Newton, Paul Queripel
Indexer Marie Lorimer

Thanks to Heather Dickson, Ryan Evans, Lisa Knights, Martine Power, Raphael Richards, Kerri-anne Southway, Gerard Walker

A

000 Map pages
000 Photo pages

B

000 Map pages
000 Photo pages

000 Map pages
000 Photo pages

000 Map pages
000 Photo pages

S

T

U

V

W

Y

Z

000 Map pages
000 Photo pages

how to use this book

These symbols will help you find the listings you want:

- Sights
- Activities
- Courses
- Tours
- Festivals & Events
- Sleeping
- Eating
- Drinking
- Entertainment
- Shopping
- Information/ Transport

These symbols give you the vital information for each listing:

- Telephone Numbers
- Opening Hours
- Parking
- Nonsmoking
- Air-Conditioning
- Internet Access
- Wi-Fi Access
- Swimming Pool
- Vegetarian Selection
- English-Language Menu
- Family-Friendly
- Pet-Friendly
- Bus
- Ferry
- Metro
- Subway
- London Tube
- Tram
- Train

Reviews are organised by author preference.

Look out for these icons:

TOP CHOICE Our author's recommendation

FREE No payment required

A green or sustainable option

Our authors have nominated these places as demonstrating a strong commitment to sustainability – for example by supporting local communities and producers, operating in an environmentally friendly way, or supporting conservation projects.

Map Legend

Sights
- Beach
- Buddhist
- Castle
- Christian
- Hindu
- Islamic
- Jewish
- Monument
- Museum/Gallery
- Ruin
- Winery/Vineyard
- Zoo
- Other Sight

Activities, Courses & Tours
- Diving/Snorkelling
- Canoeing/Kayaking
- Skiing
- Surfing
- Swimming/Pool
- Walking
- Windsurfing
- Other Activity/ Course/Tour

Sleeping
- Sleeping
- Camping

Eating
- Eating

Drinking
- Drinking
- Cafe

Entertainment
- Entertainment

Shopping
- Shopping

Information
- Post Office
- Tourist Information

Transport
- Airport
- Border Crossing
- Bus
- Cable Car/ Funicular
- Cycling
- Ferry
- Metro
- Monorail
- Parking
- S-Bahn
- Taxi
- Train/Railway
- Tram
- Tube Station
- U-Bahn
- Other Transport

Routes
- Tollway
- Freeway
- Primary
- Secondary
- Tertiary
- Lane
- Unsealed Road
- Plaza/Mall
- Steps
- Tunnel
- Pedestrian Overpass
- Walking Tour
- Walking Tour Detour
- Path

Boundaries
- International
- State/Province
- Disputed
- Regional/Suburb
- Marine Park
- Cliff
- Wall

Population
- Capital (National)
- Capital (State/Province)
- City/Large Town
- Town/Village

Geographic
- Hut/Shelter
- Lighthouse
- Lookout
- Mountain/Volcano
- Oasis
- Park
- Pass
- Picnic Area
- Waterfall

Hydrography
- River/Creek
- Intermittent River
- Swamp/Mangrove
- Reef
- Canal
- Water
- Dry/Salt/ Intermittent Lake
- Glacier

Areas
- Beach/Desert
- Cemetery (Christian)
- Cemetery (Other)
- Park/Forest
- Sportsground
- Sight (Building)
- Top Sight (Building)

OUR STORY

A beat-up old car, a few dollars in the pocket and a sense of adventure. In 1972 that's all Tony and Maureen Wheeler needed for the trip of a lifetime – across Europe and Asia overland to Australia. It took several months, and at the end – broke but inspired – they sat at their kitchen table writing and stapling together their first travel guide, *Across Asia on the Cheap*. Within a week they'd sold 1500 copies. Lonely Planet was born.

Today, Lonely Planet has offices in Melbourne, London and Oakland, with more than 600 staff and writers. We share Tony's belief that 'a great guidebook should do three things: inform, educate and amuse'.

OUR WRITERS

Emily Matchar

Coordinating author; Plan Your Trip, Diving in the Bahamas, Nassau & New Providence; Grand Bahama; Biminis, Andros & Berry Islands; Abacos; Eleuthera; Understand; Survival Guide Emily's first trip to the Bahamas, as a callow college student, was not particularly promising (let us never speak of Spring Break 2003 again, please). But subsequent trips opened her eyes to the wonders of pink-sand beaches, blue holes, sweet little colonial villages and cracked conch. In fact, she's kind of annoyed that she's not on Eleuthera's Lighthouse Beach right now. When she's not traipsing the globe, Emily lives in Chapel Hill, North Carolina, and writes about culture, travel and food for a number of magazines and newspapers. She's contributed to nearly a dozen Lonely Planet guidebooks.

Read more about Emily at:
lonelyplanet.com/members/emilymatchar

Tom Masters

The Exumas; Cat & San Salvador Islands; Southern Bahamas; Turks & Caicos Tom is a long-time lover of all things Caribbean, particularly anything to do with diving, which he's done everywhere in the region from Cuba to the Cayman Islands and from Dominica to the coast of Venezuela. Taking on the remote 'Out Islands' of the Bahamas and the little-known Turks and Caicos for this book was pure pleasure, despite a series of disasters on the road ranging from missed planes to crashed cars and lost passports. Tom lives in Berlin and can be found online at www.tommasters.net.

Read more about Tom at:
lonelyplanet.com/members/tommasters

Published by Lonely Planet Publications Pty Ltd
ABN 36 005 607 983
4th edition – September 2011
ISBN 978 1 74104 706 6

10 9 8 7 6 5 4 3 2 1
Printed in China